My Ebenezer Stone

*To Dee Dee,
Thank you for sharing us with Charity from the start! I pray that the Lord will show you how to use all He's taught you through your losses.
Romans 8:28
♡ Shirley*

Shirley Peek Graham

My Ebenezer Stone

The grace-filled story of one man's journey through cancer and the family who survives it

My Ebenezer Stone

An Amazon Company

Scripture quotations or paraphrases taken from The Holy Bible, Public Domain

Details in some anecdotes and stories have been changed to protect the identities of the persons involved.

ISBN978-1516881598

Copyright © 2015 by Shirley Peek Graham

All rights reserved. No part of this book may be reproduced or transmitted in any form or by any means, electronic or mechanical, including photocopying and recording, or by any information storage and retrieval system, without permission in writing from the publisher.

Published in the United States by CreateSpace, A Division of Amazon.

For my children:
Jon, Austin, Elisabeth, Sarah, Charlotte, Emily and Joseph
***
"I thank my God for every remembrance of you"
Philippians 1:3

Table of Contents

Introduction 1
Chapter One 4
Chapter Two 26
Chapter Three 33
Chapter Four 53
Chapter Five 65
Chapter Six 79
Chapter Seven 93
Chapter Eight 105
Chapter Nine 109
Chapter Ten 116
Chapter Eleven 122
Chapter Twelve 126
Chapter Thirteen 130
Chapter Fourteen 140
Chapter Fifteen 145
Chapter Sixteen 156
Chapter Seventeen 159
Chapter Eighteen 162
Chapter Nineteen 168
Chapter Twenty 173
Chapter Twenty-One 177
Chapter Twenty-Two 183
Chapter Twenty-Three 188
Chapter Twenty-Four 193
Chapter Twenty-Five 196
ChapterTwenty-Six 199

Chapter Twenty-Seven	203
Chapter Twenty-Eight	206
Chapter Twenty-Nine	210
Chapter Thirty	214
Chapter Thirty-One	218
Chapter Thirty-Two	220
Chapter Thirty-Three	223
Chapter Thirty-Four	227
Chapter Thirty-Five	235
Chapter Thirty-Six	239
Chapter Thirty-Seven	235
Chapter Thirty-Eight	260
Chapter Thirty-Nine	261
Chapter Forty	263
Chapter Forty-One	267
Chapter Forty-Two	272
Chapter Forty-Three	276
Chapter Forty-Four	282
Chapter Forty-Five	286
Chapter Forty-Six	289
Chapter Forty-Seven	294
Chapter Forty-Eight	298
Chapter Forty-Nine	309
Chapter Fifty	316
Chapter Fifty-One	324
Chapter Fifty-Two	325
Chapter Fifty-Three	328
Chapter Fifty-Four	332
Chapter Fifty-Five	339
Chapter Fifty-Six	335
Chapter Fifty-Seven	351

Chapter Fifty-Eight	368
Chapter Fifty-Nine	373
Chapter Sixty	379
Chapter Sixty-One	387
Chapter Sixty-Two	393
Chapter Sixty-Three	397
Chapter Sixty-Four	402
Chapter Sixty-Five	407
Chapter Sixty-Six	409
Chapter Sixty-Seven	423
Chapter Sixty-Eight	427
Chapter Sixty-Nine	440
Epilogue	446
Acknowledgements	449

Introduction

This book began as my telling of the amazing story of my husband Paul Graham for our seven beautiful children: Jon, Austin, Sarah, Elisabeth, Charlotte, Emily, and Joseph. Somewhere along in the writing of these pages, I realized that when God is working (as He always is), life experiences are never isolated. Our personal adventures are busily weaving permanent threads into the tapestries of other people's lives. My prayer is that God will use my family's journey to knit a thread of encouragement through Jesus into your own tapestry. I pray that through our story, His goodness and love may become evident in your life as well.

Paul's life-altering passages made us eye-witnesses to God's work. Sharing his journey, filled with Divine intervention, was a gift to our family and friends that I feel called to share. Watering down God's presence on this adventure or leaving Him out would make the story a lie. Traveling alongside Paul with God leading the way has changed me. This walk took me to a crossroad where I could either hang my hopes on the wisdom of the world, or desperately grab the hand of Jesus and hold on tight for the ride – a ride that ultimately brought me into a deeper relationship with God the Father, Jesus, and the Holy Spirit.

Through these pages, which begin with a little family history, I hope to pass along some of the grace I've seen. I offer this story, which I sometimes had little spare time to re-create and rarely felt competent to compose, but just as God insisted that Jonah go to Nineveh, I knew He wouldn't leave me alone about this book. I may never know the all the reasons He insisted I write this, but to leave it unfinished may doom me to the belly of a great fish. I do hope to avoid such a fate.

Writing this book has been a lot like this passage from Exodus 33:

"Then Moses said, "Now show me your glory." And the LORD said, "I will cause my goodness to pass in front of you, and I will proclaim my name, the LORD, in your presence. I will have mercy on whom I will have mercy, and I will have compassion on whom I will have compassion. "But," he said, "you cannot see my face, for no one can see my face and live. Then the LORD said,

"There is a place near me where you may stand on a rock. When my glory passes by, I will put you in a cleft in the rock and cover you with my hand until I have passed by. Then I will remove my hand and you will see my back; but my face must not be seen."

I've stood in the cleft of that rock chronicling our life, and I've seen God's glory as He passes through the stories. May the reading of this book bless you as its writing has blessed me.

"Then Samuel took a stone and set it up between Mizpah and Shen. He named it Ebenezer, saying, "Thus far the LORD has helped us."

I Samuel 7:12

For we are God's handiwork, created in Christ Jesus to do good works, which God prepared in advance for us to do.
Ephesians 2:10:10

Chapter One

My name is Shirley. I am the lucky woman who fell in love and somehow managed to win Paul's heart. We married May 30, 1992. Before I tell about him, I will share the beginnings of my life. I was born in Atlanta, Georgia, on March 19, 1955, to John and Ophelia Peek. My family already had two children, a dainty seven-year-old, Jeanne -- pronounced Jee-nee -- Marie, and a happy, lively five-year-old boy, Dale John. Two years after my arrival, Timothy Ray would complete the John and Ophelia Peek clan.

My place in our family was largely to provide comic relief. I wasn't particularly funny, but my skinny proportions and great big eyes afforded me a license to make people laugh. I often resorted to absurd, off-the-wall comments to evoke laughter. The core of my comedy was a weird sense of obligation. I bear a lifelong feeling of responsibility for the happiness and comfort of all mankind. I don't know if it is a gift, a burden, or a calling, I just know that when tension looms, and even when it doesn't, I must provide a release. I offer this example from my memory.

When I was about five or six years old, our family was enjoying supper together when one of us got called down for an infraction of some sort. This instantly killed the mood. Conversation ceased. Eye contact was avoided and the only sounds in the air were the irregular *click, click, click* of forks against plates. Swallowing became a terrible task. Suddenly, without any prior planning, spontaneity commanded me to stand up and announce one word, "Eyeball." As surprise then laughter travelled around the table, I began to relax in the grace of my family's cooperative response. Yeah, that's the reaction I wanted. Hysteria soon welled up in me, too, and I wondered how I could have known proclaiming that one word would change the collective mood. Looking back, I don't think I was trying to control anything, but I had to rescue my loved ones from pain. As an altruistic humorist, I was employing the only resource I was born knowing how to use.

My brother Dale didn't have to rely on the absurd. He was

the one with an authentic, easy humor that just flowed from him. Such a cute little boy was he. When he smiled, you had to imagine all his muscles and bones being part of the process. I stole his jokes whenever the opportunity arose, and, truth be told, I still do. He is a hero to me. He taught me to find some form of levity in all situations, especially the stressful ones. It was an invaluable lesson that has kept me on the map a time or two.

      Two characteristics set me apart from most normal children. One: I had classic migraine headaches; and two: I was very skinny with uncommonly large eyes. Headaches, the bane of my life, began as early as my recollection allows. I would be forty years old before finding the *triptan* drugs that changed that part of my life. I thank God for every single pill I have ever taken. Every school year, my unsuspecting new teacher had to be broken in. The headache usually opened its performance by gripping me with fatigue. Before I had time to remember that tiredness always preceded the throbbing in my head, pain behind my left eye would disable me. The next requirement was to drag my scrawny little legs to the teacher's desk to say something like, "I don't feel good." The teacher would send me to the health room for a temperature reading. Invariably, there would be no fever, so I would be sent back to class with a note to that effect. Protocol being what it was required the teacher to send me back to my desk with the consolation that I could lay my head on my desk for a while. It was some relief to close my sore eyes against the glaring light, but everything seemed so loud. With my cheek flattened against the cold, inflexible surface of my desk, a vivid odor of old, dirty, rubber erasers threatened nausea. I suspect that's why I don't like the smell of rubber even now. Too weak to feel anything besides throbbing, I couldn't feel sorry for my teachers as I now do. Poor things couldn't possibly know what was going to happen, and how could I explain when it took every molecule of energy in me to fight through the fog of fatigue and pain just to lie there? But the consequences would come soon enough and throwing up was always a show stopper that set the teacher in motion. Her initial panic would cause her to put down her lesson planner and remember she was supposed to call the janitor if this ever happened. The poor guy would lumber sadly into our room, hating his job, and toss that odd smelling, spongy cat litter stuff on the floor. As weird as it smelled, it was indeed an improvement over the stinking puddle of vomit it covered. Once it had sufficiently soaked up the offense, I would be accompanied by an unwitting classmate to the health room cot to lie silently in the dark until Mother could drive to Harris Street Elementary and retrieve me.

I had to do this exercise only once each year. After that, if I so much as hinted at feeling ill, someone was on the phone to my parents, I was shipped speedily to the Health Room, and a trash-can was placed within my reach. After Mother had checked me out, I would cover my eyes against the piercing sunlight, lean into her tall leg and stumble to her car. Photo-phobia is the term for when light is intolerable, and it is a hateful companion to the other mean symptoms of migraine. As my gag reflex sat on a hair-trigger, I'd crawl into the car that would take me to my own bed with clean sheets. Once we were home, Mother would always urge me to, "Sip on a little Co-Cola," which was impossible, and to "Try to take this aspirin, Honey, it'll make you feel better." But, Mother and I both knew my headache was already laughing at St. Joseph and his worthless little orange pills. I would lie as still as possible until the powerful lethargy graciously overtook my pain and brought the kindly Sandman. After sleeping for hours, I would wake to the unwelcome smell of supper cooking. Bitter bile would rise up from my belly, ushering in the migraine's awful finale. I'd throw up so violently that the strain would leave clusters of tiny red dots on my pale cheeks. When the headache was over, the pain was absolutely and completely gone, leaving in its wake some weariness and exhilaration like an endorphin high.

Perhaps my remarkably bony physique resulted from the headache's regular intestinal purging demands. Whatever the reason, I was pretty self-conscious about the way I looked. My huge eyes must have made me look even skinnier as my skinny face re-emphasized my eyes. These two factors constantly and mercilessly conspired against my self-esteem. Instead of chanting multiplication tables with my classmates, I remember canvassing the schoolroom and noting how no one else's wrist bone poked out quite as freakishly disproportionately as mine. Consequently, please don't ask me to multiple, say, seven times eight.

But, around Dale, I could accept my skinniness. He could make anything funny, even my most embarrassing trait. Because I knew he truly loved me and had not a thread of malice in him, being the subject of his jokes was actually an honor. Whether we were laughing about me or something else, laughing along with Dale was always a wonderful treat.

"Shirley," he'd deadpan, "what are those two strings hanging off your shoulders?"

As I looked down to find the errant strings, Dale would jump right to his punch line, "Oh, I'm sorry, those are just your *arms*."

"Shut up, Stupid." were the words preceding my pathetic attack as I chased and slapped him with flailing string-arms.

And there were other taunts: "Shirley, you are so skinny that you have to run around in the shower to get wet." And, "When it rains, you run for cover under the clothesline."

The best I could ever do in attack was to plagiarize his quips. Not a brilliant combat strategy, mind you, but it does take one to know one, so to speak. Dale wasn't exactly tipping the scales like a body builder. When I became a sullen teenager, Dale's talent to pull a giggle out of me did not flag. I still see him in the eye of my memory, responding to my many complaints with an upturned Brut cologne bottle 'microphone' and a horrible rendition of the popular song, *Try a Little Tenderness:*

Oh, she may be weary, young girls, they do get weary ...

Dale taught me to take a joke, to laugh at myself, and he practiced what he preached. He could dish it out, but was good at taking it, too.

Jeanne was also my hero. Because of our seven-year age and size difference, looking up to Jeanne was necessary, but worshiping her was something I did of my own volition. She was everything I was not. She had beauty and grace. Her opinions were Gospel to me. Pleasing her was my earnest desire, and her rejection was worse than death. I could imagine nothing beyond her reach. It was agony to watch Miss America on television when I knew Jeanne was the only girl in any state who really deserved that crown. Maybe some of those girls were almost as pretty as she, but they would all look like turnips if she were standing beside them. Surely her day of justice would finally come, I imagined. Some official 1960's Hollywood talent scout would be certain to discover her in perhaps, a soda shop, and bestow the honor of her true destiny. Because of my adulation, she was for me a maternal figure, taking time to talk to me and fix my hair when Mother was at work. She listened to me and sincerely cared about my feelings. Typically, she was on my side, fiercely protecting my honor. We shared a room, so there were many opportunities to gather wisdom from the wellspring of her experience. I hope she didn't realize how much I depended on her for approval.

I believe I remember the day Timmy was born. Yes, I was only two, but I have this brief memory of myself standing in the back seat of a car in front of our house in East Point, Georgia. I am between two other children, presumably Jeanne and Dale, looking out the back window. I have no recollection of where we were headed, only that we were heading somewhere because the baby had come. Maybe it is an inaccurate memory, but it surely seems real.

Timmy was a round little guy who earned our admiration by being the cutest baby in the world. One of his chubby cheeks sported a deep dimple which I will always covet. He's loved TV as long as I can remember, and was as accustomed to our adoration as he was familiar with commercial breaks. One time when we were all fawning over him for having such delightfully soft and pudgy hands, he stated this fact to us, "My hands are as soft as napkins." We all killed ourselves laughing and it became an eternal catch-phrase in our family.

After Timmy was born, he and I were often referred to as, "the little ones," a moniker we accepted as a matter of fact, without any shame. The unspoken assumption of the title seemed to be that we were fragile and valuable, so everyone should be working together for the common goal of our protection. We were, after all, the least of all. I think we were probably "the little ones" until we were mostly grown and towered over Jeanne and Dale, who had moved out.

Daddy was a sheet metal worker in the early days of our family. He later joined the ranks of the US Department of Labor in the Bureau of Apprenticeship and Training. I loved the way he said those words and willed myself to practice saying them until they rolled off my tongue as easily as they did his. Before long I could say it really fast, "MydiddyworksfortheYouessDepartmentaLabrinthaBurovApprentas hippinTrainin." I fancied that people must be utterly awed by my verbal prowess.

Daddy was the third of ten children born to Mary Lou and John W. Peek in South Pittsburgh, Tennessee, named Mary Etta, Jessie Lorene, John Lemuel, Charles "Charlie" Russell, George Arnold, Inez Joy, William "Billy" Owen, Evelyn Ruth, Marshall Eugene "Genie-boy", and Helen Marie. John W. was a barber. My father briefly took up the trade when he served in the Coast Guard during World War II. As the story went, the military assumed Daddy's proficiency in the trade by proxy because of his father's association. Having all this barber history intrigued me enough to pursue my own Barber's License when I was twenty years old. Even during the Depression, John W.'s vocation allowed a steady income. Daddy used to say his father had owned one of the first cars in town. Apparently, however, John W. was prone to gambling and drinking, activities which sometimes cost him his extra acquisitions. Daddy's patient and loving mother, Mary Lou, provided the balance and consistency in their home. She taught them about Jesus and her prayerful love offered sanction from the often volatile outbursts at home.

    John W's alcoholism altered the normal sense of cause and effect in Daddy's formative years. My father's memory was remarkable, and he fought the demons of his childhood by maintaining meticulous control over the things he was able to master. As an adult, he might have seemed a little like a control freak. He was no more perfect than any man, but his moderation, discipline, and participation in worship were three living lessons that my siblings and I eventually chose also to own. My father looked important. He carried himself with dignity and quiet authority, so people automatically respected him. If visiting a hospital, he was sometimes mistaken for a doctor. In church, visitors assumed he must be the preacher. He had the most confident gait I have ever seen -- his walk was his trademark.

    John Peek could build anything, yet he had such humility about this ability that it took me years to realize how uniquely gifted he was. Throughout my life, his hands hammered and sawed away at hundreds of things that improved our lives. Those hands of his could do more than build things, though. Over time, I observed them gently quiet a crying baby, crochet blankets for his grandchildren, and clasp together in thankful prayer.

    Daddy was always good at eating food that makes people say, "E-w-w." Under his tutelage, I learned to enjoy culinary oddities like dill pickles or sardines in mustard on saltines, but I didn't even try to acquire a taste for his pickled pig's feet. When Mother worked late on Saturday nights, it was Daddy's job to make supper and his habit was preparing hamburgers and home-made French fries. I can picture him now, in a memory ingrained on my brain forever, standing at the counter, cutting and salting the raw potatoes. His methodical assembly required scooping them into a colander and salting them before shaking them around to evenly distribute the salt. I hung around the kitchen waiting, knowing he would offer me a few raw, salted fries as he waited for the grease to heat up. They were a surprisingly tasty foretaste of the feast to come.

Daddy could also make potato soup, but I saw him make it only on those rare occasions when he admitted to feeling poorly. I think it was his special comfort food, although, with his Scots-Irish roots, perhaps it was just one of the things he was taught as a matter of course, a form of art passed through generations. Mary Lou Beene Peek -- from the Irish name McBene -- taught him how to make it when he was a child. She was also the one who taught Daddy how to crochet.

Every opinion I've ever heard about Mrs. Peek regarded her saintliness. Mother, Daddy, and his siblings spoke of her with the same reverence that Catholics reserve for Mary the Mother of God. She was only fifty years old when she died from melanoma and breast cancer, but the love she imparted to her children lasted throughout their lives. I got to read a few charming letters she had written to my Aunt Mary Etta right before Mrs. Peek died. Each letter downplayed the cancer that would soon kill her and was signed, *Oceans of Love, Mother.*

Once their grandchildren started coming, Daddy and Mother were almost always crocheting some baby-oriented item while watching TV at night. I was a teenager during this time when they taught the skill to me as Johnny Carson entertained us from a console TV in the foreground. Everyone I knew got a crocheted blanket that Christmas.

Another wonderful thing about my father was that he could play the harmonica. As young men, he and his brother Charlie actually played at various functions in an all-harmonica band. What a wonderful spectacle that must have been. I loved it when I could convince him to play for me. A couple of his favorites were *The Wabash Cannonball* and *Roll out the Barrel.* My love for Bluegrass music must have been given its first breath of life in the chords of Daddy's harmonica.

Daddy was smart, but never rushed through anything unless there was a genuine, urgent need. He operated on his own agenda. We found his school yearbook after we were grown and snickered over his ironic nickname, "Lightning." He never minded taking the time to be deliberate and fastidious, taking a little longer or even starting over to get a job done perfectly. I sincerely believe that the things my daddy built will still be standing when Jesus comes.

My mother, Ophelia Peek worked at W.T. Grant store from my earliest memories. She pinched and saved the remainder of her pay checks that didn't go into buying our school clothes. I wondered if her strong work ethic came from surviving the Depression, or maybe it was her maternal German roots from Edna Gunter's lineage.

Just like Daddy, Mother was third in her family birth order and born in 1922. She grew up with two brothers and five sisters. Chronologically, they were Anna Lou, Robert "R.L." Lee, Ophelia "Ophie" Lorene, Ruby Nell, Daisy Madeliene, Virginia "Ginny" Eloise, Barbara Jean, and William "Cran" Cranfill. Her parents, Byrd Clifford and Edna Gunter Brown farmed some land in Hartwell, Georgia. All the children worked the fields. It was a hard life. My Aunt Daisy used to say they could feed the chickens through the cracks in the floor.

As a very bashful third grade child, little Ophelia was offered piano lessons by her school teacher, Ruth Jones. She truly wanted to learn because her big sister Anne had taken lessons, but Ophie's shy personality paralyzed her from accepting the offer. Every time my mother mentioned this story to me, she confessed her regret over the lost opportunity. As a result, Jeanne and I both got to take piano lessons. Mother used her loss for our good.

Shy though she was, Ophie was a reputed force to be reckoned with on the basketball court. As a famed guard on the Allford School and Hart County High basketball teams, her natural athletic gift gave her a bold and exhilarating momentum. Describing it in her eighties, I could hear the smile in her voice when Mother said, "It was almost like you were playing and fighting at the same time." On the court, a transformation occurred. Demure Ophelia's long, sleek five-feet-seven-frame would become "Wicked Elbow," a nickname given to her after accidentally throwing her elbow into another player's teeth while fighting for the ball.

In 1934, an awful thing happened in the Brown family. It was agreed that sixteen-year-old Anne could throw a little party. Sometime during the event, a rough crew of boys crashed it. Byrd Brown asked them to leave and they attacked, striking him in the head with a blunt object. My mother remembers that he was bleeding and unconscious. She once told me, "I could see his heartbeat in the hole that was left in his head." The sheriff came and Byrd was taken to the hospital in Royston, Georgia. For the rest of his days, Byrd Brown's pain was unrelenting. In 1950, the grandfather I would never meet found a way to stop his pain. Byrd Brown took repose under his usual resting tree when my grandmother saw him alive for the last time. She went into the house to get their youngest son, Cran, a drink as he worked in the cotton field. When she returned, she found her husband shot in the heart. A sawed-off shotgun was found with him.

My mother was a worrier. She seemed cynical of nearly everything and everyone. Growing up, I was often unnerved by her protective ways. We had rules and curfews, and all of our time away from the house was carefully monitored. I suspect that losing her daddy so tragically might have encouraged the way she raised us. Much too young, she had learned the very worst of what can come from the most innocent beginnings. How could she ever again trust her loved ones to what she couldn't see around the corner?

Somehow, even working full-time, Mother managed to prepare balanced meals and clothe us, even sewing clothes for us from time to time. She drove her green, 1954 Chevy to take Jeanne and me to piano lessons, Georgia's Baptist Girl's Auxiliary, Brownies or Bluebirds. She helped Dale with his paper route and took him and Timmy to Royal Ambassadors at church. As each of us came of age, Mother entrusted us with putting supper in the oven. I can picture the notes she had carefully written in her flowing cursive script before leaving for work. I would find them written on a page of her stationary pad, lying on the kitchen table after we came home from school.

Dearest Shirley,

Pre-heat oven to 350 ° at about 5:30 p.m. Take the meat loaf out of refrigerator and put on top rack in oven. Heat up green beans on low on top of stove. I'll home around 6:45 p.m. and will mash some potatoes when I get there. You can make some Jell-o if you want to.

Love, Mother

I was grown with my own family before it occurred to me that Mother's notes had taught me to cook. What's more, they had created an impetus for my confidence and love of the culinary arts.

Oh, how I would need that in my later years.

Daddy and Mother were diligent to have us at Second Baptist Church every Sunday. Regardless of anything else that might be going on in our family, we were always at Sunday School and Worship on Sunday mornings. I was an adult before I knew to appreciate this rare discipline. Two things I remember about Worship are that Daddy used to make me tiny wine goblets out of the silver wrappers of Wrigley's Spearmint gum Mother would share with us and that I never could be still for very long. Sometimes Mother would let me fall asleep in her lap. I understand now that this was likely the only way she could concentrate on the sermon.

The old adage that *the family that prays together stays together* was something my parents boldly took on as a responsibility. At home, despite any family disruptions that came up (and there were plenty), we had devotions before bedtime. They consisted of a Bible reading, our individual prayers, and a collective recitation of The Lord's Prayer. If the discipline of Sunday Worship was rare, this worship together as a family was almost unheard of, yet my parents made it seem as normal as mealtime. Praying in public was something Daddy was often called on to do at Second Baptist. As a consequence of this example and our devotions, praying aloud is something none of my siblings and I have ever felt shy about. One of the greatest gifts in my life is that my parents taught us to worship and pray, but my brothers and sister and I had no idea how much power Mother and Daddy were passing on to us.

By the time each of the four of us reached puberty, the Holy Spirit had urged us down the aisle on a respective Sunday morning to give our hearts to Jesus. I was nine-years-old when I answered the call, and this was the first time I really remember feeling the Power of the Holy Spirit. I cried and cried as if a river were pouring out of me. I felt self-conscious afterward, but I knew no force on Earth could have stopped me from taking that walk. Like most Baptist churches, we had a Baptismal Pool behind the choir loft, and that's where all of us got baptized. I don't remember ever talking about it with my parents before or afterward, but it was to their credit that I knew the path, and I was glad I had taken my walk.

On the playground at school, I pondered my need to make a concerted effort to be mindful of my sins. My friend, Barbara and I talked about Jesus sometimes. Considering her Christian maturity, she must have received Salvation as a toddler or earlier. Along with her Gospel-singing sisters, she wore her faith like a well-worn quilt. Looking back, I see that Barbara's friendship was one of the ways God kept my mind on Him, even back then.

Searching side effects came about from being in Worship every Sunday, like having a weekly launching pad for thinking about whom and *Whose* I was, and what might be required in the future. Belonging to Jesus got me thinking about my life's path. I can remember being as young as nine and wondering how God wanted to use me. My greatest desire in life was to have many children of my own. By the time I was a teenager, I decided that I would adopt children if I never found a husband or couldn't bear children on my own. Being a mother was something God placed squarely on my heart long before any other guidance I can recall.

Great is Your love toward me; You have delivered me from the depths of the grave.
Psalm 86:13

The Move

On April 11, 1969, my family moved from Atlanta to Columbia, South Carolina with me kicking and screaming. My attempts to thwart the move by yanking up the "For Sale" sign every day after school had rendered no effect whatsoever. Leaving Atlanta en route to Columbia that Friday evening with two adult dogs and six puppies attached to the roof of the car in a U-Haul carrier, we encountered five-o'clock traffic. For some strange reason, which still makes no sense at all, there was a break in traffic around Duluth. The speed limit was seventy miles per hour, and Daddy was driving at least that fast. As a matter of fact, driving is the one thing I remember Daddy doing fast.

Seated beside Daddy was my brother, Tim, who opened up a hole by leaning down to tie his shoe at this critical moment. Beside Tim was Mother. Behind her in the back seat was Jerry, my sister's boy friend. Jeanne leaned against him with her head on his shoulder, widening the space above and behind Tim. I sat behind Daddy pressing my ear against my window and the gift of a transistor radio my boyfriend, Larry had sent with me. As I willed a few more scratchy strains of Atlanta rock music from WQXI, I also inadvertently opened the hole up another few life saving inches. No one wore a seat belt; in fact, I don't even think seat belts were a requirement in 1969.

The next thing I knew, all the windows were breaking and it felt like we were flying in a circle. Daddy was hanging over the back of his seat in a backbend position, his bleeding head lying almost in my lap. My first thought was that Russia must be attacking the United States and we were being fired on; this was a common fear of mine, perpetuated by commercials and drills of the sixties era.

I screamed, "Daddy, Daddy!" (Although my sister says she heard this as, "E-e-e-e-e-e!" in a pitch so high she wanted to slap me). Mother and Timmy reached for the brake, but by that time the car was already out of control.

It's so crazy how vivid insignificant details become in a

traumatic situation. I can still visualize my short blue skirt, white collared shirt, and sleeveless sweater that matched the skirt. I could never wear it again, as it was spattered with Daddy's blood and miniscule shards of glass gnawed tiny holes that unraveled the fabric.

What had happened was our windshield had been hit by what I remember as a large metal hook with a few links of heavy chain attached to it. It had broken off a logging truck driven by a man with no license, traveling in the opposing lane at a speed of seventy miles an hour or more. Since we were going in opposite directions, it impacted at approximately one-hundred-forty miles per hour, cold-cocking my father right below his bottom-teeth gum line. This was likely the only place on his face where he could have taken that blow without instantly being killed. The metal slung around through the blessed hole God had arranged for us, and exited the back window, with my daddy bearing the sole impact. Only God knows how we all lived.

While still in motion, Jerry reached over the seat and put the car in neutral. Our blue 1962 Chevrolet Bel-Air became airborne, turned to the left, and lifted itself over the median. It crossed over the opposing lanes of traffic backwards and deposited itself at the bottom of a fifty-foot embankment. If the car had landed any other way we would have been thrown out. Truly God's Own hand was on us and why the car never rolled is another mystery He might explain to me one day.

When we realized the car had finally landed, we tried to remember how to pull the doors open. We tumbled out clumsily with little conversation. We were a little like zombies, trying to shake the cobwebs out of our brains so that something normal would come into focus. Amazed that Daddy was also stumbling out, we began to plead with him to sit down. Instead, bleeding and talking, he started making cracks. He spat a couple of bloody teeth into his hand. Despite weaving drunkenly, he looked me right in the eye, and said, "Well, looks like you have a toothless old man now!"

It was agonizing to watch him respond so inappropriately to the situation. Where was the Daddy we counted on, who always knew what was going on before anyone else? Minutes passed before he began to faint and someone caught him. A jug of water appeared from somewhere and I don't remember what it was used to improve. Maybe someone tried to give Daddy a drink or wash his wounds.

People were lining up on the interstate rail gawking at us. As precious time passed I began to worry and climbed the hill to ask for someone to help us! I pleaded with one man to, "Please, help my father," but he never even looked at me. It was as though we were a television show he was watching. Despite the fact that I stood there talking to him, we weren't real to him. He just stared past me to the base of the bank where my family struggled to make some sense of what was happening. I finally descended the embankment in disbelief.

Joining the confusion of my frantic family, I passed my little brother, Timmy, kneeling in the grass, praying for an answer. God heard his eleven-year-old voice and caused an air traffic patrol plane flying overhead to spot us and radio for an ambulance. This brought the emergency medical vehicle fairly quickly. The first thing Daddy told us he remembered was the bump of the stretcher as paramedics pushed him into the van and en route to the next exit, where tiny Joan Glancy Hospital was located.

One of the first discomfiting memories I have of getting to our new house in Columbia was arriving without Daddy. Mother was so fragile, but she smiled on the first day we arrived, as we were greeted by the most wonderful home-made cinnamon rolls I ever remember eating. They had arrived, compliments of our realtor's mother, whom I never had the pleasure of meeting. She was compelled to do us a kindness after hearing of our plight. This might be my first cohesive acquaintance with God reaching out through the benevolence of strangers. Knowing how much we appreciated her unsolicited gift is, for me, still a beautiful ideal. This example reminds me that God sometimes uses our everyday talents to comfort people in need.

Even when he got home from the hospital, Daddy was in bed healing most of those three months. His determination to recover was almost supernatural as his penchant for discipline took over and became an entity of its own. In order to force nutrients a blender was purchased to pulverize solid food into thick liquids. Family meals were watered down and pureed for Daddy. Each day, he slowly drew three square meals through a straw, past his wired-together teeth, and into his stomach. Well, every meal except for one. One night when Mother cooked fried chicken livers as an entrée, Daddy's Tennessee voice calmly explained the aftermath through his medically-clenched teeth, "I tried to swallow it, but it went up instead-a down."

Quite a self-sufficient man, Daddy had never asked me for any help that I could recall, so it felt strange and novel when he asked me to make him milkshakes from time to time. I was honored that he trusted me to do it, yet it scared me that he had acquiesced. Between pushing nourishment, sleeping a lot and sheer will to recover, Daddy was gaining strength.

When John Peek was finally healed enough to have the wires cut that held his jaws together, he moved gratefully to the next level of his recovery. Drinking meat and vegetables from a straw was soon replaced by cautious chewing of solid food. For the rest of his life, he was committed to greeting the day with morning stretches and muscle-strengthening exercises; and as long as he was able, he practiced this physical therapy before ever getting out of his bed. Many years later, his seventieth decade would find him still strong enough to split logs with apparent ease.

Mother carried on, finding a position at W.T. Grant store in our new town. My brother and I settled in at our new schools despite my reluctance. Sooner than we could believe, Daddy returned to work at the Department of Labor in Columbia. Our lives almost seemed predictable again, but something was different. We knew God had saved us all from what should have been swift death, and now we were left to figure out why.

As soon as Tim and I were settled enough in our school in Columbia, I began to hate my situation. I wondered why friends were so hard to make in this town. All my comfort seemed very, very far away. Jeanne lived in a dorm at West Georgia College and Dale was many miles away in Atlanta. His Brut bottle sat right-side-up on a dresser in the apartment he shared with his new wife, Sally. I came to discount God's message from the car accident. Instead of keeping the assurance that there was a purpose for each of us, I began to think my life was over and I would never again find anything to be happy about. The greatest reason I was wrong was Ruthie Addison, whom I would meet at E.L. Wright Junior High School.

I had arrived with such a bad attitude Ruthie must have overlooked a whole lot in order to like me. I hadn't wanted to leave my Atlanta friends or my school, so I carried a defensive little chip on my shoulder that underscored my belief that Columbia was not as cool as Atlanta. The weight of that chip was an awful burden. I hated having left my sub-freshman status at W.F. George High School, only to reappear in South Carolina with a more juvenile ranking: *junior high school-er*!

I also hated the cliques at E.L. Wright Junior High that seemed to shun a new girl. That's when my friendship with Linda took root. Linda had a little cocky attitude going on, which may have been attracted to my negative one. I let her copy my Spelling papers, so she introduced me to Ruthie one day at lunch. It was customary to go out on the schools grounds when we were finished eating in the cafeteria and that's where Linda took me that day to find Ruthie.

"Ru-u-thie!" Linda addressed her, drawing out the "u" in her name as long as possible, "This is the girl I told you about who reminds me so much of PatZimmer!"

Linda, who couldn't decide between her previous New Jersey accent and the South Carolina one, said, "Pat Zimmer" as if it were one word.

"Ohmygosh, Ruthie, I can NOT be-LIEVE how much she looks like PatZimmer, can you?" asked Linda with no small amount of enthusiasm.

("Pat moved two months ago and I have missed her *so much!*") Linda added as an aside to me, even though she had already mentioned this point several times before. I faced Ruthie as Linda fluttered off abruptly to speak to a girl named Bethany. Ruthie chewed her gum and appeared to be looking across the grounds at something serious. I squinted at where she was looking, but couldn't find anything extraordinary enough to watch. Taking this personally, of course, I wondered if she was ever going to say anything. Maybe I ought to walk away. Her aloofness, however, was brief; actually the result of Charlie. Ruthie's intense blue eyes carried out a constant search for her heart throb when she was at school. Whatever he might be doing at any given moment was always of grave importance to Ruthie.

"Hey." She answered slow and smooth, finally making eye contact. "It's nice to meet you. Where'd you move from?"

Ruthie was kind and mature. She seemed surer of herself than I, so I countered her maturity with my self-perceived coolness.

"...Atlan'a," I answered, not bothering to mention the state. Since Atlanta was so cool I figured Ruthie would recognize and assume I was also cool.

"...Really?" Ruthie replied in her calm, sweet voice, "Why'd you move?"

She actually seemed interested in me, which was all it took for me to spill my guts. I told her about how Daddy had accepted a transfer with the *YooEssDepartmentaLabrinthaBurovApprennashippinTrainin* (I could still say it really fast). I intimated to her about the wreck, and that Daddy was still in the hospital. She listened in a way that made me believe I was mildly fascinating. Her acceptance of me was a healing elixir for which I was starving.

Sometime before the bell rang, our talk took a practical turn. We realized our sub-divisions were only across Trenholm Road from each other, so Ruthie suggested that I ride home on her bus the next day. She said one of her parents would take me home when they returned from the post office where they both worked. Riding the bus was a new and uncomfortable addition to my itinerary, but Ruthie explained where I should meet her to find the right bus.

The next day at her house, I learned all about her Charlie and told her about my Larry. We hung on each other's stories as though they were teen romance magazine articles. Ruthie brought out marshmallows and potato chips that, for some reason, were in their freezer.

"They're frozen?" I queried the statement.

"You don't freeze your potato chips and marshmallows?" Ruthie countered with a question, looking at me as though I had just grown antennae on my forehead.

"Can marshmallows spoil?" I continued in the fashion of answering a question with a question.

"I don't know." Ruthie stated, breaking the cycle. She pirouetted, proceeding to her living room with me on her heels.

"What do they dance like in Atlanta?" She asked, making herself comfortable and cross-legged like a spectator. I could have demonstrated the Twist or the Swim, but immediately felt pressure to perform something exotic for her instead.

"Well," I said, "do y'all do "Around the World?"

"No." Ruthie confidently stated, capturing a frozen marshmallow from the bag with only a dainty thumb and index finger. "What's that?"

Honestly, I had only seen the dance once. A girl named Jenny with waist length hair had mesmerized the crowd with it at a school dance. Jenny was Cher-cool, a year older than I and I didn't really *know* her, per se, only *of* her. Her mother, I heard, had died when we were in elementary school. It was a time when children traumatized by events weren't provided an outlet for their questions so Jenny's mother's death only made her more mysterious and without reproach. I slung my head around as I had seen her do, making deep arcs followed by wide circles with my shoulder length hair. It wasn't much of a dance, I remember thinking as my brain cells were being flung and slammed against the inner walls of my skull. Right before I stopped and tried hard not to act as woozy as I felt, it occurred to me that maybe, just maybe, Jenny had made the dance up.

"You're right," Ruthie lied graciously without a trace of sarcasm, "that is a cool dance."

Perceptive, even as a child, Ruthie was quick to pick up on why I was having such a hard time making friends. Surprisingly, it had less to do with my attitude and dance skills than it did with my wardrobe ensemble.

Cool or not, in Atlanta, saddle oxfords were the standard issue for girls and boys. I can't remember beginning a single school year, from first grade on, when I didn't have a brand-new pair of black and whites. If you had a second pair, they might be brown and tan. Cheerleaders wore modified pointy-toed ones with their uniforms. I had been at E.L. Wright for a month now and still hadn't noticed that I was the only one wearing the big city shoe of choice. Who knew style could be so fleeting a mere state away?

Bearing loving-kindness and wisdom far beyond her fourteen years, Ruthie saw no purpose in simply telling me I needed to get a pair of Weejun loafers to make friends. Chances are, I would have been hurt and angered, the chip on my shoulder would have grown far heavier, and I would have sunk into worse despair. Instead, Ruthie shared her concerns with her precious little mama, Louise. I don't know how many shoe stores Mrs. Louise drove Ruthie to on her day off before they found her a pair of her own saddle oxfords. All I know is that Ruthie's feet were cradled in a pair the next day. By the time I realized we were the only two people in South Carolina wearing saddle shoes, I recognized something far more valuable: I had made a special life-long friend. As I write these lines almost forty years later, I am proud and thankful to claim Ruthie as my best friend, still.

These are some of the highlights about the first hand observers of the beginnings of my life. I hope my brief descriptions provide an apt glimpse of these precious and dear people who God used to define me.

***

My teen years took me through Spring Valley High School in Columbia, South Carolina where I graduated in 1972. I met David Miller in my Art Class and we became an on-and-off couple during those years. On one of our "on again" periods, we introduced my sister, Jeanne to his brother, Scott. They married. We didn't.

After graduation I had one minimum wage job after another with no intention of going to college. I told myself I didn't want to be a financial burden on my parents and that was true, but secretly I feared I wasn't smart enough. After our move from Atlanta I'd rarely taken high school seriously and my grades were evidence of this.

At age nineteen I ended up working as a receptionist/shampoo girl at a Hair Replacement Center in Columbia. It was here I met my friend, Carolyn a twenty-three year old graduate of the barber college our employer ran. It was from Carolyn that I learned business and barber ethics and she helped me cultivate an interest in barbering. Finally, I felt like I had some direction.

After the Hair Replacement Center closed, Carolyn transferred to King's Quarter's Hair Styling which is where I finished up my On-Job-Training. It was at this time that I met Jon Thornton, a former resident of Pensacola, Florida, who was an interior designer at an office furniture business in town. We dated for over a year (with one big break-up and make-up in between) before we married. Only four months after our wedding I convinced Jon we should have a baby and we conceived soon after. Our attention, fully on being newlyweds and newly expecting made this a truly fun time of life.

Jon and I were almost two years married with a one-year-old before we realized how different our goals were and how little we had in common; but little Jon Lemuel, or "Lem" as we called him, made it easy to ignore our differences and focus on love and joy for a long time. Lem was uncommonly adorable with a happy personality and thick, pouty lips that broke out into a grin without much provocation. Having fulfilled my life-long wish to become a mother, I relished in every moment of my new role. Even with the daily disappointments my marriage brought, I was happier than I'd ever been before in my life.

When Jon was offered a job in Pensacola, Florida we moved, but the change of scenery only briefly took our minds off the marital discontent. It seemed clear that our problems had followed us to Pensacola and very soon the strain escalated to the point that we could no longer ignore it.

By the time Lem was two-years-old, none of the counseling nor our efforts to compromise had proven effective. Even though I was three months pregnant with Austin I felt we'd all be better off if I moved back to South Carolina and set up a new household alone with the children. A year-long separation later our divorce was final.

As my heart worked to recover from the divorce and my body recovered from the June 21, 1982 birth of Austin, the three of us lived with my parents. Before Austin was born Daddy fashioned the mother-in-law suite (a separate room off from their house) into a one-chair barber shop for me. My old hairstyling patrons proved their loyalty to me and soon after Austin's birth we were able to move into a small apartment. Austin was born eight-pounds, fourteen ounces, a mere ounce lighter than the birth weight of his brother, Jon Lemuel. There was never a more beautiful baby than Austin. He was fat and pink and smiled most of the time and quite a character from the very start.

Before Austin was three months old I started hearing from David Miller, who had heard of my divorce from Scott and Jeanne. Still in the Navy and stationed in Charleston, South Carolina, he began calling me and writing letters when he was at sea. I hadn't forgotten that he'd broken my heart and in the wake of trying to heal from a devastating divorce, I didn't trust him. Still, I enjoyed the attention he was giving my children and me. Before I knew it, I'd dropped my guard and let David convince me he was true blue. Not long afterward, he totally surprised me with an engagement ring. I felt rushed, but nonetheless happy that something positive seemed to be rising on my horizon again.

We moved to Summerville, South Carolina after we married and David was soon out to sea. On my trips to the grocery store with the boys I noticed a marquis on the Lutheran church near our house that advertised Vacation Bible School coming up. Small though it was, their V.B.S. catered to every age. There would be a class for Lem, a nursery class for little Austin and even a class for me. I was excited. I found the places for Lem and Austin and chose for myself a class that focused on Martin Luther. I was fascinated by his life and the changes he made in the Reformation. I remember thinking that his questions were the same as mine and agreed with his interpretation of the Bible. By the end of the week, I realized this was the church to which I wanted to belong.

It took David and me less than a year to discover we'd made a horrible mistake. I wasn't anywhere near healing emotionally from the dissolution of my first marriage and David was also having trouble dealing with his own issues. It seemed unbelievable to me that I'd navigated my little family into such a mess of a state, but here we were again, starting over and me, pregnant again. I felt like the star of my own trashy soap opera.

We moved back to the apartment complex in Columbia where we'd lived before David and I married. I took up barbering again with my faithful clientele. David and I went to counseling through the Navy when he was in port, but we still weren't getting anywhere. I was so depressed that after I got my sons to bed at night I'd curl up into a little ball on my bed and cry for hours.

The boys and I visited a Lutheran church near my apartment one Sunday. I thought I could handle it, but my tears were on a hair trigger. I managed to get Lem and Austin to their Sunday school and nursery classes then found a class for me through the assistance of a lady named Lois. Lois also had two boys and was about my age. When Sunday school ended I located my sons and we went to the Sanctuary, but I didn't get far. Noticeably pregnant now, with two little boys in tow who had different last names from mine, I felt as though I had a scarlet letter painted on my chest. My throat closed up and I realized I was too big a mess to sit in a pew for an hour. We left and my tears flowed all the way home.

The next week my car failed and I had to enlist the kindness of my father to help me to doctor appointments and grocery shopping. Lois called around Friday just to check in. I told her about my car and she offered to drive us to church the following Sunday. For some reason I felt some fortitude and accepted her offer. She taxied us to church for a couple of Sundays until my car was repaired. I lost heart again and stopped going to church. Little did I know that Lois and I would find ourselves on the same path again one day.

***

Weighing in at eight pounds, thirteen ounces, my beautiful

little Elisabeth was born on September 16, 1984 at my parents' house in Columbia with the assistance of Tavish, my friend and midwife, my barber friend, Carolyn and another friend named Jo Ann, who videotaped Elisabeth's birth. Lem, Austin and Mother were the first family members to meet her.

  My little family, now settled in our apartment in Irmo, began to grow roots there. Jon started kindergarten at Irmo Elementary and decided to go by his first name, Jon. I went to work cutting hair at Tracy's Family Hair Care and business was pretty good. I met a new friend, Cindy through my apartment manager and she charged me way less than she should have to keep Austin and Elisabeth while I worked. Jon joined his siblings at Cindy's after kindergarten.

  David was still dealing with his own issues and it seemed to be best that he wasn't around. Lem and Austin had occasional visits from their dad but as our sons grew, he wasn't a big part of their lives. When Elisabeth was two-years-old, I found Christus Victor Lutheran church and there she was finally baptized. It felt good to be part of a church community again and it felt good to feel healing in my heart. Oh, and a surprise awaited us at Christus Victor. My friend, Lois was the pianist!

*I praise you because I am fearfully and wonderfully made;
your works are wonderful, I know that full well.
Psalm 139:14*

Chapter Two

Paul's father Joe was almost perfectly replicated in Paul. Copies in face, frame, and mannerisms, genetics had built them with calf muscles enough to shame any dancer or soccer star. It was hard to believe these two had spent Paul's formative years so many miles apart, but not for lack of effort on Joe's part. The more I got to know Joe, the more I learned about Paul's beginnings. Distinguishing between Paul and his dad was easy when they were speaking, however. Though similar in timbre, their voices couldn't conceal distinctly different accents. Joe was Rhode Island born and bred. The various zip codes of his adult life hadn't muscle enough to knock the sharp edges off his vowels. By contrast, Paul's vowels were softer and never rushed. He had rarely been outside Columbia, South Carolina growing up and any addresses he had later owned were situated below the Mason-Dixon Line.

Joseph David Lionel Fournier and Betty Doris Sumner met in Tampa, Florida, when Joe was in the Air Force. Both of them very young (Betty was only sixteen) when they made the decision to marry. Soon after their marriage, Joe left Florida to report back to duty. He promised to secure housing and send for the wife he believed he loved but didn't know all that well.

With Joe gone, Betty began to concentrate on two overwhelming realities. One, she was expecting a baby and two; she didn't want to be married. Her emotions must have been at war within her. Hardly more than a headstrong yet insecure child herself, she bravely confronted the birth of a baby she already loved fiercely. Staying in Tampa became her whole focus. In her young mind, removing her husband from the equation of their life seemed like the most logical answer to the problem of her discontent. It was *her* baby, she reasoned, and Joe's paternity didn't count for nearly as much. Needless to say, communication became strained between them during the military separation and pregnancy.

After he was born on August 8, 1950, Paul was christened in the Catholic faith (Joe's denomination). Working hard to make it work, Joe saved and bought Betty a fancy car. Still, the lack of communication intensified. Over the next couple of years, Joe's efforts to visit little *Joe-Paul* and Betty during his times of leave were often thwarted. Knocking at one or another Sumner relative's house, he sometimes had to give up on what was obviously a fruitless search. These failed endeavors sent him back to his duty station wondering, not just where his family was, but also what on Earth he might have done to fall so far outside Betty's favor.

By the time little Paul was four, Joe finally agreed to sacrifice his marriage and the chase. After he and Betty were divorced, Joe began to move ahead, seeking happiness in a new life and a denomination that didn't exclude divorcees. He remarried a few years later to Rozemary and they had two beautiful daughters, Michele and Monica. Betty often told me Joe was ever faithful to send child support right on time every month. Sometimes I would hear her sigh before saying, "I probably should have stayed with that man."

After the split, Betty married Rod Graham. It wasn't long before they moved to Columbia, South Carolina. The Graham family inhabited a small house in a hilly neighborhood which must have been created with bicycling kids in mind. As a very young child, Betty had been prone to dress Paul in sissy clothes and forbade him to get dirty. Pretty soon, two more busy boys, Steve and Danny, were added to the mix of their family, and all that testosterone choked off Betty's fashion attempts. Before she was really ready, Paul had wrangled beyond her parameters and experienced mud and blood like a proper boy.

Paul's family was far from rich, but since Rod was a grocer and Betty was a waitress and a great cook, the family had plenty to eat. Three hungry boys at the table, however, left every man for himself. None of the boys were above licking all over their food in full view of the others to insure ownership. After all, food with spit on it tastes just like food without spit on it; as long as it's your own spit. Paul's ability to eat fast was learned through these early meals, and he carried the skill into his adulthood. It served him well when he became a busy pharmacist without a lunch hour, working his meals between patients, pill counting, and arguing with insurance companies. His friend, Jackie, a pharmacy tech, once told me, "Paul taught me so many things, but the best thing I learned from him was how to eat really, really fast."

Despite the small borders of his pre-adult world, Paul managed to find an everyday treasure trove of adventure. He honed a competitive marble-shooting skill that earned him neighborhood fame as the King of Marbles. His trophy was a big glass jar containing hundreds of multi-colored glass balls, all claimed fair and square, in victories over other little boys. He could out-shoot anybody.

Besides his marble collection, he also took great pride in collecting coins. Collecting younger brothers wasn't necessarily his choice. Being the oldest, he was often called on to oversee his brothers, who did their brotherly duty by trying his patience. When some of his pennies disappeared one day, Paul confronted Steve, who finally confessed to the crime. Once it was established that the money was gone – spent at a store – Steve pleaded this defense: "I only took the old ones." This may have been the very day Paul learned to practice mercy and self-control.

Other milestones in his life included taking a regular pounding from the neighborhood bully. Paul finally let him have it one day and the big boy ran away crying, never to bother him again. This experience enlightened Paul to a universal truth about bullies and gave him newfound courage and confidence.

And the Lord had plans for this little man. By his own choice, Paul made Sunday bicycle treks to a Baptist Church several blocks from his house where he gave his young heart to Jesus. As much as he loved riding a bike, his family's budget didn't always allow for an available set of wheels. He told of receiving the gift of one bike that was a special joy because he'd been without one for an achingly long time. The bike was used, and the frame had been welded together, but it was enough for a boy whose longing was to fly up and down the streets. It felt so wonderful to take the downhill ride and feel the wind bouncing off the top of his crew cut. Pedaling up a hill one day, the bike suddenly broke into two pieces. When Paul shared this story after we were married, his voice took on a quiet hoarseness when he described the break, almost like shame. As the bereavement and disappointment in his little-boy heart remained all those years later, I envisioned him standing in the hot, dusty street, many blocks from home. Maybe he had even fallen, skinning his little elbow or knee. How I wished I could give that child a brand, new bike. Paul must have felt the same, and I don't think the loss ever left him. He brought it into fatherhood and let God use it for good. I know this because on Christmas morning at our house, new bicycles would always be waiting there under the tree.

Paul appreciated his stepfather. This admiration centered greatly on the way Rod treated Paul like his own son while growing up. From Rod, Paul learned to fish, hunt, and to do other manly things like car repair, fixing things around the house, pouring a concrete patio. Still, Betty was protective of Paul, and when Rod disciplined him, she sometimes reminded him, "*that* one is *mine*." In other words, she was willing to pull rank as the blood parent should she question Rod's parenting.

Paul lived true to how God had built him. Playing football and basketball in high school, he and his teammates developed a tight group whose friendship, ribbing, and golf continued as grown men. Betty, a cute little sprite of a woman with a smallish face and strawberry hair, adored her boys, loved their friends, and rarely missed a high school game. She claimed some of these friends as her adopted children and kept cards and pictures of some of them in her Bible. They called her, *Mama Graham* and were frequent, welcome additions to the Graham household. In fact, they still speak of her layer cakes in reverent tones.

Of Paul's high school buddies, he was closest to Gary Smallen and Phil Williams. Both boys made regular impressions on the Graham furniture. Phil had a special talent with their dog as well. Meatball was the dog's name, and he was a Heinz 57 mix. It is reputed that Phil taught the dog to talk. Everyone who witnessed it swears it is true.

"Ta-a-alk to me, Meatball." Phil is said to have uttered while holding the dog's jaws shut.

"Mm-m-mmmm-m." the dog would unwittingly reply.

"Tell me what you want." Phil's urging would accompany the opening of Meatball's mouth just a little bit, two times.

"Mm-ma-a-a, Mm-ma-a." Meatball would whine, jerking his shoulders left and right in an attempt to escape.

Paul's warning comment was, "That dog is going to kill you, Phil." He'd say it with laughter, knowing fully-well what would come next.

"Tell me again who loves you." Phil begged longingly as Meatball's answer seeped past his dog lips and out through Phil's fingers.

"Mm-ma-a ma-a-a." Repeated the dog as his back legs dug

deep stripes in the pile of the rug.

Phil would keep evoking Meatball's utterances until he let him loose. The dog was so mad he would chase Phil out the screen door and down the street. Phil the daredevil always outran the dog and thus lived past his teen-age years to adulthood. Like Gary, Phil became a high school football coach. I often wonder if he used his gifted method of inspiring a good run out of a dog on his players as well.

Paul and his buddies made a mark on the world doing things that boys do, both good and bad. Some of their activities weren't very well thought out, and some were downright dangerous. For example, they sometimes tested their water sport skills while emptying a cooler of beer in a boat on Lake Murray. As a result of drunken water skiing, Paul ended up in an immobilizing leg cast that kept him watching a whole lot of TV for months.

One of Betty's favorite stories was about an afternoon when Paul was suddenly drawn to laughter by a TV chewing gum commercial.

"Mom, come here, quick." Paul had called from the living room, "You've got to see this."

Betty scurried to the T.V. where Paul was watching a commercial for Fruit Stripe gum.

"It's YOU." He informed her, amazed at the resemblance of his mother to the Fruit Stripe mouse. "You look just like that mouse." Amused, Betty giggled along with the idea of having a cartoon twin. From that day forward, she took delight in this association.

Paul's skiing injury later resulted in one of his great disappointments. Having hoped to finish ROTC in college and enter the Air Force as an officer, he tried to enlist. The military medic who did his medical assessment had this to say after looking at his knee injury: "You'll be in a wheelchair before you're forty." These words made Paul hoppin' mad. He felt the medic was over-stepping his authority – shooting from the hip. Paul used his anger to defy the prognosis. He exercised ad nauseam to build muscles around the torn ligaments and damaged tissues and absolutely was not in a wheelchair at forty as predicted.

Four years her senior, Paul began seeing Fran when she was in high school. They married soon after Fran graduated from high school. Around 1980, when Paul was still in his twenties, his half-sister Michele was touring with a Christian song and dance troupe and determinedly made it her mission to find the brother she longed to know. Traveling near Columbia, South Carolina, she chanced calling a phone number in the local book. The name beside the number was Paul Graham, and hoping it was the Joe-Paul she knew to be her brother, she dialed.

Paul: "Hello?"
Michele: "Yes, is this Joe-Paul?"
Paul: "No."
-CLICK-
Fran: "Who was that?"
Paul: "Wrong number."
Fran: "What did they say?"
Paul: "They wanted Joe-Paul."

Fran knew it was someone from his father's family. Of course, Paul did, too. What he didn't know was that he was scared – grappling with an emotion he couldn't name. It lurked from a deep place in childhood where he had no control over his own world or the ones he loved and needed. He may have seemed cold, but he was actually trying to protect himself from phantom feelings of loss way down inside him.

Michele didn't give up. I don't know how Fran did it, but somehow she convinced Paul to talk to Michele when she called back. Some healing and reconciliation took place over the years, and I will always be indebted to Michele and Fran for their parts in helping Paul risk the rejection he feared so much. Thanks to these two women, our children know their daddy's family.

Paul and Fran were married eight years before conceiving their daughter, Sarah. Paul decided to go to Law school and managed to work it in between being a full-time pharmacist and shared responsibility for Sarah's care. After he graduated, Fran was offered a promotion that required a move to Cary, North Carolina. Paul took a job there in pharmacy and in spite of their efforts, the marriage came unraveled. Fran wanted a divorce and Paul finally relented. Paul moved back to Columbia, took a pharmacist job at Kroger in Lexington and hung his Law shingle up at The Office of James Pope, Esquire.

When the divorce was finalized, Paul had pieced his life back together. Fran married a co-worker, Dave and they moved to Atlanta, Georgia. Paul began scheduling his life around the every-other-weekend visitations with Sarah that started with a drive to Atlanta.

Two are better than one, because they have a good return for their work; if one falls down, his friend can help him up.
Ecclesiastes 4:9-10

Chapter Three

May 30, 1992: Christus Victor Lutheran Church.

Alone in the Pastor's study-turned-bride's-room, I put the finishing touches of make-up on my 37-year-old face. I wasn't nervous. Paul and I had dated for almost two years. I loved him and felt sure of his love. Oh, man, did I love him. He was so strong and handsome, but it didn't end there. Having practiced pharmacy since graduating from the University of South Carolina in 1973; he had returned to college and earned his law degree in 1985. Currently, he was actually working in both venues. He seemed to know so many things about so many things. Never was he pompous about his knowledge, but over time, I realized that he was one of those rare individuals who could absorb and retain everything he had ever heard. It astonished me that he just always knew the answer to any question. I loved bragging about my fabulously brilliant, hunky boyfriend.

His love for children had also earned him a lot of points with me. He had only one, Sarah, but the fact that I had three didn't seem to shake him up one bit. Like me, he had always wanted a house full of children. He quickly came to love Jon, Austin, and Elisabeth, and we became an instant group, celebrating holidays and outings together.

I was touched one day when my oldest son Jon told me he felt happy seeing me happy. His comment took me back to the time he was six years old when Jon, Austin, and Elisabeth and I lived in a little apartment. Some guy I met had asked me out to dinner but stood me up. That night, Jon had awakened around 11:00 p.m. with an earache. He was surprised to find me instead of the babysitter, sitting on the couch still dressed for a date. Laying his little head on my lap, he said, "I thought you had a date."

"Yeah," I answered, "he never came."

Jon's need to comfort my bruised ego came in words

of wisdom beyond his years.

"Well, that's okay, Mom," he began, "at least you found out early he wasn't worth the trouble."

I had smiled at the very words I needed to put my life back in perspective. How blessed I felt to have this wise little boy in my corner.

In contrast to Mr. No-Show, Paul Graham was a man I could count on. His integrity was evident and his character upstanding. The care he took of his daughter Sarah was a love story. Paul was the most devoted father I'd ever met. Sarah, nine years old from his first marriage, received his visitation every other weekend. In order to achieve this privilege, Paul drove to Atlanta every other weekend. Sometimes he stayed with her in an Atlanta motel. More often, he made the four-hour drive, arriving in time to pick her up from school on Friday. There were then another four hours to bring her back to his home in Columbia, South Carolina. This time and mileage, along with the return drive to Atlanta and back after church on Sunday, was his willing labor of love. He was determined to be a good father to Sarah no matter what the sacrifice.

Then, there was his faith. He meant to be at church on Sunday because he truly loved Jesus. What a joy it was to know I wasn't dragging him along. Truthfully, his commitment to Christian community was greater than mine had ever been. Oh, I went and took my children most of the time, and I made sure they were Baptized and had their Communion instructions. Beyond that, though, I took little responsibility for serving. In contrast, Paul had been a church council member, served on committees, and even remained active right after his divorce. When I divorced, it knocked all the starch out of me. I was depressed and unmotivated. Elisabeth was two years old before I finally had her Baptized.

Now, here was this wonderful, beautiful man, the man of my dreams, about to profess to the world that *he* loved *me.* God was answering my prayers with someone more perfect for me than my imagination had ever allowed. At times, I was so afraid it would all go away, it paralyzed me. Lost in Paul's strong embrace, I would sometimes instruct him, "Don't ever leave me. Don't ever die." The first time I told him that, he laughed. "I will never leave you," he answered, "and I'm going to try real hard not to die."

"Well," I replied, "just don't."

Jon, Austin, Sarah, and Elisabeth would be our wedding attendants. Twelve-year-old Jon and nine-year-old Austin were already ushering guests to their seats. Sarah, also nine- and seven-year-old Elisabeth visited with my friend, Cindy before taking their places as our bridesmaids.

Looking into that mirror, I thought about the things that had brought me to this moment in my life. Two broken marriages had convinced me that I was a hopeless failure at this institution in which I longed to succeed. Though my nuptial losses hadn't turned me into a man hater, for six years I'd been very careful not to give my heart away. I still hoped there was someone who was meant to truly love me, but recognized that I really didn't deserve another try.

Finishing up my make-up, I thought about times I had prayed that God would sustain and help this someone, if he existed, that I longed to know and love. I remembered nights when my loneliness found me asking for another chance – for a husband to love, a father who would love my children. I prayed for that person, whoever he was, that God would help him in his life as I waited for him.

Loneliness wasn't my whole being, though. My children were the love of my life, and we were a team. Often when we were out, strangers would comment on their good behavior. These comments were huge gifts of encouragement that helped me feel capable during this hard time. God had sent me such beautiful children. Leading three little tow-headed cherubs with bright blue eyes was like being in a parade. Each one loved being funny and easily captured the hearts of strangers. Jon was born October of 1979, and Austin, two years and eight months later. Elisabeth and Austin were two years and three months apart.

Jon and Austin practically worshiped Elisabeth and found delight in every little thing she did. She was their princess, and they would have turned themselves inside out for her. How I loved these precious children. Being loved by them fueled my motivation. Their needs saved me from indulging in an excess of self-pity. There was little time to wallow in loneliness when a tiny shoe was waiting to be tied, another glass of juice poured, and a boo-boo trusted to a mother's healing kiss.

My trade had been barbering since the seventies, but concern that my barber's salary would never send three smart children to college drove me to re-think my vocation. Once Elisabeth started first grade, I entered college for the first time as what was gently referred to as a "mature student." I wasn't sure I could pull it off, but I was a sophomore now, majoring in English Literature. Gleefully, I counted every A as validation that maybe I had misjudged my intellect all those years before. Attending college had improved my self-image like nothing else.

Early in October, my friend Tami and I decided to have a girl's night out. Before we set out, Tami said, "Let me call Paul and ask him if he wants to go with us." Paul and Fran had divorced in April. Although Fran and I were similar in age and had gone to the same school, it was her younger sister Tami and I who forged a closer friendship over the years. Since Fran and I touched base infrequently, I really didn't know Paul other than that he was her husband. Now, they were divorced, and Tami said Paul resided currently in an apartment about a half an hour from me. She thinly veiled her effort to match us up by saying she was concerned that he didn't get out enough.

"Okay." I said, with a "more the merrier" attitude. "If you're sure he will be comfortable with that, I mean, you *are* his ex-wife's sister."

"Oh. It's fine." Tami answered quickly. "*I* didn't divorce Paul."

I laughed as Tami looked up Paul's phone number.

Paul met Tami and me at a Mexican restaurant in Irmo. It was strange after all these years of knowing him as Fran's husband, meeting up with him as a single guy. I think we both felt self-conscious and a little vulnerable. I caught myself studying his face, something I had never allowed myself before. His eyebrows held a shape that made him seem serene, thoughtful, and intelligent. The lines of his face were straight and even. He looked nothing like me. His deep-set, brilliant, sparkling-blue eyes contrasted my big round pale blue ones. Whereas my nose was a little crooked and round, his made a neat straight line down the middle of his features. It was a really nice nose, not 'too' anything. He joked about losing his short, light brown hair, but like Sean Connery and Bruce Willis, he was one of those men who could pull off a receding hairline without giving up his attractive looks. I felt drawn to him, and we quickly found rapport together.

After dinner we went to a Western bar because Tami wanted to dance. I'm not much of a dancer, but after a while, Paul asked me to dance a slow song with him. I warned him to beware my feet, but he brushed off my caution and slipped an arm around my waist. With his other hand, he held mine close to his broad shoulder. It was the first time I noticed how warm his hands felt and how muscular his arms. Before I knew what was happening, he had pulled me into motion with him, swaying left and right with a cool little rhythmic hitch in one hip, between steps. Who knew he could dance like that, and who knew he could bypass my inferior rhythm with his sure steps? I was enchanted.

"Paul." I exclaimed, "Wow. You can really dance."

He smiled confidently, and so did his eyes. However modest he was, it was plain to see he knew my words weren't mere flattery.

After that night, I thought he might try to contact me. It wouldn't have been much trouble to get my number from Tami. He didn't though. We finally ran into each other at Tami's Thanksgiving gathering. My kids and I had made Thanksgiving with Tami's family a tradition in recent years, and this year she had invited Paul. He was already there when we arrived, hunting deer, I think, that morning with Tami's husband, Karl. As I sought a cup of coffee in the kitchen, Paul appeared outside the window, waving at me. I waved back and set about pouring my coffee. Sometime before we ate dinner, I was inside talking to Tami on the couch when Paul came through the door, bleeding from an elbow scrape acquired playing basketball. As he prevailed upon me to apply first aid to his wound, Tami deliberately slipped out of the room, enjoying her new role as Cupid. I thought Paul might have felt the attraction I was feeling. I thought he was flirting, but he was too subtle to be sure. I really hoped he would call me right after Thanksgiving. He didn't.

Well into December, long after I had given up on hearing from him, the phone rang in my apartment. "Hello?" I answered.

"Hello, Shirley." Paul greeted me back, "This is Paul."

My heart fluttered around in my chest trying to decide whether or not to break through its walls. I noted a quiver in his voice. Could he be nervous? I couldn't imagine. "Hi, Paul." I answered, pretending to be confident, hoping to put him at ease. "What a nice surprise to hear from you."

"It's nice for me, too." He replied, but the tremor in his voice remained. He went on to say he wanted to take my family out for pizza on Saturday. I accepted, but wondered about his intentions. Was he interested in me, or did he just feel sorry for the divorcee and all those children? Did he hope to seek a relationship with me, or was he just looking to find his daughter some nice, same-age children with whom to do things together? I couldn't tell. I had other single father friends with whom I had no romantic interests, but I was already hoping for something more with Paul.

When Saturday arrived, I took Jon, Austin, and Elisabeth to their children's choir dress rehearsal at Corpus Christi Catholic church for the Christmas program. I smiled, watching this sweet throng of tiny choir angels take their places at the altar. They wore puffy, white choir blouses with bright red bows at the neck. As I sat in the pew listening to these Earth cherubs lift Christmas praises to the newborn Jesus, Paul slid quietly into the pew beside me. He had just gotten off work at Kroger Pharmacy across the street from this church in Lexington.

"Hi." He whispered, shyly, and my heart did a nervous little dance.

"Hey." I quietly replied, trying to pretend like my insides hadn't just congealed. Paul was sitting just close enough for me to smell his leather Member's Only jacket and a soft waft of Halston cologne, so nice, yet disarmingly manly. I tried feebly to concentrate on the choir, but I was having trouble paying attention now. Legions of butterflies had formed in my upper GI tract and fluttered furiously, threatening to burst through all my orifices. I managed to keep them subdued as time became mysterious. I don't know how long we sat there, or if we talked, or when the rehearsal ended, or how I retrieved the children afterward. The next thing I remember was sitting in the passenger seat of Paul's Ford Bronco, heading to Pizza Hut. Paul drove, and my three children sat excitedly, buckled up in the back seat. I prayed they would behave well so that I wouldn't have to call them down.

  It was stressful enough being alone with a potential boyfriend, but having my children in the mix made it impossible to relax. Yes, they were nice kids, but there were three of them, and I found that putting on the party manners of a new courtship and simultaneously tending to the demands of young children was more than I could comfortably handle, but in my wildest imagination I couldn't have concocted the mortifying event brewing.

  Arriving at the restaurant, the children unbuckled, tumbling out of their seats. To my utter horror, Elisabeth stood up, reached over the back of Paul's seat and slapped him soundly on the head.

  "Owww!" Paul yelped. "Why'd you frap me in the head?"

  Then, he coughed up a little laugh trying to cover his embarrassment.

  When Elisabeth climbed out, I met her at the car door with a whispered scathing, "Child! Why on Earth did you slap him? Do you want me to spank you right here? Don't you *dare* embarrass me that way again." Her bottom lip slid forward. We both wheeled around and headed through the red door with the others with Paul following behind us. "What was she thinking?" I wondered. I had never seen her do such a thing. Somehow, Elisabeth must have known Paul was playing for keeps and felt threatened by the possibility of losing my attention. Whatever the reason, her behavior had caught me completely by surprise.

The next memory I have of that night was after Paul took us home. He walked us to the door, and the children disappeared inside. As they busied themselves getting ready for bed, there was a perfect opportunity for him to kiss me, but he didn't.

"Thank you for going with me." Paul said before he headed down the metal steps from my apartment door.

"Thank *you*." I answered. "We really had fun."

He was gone without allowing me a single clue as to his intentions. I hurried inside so I could peek through the blinds and watch him walk to his car. I noticed his cute gait. It wasn't a limp, but something that bounced a little with each half-step; a repercussion of his water skiing accident that I'd learn about later.

"I like you, Paul Graham." I whispered through the sliver between two blinds. His Bronco backed out and I prayed a little prayer, "Do I get to keep him, Lord?" God said nothing, but I am pretty sure He was smiling.

Right before Christmas, Paul called again, asking if we wanted to join him for a trip to Riverbanks Zoo for *The Lights Before Christmas* display.

"That would be great." I answered. "Will you be coming after work?"

"That, I will." He said.

"Would you like to have supper with us?" I asked.

"Is it ham sandwiches?" He asked, joking. "I usually eat a ham sandwich."

"Well, I was planning beef stew," I replied, playing off his comment, "but I can change the menu to ham sandwiches if you'd rather have one."

"No way." Paul answered with mock anxiety, "I love beef stew."

"Okay. What time can we look for you?"

He said he was getting off work at 6:00 p.m. With Kroger Pharmacy only a couple of blocks from my apartment, I guessed he would arrive about 6:30.

"One more thing," I added, "is there anything you don't eat?"

"Onions." He answered.

"Serious?" I responded.

"I don't like them."

After we hung up, I sat on my bed for a few seconds speculating on a possible future with a man who didn't like onions. I loved them. What would my beef stew taste like without them? What if we got together and I had to learn to cook everything without onions. Could I make him like them, and why was I off on this onion tangent anyway when there was the problem of what to wear on another family-style date to contend with?

Paul arrived the evening of the zoo trip with bags of Skittles and M&M's for the children. I hoped Elisabeth would recognize this peace offering and avoid making tiny red hand-prints on his head this time. Paul seemed to be comfortable enough, eating his onion-less beef stew and complimenting it several times. Remarkably, it didn't taste that different without onions.

The Zoo was beautiful at night. The five of us meandered around the animal cages illuminated by Christmas lights in animal shapes. I was relieved when we were home without incident from any of the Skittle-stuffed children.

Saying "goodbye," Paul gave no indication of his interest in me, or us, or whatever it was. He mentioned that he and Sarah would like to stop by on Christmas Eve, and I surmised that he would be bringing some Christmas gifts. Again, I thought he might just be a sweet, lonely guy wanting to do a good deed. Now I would have to figure out appropriate gifts for him and Sarah. Come to think of it, I wondered what he would find as appropriate gifts for Jon, Austin, Elisabeth and me. Maybe his choice of presents would give me a clue about his intentions.

As part of the Creative Writing class I was taking at Midland's Tech, I kept a daily journal. The entries during this time describe the anticipation I was feeling about being alone with Paul. That night, alone in my apartment, I made this stream-of-consciousness entry in my journal:

He didn't go for the "Departing Kiss"- which is both good and bad. Good, because it is so awkward and nerve shattering and what if I have bad breath or he slips me the tongue and I'm not expecting it and I end up looking real stupid or suddenly become nauseated and have to go throw up or worse yet it changes the proverbial safe friendship into a dangerous unsafe potential romance that might not work out. What if somebody gets hurt and it might be him and I would be responsible for hurting this sweet man or what if I am the one who gets axed in the end? GOD-HELP-ME. This heart of mine is far too fragile to withstand another assault. So, yeah ... It's better that he didn't go for the "Departing Kiss."

On the other hand, had he gone ahead and done it, at least it would have been OVER and I could have relaxed some. As it turned out, he asked me to go on "The Second Date" with him. I considered this.

"Hm-mm-m," I mused, "he is a decent and respected person who is not only intellectually stimulating, but also believes in God and, what's more, seems to be devoid of mental illness (and did I mention so handsome?) so WHY in the world would I want to see him again? He can't be real."

But my curiosity prevailed and I said, "I think I would like that ... a lot."

Now I guess I'll have to do that "Waiting Thing" that I so hate that precedes "The Phone Call" anticipated, regarding "The Second Date." If it happens, then maybe he'll go for "The Kiss" –which will be warmly received. Or maybe he won't ever call again and when I see him he'll act like we never met. Then I'll feel so foolish for a while. Then I'll think, "I don't care about those mean old boys anyway!"

Then I'll gain thirty pounds just to show 'em, damn 'em, just to show 'em."

On Christmas Eve I baked Swedish Lace cookies for Paul and Sarah, packing them in three oval balsa wood boxes with Christmas geese painted on top. ...*tasteful without being pushy or desperate,* I thought. Paul knocked on the door with Sarah and her cousin, Jennifer, who seemed to be already enjoying a pretty intense sugar high. As the children bounced all over the furniture in my apartment, I wondered if Paul was always this permissive. He sat beside me on my couch without so much as a hint of discipline toward the girls, and we struggled with a little conversation. A purse-size, leather,

Etienne Aigner tissue holder was his gift to me, and I have it to this day. Jon and Austin's gifts were lethal-looking slingshots which simultaneously added to my horror of raising boys and made them hysterically happy. I don't remember Elisabeth's gift; some Sarah-endorsed girly thing, no doubt, as she had already taught her daddy what little girls liked.

Christmas Day, after we opened gifts at home, the children and I would be traveling to be with my parents, Grandma and Papaw in Hartwell, Georgia. As best they could, my parents had helped to fill in the empty space of daddy and husband in our family. They invested as much time as possible in our lives by attending my children's recitals and ball games, delighting in their achievements and sending me twenty dollar bills from time to time. In part, my children knew love of family because of Papaw and Grandma.

Thinking about Paul and wondering what was going on in his head was becoming my favorite pastime, but I was afraid to drop my guard until I was sure I understood his intentions. My friends Tracy and Dupre had planned an after-Christmas party on December 27th. I didn't want to seem forward, but I wanted to take Paul with me and figured that if we were alone for a while, maybe his motive would crystallize. I decided to ask him. As the sucrose-induced children ran amok in my apartment, I took a chance.

"I'm going to a party after Christmas," I began. "It's on the 27th. Do you think you'd like to go with me?" I asked him, making sure he understood it was *with me* that he was being invited.

Paul smiled. "Yeah, I would go to a party with you."

He seemed happy, but kind of nervous, too.

"Good." I said, thinking, "*Maybe now I will finally understand where you are coming from*".

I was excited about this possible new turn in our relationship, and my close friends were following the drama. I borrowed a slinky red dress for the occasion. School was out for Christmas holidays, and my children had stayed behind in Hartwell after our visit. Since they were spending a few days with Mother and Daddy, I didn't have to worry about a babysitter. Paul came to my door smelling good again and not looking as though he had just worked for eight straight hours. He wowed over my outfit, and we exited by the metal stairs to the parking lot. Paul opened the passenger's door to his Bronco which prompted me to fail in my attempt to climb gracefully into the high seat. We made some inconsequential small talk en route to the party, a trip which took about thirty minutes.

When we arrived, Tracy answered the door and smiled her thousand-watt smile at us.

"Ha-a-ay, Shirley." She sang, "This must be Paul."

I made introductions, then Paul sat beside me on a couch with Tracy perched on its arm.

"I love your hair." She cooed, then, "Does it take very long to get it like that?"

"Not at all," I answered. "This only took me twelve hours today."

"Oh, that's really good." Was Tracy's distracted answer.

Paul hid a chuckle as Tracy's interest in my hair segued into some other hostess fodder. She forgot to excuse herself before joining a new cluster of guests. Tracy's drinks had already defined her tonight. I, on the other hand, was feeling a different kind of intoxication as Paul appeared more and more taken with me. Tracy's attention-deficient visit is the only specific thing I remember about the party, other than laughing a lot and feeling Paul's arm slide warmly around my waist when we stood outside talking to a cluster of party guests.

Leaving the party in Paul's Bronco, I was talking quite a lot. Paul pulled the Bronco into an empty parking space outside my apartment building and I looked out the window, yammering away about something useless, taking nervous glances at Paul and wishing silence between people didn't make me so anxious. Paul turned off the car and watched me talk with enormous interest. Now, I was really feeling self-conscious. I was pretty sure my comments weren't all that fascinating, yet he seemed to be hanging on my every word. Perhaps he and Tracy had been drinking from the same wellspring. I suddenly felt like a dog chasing a car, only now I had caught the car and didn't know what to do next. I began trying to explain whatever it was I was saying in a different way, keeping a nice buffer of verbs and nouns between us. Still, he gazed at me. Right in the middle of my inane oratory, Paul just leaned into me, graciously interrupting me with a kiss right on the mouth.

"Whoa. He's a good kisser." I thought delightedly and let myself get lost in it. "He must like me."

Talking for hours that night, Paul solved the mystery of his puzzling behavior. He explained how he had been fighting his feelings. Liking me was not part of his planned itinerary, yet he kept being drawn to me. He was an attorney, bound by logic. If his divorce had been painful, he had reasoned, spending the rest of his life without making another commitment was the rational way to avoid problems. Despite this mature rationale, he finally had to admit that he hadn't stopped thinking about me since that night out with Tami. The more he talked, the more my heart filled to bursting.

Paul called me the next day. The quivery shakiness in his phone voice had disappeared, leaving behind a confidence that calmed me. I loved that he was checking in. What a gentleman. I was leaving soon to get my children from my parent's house and wouldn't be back for a couple of days. How nice to leave knowing he was thinking about me. He asked about seeing me again and, well, I said "Yes."

Once Paul gave in to his feelings, our lives were filled with romance. The smallest activities were joyful and exciting. On one of our first post-kiss, family-style dates, we took our four children to a movie one bright afternoon. They wanted to sit on the front row. We let them, as we sat behind them at a reasonable distance. When Paul reached for my hand, it felt as if all the nerves on my skin were exposed. His hands were so warm. Almost instinctively, our hands began to do a little dance. Sliding back and forth across each other's palm and knuckles, touching thumbs and fingertips; it was as though our hands had been waiting all our lives to find each other, and now wanted nothing more than to feel the presence of the other. In the blackness of the theater, not seeing the hand we were caressing, we were blind, yet able to memorize the curves and nuances, hills and valleys of each other's skin. Dancing our wonderful electric hand-ballet in the darkness, I thrilled at this new feeling the mere act of holding hands had become.

Back at school in my second semester at Midland's Tech, I was approached by my Creative Writing teacher in class as he returned our journals with his comments. He smiled as he opened mine to one of the entries.

"I really liked this." He offered, handing it to me. "This is really good stream-of-consciousness writing. With your permission, I would like to enter it into the *Stylus*."

"The *Stylus*?" I parroted.

"The *Stylus* is a compilation of students' work. The Language Department publishes one every year. Anyone can submit an entry, but the best work receives honor and even a cash prize."

"Yes." I responded. "I'd love to submit it."

Promising to help me prepare my work for publication, my professor walked away to finish class. I couldn't wait to get to my crummy typewriter and polish up 'The Kiss.'"

When Midlands Tech presented its awards ceremony, Paul was sitting in the front row with Jon, Austin, and Elisabeth. He beamed proudly along with my children when my name was called. I accepted the first place honor and a $100.00 check for "The Kiss." I smiled at Paul as my cheering section delivered applause that must have left their palms stinging. They were my best cheerleaders, and I cherished their sincere belief in me.

"Oh, Lord." I prayed. "Let me be the person they think I am."

***

By this time Paul had moved from his apartment in Irmo to a trailer situated on a piece of lake property in Winnsboro that he'd bought from his stepdad, Rod. The lot was lovely, but the trailer? Not so much. This brown-and-tan single-wide did, however, accommodate Paul's needs during the week and Sarah's needs every other weekend. It was almost an hour's drive from Paul's job and my apartment in Lexington but even considering commuting costs, it was a more economical way for Paul to live.

The first Saturday Paul drove our collective group to the lake lot, I wondered if we'd ever get there. Four pre-teens in the car may have had some bearing on why the trip seemed longer than it really was. When the Bronco's tires finally crunched over the gravel drive, I read aloud from hand-painted words on a wooden sign nailed to a tree, "NO ALCOHOL ALLOWED."

Paul laughed while putting the car in park.

"That's supposed to be a joke." He explained. "When Dad lived here he appreciated its irony."

Paul unlocked the trailer door and we entered with a few bags of groceries. Sarah led the others out the back door and by the time Paul and I stepped onto the deck, the children were down at the dock daring each other to jump in the chilly late-January water.

"What a cool place!" I told Paul.

"It has utility." He answered. "Dad used to lease this land from the power company. When they decided to sell it all off, they offered it to the leasers before it was put on the market. He bought this lot for only $6,000.00!"

"No kidding?"

"I'm serious. When he and Millie married and bought a house in Chapin he sold it to me."

"…for $6,000.00?"

Paul laughed, "No, but $20,000.00 was still a pretty good deal for almost an acre of lakefront property!"

"Truly!"

We walked slowly around the land, the children's excited voices making a contrasting backdrop to our calm conversation.

"It's woodsy!" I noted.

"Yeah." Paul agreed, "Lots of pine trees. One of these days I'd like to build a house here. I'll get rid of all the pines but leave the hardwoods, like this little maple here."

"You like maple trees?"

"I do! I like the leaves." He answered and I made a mental note to remember this fact when his birthday rolled around.

"What's this?" I pointed to a pear tree.

"I'm not sure. I haven't paid too much attention to it.

There's fruit on it sometimes. Pears, maybe? The birds make a real mess of it."

By the time we made it down to the dock the kids were threatening to push each other in."

"DAD!" Sarah shrieked. "CAN WE JUMP IN?"

"Sure!" Paul replied a mere fraction of a second before I screamed,

"NO!"

I was too late. Four fully clothed children were already in mid-jump before my single syllable left my lips. It didn't take long for the children to ascend the ladder and stand, drenched and giggling, on the dock.

"What are you going to do now?" I posed the question to my three fourths of the dripping wet people. "Did you think about not having a change of clothes here?"

"Well, *I* have clothes!" Sarah bragged.

"There's a washer and dryer inside." Paul assured me. Then, to Sarah he said, "You'll have to share your clothes with the others while their things are being washed."

Heading back inside, the mental image of the two boys sporting Sarah's attire was greeted with much hilarity.

Most of our courtship consisted of this kind of group outing. Our families went on trips and shared meals like a single unit when Sarah was in town. I guess the process of blending our families began early on so we'd worked out some of the kinks before we really were one family. Still, melding our two households was often a difficult endeavor and we made as many wrong decisions as right ones. Paul and I were in total agreement on some issues, but for the others, we worked out our differences in private and showed a united front to the children in public. This parental solidarity is something I think we did right from the start.

***

On one of our rare outings alone, Paul and I stopped at Kroger for something and he ended up buying a chocolate cookie. After we got into the car, he took a few minutes to eat it.

"Mm-m-m," He moaned, trying to entice me. ". . . want a bite?"

"No, thank you," I answered. "I'm on a diet."

I neglected to mention that I was usually too excited and nervous to eat around him. "You enjoy it."

"It's really good," he continued, "and here, this is the best bite." He offered me the last bite. It had lots of nuts and chocolate chips.

"No, Paul." I refused, "I couldn't take your best bite."

"I want you to." He insisted, "Please, it's so good, I want to share it with you.

"Okay" I relented, seeing that he wasn't likely to give up. I took it from him with my fingers, only biting half of it. I handed him the other half.

"Here," I said, handing him what was now the last bite. "I want *you* to have the last bite."

He turned the small morsel over in his hand and examined it. He would not go down easily. I watched as he bit it gently in half with a pill cutter's precision and put the other minuscule half into my open palm. We were both giggling now. I wondered if it was possible to bite this minute crumb in half. I had to try. With my small motor skills in check, my teeth managed to slice through what was now an almost imperceptible molecule. I can't remember which one of us finally ate the actual last bite. The important thing was that we had started a new competition of being the most sacrificial giver, and it wasn't about to be over.

We left for my apartment, and Paul walked me to the door. I loved his gentlemanly ways, like opening doors for me and kissing me goodbye. He stepped inside for a minute and held me. I slid my hands around his ribs and under his jacket, melting into his chest with the mingled smells of leather, cologne, and man. He sighed and I smiled.

"You haven't done anything wrong yet." He didn't mean to say it out loud.

I let him go and stepped back, stung by his comment.

"I haven't done anything wrong yet?" I challenged him. "Is this a test or something? Do you have rules for me?"

He opened his mouth and closed it just as quick. Trying again, he replied, "Well, I just mean I didn't expect you to be, you know, to do everything right."

"I don't." I answered. "I'm not going to always do everything you like. Love me or not, but don't try to fit me into your prescribed ideal."

"I just don't want to make a mistake again." He explained.

"Maybe you just did." I answered sarcastically. "You're not the only one of us taking risks, Paul."

"I know." He answered.

I walked past him into the kitchen to load the coffeepot. He worked long hours, and I always worried that he might fall asleep on the way home when it was late. Now that I had found him, I didn't want to take a chance on losing him, so I had adopted a ritual of making him a big thermos of coffee and a bag of microwave popcorn for the road. I sat at my kitchen table, and Paul joined me in an adjacent chair. Steam rose from the coffee maker as hot grease knocked the popcorn kernels about. He started to brush a crumb off my table, but put it between his fingers to examine it instead.

"I didn't mean it the way it sounded."

"Maybe," I allowed him, "but, it seemed more like a Freudian slip to me."

The coffee hissed angrily and splashed into the pot.

"I guess maybe it was." Paul confessed, offering, "I do love you - so much."

The strange but pleasant combination of smells, bursting popcorn kernels and brewing coffee, mingled and filled the room. We inhaled the rich aroma of this splendidly charged air and held our breath to keep its lovely warmth inside our chests a little longer.

"I love you, too, Counselor."

Some precious moment in the second year of our courtship, Paul finally surrendered his post-divorce decision to forever avoid another marriage. We had traveled to Charleston, South Carolina, one weekend in January of 1992. It was in that romantic, historical city between tours and a carriage ride that he asked me to marry him. I remember his words,

"Shirley, I think I want you to be my wife . . . no, I do. I mean, I know I do."

Even though I expected this sooner rather than later, I was nonetheless startled by the words of his proposal. In an instant, my throat was dry and my eyes were wet.

"Me, too." I smiled, watching the lines in Paul's face soften through my tear droplets, wishing I had prepared a more eloquent response. We embraced and kissed for the first time as fiancés.

On a Friday afternoon late in February I packed up some food including a special cake I'd made and headed out to the lake with my kids. Turning out of the apartment complex Jon asked,

"What are we going to the lake for?"

"A surprise." I answered with an air of pronounced mystery.

From their seats in the back, Austin and Elisabeth perked up at the mention of a surprise.

"What surprise?" Austin asked as Elisabeth covered her cheeks in an effort to contain excitement.

"The surprise Paul and I have planned!"

For the rest of the way there were hundreds of guesses about the surprise but I evaded giving them a single clue. Finally, Dutchman Creek Volunteer Fire Department came into view on my right and I breathed a sigh of relief that I'd made it without getting lost. I turned right and we counted the lots on the left together until the trailer came into view. Spotting the Bronco, I knew Paul had made it back from Atlanta with Sarah, who bounded out the door. Jon, Austin and Elisabeth exited my car and all four were drawn to the dock by some magnetic force.

Paul stepped through the door and wrapped me in his arms. "Is that my bride-to-be?"

"Sh-h-h!" I scolded him. "Don't spill the beans! Did you get the ice cream?"

"Didn't I tell you I would?"

"Good job!" I grinned.

We went to the hatch and Paul lifted out a bag of drinks. I carried the sheet cake that I'd decorated with cartoon pictures of Paul, me, each of the children and *Prospective Graham Family* emblazoned across the top to announce our engagement. We'd managed to keep it a secret from everyone we knew until we had a chance to share it with the children first.

* * *

Now, almost two years after our courtship began, I was actually stepping into the narthex and down the aisle to marry Paul. Rising to the occasion, my beautiful sons looked and behaved like gentlemen in their neck-ties and dark suits. I met them in the Sanctuary where they took my arms, ushering me to the altar where my friend Lois was playing *Pachelbel's Canon in D* on piano.

The church was full. I could see the backs of Dale's and Sally's heads. They were sitting with my parents. Sally had been married to my brother since they were teens and was one of the people whose shoulder had been dampened by my tears over the years. She could also make me laugh until my cheeks and ribs hurt. She and Dale were a perfect set. I giggled, remembering how she took the news that Paul and I were engaged.

"Have you picked out the music?" She had soberly asked.

"Lois will play *Canon in D* until I walk down the aisle," I answered, "and then she'll play the traditional *Wedding March*."

"Oh." Sally had quipped, "I figured it would be, *Two Out Of Three Ain't Bad*."

Pastor Eiwen was smiling his head off when we got to the altar. He and Paul had been friends for several years, and I was his family's hair stylist. We were all charter members of Christus Victor and had seen each other through ups and downs.

"Who gives this woman to be wed?" He asked.

"We do." my sons replied as their warm little hands released my arms.

I faced Paul as my boys moved to our right. Opposite them, on our left, Sarah and Elisabeth looked like fairies dressed in ivory and lace. Cindy had made dainty garlands of tiny red roses which now encircled their crowns.

Paul stood before me, joy and fear both reflecting in his eyes. I thought I might cry until, at last, he began speaking his vows to me. "I, Paul take you, Shirley to be my wife . . ." His bottom lip trembled, silently announcing the tears that would follow. I had not considered public tears from this confident, masculine man. I was overcome with the precious burden of knowing the depth of his love. I wanted to embrace him as I promised him he could always trust me to love, honor, and never leave him come richer or poorer or sickness or health. I felt God pouring His strength into me and I knew I wouldn't cry. I knew Paul and I would be taking turns being strong, depending upon who needed support most, and I knew I was taking one of my turns now.

I am my beloveds and my beloved is mine.
Song of Solomon 6:3

Chapter Four

After a beautiful honeymoon to Cancun, Mexico, Paul and I returned to Columbia, South Carolina, where we spent the next several weeks moving our newly blended family into a new house in the Summit subdivision. It was an exciting time. The subdivision was a planned community with sidewalks and bike paths, basketball courts, and two swimming pools. The children made friends quickly, and a perfect summer began to spread itself out ahead of us like warm honey-butter on toast. The week after our return, we completed all the legal paperwork for Paul's adoption of Elisabeth. Unpacking and putting our new household in order was a labor of love for me. I was exquisitely happy, yet self-doubt kept poking a pointy finger into my ribs and whispering, "This happy life is a cosmic mistake. It's not really yours. You'll have to give it back."

"Be gone with you." my mind would scream, refusing to let foul thoughts steal the joy opening up my heart like a daffodil. I had fallen in love with the garden of life God had allowed to grow around me and mine. I couldn't remember ever feeling so content. Besides, I had ordered Paul to never leave me and never die.

As soon as paperwork was complete and we made our house presentable, we had our first gathering in the new house. An adoption party for Elisabeth Graham came together on a Saturday with friends and family. Paul wanted to adopt Jon and Austin as well, but respected the allegiance they had to their biological father. At ages twelve and nine, the prospect of a name change was something they couldn't imagine, either.

Paul understood. He had been born Joseph Paul Fournier, but when Betty and Rod married, they simplified their lives by calling him Paul Graham. He started and ended public school with his step father's last name. By the time he was eighteen and had to sign up with the Selective Service, none of the people he was associated with knew him as Paul Fournier. The Selective Service was unyielding. If he wanted to be Paul Graham, then he would have to have his name legally changed, so he did. This would come up from time to time, and Paul would always say, "So you see, we are really imposters."

Elisabeth was graced with a joyful spirit and abundant personality. She was ecstatic on her special adoption day. A social butterfly by nature, she flitted from one guest to another, answering questions about her new life and name. As they would for a birthday party or a baby shower, the guests brought gifts to celebrate this part of our daughter's life. Elisabeth opened each gift, gushing over the contents.

"Thank you, Miss Donna." She exclaimed with rapture, lifting a turquoise T-shirt out of the packaging.

"Look on the back." Miss Donna suggested, as Elisabeth ceremoniously turned it around for all to see. Emblazoned across the shirt, the air-brushed flourishes heralded her freshly legalized moniker: "Elisabeth Noelle Graham."

Elisabeth loved being the center of attention, but was unaccustomed to owning the limelight for such a long period. She adapted quickly, however, and was reluctant to step out of it when the party guests began making conversation in adult clusters. Five of Paul's buddies stood in our small kitchen sharing their thoughts on the state of the world. Elisabeth bounded into the room bursting, "Is my daddy in here?" Before stating the obvious, they all looked around for Paul, thinking they had missed him somehow. Not in the sink or under the refrigerator, one of them concluded, "Um, no, he's not here."

"Okay." Elisabeth responded and skipped merrily away. Watching from the opening to the dining room, it took me a couple of seconds to figure out that she merely desired to feel the words, "my daddy" slip easily from between her pretty lips.

The wedding and Elisabeth's adoption party opened the way for Austin and Sarah's shared birthday party in the park. With birthdays only eight days apart, a tradition of sharing their party happened easily.

Before we could blink, it was August 8 and time to celebrate again. For Paul's forty-second birthday, a new camera seemed the right gift. He loved photography, and four children produced lots of reasons to take pictures. I was rather proud of this gift. Paul probably wouldn't have bought it for himself, but I had noticed him looking at it longingly the last time we were in Service Merchandise. I had wrapped it in birthday paper the day before and had it ready to open the minute the alarm clock heralded his birthday morning.

"*Happy birthday, to you*" I sang, setting the gift on his chest. Paul picked up the package and sat up.

"You don't waste any time, do you?"

"You're getting older by the second. I've got to make sure you don't miss anything."

He tore off the paper. "Thank you, Darlin'." Paul rubbed sleep from his eyes and examined the camera. His attention turned to the camera's small instruction book and he turned a page slowly. I leaned over his shoulder to read along.

"Oh, well." I said, noticing the words were written in German, "I don't guess you can interpret German."

"Yes." Paul replied modestly, "I can." He looked back at the pamphlet seriously. With my mouth a gaping hole, I listened in amazement as Paul read the German text in unhesitating English.

"Wow." I finally replied as I looked at my brilliant husband in utter wonder. "That was incredibly fluid. You translated so fast. I didn't know you could even *speak* German, much less, *interpret* it so well."

Paul smiled and said nothing, but his eyes were dancing. His smile looked suspicious, threatening to morph into a grin and snort any second.

"Hmmm." I snatched the pamphlet from him. What a cool trick. I had really let him get me this time. The German text was all I could see as Paul read, obscuring the English side of the instructions from me. He broke out in a guffaw as I cut my eyes at him, giggling in spite of myself. Now I really owed him one.

Thanks to our recent wedding, we had current addresses for friends, coworkers, and relatives. When his birthday passed, I realized how easy it would be to throw a surprise party. He wouldn't expect it at all, but if he found out, I knew he'd try to put a modest end to my plan. I obviously couldn't stockpile party fare without tipping him off, so invitations requested that guests bring hors d'oeuvres instead of gifts. As Paul innocently filled prescriptions at Phar-Mor by day, the children and I conducted a subterfuge at home. Our friends and next door neighbors Rick and Charlene were willing co-conspirators. With every grocery store visit, I covertly added to a small collection of soft drinks and beer in their garage. I made up invitations and copied, stamped, and mailed stacks of them. Nearly everyone Paul knew was in on our plot.

On the day of his party, I had arranged for Earl Stalbaum, our friend and life insurance advisor, to come to the house and talk to Paul about our insurance portfolio. Earl was great, droning away at nothing in particular. Paul was really trying to follow along, but kept thinking, "Is he ever going to get to the point?" As Earl expertly distracted Paul, our cul de sac quietly filled up with familiar cars. The clandestine guests gathered at Rick and Charlene's until most had arrived.

After a half an hour that seemed much longer to Paul, the doorbell rang and he excused himself to answer it as Earl silently congratulated himself. Opening the door, Paul found no one on the doorstep, but our lawn was a newly sprouted carpet of people he loved yelling, "SURPRISE!"

For a minute, Paul let all color seep out of his face and couldn't respond for wondering, "How am I supposed to feed all these people?" Quickly gathering his wits, he opened the front door, and the party entered. We spent the next many hours laughing and celebrating Paul.

Surrounded by all the "adopted" children she hadn't seen in years, Betty "Mama" Graham may have had the most fun of all. Truly a character; she teased Paul's old high school chums, saying every unexpected thing that came into her head. She loved to make them laugh at their expense.

"Rusty." She exclaimed to one of Paul's old pharmacy school mates. Rusty had been a late-bloomer and classic runt, but finally grew to an average-sized man. "You got fat." She accused him. Rusty laughed out loud. She could catch her audience off guard and somehow get away with such comments.

Mama Graham looked over my shoulder as I showed off our honeymoon pictures to guests. When I came to a photograph of our feet, bare but for the wedding bands on our toes, she ignored the romance in the snapshot and whispered, "Look at your feet in this picture, Shirley. I had no idea they were so ugly."

"My feet are not ugly." I replied in defense of my foundation.

"You shouldn't be taking pictures of them." She proclaimed quietly, eyes twinkling, shaking her head. Paul loved his mother deeply, but had never quite known what to do with her. She cracked me up.

Betty would mingle awhile then sit talking one-on-one with these adults; the same teenagers who had spent so many hours at her table and in her living room. They were the ones who had slept over at her house, gotten in trouble along with Paul, and found comfort in her kindness when their young worlds were too much to bear. They all respected and adored her. She was as happy as I had ever seen her, partying in her favorite element.

I suppose that she and I were kindred spirits, considering we had similarly damaged track records in marriage. Our wedding could have been hard for Paul's mom. She had been divorced from Rod when Paul was a young man, his brothers still in high school. Both Joe and Rod, remarried now, had attended the wedding with their wives. Instead of focusing on her losses, Betty Graham had shopped for the prettiest coral-colored suit she ever owned. She'd cut quite a figure, exuding joy and social confidence and greeting everyone there. Her focus was obvious: her son was having a wedding and she'd come to celebrate.

* * *

The months following our marriage had been full of firsts. Elisabeth and I had new names, Paul and I now had four children instead of one or three, a situation which gave us the new titles, "step parents." Jon, Austin, Elisabeth, and

Sarah had new siblings. Austin, Elisabeth, and Jon were in new schools: North Springs Elementary and Summit Parkway Middle School. All were making new friends. The layout of the subdivision necessitated only a short walk to the library, pool, basketball courts, or school. Consequently, the children had more freedom than ever before.

Paul and I were making new friends in the neighborhood, too. We had met Carlos and Ann at the pool as their daughters Mariel and Sarah swam with Elisabeth. Old friends turned out to be serendipitous neighbors, too. Among them were Tim and Gale, a couple of my old running buddies from high school and Rick and Charlene, our next-door neighbors. Rick and Paul had attended Dentsville High School together. He and Charlene had been married for only a couple of years. We enjoyed sharing excitement over decorating our new houses and being an otherwise silly combination of people whenever possible.

A few weeks after we moved in, Rick and Charlene began building a deck on the back of their house. They spent their weekends sweating, hammering it together. We quickly dubbed Rick "Deck Boy." Paul and Deck-Boy really liked talking about their home improvements, and I was amused by the way they used deeper voices to do so. Paul would frequently wander next door to observe and discuss progress from time to time. One afternoon, Paul and I were drawn to the not-so-distant drumbeat of Rick's hammer. As the men began discussing the prospective length of the deck, Paul offered, "I've got a twenty-five-foot tape measure."

"No thanks." Rick declined, "I've got one." He reached into his toolbox coolly extracting a one-hundred-foot measuring tape. Both men strained, Rick to hide his smirk, Paul to conceal his surprise.

"Deck Boy," Paul dryly managed, "That IS a tape measure."

They had a short laugh, but the quest for superiority rose up in their man-hearts. Paul's nostrils had already flared at the sweet aroma of the contest. The baritone voices in Paul and Rick's brain centers were boldly ordering them to "let the games begin."

On his next trip to supervise Rick's construction, Paul

waited, somewhat patiently, kicking at the dirt until Rick reached for his tape measure which cued Paul to whip out the shiny new *two-hundred* foot tape measure he'd hefted over on his belt loop. Revising a quote from *Crocodile Dundee*, Paul gleefully announced, "That's not a tape measure, my friend; *this* is a tape measure." Charlene and I covered our faces as they laughed and hooted like little boys.

    Their competition finally came to an end one day after Deck Boy sprang for a three-hundred-foot tape measure. I shudder to guess how much it cost. Unable to stand the wait for Paul's next visit, Rick limped over to our house one afternoon. Lugging the additional weight of his prize, the twenty-foot journey must have taken longer than usual. Eventually, he made it to the garage where Paul was performing some masculine function at his work table. Alerted by the scraping of Rick's shoes across the driveway, Paul looked up, surprised by the huge, heavy-duty hardware treasure Rick labored to raise. Fueled by a sudden, unexplainable moment of reason, Paul relented, "Okay, Deck Boy," He answered, holding up both palms, "I give." Satisfied, having defeated Paul, Rick dragged his laden body back home, bearing a happy victory smile. He couldn't wait to tell Charlene – who didn't care at all – that he had won the championship.

    Amid our new friendships and activities, we continued some old traditions, like celebrating at the trailer on Lake Wateree. We could be found there on New Year's Eve, popping fireworks off the dock and eating ham with collards and Hoppin' John. Sometimes Paul and I carved out some alone time there on a rare weekend. Fourth of July sometimes took us to the lake for more fireworks and when Thanksgiving rolled around we were there again, fishing off the dock and smoking the turkey nearby. The only real predictable thing about the weather in the South Carolina Midlands is that it's never quite as cool as you think it ought to be. It was the stuffiness of the trailer that pulled me out of the kitchen and onto the deck that first Thanksgiving after we married. I set my iced tea on the wooden picnic table as the smoker seeped lovely turkey smells into the air. My eyes traveled down to the dock where Paul and the children chattered easily while casting their fishing poles into the water.

I smiled thinking about how much had changed over the past couple of years and breathed a prayer of thanks. Looking out over the yard, I made a search for the small new maple tree Paul had planted a few feet from the other maple. It had been a birthday gift from the children and me back during our courtship and it seemed to be thriving despite our less than regular visits.

Remembering the other tree Paul had shown me the first time he brought me here to the lake, I did a panoramic search of the yard, picking it out among all the pine trees. It was an easy task. I just followed the voices of many birds gathered in its branches. Leaving my tea glass to soak into the wet ring it made on the picnic table, I sashayed over to see what was causing such a ruckus among these birds. A breeze caught my nose and I could smell a thick, yet not unpleasant scent of fruit rotting on the branches as well as the ground. No wonder the birds were so happy and vociferous. Whatever kind of fruit tree this was, it had been transformed into a natural Sangria bar for these winged members of the Animal Kingdom. I watched them weave uncertainly from branch to branch, feasting on fermented fruit.

"This must be the mess Paul told me birds could make of this tree." I thought, and grieved a little for this fruit we had missed. It would be hard to tell what *kind* of fruit, in its present state, but pears would probably be a pretty good guess.

I walked back to the trailer thinking about our new family life. We hadn't been willing to give up the hour's drive to Christus Victor Lutheran Church for Worship since so much of our history had begun there. Finding a new church would have been as traumatic as leaving home. It had taken my usually prompt husband a long time, but he was finally relaxing a little about being late every Sunday. Paul was a good sport, though, and finally began to joke that we attended the 9:45 am Sunday School Class (The class started at 9:30 am.).

Austin was now old enough to serve in Worship as an acolyte. One Sunday morning, he was asked to assist with

Communion. He was so honored to be trusted with his new responsibility that he didn't mention that no one had actually instructed him in this particular field as yet. After donning his little robe, he followed the pastor around the Altar area. His duty was to hold a golden platter designed so that Worshipers could discard their empty Communion glasses. Paul and I beamed with pride.

Seated in the front pew, we were some of the first worshipers the ushers called forward to kneel at the Altar. The Pastor approached me, broke a chunk of bread off the round loaf and placed it in my left hand with these words, "The Body of Christ broken for you."

I responded, "Amen."

My family members kneeling beside me repeated the ritual. Our resident Seminary student followed the pastor pouring Communion wine into our tiny glasses.

"The Blood of Christ poured out for you." She reverently announced.

"Amen." I smiled humbly as Austin followed with his tray.

Still kneeling, I looked up at my sweet little boy and deposited the spent cup into one of the holes in his platter. The corners of his mouth curved proudly upward as Austin looked into my eyes. We returned to our pew as, one by one, ushers led the rows behind us to the Altar. I wanted nothing more at that moment than to watch my son, but remembering that *pride goeth before a fall*, I tried to busy myself tearing off little pieces of the bulletin to bookmark the upcoming congregational hymns. Studying the ripped paper sticking out the top of my hymnal, my gaze kept drifting up to the Altar sneaking glimpses of Austin serving.

About halfway through Communion, I looked up at Austin and something just didn't seem right. Paul noticed it about then, too. Upon squinting for a better view, I tried to understand what appeared to be Austin carrying a massive ice pyramid. My jaw dropped as I noted scores of tiny Communion glasses stacked ten high on Austin's platter. He had seemed so confident that none of the other servers thought to check on him. If they had, Austin would have been instructed to replace the platter with a fresh, empty one.

Much too late for that now. Immediately, Paul and I both felt compelled to help in some manner, but quickly became powerless. Disabled in our alarmed state, we continued to watch in equal parts horror and hilarity as Austin approached his next Communion victim, an unsuspecting man who paused in reverence after emptying his small chalice. Austin stood smiling before him, offering the untrustworthy place of repose for his container. The man stopped cold at the sight of my son's gravity-defying tower and drew his cup back protectively. Austin brought the plate forward as gently as possible without upsetting the precarious triangle of glass as if to say, "Go ahead. It's okay, man, trust me." Confused and clearly disturbed by Austin's challenge, this man nonetheless gingerly added his teeny cup to the top of the heap. Austin stepped to the next unwitting soul as the relieved man rose and hurried to his pew, no doubt wishing to put as much distance as possible between himself and the almost certain crash to come.

  How long must Austin have been repeating this exercise while we sat, falsely trusting in the system? Sooner or later it was going to topple. Could we be the only ones who noticed? I gasped, and that's when the silent giggling started between us. The idea was so funny that our bodies began to tremble and shake within. We were kept silent only by an unreliable veil of false composure. Limp and shuddering in our bones, we yearned for an elusive portion of self-control. Weakness worked its way into our lungs with suffocating power. Neither of us dared attempt heroics. Thankfully, something merciful in the universe caused the Pastor's head to turn toward Austin. After a little flurry at the Altar, Austin's glass tower of doom was replaced with a clean platter. Worship continued without interruption. It took Paul and me the rest of that Sunday afternoon, however, before we could function without falling in the floor laughing over what we had witnessed.

  Paul and I shared a love for the written word. I say, "Language is my strength," but that's because it sounds so much better than, "I stink at math." Paul said he was better at science and math, that he was left-brained, more analytical and less creative. True, his math and science areas were really strong; however, electrodes fired like Independence Day on the language side of his brain, too. There didn't appear to be a weak side in there. Humbling, yet mildly irritating to me was the fact that he always read faster than I. He was really good at editing my college writing and expertly showed me the unnecessary verbiage in my required papers. We loved reading together. Now that we were married we'd sometimes check out two copies of the same library book, read them together before falling asleep then discuss them later on. It was our own intimate book club.

One of the agonizing side-effects of single parenting had been watching Jon, Austin, and Elisabeth grow up without a father's interaction. In the same way that a person who loses a leg feels a need to scratch the phantom itch, I never lost my compulsion to say, "Look at our great kid" to a husband/father who wasn't there. My heart stung knowing they suffered in that loss, even if they hadn't figured it out yet. I had tried to provide for them as a father by turning the mother in me on full blast, but their need for a daddy remained. Having grieved over this, I took great pleasure in relinquishing my quasi-paternal role over to Paul. The new privilege of having a loving husband who enjoyed being a good father to our children was joy to my soul.

And God blessed them and said unto them, 'Be fruitful and multiply and replenish the Earth.
Genesis 1:27-28

Chapter Five

A few months after our wedding, I felt an urging to discuss our family with Paul instead of having our usual book-fest. We lay beside each other with our books open. Paul was reading, but I was having a hard time concentrating. I knew he'd always dreamed of having a big family – we certainly had one already – but I wasn't sure whether or not he wanted to have *another* child, one from our union. Personally, I was feeling a real longing to have our baby.

"Paul," I began that night, "My biological time clock is ticking away." He put down his book and looked at me seriously. I went on, "I don't know what you are thinking about having a child together, but if you think this could be something you might want to do, I believe we should go ahead and start talking about it." I always talk too much, so I continued. "Yes, I know we have a lot of children already, and if you are satisfied with the size of our family, I am okay with that. I realize that maybe we really can't afford it, but if we had a baby, I think I could still work part time and make a financial contribution while I was finishing school."

Looking back, I wonder if I was conscious on some level of how flagrantly I was lying to him. Maybe my wish for us to have a baby had merely driven me to delude myself about school and work. A faint, but satisfied smile kept the corners of Paul's mouth busy throughout my monologue. I don't think he really cared whether I kept working or not. Paul wanted a baby, too, and when I finally found a stopping place, he replied, "Shirl, I want a baby, too." He hugged me and continued, "…and I appreciate your willingness to go through a pregnancy in order for us to have one." I thought he was very wise not to end with, ". . . at your age."

An uncommonly fertile woman, I tested positive mere weeks later with the pregnancy test I asked Paul to bring home from Phar-Mor. Of course, we didn't believe the results, so I scheduled an appointment with my OB, Doctor Freddie. Paul and I took his last appointment of the day so we could make it to a dinner and birthday party for Paul's best friend, Phil Williams, right afterward. The party guests would be mostly Paul's friends, people with whom he had walked the halls in high school and college.

I lay on my back supported by the metal examining table. Paul stood beside me, looking around at all the gadgets. He knew a lot about the gadgets. When his dream to join the Air Force was crushed, he had hoped to study medicine at the University of South Carolina. Much to his chagrin, he had encountered another road block: lack of available funding prevented this pursuit as well. He responded to this new disappointment by walking down to the end of the hall and signing up for the Pharmacy School.

I, on the other hand, was a purist who didn't appreciate the gadgets of modern medicine, at least so far as giving birth goes. I believed since birthing babies is not a disease, having them in hospitals where people are sick is a negative approach that defies nature. Didn't God specifically design a woman's body to perform this unique function? Wasn't the addition of obstetric bells and whistles audacious? Didn't it interfere with God's perfectly implemented plan? So, I had always refused ultrasounds and other such tools I considered invasive. That's why I didn't recognize the ultrasound machine when it was wheeled over to my belly without my knowledge or consent.

"Oh, my," Dr Freddie exclaimed with inflated gravity in his voice.

I tried to ignore his drama, but he went on, this time a little louder with the same slightly exaggerated seriousness. "Hmm. Oh, boy."

His playful manner only pretended foreboding. I feigned patience, figuring he'd be serious in a minute, but I was wrong. "Looks like trouble."

"Come on, doc. What?"

Dr. Freddie smiled. "You don't want to know."

"Yes I *do*. WHAT?" I repeated, noting that Paul's face registered amusement, not alarm.

Dr. Freddie turned the screen so I could see. "There's

a baby."

"Okay," I replied, smiling, "I kind of see that."

"And it sure looks like," Dr. Freddie continued, "there's another one right there."

I burst out laughing. My tummy began shaking, so the picture on the screen got all wiggly. "No way. Is it really?" I queried, "I can't believe it."

Dr. Reynolds explained that lots of pregnancies start out as multiples. Strangely, the body sometimes "reabsorbs" one of the babies. "At only five-and-a-half weeks of pregnancy," he lectured us, "I don't recommend telling anyone. Wait until you are at least seven-and-a-half weeks along and we can confirm both babies with another ultrasound."

In the time it took to understand there were two babies, this purist mama couldn't wait for the next ultrasound. I was suddenly excited to be living in a time of gadgets that could reveal the truth of desires too heady to wish out loud: God was sending two babies!

As Paul drove us down the interstate, I got lost in the crazy momentum of my thoughts. It felt like we had just won a monumental jackpot. Would they be identical? How can people really tell identical twins apart? Don't twins usually come too early? I hoped I would carry them to term. Were they two girls? Were they two boys? Maybe they were a girl and a boy. I guessed I'd have to quit school, but exchanging a degree for two sweet babies seemed like a wonderful trade. How quickly a dream can change.

Remembering that I was not alone in the car, I slowly turned toward Paul. His thoughts must have been racing as well because he slowly turned, too, as though he'd just remembered me. We were like two Stooges. Cracking up together ensued, following some more silent wondering. We must have repeated this new exercise four more times before we were able to talk. How much self control would it take to wait two weeks to tell? It didn't take long to find out.

Being late to the party, we made an inadvertent little entrance before finding our seats. It was rumored we might be pregnant, and everyone there was hoping for a confirmation.

Before we sat down, Phil began prophesying loudly enough for everyone to hear: "Paul, my friend, he announced, "I had a dream that you had a son."

"Well," Paul began, his will and resolve melted clean away, and feeling pleased that Phil had set him up, "you better go back and dream another one, because there are two!"

* * *

My classes at the University had to end after the spring semester. This became evident when, in my fifth month of pregnancy, I had to squeeze into the desk in my Philosophy class. Current study of multiple pregnancies had informed me that by six months, a twin pregnancy measures a nine-month-pregnant belly. I soon discovered that everything after that simply looks surreal. I was growing to mammoth proportions.

It was in my Logic class that I first felt both babies kick me simultaneously. It seemed ironically *ill*ogical that I should have to sit composed while feeling this wonderful miracle. The logical thing to do *if* two babies kicked seemed to be to *then* interrupt the lecture and announce this momentous milestone.

Paul's father, Joe, had given us a car around this time, but reaching beyond my stomach to steer was already becoming a chore. I began having nightmares that I couldn't reach the brakes when I drove this car. As my girth grew to a seemingly impossible size, I realized a new opportunity to amuse my audience. I loved finding Paul comfortably relaxing in an armchair, maybe reading the newspaper. I would walk deliberately toward him, adapting my walk to suggest I was coming to sit on his lap like some big old Baby Huey. He always responded in horror, because he never knew if I was really crazy enough to crush him under me or not.

Paul proved to be functional in a lot of ways I hadn't expected. One such example of his wonderful, willing utility came to light around my sixth month of pregnancy. This was when getting out of bed to go to the bathroom became necessarily frequent, yet my body's heavy and weakened state made this exercise an awful challenge. Together, we perfected our cooperative effort to get me into a standing position for the journey from bed to bathroom. Paul was reluctant at first, but thanks to my need and the confidence I felt in my heretofore untried plan, I finally convinced him to place the soles of his feet square against the small of my back and push. I leaned into his feet and he didn't stop pushing until I was standing and balanced. *Voila.*

Another fun thing I enjoyed during the later months was catching the children off guard and making them recoil. One such day around my seventh month (visual description: eleventh month), we were at the lake trailer in Winnsboro. The children were down on the dock, absorbed in their pre-teen coolness. I'd walked down to the dock with them but realized almost immediately that my brain would explode if I didn't distance myself soon. Sarah and Elisabeth's water shrieks would have made an apt background for a B-rated horror flick and I was pretty sure my eardrums were beginning to bleed. I lumbered along through the yard elephant style, stopping to observe the pear tree which was becoming sort of a little pet. It was June and not much was happening on the branches so I wandered along, looking for something else to relieve my boredom.

The trailer door slammed and I noted Paul in his swim trunks headed toward the dock, looking slim just like everybody else in the world except for me.

"Hey." I called to him.

"Hey." He called back. "Didn't you want to swim?"

"You're so funny. Maybe I'll surprise you and jump off the dock. Maybe I'll jump into your arms so you can catch me. Maybe I won't sink like a rock with you under me."

Paul smiled as he passed me, but he looked a little wary if you ask me. Anyway, I figured as long as he was down on the dock I was off life guard duty, which was really a pretty hilarious notion when you thought about it. The air condition called to me like a siren from inside the trailer so I obeyed the call. There wasn't anything to do inside either so I went into one of the small bedrooms and opened a drawer in an old chest of drawers.

"What do you know?" I said to myself as I pulled an ancient neon-orange bikini out. Suddenly, I didn't feel so bored as I gleefully stripped myself of maternity garb, donned the two tiny excuses for apparel and waddled off to the dock. I swear the Earth seemed to shake. Paul spotted me first and just shook his head as the children first stared in disbelief, then started screaming and covering their eyes.

"No, no!" Their cacophony rose in evidence of the horror of this moment.

"What?" I innocently queried, barely able to stand for laughing. "What?"

Paul would never have thought up, much less carried out such a vulgar display, yet my antics amused him. I think he and I appreciated our dissimilarities as much as our similarities. We were alike in our standards of faith, family, and work yet Paul's reasonable, appropriate personality presented a complimenting balance to mine, which sometimes took levity right to the edge – okay, sometimes over the edge. We found ourselves admiring these differences and basking in the vicarious living afforded by our relationship. As I began to take myself more seriously, Paul began to loosen up a little. It was good for us. The changes gave us new confidence as they increased our respect for each other. Even as God had multiplied me into three people, He was truly in the midst of our marriage making Paul and me one. It was fun recognizing the many different ways He was completing His promise to do just that.

The pregnancy with twins was different from my singleton pregnancies. Instead of feeling healthy Earth Mother connections to the Universe, my body seemed to betray me. With double the blood and water volume, my vision and hearing actually decreased. I even developed carpel tunnel syndrome in my wrist. Sometimes I felt less like a human incubator than a human aquarium. Being in such an odd situation isn't without its advantages, however. Caught off guard and not intending to, I could really impress my children. One of my new abilities actually rendered Sarah and Elisabeth speechless one hot, summer afternoon in Taco

Bell. As they sat across from me at the little table pretending I wasn't really with them, the liquid in my forty-four-ounce-drink began to drop like a thermometer in a flash freeze, rendering them unable to ignore me. With only a couple of vacuum-force pulls on my straw, I'd become a shameless slave to the needs of my gestational thirst. "O-o-oh." I exclaimed in the tone of a well-bred Southern lady, "I was *thirsty*."

Sarah and Elisabeth simply stared in shock. When they were composed enough to speak, they begged, "Do it again. That was so cool."

One of the smartest things I did in preparation for the future was to teach Jon, Austin, Sarah, and Elisabeth to do their own laundry. Right after we blended our family, I had designed a "Rotating Chore Chart." Daily jobs included emptying the trash, unloading the dishwasher, sweeping, and vacuuming. Cleaning the bathrooms was the weekend duty shared by all the children. The next week, everybody would rotate to the next chore on the list. The idea was fairness, but they hated it anyway. Blending a family is tricky because children are constantly keeping score, and their score cards are painfully self-focused.

As happy as we were, this time in our life was not without challenges. As my girth ballooned, Paul's position at Phar-Mor looked more insecure with every news report. There had been embezzlement at the top, and Phar-Mor was sure to Chapter 11 any minute. It wasn't that Paul couldn't find a job in Columbia. He had a trusted reputation in Columbia's pharmacy network. Those who knew Paul would jump at the chance to hire him. The problem was health insurance. If Paul changed jobs, we would have no health insurance until he had been employed for three months. Our babies were due right about the time we anticipated his transition and the subsequent lapse in insurance. We handled this problem in the only way we could: by praying and asking God to guide us. Phar-Mor did close, and Paul went straight to work at Kmart's Two Notch Road pharmacy where he had worked after he graduated from Pharmacy school. In a lot of ways, he was coming home. God answered our prayer by giving us enough resources to pay through the nose for Cobra insurance until the Kmart policy became available, so we were never without coverage.

Paul came home early one afternoon as I was cleaning out my bedroom closet.

"Hey." He greeted me as I looked up from the rubble.

"Hey, Counselor." I answered, surprised to see him. "I thought you worked until 6:00.

"I had a dermatologist appointment, so I took off early." Paul answered.

"Oh. I replied, "Did you have fun?"

"I wouldn't call it fun," he said, "but it wasn't too bad. Dr. Chow cut a big hole in me."

"Yeah?" I responded, "Couldn't you stop him?"

Paul pulled his shirt open and showed me his battle scar. "I guess I could have taken him if I'd had to, but he was really nice about it." Paul said.

"Durn." I reacted. "What was it? He made a huge hole."

"They do that so they can be sure they have clean margins." Paul explained. "The spot wasn't really all that big."

"Well," I repeated my question, "what was it?"

"It was melanoma." He casually answered, looking guilty.

"Melanoma?" I repeated with no small amount of alarm. "That's bad, Paul. Were they sure?"

"Yes," he said, "yes, but he said the margins were clean. That's what you want, clean margins."

"Paul?" I asked him, standing up and coming closer, "Are you sure?"

"Yes, Sweetie." He said, putting his arms around me, "It's really okay. Dr. Chow just told me to come in every six months instead of every year now, but it's not a big deal. I promise."

"Okay, I believe you," I lied, "but you sure can kill a mood, can't you?"

"Yeah." Paul laughed, "I guess I can."

Following his lead, I pretended to put alarm aside, but knew I would be counting his freckles carefully from now on. I also thought about the times his mom had asked me to be sure Paul was wearing his sun screen and wondered if she knew something I didn't know.

In the eighth month of pregnancy, my blood pressure, which is commonly on the low end of normal, began to spike. This had never happened in my other pregnancies. The insult added to this injury was illuminated by people who felt the curious need to tell me it was only because I was older this time. These were the people I secretly wanted to sit on. I was prescribed bed rest around seven-and-a-half months. My days were filled with sleeping and reading paperbacks light enough to hold while lying on my back. A heavy book would put pressure on my carpel tunnel. Of course, there were also frequent visits to the bathroom precipitated by two babies' who were using my bladder as a trampoline.

Still, I managed to be the cool mom thanks to bizarre new ways of bonding with my children that arose from this strange pregnancy. With all that extra water sloshing around in me, my legs developed edema. I discovered that poking a sinkhole in my shins left a deep depression for several minutes. My legs seemed much like Silly Putty. Naturally, I shared this newfound skill with my children. At thirteen and ten Jon and Austin, found it especially entertaining.

"That is so cool, Mom." They would exclaim, "Can I do it?"

All good things must end, they say, and the edema was a precursor to possible problems such as pre-eclampsia. After one of my weekly obstetrician's appointments, I was instructed to check into the hospital for induction of labor. Calcifications had been spotted in my amniotic sac, bringing urgency to the births. I was disappointed, having hoped to carry the babies to term. They were going to be four weeks shy of complete gestation. What's more, Doctor Freddie wasn't on call. I had seen Dr. Michael, his partner, only a couple of times. He looked a lot like young George Stephanopoulos to me, but even handsomer. Much too young and cute to be an OB doctor (you could cut a diamond with the perfect lines of his jaw), he was nonetheless kind and capable, but I didn't know him like I knew Dr. Freddie.

Even though I was nervous, it was a comfort to be going through this with Paul beside me. He was so self-assured, intelligent, so respectable, it was easy to trust him. Standing at Lexington Hospital's check-in desk, we looked at each other. Paul gazed lovingly into my bloated face. "We'll have babies soon."

"I wish I could deliver them cooked all the way." I said nervously.

"They *are* cooked all the way." Paul assured me. "They just won't be very fat."

"I know." I answered, "It's just that I don't want them to struggle."

"I'll make sure they take good care of our babies," Paul assured me. "I won't let anybody do anything you don't want." I leaned my head against him breathing in the comfort of his familiar smell. I knew I really could lean on him to be true to his word. Paul didn't let himself be intimidated by people or circumstances. "Remember," he reminded me. "I am protection of you. I nodded my head as he continued, "I am protection of our babies, too."

Way back in 1979 when Jon was born, my contractions had been induced with a Pitocin drip. It made labor so overwhelming that I swore I would never let a doctor use it again for my labor. I didn't. I birthed Austin at a birthing center with a nurse mid-wife named Marie. When Elisabeth was born, my friend, Tavish, a lay midwife, helped me with a home delivery. Now, understanding that Pitocin might be required to start my contractions, I willed to do everything in my power to bring about labor. The best power I had was prayer.

"God?" I called, pleading, "I know You can make me go into labor if You will. Please bring it on, and bring our babies here healthy. Don't let them struggle, Lord. And, thank you for this beautiful family."

After my membranes were stripped, Paul and I walked and walked the hospital corridors. It felt so good to rest against his muscular arm. God answered my prayer by bringing me into labor fairly quickly. It's funny. I don't know why, but no matter how often God answers with exactly what I request, I am still usually surprised.

Our friend, Jane arrived at the hospital straight from work. She was wearing a dotted cinch-waist dress, and told us she had dressed as Minnie Mouse for this occasion. Hers was obviously the only waist between the two of us, and while I recognized the innocence of her waif-ness, I thought it was especially cruel of her to wear a belt. I was the Stay-Puft Marshmallow man to her Minnie. With our video camera in tow, Jane set about to chronicle the making of Graham history. From her position in the labor room, Jane focused the camera on my swollen frame which mostly obscured the hospital bed on which it reclined.

"Hey, babies." I called to the camera while placing my hand, minuscule by comparison, on one side of my massive abdomen. "This is one of you over here," I continued, moving my hand to the other side, "and here's another one. Y'all have very expandable living quarters at this point. Y'all hurry." I instructed, adding, "Your daddy said to tell you that labor started at 3:00. Y'all come on."

"Y'all" was the term Paul enjoyed using to define me since we learned there were twins, i.e., *y'all* come sit over here, or, what did *y'all* say, etc. Consequently, I, too referred to myself in the plural. It made me feel regal; something like Jabba the Hut playing Queen Elisabeth.

"Smile, kids." Jane called, moving the camera to a chair beside my bed which held eleven-year-old Austin and Elisabeth, almost nine.

"Hi, babies." I added from the background, "Here are your brother and sister, two of them anyway."

Austin rose, dressed in a red T-shirt and shorts, his blonde curls following the different beats of many drummers. He seemed confident, ready to take on whatever was ahead.

"Okay." He began and took a breath. "I'll go. When you're my age, I'll be twenty-two, okay? And it's 1993, and I know that seems like a long time ago," he hesitated, reaching for words, "cause - and, so - that's all."

Austin returned to his seat as Elisabeth simultaneously stood and prissed self-consciously over to the camera, wearing her obligatory pink with flowers. The first girl after two boys, Elisabeth had spent her beginnings in nothing but pink with at least thirty pounds of lace. The lace had been discarded, but pink remained a staple in her wardrobe. "Hi." She began, "I'm Elisabeth, your sister," she paused, feeling the magnitude of being in the spotlight, "and it seems like a long time ago for you." She added, feeling suddenly guilty for so shamelessly plagiarizing Austin's monologue. Embarrassed, she turned to Austin, apologizing "I know you already said that." Austin shrugged and leaned back in the chair. Elisabeth continued, "and, um, um, I hope you get out safe," she paused, putting her hands on her hips, rocking back and forth, "and, soon." She added with relief, and smiled, pleased that she was finished.

"What are you going to do when they get here, Elisabeth?" I asked her from the sidelines.

"I'm going to stroll you in the grocery store…" she announced to the camera, "…and how old will I be when they are my age?" She asked, swirling toward me.

"You'll be nearly nine when they get here, so you'll be nine years older your whole life.' I explained. Austin rocked quietly in the chair behind her.

"So, you'll be eighteen when they are nine." Paul's brother Steve's wife, Wanda, called out. Coincidentally, she was an identical twin. She immediately regretted her statement as the camera panned over to the origin of her voice. "I don't need to go on there." She quietly rued, but the unsympathetic camera demanded a comment. Wanda relented, "Hey, babies. Hurry up and get here. We are anxiously awaiting."

Anxiously awaiting, we were. Excited family-in-waiting filled up the waiting room where Jane followed behind Elisabeth, taping her every footfall. By 6:28 p.m., Mother and Daddy had made the almost three-hour drive from Hartwell, Georgia. I am guessing Daddy probably made the trip in two hours with Mother biting her tongue, no doubt caught between hoping they made it in time for the birth and just hoping they made it there in one piece. She hadn't relaxed in the passenger seat since our wreck outside Atlanta in 1969.

Our friends, Gale and Tim soon brought Jon to join his siblings. Sarah was with her mom in Myrtle Beach, South Carolina and wouldn't be with us for this milestone. Jane, taking a break from birthing babies to visit with the others in the waiting room, knew our family well. She'd started out as one of my haircutting customers, and somewhere along the way, we had become buddies.

By 10:30 p.m., Paul was back in the room with me, dressed in light blue hospital scrubs. He reached for my hand and gripped it as I confronted a hard contraction. Whispering, he gave me a read-out from the machine as *Pachelbel's Canon in D* softly soothed the atmosphere around us.

An hour later, Paul unfolded my list of requests and read them quietly to our nurse. "No sugar-water in the nursery," he instructed, "only breast milk." Our nurse nodded patiently in reply.

Paul and Jane's tolerance for stress began to wane. As I braced for another hard contraction, Jane taped Paul putting his hospital mask guard on. Paul responded by covering his eyes with it.

"Where's everything *at*, dad-gum-it." He joked.

As Jane giggled at Paul's annoying antic, I realized I could strangle both of them if not for the contraction. I must have been in the transition stage of labor, making the timing of their exchange particularly poor. Wisely, they gathered self-control before the contraction's end.

At 12:19 p.m. Jane took the camera to the waiting room to give everyone a progress update. Paul and I were now moving to the delivery room. Jane panned to Elisabeth, lying on a couch pretending to try to go to sleep. "I'm *tryin'* to go to sleep." She explained in exaggerated tones, convincing no one.

With a twinkle in her Papaw's eye, my Daddy advised her, "If you'd be quiet long enough, you might."

Jane entered the delivery room with the camera at 12:32 a.m., where my pushing was being emphasized with lots of volume. Almost half of the baby's little head was visible.

"Push, push, push, push, push." Commanded Dr. Michael, whose Hollywood good looks would have seemed more at home playing an obstetrician in a soap opera, but I wasn't noticing that at the moment. My legs trembled uncontrollably as I let out a short cry. In that same moment, the rest of the baby's tiny head slid into the doctor's hands with a slippery little "plop." My perfectly manicured hands,

hands that hadn't done a lick of work for those last weeks of bed rest, reached instinctively for the baby. My body was certainly making up for all that leisure now. Anxiety showed in the worry lines on my face, and I quietly inquired, "Is she okay?"

Charlotte gulped air and answered my question with a series of loud, beautiful, *"Wah's."*

"Is this Charlotte or Emily?" I heard someone ask.

"This is Charlotte." The reply came from another part of the room.

Dr. Gold, the pediatric doctor, held Charlotte's wobbly, slippery infant body in something that loosely resembled a sitting position. "Hold your head up. Be proud." Dr. Gold instructed her, "Happy birthday."

I lay on my back, exhausted from the physical effort of childbirth hoping for a long rest before doing it all over again. Charlotte, swaddled in the blanket like a stiff burrito, was gently handed to Paul. Smiling, he gently gave the beautiful little bundle to me, blinking to keep his tears from falling.

Charlotte was soon whisked away to the neonatal nursery while Jane continued to film through the mist of her own tears. Dr. Michael handsomely noted my exhaustion and apologetically told me to go ahead and push the other baby out. A few pushes slipped a little gray Emily into the world. My face registered distress over what sounded not right. Emily sneezed once, sputtered, and as I looked down, the scene wasn't right. She was the wrong color, and I didn't hear her cry.

"What's wrong?" I demanded weakly, and then I heard Emily scream twice. The tension in our faces fell partly away, and I looked up at Paul by my side. "Two screams." I intimated to Paul, holding up two fingers. The words I spoke were like a quiet victory prayer of thanks, a relieved confirmation that Emily was alive. Paul leaned in, kissed me and hugged me softly. Good gracious. We had six children.

But seek first his kingdom and his righteousness, and all these things will be given to you as well. Therefore do not worry about tomorrow, for tomorrow will worry about itself. Each day has enough trouble of its own.

Matthew 6:33-34

Chapter Six

July 20, 1993

Emily was in the neonatal nursery attached to oxygen. My arms longed for both babies. I got to nurse Charlotte in the post delivery room and take her with me to my hospital room. The nearly overwhelming exhaustion I felt only delivered sleep to me as long as at least one baby was snuggled up beside me. Charlotte and I slept for a few hours before a nurse came to check her oxygen levels. Reluctantly, I relinquished her to the nurse and whispered, "Bring her right back."

"I will as long as everything checks out good." she answered, taking my wee baby out the door, leaving behind my empty arms.

The nurse returned a little later, apologizing, "We need to get her oxygen levels up, then we will bring her back to you."

"Okay." I replied sadly, lying back on the pillow, unable to rest.

I enjoyed the privilege of rooming-in when my other babies were born, so this feeling of being without a child in my post-delivery state was uncomfortably new to me. I turned and looked at Paul, zonked out in the chair by my bed. I had gone to sleep easily with the three of us in this room, but now my maternal hormones yearned restlessly for newborn babies. In spite of my weakened, tired body, I had to find a way to be near Charlotte and Emily. Paul breathed evenly, and I didn't have the heart to wake him. Drawing my deflated frame out of the bed, I ventured a walk. It didn't take long for me to realize what a weakling I was, so I crept into a vacant wheelchair parked nearby. The cold metal of the chair felt strange. I felt strange. My hands gripped the wheels and made a little slow momentum, and tried to act as if I weren't an escapee. I found Charlotte and Emily in the neo-natal nursery down the hall without anyone stopping me. Neither baby looked nearly as robust as their siblings had been at almost nine pounds apiece. Charlotte weighed in at a wee five pounds, fourteen ounces as her sister Emily barely tipped the baby scale at five pounds, twelve ounces. Their little legs bore no fat at all, and miniscule ribs labored up and down as their lungs gulped oxygen. I sat next to Emily with my hand touching the incubator.

"Make her strong, Lord Jesus." I prayed for my miniature baby whose petite chest rose and fell frantically. I would have cried, but I was actually too exhausted. "Let her feel Your presence." I added. "In Your Name."

Suddenly, I realized my body was uncommonly weak. My blood pressure must have been dropping. I gathered the little energy I had left to turn the wheelchair around and leave. Just as I exited the nursery, a lactation nurse approached. She reiterated the name on her name tag and asked if I had thought about nursing.

"Oh, yes," I answered, "yes."

"I want to talk to you, then, about breast feeding." She said brightly.

"I'm okay," I answered feebly, "I breast-fed my other babies."

I had nursed Jon, Austin, and Elisabeth for over a year each, but I didn't feel well enough to say it to her.

"Would you like some help back to your room?" She asked me, noting my weakness.

I smiled, nodding as she walked behind my chair to comply.

When we arrived, Paul was still soundly asleep and I let the nurse help me into my bed. It had been such a little trip, yet I was completely worn out. It was going to take a long time for my poor body to recover from this multiple pregnancy and birth feat.

After three days, we all got to go home with our fraternal twin daughters. We packed our two diminutive babies into car seats that seemed to gulp them up. As the Bronco turned up Red Cedar Lane, we saw our friend Gale waving as she tied two pink ribbons on our mailbox with "Charlotte" and "Emily" scripted in gold glitter. Our freezer had been stocked with ten or twelve huge casseroles, compliments of our friends at Christus Victor.

"We usually send a meal when a family has a new baby," explained Beth, my choir-mate at church and wife of Earl our insurance agent, over the phone, "but there are so many of you, this seemed like the only answer."

How thankful I was for those casseroles. I was enjoying the most excellent eating disorder imaginable. Six large meals were absolutely necessary as my body produced enough milk for two infants. My weight was dropping rapidly, yet I ingested thousands of calories. What fun! I had a nursing pillow shaped like a "C" that went around my middle. It was designed so that I could sit cross legged in my bed with an infant's head resting on either side, and it worked great. Another feature I came to find was that I could put a big plate of food right in the middle, nurse two babies, and eat with both hands free.

It wasn't all fun, though. By the time I had been home for a couple of days, I was fighting a headache that got more severe over time. Since I'd gotten relief from Chiropractic in the past, during and after pregnancy, I scheduled an appointment and hoped for the best. Paul and I loaded the babies into the car and set out for my appointment. I sat in the back seat with our tiny passengers while Paul drove us. When we walked into the office, the receptionist came out from behind the desk.

"Oh, my goodness!" She exclaimed. "Twins!"

She squatted in front of the two baby carriers on the floor smiling at . . . oh, no. What were their names? With my pounding head and sore neck, I thought I must surely be losing my mind because if she asked me the babies' names, I honestly couldn't tell her. What was wrong with me? I did recall having moments of stupidity after having my other children, but this episode was over the top.

"Dear God, please don't let her ask their names," I prayed. God was merciful and granted my request, but this case of amnesia, or whatever it was, made me nervous.

Seconds later, we were called into the chiropractor's

treatment room. Once inside, she asked me to contort myself on a short contraption built into the middle of the floor. As she skillfully thrust the heels of her wonderful hands against the most excellent spot on my body, I heard a perfectly glorious "POP."

I felt some measure of immediate relief before she said, "Try to rest and even sleep for a couple of hours when you get home. The pain will subside completely by tomorrow."

Oh, how I wanted to believe her, and resting was the only thing I longed to do. She seemed awfully sure in her prophecy and I fell off to sleep soon after returning home.

Waking up hungry after two hours, I could really tell a difference. Paul tip-toed into our bedroom just as my eyes opened.

"You're up." He said proudly.

"Yeah, I feel better," I said before he had a chance to ask, "but I'm really hungry."

"What do you want?"

"It doesn't really matter, but make sure there's a lot of it."

Paul smiled, thinking I was kidding. He disappeared into the kitchen and pulled a wonderful steaming casserole from the oven, compliments of Christus Victor Lutheran Church. In minutes, he returned with a plate of something with chicken and flat noodles in a delicious cream sauce. I didn't know which parishioner's kitchen it had come from, but surely Christ's Own hands had been borrowed to blend the ingredients. I finished and begged for seconds before Paul had time to leave the room.

"Are you really finished?" He said, disbelieving.

I wasn't even embarrassed, "Hungry... food... more... now." I ordered as Charlotte said something similar from the crib by the bed. It was just a little baby cry, but it was every bit as demanding as my own request.

Emily made a tiny squeak as I lifted Charlotte in my arms. I adjusted the covers and my nursing pillow, taking care to leave plenty of room for dinner, stage two. By the time Paul returned with it, Charlotte nursed soberly. Emily squeaked again and Paul backed away from our voracious eating frenzy to lift her from the crib.

"What's the matter there, little bullet-head?" Paul asked Emily's small face. She squeaked again, presumably in protest to the nickname he'd bestowed.

He looked on helplessly before laying her gently on the left side of my nursing pillow. I positioned baby Emily awkwardly at my other breast and she struggled to latch on. Once she was attached, I voraciously attacked the second casserole perched neatly between babies.

"What?" I asked, looking up at Paul staring at me with something like shock or amazement.

"I don't know." He answered. "I just wish I could do something to help."

"You did." I assured him. "You fed me twice and handed babies to me."

"I know." He agreed, "I just wish I could do more."

"You are feeding two babies when you feed me." Paul shook his head. I'm sure he would have breast fed the twins if he could have figured out a way. I sat with bovine regality on the bed and lifted an eyebrow.

"Well," I said in my best scientist voice, "You do realize that with enough stimulation, men can produce breast milk, although the quality of their milk has never been confirmed."

"You're so cute." He answered without sincerity. He had laughed the first time I said this to him, but after a hundred repetitions, my joke had aged gracelessly. Paul could now muster only an eye roll and a shake of his head.

"Hey." I changed the subject, stretching my neck and turning my head, "I don't hurt."

It wasn't nightfall quite yet, and I was pain-free. Hallelujah.

* * *

With a couple of weeks off work for paternity leave, Paul adapted easily to his father-of-twins role. When they cried, we each took a baby, but we would soon learn to carry crying babies in each arm. When they woke in the middle of the night, I would rush to the bathroom while Paul retrieved the babies. When I returned he would have their diapers changed and ready to hook up to the milking machine (otherwise known as me). He'd lie there for a few minutes wishing he could do more before going back to sleep.

In order to regain strength and nurse twins, my routine was simple: eat, rest, eat, rest, repeat. The urgent things got managed but it was often in lieu of the important things. I was pretty sure I would moo soon, but at least I washed a load of clothes most days, and eventually got them into the dryer. Once they got as far as the clothes basket, another task or need usually presented itself, and that was the extent of my housework. We all learned to adapt to wrinkles. Thanks to the support and helpful ways of our family, I would be able to nurse Charlotte and Emily for a whole year.

Emily concerned me, though. She was so very little and didn't seem happy. When she cried, which was often, her little body bowed and her fingers splayed. The cry she made sounded like a high-pitched screech. Her eyebrows knitted together which made her tiny face look old, worried, and anxious. I had learned that the second-born twin sometimes has problems. I wondered if she was really okay but I was too scared about it to verbalize my unease to anyone except God.

Charlotte, on the other hand, continued to thrive. She nursed well and seemed happy. Her progress was on schedule. When our family went out together into the world, Paul would always end up holding Charlotte as I nursed Emily. It seemed that the only time Emily came close to relaxing was when she was nursing, although she still acted unsatisfied.

I finally called my local La Leche League chapter. Having already nursed three babies with success, I hadn't expected to need any instruction but nursing premature babies called for a new strategy. The problem was that Emily's sucking reflex wasn't strong enough. A league lactation expert came to our house right away to show me how to re-position my breast and Emily so that she could nurse better. Finally, little Emily began to relax, proving that you really can teach an old . . . cow new tricks. By three months, I happily noticed a double chin and little rolls of baby-fat forming around her middle. But developmentally,

Charlotte was still ahead, smiling and rolling over long before Emily showed any interest in trying.

Too soon, Paul's paternity leave ended. Sarah was back with us, and I thought I was braced for my first day with six helpful children. By afternoon, it looked like we might really be getting used to our new life. Austin, Sarah, and Elisabeth hesitantly asked about riding their bikes to the library, and it seemed like a good idea. Jon stayed behind in case I needed two good arms.

Alone in my bedroom with two pink babies, we dozed off together. I was awakened abruptly by Sarah rushing in.

"Austin fell off his bike on his head," She announced, alarmed. "He's talking crazy."

"Where is he?" I quickly asked her.

"Elisabeth is helping him," She answered. "We were almost home."

"Okay," I told her shaking the cobwebs from my newly awakened brain. "Stay right here with the babies while I go find him."

I exited via the garage door and met Elisabeth leading a stumbling Austin up the driveway. I approached him and asked, "Honey, what happened?"

"WHAT?" Austin exclaimed.

"How did you fall?" I tried again.

"WHAT ARE YOU SAYING?" Austin yelled, "I DON'T KNOW WHAT YOU'RE SAYING."

I pulled him to my side and led him into my room, hoping he wouldn't fall. How on Earth would I catch him, as atrophied as my muscles had become?

"Austin, I want you to lie down on my bed," I tried to explain, but he was still unable to comprehend. I gently guided him to the side of the bed, helping him lie down. He complied and began to regain some comprehension. As agitation re-wrote itself on his face as fear, my shaking fingers dialed 911. I gave the operator a synopsis of our situation and Austin lay quietly. We waited nervously for the paramedics.

Sarah and Elisabeth followed my instructions. Sarah went upstairs for Jon, and Elisabeth brought a cool washcloth for Austin's head. I called Paul at the pharmacy and gave him an update of events.

The paramedics arrived, carefully moving Austin onto a board and strapping him down.

"Jon," I directed, handing him one of the cloth Snugli carriers, "you put this on and I'll wear the other one. We've got to buckle the babies up in the car because we can't ride in the ambulance with Austin. I'll need you to come to the hospital with me to help with the babies so I can tend to Austin."

Ready and able Jon replied, "Yes, ma'am."

I was overwhelmed, so to minimize my responsibilities, I left Sarah and Elisabeth at the house and let a neighbor know they were there. Sarah, resenting being left behind, wondered to herself, "Why is she making me stay here?"

Re-familiarizing myself with the task of driving, Jon and I followed behind the ambulance to the emergency room entrance. I parked, and we awkwardly tucked helpless newborns into our Snugli pockets as fast as we could. Even though it was a short walk, I was huffing and puffing long before we entered the hospital. Jon and I were led into a private room with a couch and a couple of chairs. We lay Charlotte and Emily on the couch. Together, they didn't even take up half of one cushion.

"Are you Austin's mother?" A nurse inquired at the door.

"Yes," I answered. "Can I see him?"

"Wait just a minute," She replied. "We have to give him a catheter, and we need your signature." "Uh-oh," I thought, "He is not going to like that." I looked over at Jon, who was wincing.

"She can come on back," we heard another nurse say as she stuck her head through the door. "They're out of x-ray."

I followed her through double doors and found Austin on a gurney; curtains drawn around the sides providing a loosely private room.

"Hey Oscie," I said, using his nickname. When he was a toddler, I would introduce him by his name, but often, people thought I was saying "Oscar." After a while, I just gave in and "Oscie" became a term of endearment. It stuck as fast as "Jon-boy" and "Lizard" for Jon and Elisabeth. Paul called Sarah, "Sare-bear" but she never liked anybody else using it for her. Paul called Charlotte and Emily "Cabbage-head" and "Bullet-head," but they would soon adapt to the more feminine nick-names, "Chah-Chah" and "Mimi."

Austin looked weakly at me and I could see terror in his eyes.

"Mom," He pleaded, "Don't let them put a catheter in me."

"Oh, Austin, I'm so sorry," I answered sadly. "They have to do that because you might have a concussion. You aren't supposed to get up. Even for the bathroom. You can pass out and hurt yourself even worse."

I felt awful. The one thing my injured son requested was something I couldn't provide. I gently stroked his hair. "I'm so sorry." I repeated to his strained face.

I hadn't been in with him long before being deported by the catheter inserters. Regretfully deserting my son, I returned to the room where I found Jon playing with the fingers of his new sisters. "Look how little they are," he marveled, smiling at an impossibly small thumb.

Before I could reply, I heard a nurse outside the door remark, "They are right in here."

I turned, surprised to find Paul quietly hurrying in. "Hey." I greeted him, "I thought you worked until nine."

"I thought you might need me." He answered. "I'll stay here with Austin, and you can go on home."

"But, it's your first day back to work," I argued.

"It's okay," he explained. "This is where I need to be. You go home where you need to be."

Jon and I returned to the car, strapped in the babies, and headed home. Even in my relief, it felt strange and wrong to leave Austin at the hospital and go home. I had been a single parent for so long that it seemed perfectly normal to be overwhelmed with my required duties yet do them anyway. Life was easier now with two parents, and the children's needs were met sooner and more efficiently. This was how it was supposed to be, a dynamic I had missed out on without knowing the difference.

Paul called after the x-rays were read to say Austin didn't have a fracture, but the doctor wanted to keep him overnight for observation. The blow to his head alone could still cause nausea and other symptoms of concussion. Paul slept in a chair beside Austin that night. Meanwhile, the house felt empty despite the six of us at home. Paul called me from time to time until it got late.

Just before 9:00 pm, Austin thought he might be able to eat something. Paul doubted it but asked, anyway,

"What sounds good to you? I'll bring you whatever you think you can eat."

"I want a submarine sandwich," Austin answered optimistically.

"Do you still feel sick to your stomach?" Paul cautioned.

"Yes, sir, a little bit – but I think I can eat anyway."

"Okay, buddy." Paul gave him a fatherly pat on the shoulder. "You're the boss."

The hospital cafeteria was closed, so Paul walked across the street to fulfill Austin's request at a Subway restaurant. Returning to the room, he handed Austin the sandwich. Austin slowly removed half of the sandwich from the bag and began to peel the crinkly paper from around it. He opened his mouth, smelling the spices and gravely anticipating a bite. Thinking better of it, he slowly closed his mouth and weakly lowered sandwich onto his lap.

"I can't really eat it right now," he whispered as his limp arms fell weightlessly to his sides.

"It's okay, buddy," Paul reassured him, smiling. "Just let me know when you're ready."

"No, sir," Austin shut his eyes and concluded. "I don't want it."

Austin found a comfortable position and drifted off to sleep. Never one to waste food, Paul peeled back the sub wrapper and had supper.

If I asked today what he remembers about this adventure, Austin would say the only vivid memory is of the catheter.

Our first ordeal with six children had gone off reasonably well. Austin recovered, returning home the next day, and I put some extra energy into making sure helmets were in place for our bikers. At home, we were acclimating to the new logistics of living with two babies. There were new discoveries, and I offer three of them:

1.

You can't carry two babies and an umbrella at the same time. I tried. It just can't be done effectively. A Snugli and stroller are vital tools for twin handling unless you have a double stroller. The fancy double-stroller we had bought before the births proved to be too cumbersome to operate. A cheap double-umbrella stroller became my vehicle of choice.

When Charlotte and Emily began walking well, I learned that:

2.

Two babies are capable of lots of things one baby doesn't discover until later. While a single baby cannot open a chest of drawers, two really young babies are able to open drawers almost effortlessly. We found ourselves child proofing the house in a whole new way, i.e., screwing the chest of drawers to the wall. It was like learning to parent for the first time.

3.

There is a certain celebrity in having twins.

As to the kindness of strangers, people would go out of their way to open doors and even offer to hold a baby so that I could write a check. We were always a parade.

I rarely ventured out alone, though. It was just so much work to do it. At thirty-eight, my muscles weren't exactly bouncing back. Paul and I started walking in the neighborhood in an effort to improve my strength. The first time we tried, I sat on the curb after only a few blocks and cried. Paul was my great encourager and protected me from beating myself up.

"You've done an unusual physical feat, Shirley," he would remind me. "You can't expect to get right back overnight."

Another new observation was Emily's behavior. She often looked serious, as though she were analyzing everything. All of a sudden, at about six months of age, Emily began to catch up to her developmental expectations.

She learned how to scoot, sit up, and crawl practically all at once. In fact, she was crawling ahead of Charlotte. Still, I wondered if she would have cognitive challenges. One day, however, she did something that quieted my worry entirely. As Charlotte laid on her back, fat little fingers holding a red baby rattle up to her face, Emily watched her intently. When Emily reached for the rattle, Charlotte pulled it back. Emily, looking thoughtful, retreated and crawled across the floor. She chose another toy nearby, and instead of playing with it, she clutched it in her wee fist and banged it in rhythm as she journeyed back across the carpet to Charlotte. "What is she doing?" I wondered, holding my breath as she balanced on one hand and dangled the new toy over Charlotte's face with the other. Interested, Charlotte opened her hands to reach for it, a move which forced her to release her hold on the red rattle. As the prize fell to the floor, Emily took it and crawled off. Both babies were perfectly happy. This was the end of my angst over Emily's development. Not only did this incident seem to prove she was smart, but that she was diplomatic as well.

Paul, concerned about our money situation, took a pharmacy floater position the minute Kmart offered it. He would now be traveling from store to store in a large territory, and his salary would increase. The babies woke up a lot at night, so we were both fighting sleep deprivation by day. Sometimes, Paul would wake up just before running off the road. He usually didn't tell me, and I didn't know just how bad it was for him.

Back in 1983, there used to be a Dunkin Donuts commercial on television. To personify the company's standard for freshness; the advertisement depicted a tired, yet faithful employee waking up to his alarm clock in the dark to go to work. The doughnut maker shuffled across the floor, repeating his only line, "Time to make the doughnuts." Morning seemed to come so early for us that Paul adopted the doughnut man's mantra. Every morning when the alarm clock went off, Paul would utter the words that always made me giggle: "Time to make the doughnuts."

I was still fighting my own exhaustion and carrying around about ten extra pounds. The initial pregnancy weight fell off almost immediately but I was already tired of the little cushion that I knew would come off more slowly. Along with having to eat so much all the time for lactation, I just felt like a cow. I needed a shower most of the time because if both babies fell asleep simultaneously, I was more apt to choose sleep over a shower.

"Paul and I are still newlyweds," my sleep-deprived mind tried to reason, "why does he ignore me when he's home?" It should have been obvious to me that we were both worn out, but maybe that's why it wasn't. I felt ugly and fat. I couldn't get any work done. I was too tired to do any extra things for anybody in the family. Instead of recognizing this as a temporary season of our lives, I counted myself as an unlovable failure. I decided to talk to Paul when he returned from work one evening. Entering through the front door, Paul didn't look excited when I asked him to sit with me. Too tired to object, he pulled up two hard-backed dining room chairs and I began.

"I am so lonely," I started. "It just seems like you don't like me anymore. You never talk to me, and I need some reassurance." I looked at my hands and continued pitifully. "We're still newlyweds, but it feels like the thrill is gone. I mean, I look so forward to having you home, but when you are here, you don't seem to notice me at all. Paul," I pleaded, finally looking up at him, "I miss you."

What I saw before me was my poor, tired husband's head, bent only slightly forward. He had fallen asleep in the hardest chair in the house. My heart began to break for him. It suddenly became obvious to me that both of us were doing the very best we could. The last thing he needed from me was more pressure to keep up. I gently woke him and he shook his head, ready to make more doughnuts. "Come on." I told him, reaching for his hand, "You need to go to sleep."

I climbed under the bed-covers and watched Paul slip off his pharmacy jacket. As he stood by his side of the bed, I braced myself for the impact I knew was coming. Ever since knee surgery in his early twenties from the water-skiing accident, Paul fairly *fell* into a sitting position on the bed. I bounced in response, waiting patiently as he untied his shoes and sank soundlessly into the mattress. There would be no bothering with a book or crossword puzzle tonight. As his tall body stretched along his side of the bed, I scooted up beside him, threading my hand under his arm and around his chest. He was asleep before his head hit the pillow. I closed my eyes and thought about how lucky I was. I only had time enough to pray that our season of exhaustion would pass without killing us before I was also sound asleep.

To everything there is a season, and a time to every purpose under the heaven: A time to be born, and a time to die; a time to plant, and a time to pluck up that which is planted; A time to kill, and a time to heal; a time to break down, and a time to build up; A time to weep, and a time to laugh; a time to mourn, and a time to dance; A time to cast away stones, and a time to gather stones together; a time to embrace, and a time to refrain from embracing; A time to get, and a time to lose; a time to keep, and a time to cast away; A time to rend, and a time to sew; a time to keep silence, and a time to speak; A time to love, and a time to hate; a time of war, and a time of peace.
Ecclesiastes 3:1-8

Chapter Seven

     Summer ended, school resumed, and we journeyed down the path of an exciting new normal. Jon and Austin had new braces. Sarah was back to visiting us every other weekend and Elisabeth seemed to have an endless social calendar. Our dinner table was frequented by the children's friends. Paul was still a floater -- or "drifter," as Austin told people -- for Kmart Pharmacy.

     I was finally gaining strength, and it thrilled me that rising from a squatting position to get a pot from the lower cabinet now didn't require hauling myself up with my hands on the counter top. My legs were working right again. Driving my school-age children hither and yon, Charlotte and Emily in tow, was a smaller problem than before. Big enough to safely face forward now, my twin babies filled up their car seats a little better. Before we knew it, Charlotte and Emily were a year old and amused us regularly as they experimented with the art of conversation. We were all falling in love with them more every day.

     There were very few things the older children couldn't do to tend to the babies. They were quick studies in meeting the demands of our household. With everyone home, it almost seemed like Charlotte and Emily had six parents. Even the youngest was a capable diaper changer and I was often amazed at the patience my children showed for their tiny, yet strong-willed sisters. Charlotte was getting the hang of feeling words roll off her tongue as I buckled her and Emily in the back seat of our white Lumina one afternoon and dropped Elisabeth off at the library. It must have seemed odd to the toddlers when their siblings came and went; now you see them, now you don't. As I drove out of the library parking lot, Charlotte piped up from the back seat, "Where Lib-bet go?"

"Mommy dropped her off at the library, Sweetie," I answered.

"Oh." Charlotte responded after a pause. Apparently wishing to feel the power of words again she repeated her question, "Where Lib-bet?"

"She's at the library." I answered again, enjoying hearing her tiny, new voice really communicating.

"Oh," She replied, then, "Lib-bet gone? Mommy?"

"Yes, honey, she's at the library," I answered brightly, hoping she wouldn't stop talking to me. I looked in the rear view mirror and watched as Emily cut her eyes at Charlotte. She was studying Charlotte impatiently, and I thought she looked the slightest bit irritated. I wondered what was going on in her little mind.

"Mommy?" Charlotte called.

"What is it, sweet Charlotte?" I asked.

"Where 'Lib-bet go?"

At this point, Emily could stand no more. She shot Charlotte a look and with the intolerance only a sibling can understand, Emily explained, "She AT the LI-BEAR, CHAR-LOTTE!"

Charlotte looked blankly at Emily then turned away from her as though her sister weren't there. Continuing to ignore Emily, Charlotte immersed herself in the show of trees swishing past the window.

We pulled into the driveway of Austin's friend, Jimmy. I had told Austin he could visit Jimmy and I'd pick him up so that I could meet his mom. "Uh, Mom, I don't know if you really want to," Austin advised me.

"Of course I do," I answered.

"Well, she doesn't exactly speak the same language as you."

"That's okay," I cooed.

Austin continued, "Some people are scared of her."

"Why?"

"She's just kind of, you know, weird."

"Oh, for Heaven's sake, don't be saying that, son."

Jimmy's mom was Asian, maybe Korean, and had a loose grip on America, its language, and its customs. It couldn't have been easy to raise children in a culture she didn't quite understand, but it was clear that she worked hard to uncover the mysterious answers to questions she had. Questions like why Americans do things the way they do. I figured all that out after I met her. Parking the Lumina in Jimmy's driveway, I turned around to Charlotte and Emily, packed neatly into their car seats in the back seat. Charlotte was still mad at Emily and didn't ask where Austin was.

"Mommy's going to knock on the door here and get Austin, okay?" I sang. The girls stared at me and didn't answer. I started out of the car as Jimmy's mom ran out of the house. She was a little round woman with flailing arms. I could hear her chatter but hadn't an inkling what she was saying, but she seemed upset. I didn't realize this was her normal demeanor.

"Hi, you must be Jimmy's mom. My son is Austin." I said, enunciating carefully.

"Aussin?" She attempted to repeat my meaningless word.

"Yes. Aus-tin." I agreed as clearly as I could. "Is he here with YOUR SON, Jimmy?" I hoped that mentioning Jimmy's name along with the word "son" might clue her that we were on the same side, sisters of a kind. Austin and Jimmy appeared from inside the house. I was relieved.

"Hey, Mom," Austin said, trying not to grin as he got into the car. I looked at him helplessly.

"What is your name?" I took another jab at conversation. What was I thinking? She tilted her head like she didn't hear me right and I wondered fearfully what Asian word I may have inadvertently said. Unable to stop my foolish mouth, I continued. "Uh, I am Austin's mom. I am Shirley."

"Sheem tok?" She answered.

"These," I pointed at my bald-headed babies, "are my twins!"

Finally, I had hit on a word she recognized. "Twin?" She asked, "Girl?"

"Yes!" I answered proudly. "Two girls!"

She stuck her head in the open window. Charlotte and Emily gave her identical expressionless looks. She pulled her head out of the car and faced me.

"They cute" she said finally. "But, why you shafe they heads?"

* * *

Betty, Paul's mom, loved all our children and got a special kick out of being a grandma to twins. However, she began refusing our invitations to visit. Paul and I suspected that she was fighting depression, so we tried to check on her and visit her little house on Lake Marion Circle as often as possible. She didn't always cooperate, although when we were successful in drawing her out, she seemed to enjoy it. At the end of a visit, she always leaned close to Charlotte and Emily and said, "Let me tell you a secret." Then, she whispered into their roly-poly necks, *"I love you, I love you, I love you!"* At Christmas, however, she surprised Paul and his brothers by giving them each professional sketches of their baby portraits. Paul was delighted with his gift, but it worried him a little.

"Mom always buys gifts for the grandchildren," he explained, "but it's been years since she gave me a present for Christmas."

Betty had been somewhat reclusive as long as I had known her, despite the efforts of Paul and his brothers, Steve and Danny, to draw her out. She enjoyed working at the University of South Carolina as a switchboard operator, but that seemed to be as much socializing as she wanted. If we saw her during this time, it was usually because we visited her.

Gran loved all her grandchildren. I especially

appreciated her for accepting Jon, Austin, and Elisabeth as though they had always been her grandchildren. Each of them held a special place in her heart. She had nothing but compliments for Jon, and she always included Elisabeth when she paid for princess outings with Sarah and her other grand daughter, Rachel. She had a cool rapport with Austin. She liked telling him, "Austin, you are my main man," and he would answer, "You are my main lady, Gran!" Then, they would giggle.

Austin was experiencing the troublesome time of puberty and had started acting out in school. He was forever getting in trouble lately and Betty worried about him, too. When he failed to come home from school one afternoon, Betty broke out of her seclusion to drive around looking for him. We all made calls to his friends and looked for hours before Austin finally turned up on our doorstep, his head down, waiting on the porch with the Security Guard from our neighborhood.

"Thank God!" I said, opening the door.

"I found him at the community gym by the elementary school," The officer explained before saying the words that indicated he had saved Austin's life. "He tells me he was waiting for a guy in a van who promised to give him a job making twelve dollars an hour." My breath caught as it sank in. My little boy had probably come just short of riding off in a van for the last time. "Thank you, Jesus!" I whispered as I ushered them in and called a worried Gran who relaxed for the first time since Austin's vanishing.

* * *

Paul was making a little more money as a floater, but his ability to make the Atlanta drive had become rough with our new parenting demands. These days, Sarah's weekend visits were more often accommodated via the airlines. Worldly-wise at age eleven, she seemed as comfortable flying as riding her bike. Jon was attending ninth grade at Spring Valley High School, which happened to be my own Alma Mater. He took Sociology from Miss Powell, who had also taught me years before, God love her.

In many ways, it felt as if I had made a big circle in

my life. One of the perks of living here, where I had grown up, was running into people I hadn't seen for years, like Tim and Gale. Tim was one of the youth directors at Spring Valley Presbyterian Church across from the high school. Only a couple of years before, this church had come up with a fund raising idea they called "A Souper Bowl of Caring." Members of the youth group collected money in big soup bowls for the poor in our community on Super Bowl Sunday. Spring Valley challenged their neighbouring churches to do the same, and before long, this mission became a nationwide fund raiser in churches of many denominations. Spring Valley Presbyterians' youth program was really on fire, and Tim had started taking Jon and Austin with him to the Sunday night youth meetings.

Since Paul and I married and his father now had twin granddaughters, sometimes Joe came to visit us by himself. He came one weekend in February when Sarah was also with us. Late that Sunday afternoon, after Tim had picked up Jon and Austin for Youth Group, we had to take Sarah to catch her plane. Paul and his dad wanted to bring Elisabeth, Charlotte, and Emily along to the airport. I suddenly realized I could stay behind and have an uninterrupted shower. I waved goodbye and tried not to seem too happy about it, but I was pretty excited at the thought of shaving my legs. My shower was glorious, and I was drying my hair when the phone rang. It was Steve, Paul's middle brother. "Hey," he began, his voice sounding more like gravel than usual, "How are y'all?"

"We're just fine, Steve!" I answered, wondering why he was calling, "Paul just left, though. He's taking Sarah to the airport. Can I tell him you called?"

"Yeah," Steve replied, his voice breaking, "but I need somebody to come over here. I just got to Mom's house and, and she's in the bed -- she's dead." He began to cry.

"Steve, I'll be right there," I promised, shifting into panic gear. "I'll find a way to get Paul a message and I'll be over as soon as I can."

I realized God's orchestration even as I dug my feet into a pair of shoes and headed to the door. This time that He had carved out wasn't mostly for my shower after all. It was for me to be with Paul and his brothers as they dealt with the loss of their mother. I could see God's hand in the events that had made me available. If I had gone to the airport as usual, or if Steve had called a few minutes sooner, the phone would have rung and rung.

I steered onto Claudia Drive, entering the neighbourhood where Betty and Rod had raised three boys. Their bike-riding childhood ghosts swished past me on the streets that led to Betty's steep driveway. At that moment, I wished I could slip Paul, Steve, and Danny into my pocket and take care of all the sad things that lay ahead of them. I let myself into the carport entrance, stepping gently into Betty's small living room. It took a few seconds for my eyes to adjust to the darkness inside. Steve sat at the kitchen table in his customary place across from Betty's customary place. This was where they had spent many evenings joking and smoking, arguing together and sharing a beer in their designated kitchen chairs. He didn't hear me enter, so Steve continued to sit with his head bowed, like a diner praying over a meal that would never be served.

"Steve?" I whispered. He stood up and I hugged his sobbing frame.

"I came over here to see her, and she didn't answer me!" He blurted the explanation like a small boy. "I finally went in her room . . . I thought she was asleep." He continued. "I tried to wake her up, but she didn't answer me. I put my hand on her shoulder . . . she didn't feel right, and I knew she was dead. Mom's *dead*, Shirley!"

"I'm so sorry, Steve!" I answered, not knowing what else to say. The smell of Steve's fresh cigarettes mingled in the air with Betty's old smoke. When my vision cleared, I noticed Puppy-John, a little Pekingese Paul had given Betty on her birthday the year before we married, scratching the side of the playpen Betty used for a containment area. Unknowing, Puppy-John wagged his tail and whined for attention. I wondered how long the poor creature had been waiting and what fate would await him now that Betty was gone.

Steve went to the refrigerator to compose himself with a can of the Busch beer his mom always kept in the refrigerator. Running my pointer finger down the list of numbers on a yellow page of the phone book, I heard the *crack-phew-w-w-w* of the pop top before the refrigerator door shut. I picked up the telephone on Betty's table and dialed the airport number. Waiting for the ring, I studied the items on the table that revealed the many hours Betty had sat here. The clean surface supported her telephone, phone book, a little pad and pen, a salt and pepper shaker, a couple of open utility bills, a stack of napkins, and a paperback book. Betty loved to read everything. Lately, she had been feeding her new passion for philosophy. An airport information operator startled me back from my study of table artefacts. "Columbia Metropolitan Airport," I heard her announce brightly.

"I have an urgent situation." I advised her with my false bravado, getting right to the point. "My husband is somewhere in the airport and I have to get a message to him. His . . . his mother has died."

"Okay," the operator answered, taken aback but nonetheless helpful. She took down the information that would help her locate Paul via a loudspeaker announcement throughout the airport. God's timing was still at work. Sarah had just been boarded, and the rest of the party, headed to the exit door, stopped when the loudspeaker announced Paul's name.

Waiting for Paul's call, I jumped when it rang, as though it were a Jack-in-the-box. "Hello?" I answered halfway through the first ring.

"Hello," Paul answered, and I knew from the sound of his "hello" that no one had yet hinted at the tragic news.

"Paul," I began, "Steve called not long after you left. He found your mom at her house. She has died, Paul, I'm so sorry!" I winced as an image of Paul's tightening jaw muscles filled my mind's eye.

Paul hesitated. "Are you at Mom's?" he asked, trying not to seem shocked.

"Steve and I are here now. Just ask Joe to bring you over here. Ask him to drop you off, then he can go home and stay with the children until we get back. Jon and Austin will be home soon."

He would remain calm, quietly riding with his father

and three of our girls. Entering the door of the house where he'd grown up, his eyes embraced Steve and me. He wrapped us up in his big arms and we cried together over losing Mama Graham. Steve was the first one to step away from our huddle. He shook off his grief to explain again the events that led to his terrible discovery. Paul needed to hear it but Steve needed to say it some more in order to convince himself that it really was true.

"Do I need to call Danny?" Paul asked Steve, concerned about their baby brother in North Carolina.

"I called," Steve replied, "he's on his way now."

"Probably speeding down the interstate like a wild man," Paul added, with some worry. He looked at me.

"Have you been in there?" Paul asked me directly, referring to Betty's bedroom where her little body lay.

"No," I answered, suddenly aware that I wasn't at all sure I wanted to be in there. I had never seen a lifeless body before unless it was prepared in a casket. Even then, looking at a corpse, I remembered feeling like I must be violating the privacy of the person who had once inhabited its flesh. Yet, I sensed a plea in Paul's eyes when he asked, "Do you want to go?"

"Yes," I replied. The truth in my answer was that I wanted to do whatever he needed, and I knew he needed me beside him. Had I refused, I'm sure he would have gone in alone out of respect for my feelings. We walked together through the kitchen, past the stove that had once caught fire, down the little hall where, even as a young man, Paul had slept on a twin bed in this tiny bedroom on the right. As we passed the bathroom on our left, I remembered a story that Paul had once told me: he bathed in the mornings before school, usually falling asleep on his back, comfortably submerged except for his eyes, nose and mouth. It took his mother knocking on the door to wake him.

We walked reverently into Betty's room, leaving the light out as though it might disturb her. She lay in a fetal position on her right side. We could see that she had been quietly carried to Heaven in her sleep. Paul sat on the bed beside her, so I did, too.

"Is she really gone?" I asked hoping for a mistake.

"Yes," Paul answered, gently touching her shoulder. I was silent.

"She died in her sleep," Paul continued, and I nodded my head in agreement.

"She's the only one who has really known me my whole life," Paul said, then lowered his head and began to cry. I leaned toward him as this big, grown man reached for me and sobbed like a broken-hearted toddler. Subduing the hole in his heart, he began to talk.

"See those pink lamps?" Paul pointed to the glass lamps on either side of her bed. "I remember when she got them. She thought she *had* to have them!" I looked at the lamps, glad he could talk about her, glad to have a diversion more familiar to me than watching that still little lump that used to laugh and love.

"She always said you appreciated nice things like she did."

"I guess everybody likes nice things," Paul smiled a tiny bit. "I never really understood why she said it like I was unusual." We found ourselves mute once again in Betty's softly lit bedroom.

Paul broke the silence again by re-telling a funny family story, but he was unprepared for its sudden loss of humor. In the wake of Betty's death, it had become a confession. "We were about to replace an old water heater when I was just learning to drive." He hesitated, recognizing the burden of guilt on his heart. "The new one was out there at the end of the driveway and I accidentally dented it with the car." Paul hurried to the end of the rehearsed story. "Mom was so mad and she said, 'I can't have anything nice!'"

I could feel the weight of Paul's longing to give his mom something nice right then. I felt as well the dirty pain of knowing that chance was gone forever. Paul squeezed his eyes shut, releasing a trail of tears down his cheeks. Grief seeped over the floodgates of his heart in heavy waves. After a while, this painful tide began to ebb and Paul stood up, ready to leave his mom's body. We held hands and walked solemnly back to the kitchen table. It wasn't long before Danny arrived. He headed straight for the refrigerator. Well over six feet tall, he had to lean way down to open the ancient little door and take out a Busch.

"I don't guess Mom would mind me getting a beer," he said, joking, avoiding the dark reality. Steve smiled and politely agreed while Danny worked hard at being aloof. He opened the freezer to take a little inventory of his mother's frozen food.

"She must have shopped recently," he calculated, probably drawing on deductive reasoning skills he had practiced as a police officer. He walked back into the living room and stood beside Paul. It always disturbed my eyes when they stood together with Danny towering over Paul. In my mind, there was no one taller than Paul.

"Did Paul ever tell you how mad she used to get if we drank the last Coke in the Fridge?" he asked me, grinning.

"Yeah," I answered, "he did."

Danny turned to Steve and asked how long he had been here. Steve relayed his story again as Danny digested Steve's details with a business-like reception.

"Did anybody call the coroner?" Danny asked crisply in response.

"No," Steve answered. "We wanted to wait for you."

"They had better not take her anywhere but the medical school." Danny raised his voice slightly for effect, reminding his brothers, "You know she donated her body."

"She has a Gift of Body card in her wallet," Paul answered reassuringly. "We just have to give it to the paramedics when they come. They'll make sure she gets there."

Danny went on, determined to protect her wishes, "I'll drive her there myself if I have to." Failing in his attempt to trade grief for anger, Danny finally made his inevitable walk down the hall to his mom's bedroom. As he found his mother's body, the reality of the situation quickly dug spiteful talons into Danny's heart. His brave facade crumbled quickly. Covering his eyes to hide tears, Danny submitted to his brothers' embraces.

The coroner arrived and Betty's body was put in a zippered bag. In a final, touching act of love and courage, Betty's three sons carried her body to the ambulance. Then, there was nothing left for us to do but go home. The most familiar presence in their lives was really gone. Just like that, after sixty-three years of living, Betty Graham's little heart had worn out and stopped beating, and she was really gone.

And it came to pass, as they still went on, and talked, that, behold, there appeared a chariot of fire, and horses of fire, and parted them both asunder; and Elijah went up by a whirlwind into heaven.
2 Kings 2:11

Chapter Eight

    Waking early the following day, I began preparations for Betty's memorial service. I had to use all the adrenalin pumping in me. I reasoned that the harder I worked, the less Paul and his brothers would have to do. That was motivation enough. I busied myself calling all the people I knew, then asked Betty's friend Helen to help me locate other key family members and friends. I collected pictures of Betty at various stages of her life and made a photo collage to set out in the narthex of Christus Victor Lutheran church where she would be memorialized. Pastor Eiwen had baptized most of our babies, administered their First Communion and Confirmation instructions, and married Paul and me. He was the only one Paul wanted officiating at his mom's service. Pastor Eiwen was out of town but cut his vacation short in order to be there for us.

    At home, loved ones and church friends brought casseroles and comfort visits as Paul sat listlessly in his favorite blue chair, tearing up frequently. Charlotte, Emily and I sat directly across from him on our stiff, antique sofa. Only one-and-a-half years old, the twins couldn't possibly have understood what was happening, yet staring at Paul, Emily began to cry softly. As I turned to comfort her, she shimmied off the sofa and crawled into her daddy's lap. They folded into one another as Charlotte looked on sympathetically. Even though Gran's death wasn't clear to them, their Daddy's sorrow was plain. In their dear little hearts, they instinctively bore part of his burden.

    Betty's memorial service turned out to be a lovely tribute to her life. Thanks in part to the eulogies of her sons' friends who rose up and called her blessed, there was no doubt that she was a woman who had been loved and whose presence would be sorely missed. Our church was filled up with people who loved her. Those who had celebrated Paul's surprise birthday were there, plus many others I hadn't met yet. Gary Smallen was one of these. When Gary walked over and introduced himself, I gasped, "Oh, my goodness. Your tenth grade school picture was in Betty's Family Bible."

Gary looked surprised for a second before his eyes filled with tears, and it seemed he stepped back a little. I don't know why I didn't anticipate this reaction, but fortunately I recognized his wish to maintain composure.

"I'm so happy to finally meet you," I blurted out, changing the subject in search of a comfort zone. "Thank you so much for being here. Has Paul seen you yet?"

"Not yet," he answered, recovering his voice, "I wasn't able to make your wedding, and I wanted to meet *you*."

"Well, let's find Paul," I suggested, and we began scanning the room.

Gary and Paul had a long history, and I would learn that Mama Graham had really counted Gary as one of her own. He had practically grown up in the house alongside Paul.

Visiting with those who had known Betty was a comfort to all of us. The flowers and plants sent in condolence were packed into our cars. We left the church bearing both warmth and sorrow.

Now that we were home, I felt able to rest for the first time in days. The rush of adrenaline that had fueled me for days was running out. Paul seemed stable for the first time since Betty died. As he played with the twins, I asked him if he would mind if I lay down for a few minutes.

"That's fine," He said, convincing me, so I headed to our room and closed the door.

I will explain what happened to me then, although it was years before I understood why God had shown me this. First of all, I must insist that I was not asleep. I was sitting on my bed, but not lying down. It felt good just to sit alone, still and quiet for a while without any urgent responsibility. I didn't close my eyes. I remember feeling grateful that God had allowed me to be there for my husband and to honor his mother. Suddenly, I realized I was having a vision, although I had never had one before. I also knew I could have stopped it had I wished but I wanted to see its completion. Strange, though it was, I didn't feel afraid and I was totally aware of my wakefulness. Here is what I experienced:

I was riding down Clemson Road in a car with Betty. It truly felt as though I was with her and not sitting on the bed seeing it happen. Neither one of us was driving the car, although I was on the driver's side. Looking to my right I could see her beside me, and she seemed to understand what we were doing, whereas I did not. She wore a serene smile and appeared to want me there with her. As we continued, the car began to go faster and faster. I could feel the great speed as we traveled, yet I still wasn't frightened. The car lifted itself off the road, flying, and then the sides and doors fell away from around us. Side by side we flew now, without the benefit of a vehicle. Even though we traveled very fast; faster than I liked, I still wasn't feeling fear – discomfort, maybe, since I was not controlling our travel – but not fear. I looked toward Betty again, and her eyes met mine, clearly unafraid. I looked ahead of us and saw a large, solid gate opening slowly. I remember thinking, *"We are going to slip right into that opening,"* but I was only partly right. Still gaining speed, I finally began to feel some real anxiety as we sped toward the widening space in the gate which closed immediately, but not before Betty's frame slipped perfectly into the gap. My own journey halted abruptly, leaving me outside. I marveled that I had felt absolutely no impact from the instant stop, yet was certain there should have been a crash. The vision ended as suddenly as it had appeared. I sat on my bed wide-eyed, aware that I had just experienced something real and alive but not understanding the meaning. I had actually been *with* Betty Graham and had shared something with her that was absolutely vivid and vividly absolute.

"But, what was it?" I wondered, "And why . . . and why *me*?"

The answers would be forthcoming but it would take almost a decade. I believe God was giving me something of comfort to hold on to; something to remind me that He knew everything. He was preparing me for events that lay ahead.

Though you have made me see troubles, many and bitter, you will restore my life again; from the depths of the earth you will again bring me up. You will increase my honor and comfort me once again.
Psalm 71:20-21

Chapter Nine

Winter - Spring 1995

Paul had cried openly over losing his mom. We, along with his brothers Steve and Danny and their wives Wanda and Phyllis began the awful job of sifting through Betty's worldly treasures, emptying the house to sell it. As dreary as the task was, there were blessings in her house as well. We found a mound of children's toys that showed she had already been shopping for birthdays. Even better than that, every few minutes, one of the Graham boys would find something that sparked a memory, and we would hear a tale from their lives. The Graham brothers had been lively and sometimes exasperating, but Betty left them with no doubt she had loved them.

She had also loved all the grandchildren. From the time they were old enough to walk, Gran delighted in hiding pennies all around her house. Visits from Sarah and Danny's daughter, Rachel always inspired penny-hunts. This was one of the things I learned about as we uncovered the copper treasures in every nook and cranny of each room. Charlotte and Emily would miss out on this game.

For two weeks following Betty's death, Paul seemed uncharacteristically fragile. He began to dream about her. One night he awoke with a start, breathing fast. I woke and sat up beside him.

"What's wrong?" I asked.

"Man," He said, relieved to be awake. "I just had a crazy dream. I thought it was real."

His side of the bed was mangled. I straightened out his knotted sheet and handed it to him. The wrinkles disappeared as he drew it to himself.

"What happened?" I asked, alarmed that it had shaken him so badly. He made a noise that was like a forced laugh.

"Mom was mad," he answered. "She walked in wanting to know what we had done with all her clothes."

"What did you say?" I asked him.

"I didn't know *what* to say," Paul said, still disturbed. "She was furious, though." He shook off a chill.

"Can I do anything?" I asked him.

"No, Sweetie, I'm sorry I woke you," Paul answered. "I know it was only a dream," He said, more to himself than me, I think.

"That's what I'm here for," I reminded him.

He'd lain awake, allowing grief take him on a guilty little trip before letting sleep take hold again. I lay in the bed beside him listening to his nocturnal breathing and the dogs barking in the back yard. We had taken in Gran's Puppy-John soon after her death. Since our yard was fenced, we were the most logical choice. We already owned Gabby, a Llhasa-Apso bulldog mix, who wasn't overly hospitable to Puppy-John. Sometimes she would find herself irritated for reasons unknown and jump all over poor Puppy-John.

Paul returned to work, but seemed distracted. I had never been this close to someone who was grieving a mother, so I didn't know what to expect. I let him be my barometer.

"Do you want to go to that new chicken wings place?" Paul asked me one afternoon when he was off work.

"We can do that," I answered, thankful he wanted to do something, but more grateful that he wanted me with him. He was so reserved, so aloof these days, it was a relief that he wanted to seek out something together. I continued, "Jon will be home tonight, so we can leave the babies here."

He was quiet all the way to the restaurant. We sat against the wall at a table for two. I tried, but couldn't engage him in conversation. He avoided making eye contact.

"Can you talk to me?" I pled. "You are so far away."

There was a flash of anger in his face when he looked at me. "There's nothing wrong," he said without convincing me. "I'm fine." He gnawed the meat off another hot wing without looking at me. He wasn't enjoying these wings, but was determined to finish.

"Why are you mad at *me*?" I asked, but he continued to be silent.

His anger was confusing, and over the following days, Paul struggled to deal with a lost something he couldn't name. This was a turning point for him. He stopped crying and dreaming about Betty. He didn't bring her up again but sometimes he would insist that I didn't love him. I didn't understand how he could think so ridiculous a thing.

His feelings continued to torment him. Instead of being thankful we had found one another, he would agonize over the years we'd spent apart. He made me feel I was somehow to blame. If I were a psychologist, I might say that he had transferred to me his feelings of loss and abandonment over his mother. His jealousy and unwillingness to trust me made me wonder who this frustrated man was who looked just like my husband. I walked on eggshells trying to avoid any subject that might send him into another funk.

Just as confusing were the times he would switch gears, bring me little gifts and tell me how wonderful he thought I was and how much he loved me. One such time he asked me to find a weekend babysitter and he made a reservation for us at the Ramada Inn. It was a relief to be with Paul without him seeming so depressed but his adoration of me was so over the top it was almost as uncomfortable as his agony. These were strange times, but sooner or later, I thought, he would walk through the necessary steps of his grief and become my husband again.

Paul got home from work early that Friday. We packed, dressed up and drove to the motel. He was in a festive mood.

"What's so funny?" I asked.

Something had cracked him up at work, he said. He wanted me to ask.

"Tell me," I begged.

"Alright, this old hippie guy came to the pharmacy today asking me about his bulldog," he began. "He was pretty scruffy-looking. He was trying to be all serious telling about how his dog had gotten himself into a fight."

Paul threw a little giggling fit and his face turned

ruddy-red.

"Come on," I smiled, urging him to finish.

He wiped his eyes and continued.

"I'm sure he must have meant *a hematoma*, but what he said was that his dog had a *hemostat* over his eye. All I could picture was a pit bull with hemostats hanging off his eyebrow. It was killing me to keep a straight face, but this ol' boy was so worried I thought he was going to cry. It took everything in me not to laugh."

I joined him in the hilarity, "You have more self-control than I do."

We pulled into the front of the motel and Paul put the car in *park*. I watched him enter the glass doors and return with our room entry cards. He slid back into the driver's seat and handed me the keycards.

"I think they are already cooking for us." He teased. "I smelled the aroma."

This was the Paul I knew, and I began, albeit cautiously, to drop my guard.

The main floor dining room displayed a wonderful weekend seafood buffet that we liked to indulge in on special occasions. We dropped our bags in the room and hurried to the dining room to enjoy a great meal. Next door was a lounge featuring a dance floor. I have mentioned before that Paul was a terrific dancer. In South Carolina, beach music can be heard in most public places. For South Carolinians, knowing how to do The Shag (a slow Jitterbug), the official State Dance, is the Eleventh Commandment and one that Paul didn't break. Somehow he managed to dance fabulously in spite of me. He even made me appear to be dancing, too. Amazing were his feet.

After about half-an-hour we went to our room, shared some champagne then donned swim suits. I looked in the mirror. The champagne was already making me stupid.

"Look at this, Paul." I faced the mirror and grabbed fists full of what I call my Lower Stomach. "If I could just cut this blob off, I would have a hot bod, wouldn't I?" Paul laughed at me to avoid answering such a dangerous question. "Come on," he implored me, "Let's get down to the pool before it closes."

"Okay," I agreed, "but you know it's true."

We splashed around for a while. After the glamour of being wet wore off, we went off on another champagne-induced adventure that seemed like a good idea at the time. Maybe we felt a little bullet-proof entering the motel's workout room that night. We were the only ones in there, a fact for which I am most thankful. Paul picked the rowing machine and I faced the treadmill beside it. They were situated so that we were able to face each other as we buffed-up, so to speak. Paul mostly smiled as he rowed, listening to me with amusement while I talked incessantly and laughed with great gusto at my own jokes.

"This isn't very fast." I observed. "I think I'll crank it up a few notches and see how that feels."

Paul, rowing methodically, watched me warily.

"This is really okay." I said as my bare feet slapped the treadmill in brisk rhythm. "It doesn't even feel like I'm moving all that much."

"You might want to be careful," suggested Paul. "You can get hurt on those things."

"What?" I brushed him off, dismissing his worries with a hearty guffaw. "Are you scared I'll get a hemostat? This is nothing. I wonder, though," I pondered aloud with faux intellectualism, "why you never see people walking the *other* direction. Doesn't it seem like walking the other way would, you know, work different leg muscles?" After that statement, and without any forethought, I let loose my grip on the handrails and pirouetted in mid-air, landing the opposite direction on the treadmill. What happened next? Well, I'll use Paul's words that explained the chain reaction later to our friends and family:

"In the space of about one second, she flipped around, her feet hit the treadmill, and both legs flew up. Her butt slammed down on the moving belt which shot her right off the end of it."

I wasn't hurt, but I must admit I was taken a mite aback to find myself on the floor so abruptly. Paul was crumpled up on that rowing machine laughing his head off. I don't think he could breathe. It cracked me up to see him like this, so I started laughing, too. For weeks we couldn't talk about it without coming apart.

Two significant things had happened that weekend, the most obvious being the healing that was taking place in Paul as he grieved his mother. The other thing, a big surprise, would be revealed to us in a couple of months.

* * *

Several weeks later Paul's father Joe and his wife, Rozemary came down from Missouri to visit us. The four of us went out for the Ramada seafood one night, skipping the champagne, pool and work-out room. On the ride home, Paul wasn't very conversational.

"Are you okay?" I whispered to him as we rode in the back seat behind his father and stepmother.

"I've got a headache." He answered, but didn't elaborate. The rest of us continued talking.

"Stop the car." Paul announced quietly, but Joe didn't hear him.

"Now?" I asked Paul.

"Right now." He answered flatly.

"Joe," I said, with urgency, "Paul wants you to pull over. There's a gas station on the right here, I think we should pull in."

"Oh," Joe said, surprised, and quickly drove around to the back.

"Here, stop here," Paul said, "stop the car."

Paul opened the car door, the usual bounce absent from his gait. Disappearing behind a building, we heard the loud, disconcerting roar of vomiting. We sat helplessly in the car, knowing he would be mortified if any one of us approached to comfort him, so we waited, empathizing from our seats in the car. He didn't have headaches often, but when he did, they were as bad as any I ever suffered.

He finally lumbered back to the car, and we drove home without much conversation. He didn't like to be touched when he had a headache, so once we arrived at home, I didn't offer cool wash cloths or massages, the things that soothe my own headaches. His nausea had subsided, but he was exhausted. His head throbbed as he lay on the bed and shivered, longing to submit to sleep's sweet escape. I pulled the covers over his shoulders and thought about my Grandma Brown.

"When you shiver, a rabbit's running across your grave," she used to say. I wanted to ask how anybody could know that, but never asked her. It was a creepy thing to say. I felt like shivering just thinking about it.

I have thought about this incident over the years and wondered about Paul's headaches and his struggle to sort through all his feelings as he grieved his mom. Was he really having a migraine that night, or was something else happening to him? Migraine or not, change was definitely taking its course in our lives. A total metamorphosis perched menacingly on our horizon, but first, something wonderful was about to unfold.

> *Delight yourself in the Lord and He will give you the desires of your heart.*
> *Psalm 37:4*

Chapter Ten

Spring, 1995: The baby monitor made a scratchy noise alerting us that a toddler was waking up.

"Goo' mo'ning!" Charlotte's little voice sang through the speaker. "Goo' mo'ning, Mimi!"

We heard another scratchy sound which indicated Emily was climbing off her bed. I gave Paul a soft kiss before leaving to greet the morning fairies.

"Goo' mo'nin', Mimi! Goo' mo'ning!"

Charlotte's joyful salutation was falling on my ears from the top of the steps now. I took the last step just in time to see Emily glaring at Charlotte from their usual post at the baby gate.

"Stop saying, "mo'ning" to me, Char-LOTTE!"

Emily clutched the stuffed kitten she carried most everywhere. I lifted her over the gate then reached in for Charlotte.

"What do you have, Emma?" I engaged her.

"It's my Kit," she answered, adding, "I want a weal kit."

I sighed and held their hands. We wobbled down the stairs.

"We already have two dogs," I reminded her.

"I want a weal kit."

This had been her mantra a few times a day since she was old enough to say it. She prayed for a "kit" every night at bedtime. I felt myself beginning to cave in.

"All right, maybe we should talk to your daddy. You've been pretty patient."

Emily danced. It wasn't really a dance so much as manic jumping with a little knee action on one leg. We called it her Crazy Leg Dance. Once she got started, Charlotte joined her. I laid my hand on my tummy, remembering they had done this in the womb. On my bladder.

Paul was out of the shower and almost finished dressing when we got to the bedroom. He scooped both babies into his arms in one fluid motion. "Good morning, girls!"

Emily smiled so hard I could see the dimple just under her eye. Obviously, Paul's good morning had amused her more than

Charlotte's had. Paul kissed them and carried them into the dining room where two high chairs awaited.

"I'm giving up," I said. "It's time to get a cat."

Paul looked over his shoulder at me and continued buckling in the second twin.

"You want me to call Coach? He told me he has about eighty cats now."

Paul had sort of a man-family that included the guys with whom he had grown up. Coach Richardson had mentored them in high school sports and held them accountable. As they grew into men, he remained available until the relationship developed into a genuine adult bond. Coach was proud of his boys and still held them accountable. He was like family to Paul but I hadn't been around him long enough to know him very well yet. When I found myself at a gathering with him, Coach was always in earnest conversation with one of his boys. He was more like a beloved Uncle than a former high school teacher.

The other thing about Coach was his cats. At one of his last school jobs, a bunch of stray cats managed to find shelter in an old building that wasn't being used by the school at the time. They lived off school cafeteria food that ended up in the dumpster and procreated effortlessly and innumerably as feral cats are prone to do. As Coach's time at this school drew to a close, so did the school's need of this building that was being inhabited by all the cats. When school management decided the cats would have to be picked up by Animal Control, presumably to meet untimely deaths, Coach Richardson objected. When his efforts to save the cats failed, he simply transported the animals to his home in Red Bank, South Carolina and made them his own pets. Besides feeding them, Coach made sure they had all had their shots, thanks to his friend and local vet, Max.

I realize eighty cats may seem excessive, but if Coach was a hoarder he was a very organized one. *Cat Shepherd* might better describe his business. When we arrived at the home he shared with his wife and daughter, a few cats were inside, but the greater bulk of his furry friends were outside on his woodsy acreage.

Fran, Coach's daughter, answered the door and led us to the den where we found Coach, still strong and sinewy, seated in a massive lounge chair petting a black and white kitten. Emily and Charlotte peeked out from behind my dress, fighting around their shyness to get a closer look at the kitten.

"Fran, how 'bout go find that little male I picked out for Paul."

"Where is he, Daddy?"

"I believe he's right there in the front room."

Fran returned with another black and white kitten which she placed onto her daddy's lap. He looked toward Charlotte and Emily. "You girls think these are the right ones for you?"

Emily stood up as straight as she could and forced her little head to nod affirmatively. Paul and I encouraged the twins by walking with them toward the kittens.

Coach handed the female to Emily. "Hold on to her like this."

Emily watched him carefully, studying the way Coach held the kitten she would soon stroll around in her baby-doll stroller and try to teach to do the Macarena dance. Charlotte stood behind her, curious, but happy to let Emily go first.

"Do you like her, Mimi?" Paul asked.

With her Kit finally snuggled safe in her arms, Emily's mouth stretched wide enough to see her little teeth sparkle. She nodded, and the crazy little curls on her head bounced happily.

Prompted in the moment by a sudden boldness, Charlotte moved in front of Emily. Coach handed her the little male cat she had already decided would be named Charlotte, but upon our urging, would finally relent and name him Charlie.

"You have to take good care of them," Coach instructed. "You have to play nice with them and give them their food and water."

Charlotte pressed her pink lips together and gave Charlie a motherly look. Charlie batted at the silky, white hair Charlotte inadvertently slung in his face.

"Are you going to be able to do that?" Coach asked.

Charlotte nodded slowly, keeping her eyes locked on Charlie.

I smiled at my daughters, aware that we'd just become cat owners to two wiggly balls of fur who were already writing themselves on our hearts.

***

A few months after Charlotte and Emily's birthdays we implemented birth control. One morning I checked the calendar, thinking a cycle was due. Sure enough, I was late. I smiled at the prospect of a baby but shook off the idea just as quickly. Our house was already full. Who has seven children? Ridiculous.

A couple of weeks later I was still waiting. I mentioned this to Paul as he dressed for work one morning.

"Seriously?" Paul looked up from tying his shoe with a smile and a sparkly crinkle in his eyes.

"Well, not really seriously." I began. "I mean I am late, but…"

"I can bring a pregnancy test home." He offered hopefully.

"No, let's wait."

Paul left for work and I spent the rest of the day trying to stay on task. After a mostly unproductive day I dialed the pharmacy just before Paul got off work.

Absentmindedly, I listened to the entire prompt menu, forgetting to skip over the spiel by pressing the numbers I knew well.

If you're a doctor and would like to leave a prescription, press one. If you'd like to hear the store hours, press two. If you are a customer and would like to speak to a pharmacist, press three. To repeat the menu…"

I finally pressed the number and Paul's voice made me smile, "Thank you for calling Kmart Pharmacy, this is Paul."

"Yes, I'd like to speak to your handsomest pharmacist, please."

Oh, I'm sorry; he's already gone for the day."

"Humph," I replied, "why are you answering the phone? Did you get demoted?"

"It's almost time to go home and we were slow," Paul explained in a gravelly voice, "so I let the tech's leave."

"Well, I'm relieved you still have a regular job." I carried on. "By the way, you sound like Barry White. Are you getting a cold?"

"My throat's sore. Does the deep voice make me seem irresistable?"

"Yes," I answered, "but not as much as when you use big words."

"Do try to control yourself. Do you want the

pregnancy test?"

"Yeah, just to rule anything out, I mean I'm sure it's a waste of money but still…"

"I'll bring it." Paul interrupted before I could talk myself out of it.

I awoke the next morning to Emily climbing into our bed. She was always the first to wake up. Emily loved me but if her daddy was home, he was her pick, Charlotte's, too. I took this opportunity to slip into the bathroom and use the pregnancy testing strip which instantly turned a brilliant blue. I made myself close my mouth but it kept coming back open until I looked away from the blue dot.

Climbing back into bed I dragged a sleeping, weightless Emily over to my chest so Paul could take his turn in the bathroom.

Few things are sweeter than a sleeping toddler on your chest, even with the background of Paul emptying his bladder (for what must've been ten minutes).

Emerging from the bathroom Paul asked, "Did you do it?"

I nodded my head over the curly fuzz of Emily's little head.

"Was it positive?"

I nodded my head and smiled.

Paul's teeth peeked out from behind an open grin, "Whoa!"

He slid back into bed just before just as Charlotte toddled in like a little old woman with half-closed eyes.

"Good morning, Chah-Chah!" Paul greeted her and pulled her onto his chest where she fell magically back to sleep.

"I love you, Shirley." I heard Paul say into the morning light.

"I love you, too, my husband, Paul Graham."

"We're going to have seven children!" He said proudly.

"Paul, what if I have twins again?"

Paul didn't say anything for a minute and the only sound in the room was the rhythmic and simultaneous breathing of sleeping toddlers.

"If there are twins in there," Paul answered soberly, "Then we will have eight children. Math just isn't your area, is it, Shirl?"

"Yes, smart-aleck," I replied," I know how many it will make but where on Earth will we put them?"

"If we run out of room, "Paul said recklessly, "we'll just stack 'em like cord wood!"

"What if they're boys?" I asked.

"Then we'll buy more accident insurance!"He answered without any hesitation. Then, Paul was quiet.

"I'm just proud," he swallowed before continuing, "that the Lord will trust us with so many."

He closed his eyes and smiled. God had gone and intercepted Paul's reasonable plans for the future with another extravagant blessing and he already liked God's plan better than his own. Our dreams of having a houseful of kids had come true with great multiplicity as God gave us the desires of our hearts beyond our imaginations.

Our peaceful moment was interrupted abruptly by disturbing *beep-beep-beep's* from the clock/radio on Paul's bedside table. Charlotte's eyes popped open as the alarming racket crashed into her pretty dream. It took Paul several seconds to reach way over the lump of baby-girl on his chest to shut off the alarm button.

Quiet once more, Charlotte made a somber declaration which aptly described our collective feelings.

"I don't like that song."

Don't use foul or abusive language. Let everything you say be good and helpful, so that your words will be an encouragement to those who hear them. Get rid of all bitterness, rage, anger, harsh words, and slander, as well as all types of malicious behavior. Instead, be kind to each other, tenderhearted, forgive one another, just as God through Christ has forgiven you.
Ephesians 4:29, 31-32

Chapter Eleven

    As wonderful as our new baby discovery was, I wasn't yet ready to proclaim it to the world. I'd long grown weary of the inane or negative comments that even strangers felt compelled to verbalize about the size of our family. It wasn't the attention to us that became so tiresome but rather the assumption that we were either idiots or sex freaks. *"I feel sorry for you! Didn't you have a T.V.? Haven't you figured out what causes that yet?"* These were the kinds of stupid quips we sometimes had to endure.

    My heart was being shanghaied by pregnancy hormones. That little blue dot on the pregnancy test had morphed me into a protective lioness. All those dumb cracks were a terrible disgrace, a shameful attempt to reduce our rare blessing to a joke. I got tired of being polite and started making a mental list of things I should have said. Things like, *"You feel sorry for me? Oh, my goodness, I feel sorry for YOU with your big old ugly self."* Nobody said pregnant women are perky. Besides, I never actually said any of the things I thought. At least, I don't think I did.

    In contrast, Paul's answer came always from a place of gratitude, *"I'm just proud the Lord trusts us with so many."*

    Since I had been single for so long, my side of the family had long paid Jon, Austin, and Elisabeth special attention. Consequently, my parents had been wearing their own protective lion suits for years where my kids were concerned. They laid their claim in part because of the concern and care they had invested in our broken little family. Truly, it blessed us to have them in our corner. No doubt, the children are more secure adults today for having their grandparent's unconditional love and support back then.

    But when Paul came along, Mother and Daddy may have felt

shoved aside. They might not have felt like he was able to do as good a job as they had done. They probably didn't appreciate or trust his first attempts to be my children's father. As a result, they may have been a little hard on Paul as the newcomer. Truth told, daddies are characteristically rough on prospective husbands of their daughters, no matter how old we daughters get.

Outside our families, Paul and I began to find comfort in our new step-parent roles, yet we also realized that the Grimm Brothers of fairy tale fame had pegged all of us wicked and the name had stuck for decades. If it hadn't hurt my feelings so much, I might have found it comical how often I heard things like, *"How many of the children are really YOURS?"* or, *"That's nice that Paul adopted Elisabeth, but he'll never be able to love your kids like a real blood-parent."*

To all that I still say "Pshaw," All seven of our children are equally precious yet unique. Paul and I always strived for fairness, but in order to effectively parent them, each child required a totally unique response. Disciplining behavioral issues is difficult for every parent, but in the case of a blended family, it's even stickier and trickier. Children just naturally worry that someone else might be getting a bigger piece of the pie. More than that, they are always checking to see if the parents are favoring somebody. At some point on the road to maturity, we humans come to realize that life is not fair. It is only then that we take what we have to work with and cope. As parents of people who don't know this yet, we just try to keep balance, which is usually impossible. I decided to make "That's not fair" a forbidden whining in our family.

Punishments in a blended family are especially hard to balance. For children who, like Sarah, come home only every other weekend, restriction is an absurdity. With two lives in two places with two different sets of rules for different reasons, how could we respond to her infractions? We never figured it out perfectly.

Imagine, for example, that Jon, Austin, Sarah, and Elisabeth behave like equally horrible little monsters in church on a given Sunday. Restriction might seem the most reasonable response, but Sarah is leaving for her other home in a couple of hours. Where does that leave the discipline? Should we punish just the ones we are totally responsible for and send one away Scot-free? Should we spank all four? How would we divide that? Neither Paul nor I felt comfortable spanking our step-children. Would Paul spank Sarah and I spank the others? What message does that send? There are just too many variables.

It may seem silly to someone who has never been there, but we over-analyzed everything we did. Having great love for all children, we had both hoped to be exemplary step-parents. I usually had an easy rapport with kids of any age, but the harder I tried, the more Sarah did not seem to like me. It wore Paul and me out, drove us crazy, and accounted for many of our disagreements.

Even though our hearts were in the right place, we made plenty of mistakes with each of the children. We sometimes got frustrated or reacted poorly, and our mistakes came home to us often. God was gentle, even funny about opening our eyes to some of those moments when we had to say, "Oops." One such time, the older children were all in school, Paul was at work, and I was home alone with Charlotte and Emily. I heard tiny feet padding down the stairs but the pitter-patter stopped fast. Neither of my feathery-haired twins turned the corner, so I left my kitchen project to inspect. Peeking around the corner, I found Charlotte sitting at the bottom of the stairs.

"Good morning, Charlotte." I greeted her, but she sat silently and seriously with a baby-doll between herself and the wall.

"What are you doing?" I whispered.

"My baby hadda go in Time-Out."

"Oh. I'm sorry. What has she done?"

Charlotte brushed a few scarce strings of silky white hair away from the satin-soft skin of her forehead and continued watching the errant baby-doll: "She pissed me off."

I forced my jaw closed, trying hard not to reveal the alarm that her teeny potty mouth evoked, "Did she disobey you?"

"My baby weft cwap aw ovah her woom." Charlotte explained. She began shaking her head, "Her din pick it up."

Oops. The guilty parent in me was shamed that she had picked up words we hadn't meant for her to hear. The comedic bystander within me was nonetheless cracking up. When the twins went down for their nap a few hours later, I called Paul at work to share the evidence of our lack of judgment. After I uttered the paraphrased words, "crap all over her room," Paul made a little chuckling sound in his throat that said he knew he was busted.

"She said that? Where do you think she heard it?" He asked, feigning innocence.

"No idea." I answered.

Yet, the lesson was learned. Thanks to Charlotte, we were careful to clean up our mouths when encouraging the big kids to clean up their rooms.

Although this is but one of our many failures as perfect parents, there were a couple of things I think we did right. Being consistent participants in church was one. The benefits and blessings of being part of a church family are too many to count. The second was dealing with our disagreements over the children in private. The good part about that was being able to present a united front to them afterward. I suspect there might have been a few other things we did right but those are two that stand out.

Honor thy father and thy mother, as the LORD thy God hath commanded thee; that thy days may be prolonged, and that it may go well with thee, in the land which the LORD thy God giveth thee.
Deuteronomy 5:16

Chapter Twelve

It's so easy to judge. As our adolescent Austin explored his newest sport: challenging authority, my parents were suspicious of why he would begin acting out. After all, Austin had been a pleasant little tow-headed angel from birth. He appreciated the smallest gift and smiled easily. He obeyed without a bad attitude, was sweet and funny, and nobody could beat him in video games. Mother and Daddy were unable to dismiss their roles as protectors. Instead, they jumped to the conclusion that Paul must be the cause of Austin's changes. There is still the old stigma about step parents being the embodiment of evil and all. But, that wasn't the case. Paul's presence, assurance, and confidence had made all our lives much better. Recognizing that Jon and Austin longed for an adult male to emulate, Paul would sometimes take them on guy-type excursions. They would be almost giddy, the three of them, heading out to the driving range or the shooting range. Sometimes Paul took them to play tennis or racquetball or maybe to knock at baseballs in the batting cages near our house. Unfortunately, the constraints of time and space interfered with our many of our good intentions. Paul's work schedule, coupled with necessary trips to Atlanta on his weekends off, didn't allow for many of these excursions. Ever seeking to compensate, he would sometimes let the older children take turns riding to Atlanta with him when Sarah was returned after her weekends with us. Besides helping him stay awake, this also allowed some one-on-one bonding on the way back home. In a big family like ours, that kind of private time has to be deliberately carved out within some of the necessary tasks of living.

My seventy-year-old parents were now battling a terrible demon. Daddy, whose tall, sinewy frame could still be found wrestling his cattle with apparent ease, had recently received a diagnosis of Parkinson's disease. It wasn't long before he began to show subtle signs of losing himself. In the past, his positive attitude had provided a healthy balance to Mother's tendency to see the dark side of things. Now, instead of his typical encouraging spirit, he began sharing Mother's suspicious nature. In an effort to make it easier for them and more comfortable for me, I stopped sharing any personal family information unless it was good or amusing news. Even then, their responses seemed to thinly veil traces of suspicion.

It was a good time to be a Christian, as God was the only One in my life who hadn't changed. I felt as if I were losing my little boy *and* my parents, not to mention my husband. Paul was still grappling with his mother's death but his grief manifested in a depression that he was not willing to admit, and I'm sure our family problems weren't helping him work through his loss. No matter how much reassurance I offered, Paul couldn't get entirely loose from his irrational fear that I didn't love him. Sometimes he couldn't sleep, he couldn't eat. He was noticeably miserable at work. As his trust in me eroded, I lived as one under the glass of a microscope, succumbing to this stress with headaches. Sometimes I wondered if Paul thought he had made a mistake by marrying me and inheriting all the new challenges that come with a family. He never said such a thing, but I had this frustrated idea that if I could just make order of all this chaos, I could help him reason through the depression.

Then, there was Daddy's diagnosis. Like a lot of people, I didn't know too much about Parkinson's disease at first. Daddy's first symptoms were imperceptible, really except that he seemed quieter than usual. Months went by before I saw the tremor in his hand that he had managed to hide at first, but surely, he could beat this intruder. Who had a will stronger than my Daddy? It was hard for me to imagine him having mortality. I had heard stories about how he practically rose from the ashes as a young man overcoming pneumonia. I had seen for myself the kind of discipline that brought him to health after our car wreck in 1969. I wasn't prepared for the side effects already gnawing slowly at Daddy's many abilities.

Just like in many mother and daughter relationships, Mother and I had a long-lived history of disagreements. Daddy had been easier for me to talk to, especially during my teen years. Diplomatic to the bone, he always tried to see two or more sides of a situation. If approached respectfully, he was usually willing to consider my side. I decided to call him one afternoon and try talking about this animosity that he and Mother seemed to have toward Paul and me.

"Daddy," I began, "Are you busy?"

"I'm just sitting here answering the phone," he joked.

"What are you up to this morning?" I asked.

"Oh, about six-feet-one," he quipped, then, "Your mother just went to get her hair done. I'm cleaning up my breakfast dishes."

Without asking, I knew he had consumed two poached eggs, a couple strips of bacon, grits if they had them, and toast with a quarter-inch coating of grape jelly. His first cup of coffee would have sugar lumps stirred into it and the rest of the coffee in the pot would sit on the counter waiting on him. When lunchtime rolled around, he would pour cold coffee into the same cup which would have been washed out meticulously. A ride in the microwave would make it fit enough for him to drink alongside a sandwich. Having survived the Depression, Daddy lived his days in a predictable format, relying on the motto, *waste not, want not.*

I continued our dialogue, glad Mother was out. Maybe this privacy would give him the freedom to speak candidly.

"I wanted to talk to you about something that upsets me."

"Why, sure." His reply was friendly, albeit cautious. He had lived long enough to know that to approach an upset woman otherwise would be reckless.

"It just seems like you and Mother don't like Paul. Like maybe you blame the two of us for the problems with Austin."

"Why, who told you that? What in the world are you trying to stir up?"

My usually confident father was caught uncharacteristically off guard. He recovered his composure and said something about Paul picking on Austin, referring to a recent visit at their house with most of my siblings and their children. Austin had refused to settle down as the others tried to watch a home video on Mother and Daddy's television. Paul had finally reprimanded Austin in front of the others, an act which apparently set him in a bad light. As mentioned, Mother and Daddy claimed Austin as their own. They probably wondered who Paul thought he was, calling Austin down in their house.

"Daddy, we are just trying to guide him. Parents have to discipline their children." I explained.

But I was getting nowhere. I hated putting him on the spot like this. I told him I loved him and let the conversation end gently, like a swing slowing down enough to jump out of it. When I put the phone down, I cried, understanding at once that Parkinson's was already nipping away at Daddy's judgment. I never tried to make him explain himself to me again. Daddy had embarked on a terrible journey that my brother, Dale called "the long goodbye."

With God's grace, I chose to forgive the misunderstanding, to agree to disagree, so to speak, with this position my parents had taken. Paul did, too. It was the fair and honorable thing and I don't regret it. After all, over my life, I am sure there had been countless times that I disappointed them, misread their intentions, and expected more from them than was reasonable. Yet, they continued to pray, hope, and rally for me. They still wanted the best for me, whether or not I deserved it. I owed them at least a portion of the same grace and forgiveness they had shown me.

The playing field becomes level. Parents aren't perfect; we were never meant to be. We're just people: humans shaped and limited by all manner of variables but that doesn't mean we don't love our children. God used this hard experience to remind me that He is the only Father with perfect ability and perfect love. He gave me eyes to see this so I *could* forgive Mother and Daddy. Time eventually grew skin over my wound as God helped me to remember that we are all flawed, we all make mistakes, we all jump to the wrong conclusions sometimes, we all disappoint people; yet the blood of Jesus is powerful enough to cover all of that for all of us.

Love does not delight in evil but rejoices with the truth. It always protects, always trusts, always hopes, always perseveres.
1 Corinthians 13:6

Chapter Thirteen

1995: As difficult as this period of our lives was, by contrast, my pregnancy was easy. With the exception of frequent migraines, I bore no alarming physical maladies. My blood pressure was regular and normal. I did not have carpel tunnel syndrome in my wrist. There was no hearing or vision loss. I make these points to dispel the myth that my pregnancy with Charlotte and Emily was weird merely because of my age. Pregnancy with twins was indeed the strangest physical adventure of my lifetime, yet even at forty years old, this singleton pregnancy was no more remarkable than the other singleton pregnancies, so, there. I just want to make that clear.

It was evident that Charlotte and Emily were still satisfied wearing diapers, a fact that was okay with me, too. Getting around with my ballooning belly was becoming a mammoth chore, and I recoiled at the prospect of potty-training them. Being a seasoned potty-trainer already, I was well aware that ascending to the next level of bathroom maturity would just add another logistical cruelty to the current struggle of going out alone with my toddlers. I remembered all too well that the entry into a structure of any kind requires a ninety-minute perusal of its bathroom facilities by little girls newly freed from diapers. This significantly interferes with expedience when one is running errands. I knew we could be stranded from dawn to dusk for hours of purgatory in supermarket ladies' rest rooms all over town. I doubted that Charlotte and Emily's plumbing would be in sync, so I further envisioned a doubled term of waiting. I predicted that frozen food would never stand a chance in my grocery cart when Charlotte and Emily kicked their diaper habit.

Intercepting the dangerous stuff twins are able to do was something I was still getting used to. True, they were the cutest partners-in-crime you ever saw, but child-proofing had to be raised a notch in order to keep this tiny demolition team safe *and* functional at home. I gated the kitchen in order to make meals without their "help." I can still see them in the eye of my memory. Their round blue eyes are locked on me stirring a pot of Hamburger Helper as I babble on about some musical thing I hope will keep their attention to the completion of the meal. I see their tiny, dimpled fingers gripping the white plastic barrier as they listen soberly to their mama's strange monologue.

The stairs leading to the top floor were also gated, which, as an unexpected consequence, developed superior leaping skills in the older children. I rued the fact that pole-vaulting wasn't a collegiate sport offered at their schools. Had it been, all four of the older kids would have earned scholarships. Anyway, I foresaw a future including three diaper-wearing babies and a very harried mother.

At sixteen years old, Jon would be driving age by October's end. I hoped he was mature enough for this challenge because I had a self-serving dream that he'd be driving to the store for me in just a few months. For me, having to get dressed and get out seemed like an unnecessary expense of time and energy. Even now, leaving the house was a lot of work that interfered with daily survival. Shoot, it seemed to me that *getting dressed at all* ought to be optional. Besides, we were managing just fine on whatever groceries I asked Paul to pick up on the way home from work. Other than maneuvering our car down the road a mere eighteenth of an inch from the curb, Jon was showing remarkable progress as a young driver. Teaching driving skills was a lot easier than I expected it to be; plus he had a great time in Driver's Ed at Ridge View High.

"My driver's ed teacher is pretty cool," Jon informed me after school one day. "He lets us stop at the B.P. and get Cappuccino." I thought to myself, "What teenage boy doesn't need a shot of caffeine and sugar to make it through the day?"

Jon's part-time job at Bo Jangle's Fried Chicken

drive-thru near our house allowed him to work a couple of hours after school during the week, but *no Sundays*. As a lovely consequence, he had a little of his own spending money.

Jon had a slew of friends in our neighborhood, but his best friend was Josh. These guys were funny and irreverent and cracked each other up trying to learn what made the world tick . . . or rather how to make it tick.

Sixteen is one of my favorite ages for boys. I love to hear them kidding with each other. Humor is a tool for which they are justifiably skilled. To find one's self around teen-age boys is a pretty sure deal that you are going to be laughing pretty soon. The first rule of their comedy is that nothing and no one is spared or sacred.

One of the things Jon and Josh were exploring was how to play guitar. While riding home after school on what they called The Big Yellow Cheese Wagon, Jon and Josh had a stroke of musical genius. They spent the rest of the afternoon jamming then called everyone into the living room for a private performance of their masterpiece. The song they presented glorified their bus driver, who, like the song, was named, Desiree. Most of the words to the song were simply "Desiree." The other lyrics were mostly garbled because the music lapsed every few minutes while the boys laughed maniacally at each other.

* * *

Besides preparing Jon to take over grocery shopping, I thought of additional ways to cut myself some slack. One such strategy was awarding all the children lessons in laundering as well as a personal day during the week for doing their own clothes. Four chores were rotated weekly to keep them from complaining that one of them did more than the other. That was the idea anyway. A chore chart taped to the pantry door looked something like this:

1) Empty the dishwasher
2) Sweep
3) Vacuum the carpet
4) Empty garbage.

Everyone was required to help with clean-up after meals, although Austin found it necessary to go to the bathroom about that time, and Jon learned to work the girls with pleas like, "Sarah/Elisabeth, I don't know how to rinse off the dishes right, will you please, just show me how you do it? You're always really good at it." If I didn't catch him in this act, Jon would spend the rest of clean-up time walking around the kitchen doing very little while blowing sunshine up his sisters' dresses. "Wow, Sarah/Elisabeth, you are really skilled. I wish I could rinse dishes like you." They rolled their eyes, yet submitted for some reason to Jon's shameless exploitation.

Gran's Puppy John was now a part of the family, although Gabby, our Lhasa Apso never accepted him as such. We hadn't stopped hoping they would all just get along, but so far that hadn't happened.

I enjoyed having my sister Jeanne's kids visit us from Atlanta that summer. Ben, Valerie, and Karen were close in age to our kids. One afternoon, I heard the girls screaming their heads off, so I left my laundry to find out what was the matter. As Karen, Elisabeth, and Sarah looked out the window into the back yard, I heard Valerie running upstairs saying, "I can't look. That's awful . . ."

"What's awful?" I asked them.

"Mom, Puppy John's eye is out."

"No. I don't think so."

"Mom, look at him."

"I'm sure he's fine." I pushed the curtain aside and peered through the window. My disbelieving eyes slammed shut, and I turned away from what my mind tried to deny. Did I really see Puppy John walking around with his left eye hanging out, attached only to slimy membranes? Shocked into action, I began assessing the situation. I hadn't been pregnant long, but my gag reflex was precarious.

"Gross," I heard Sarah gasp as she ran up the stairs. Elisabeth screamed again.

"Don't let the babies see this." I called up to them.

Obviously, I was going to have to drive him to a vet, and somebody was going to have to hold the poor creature.

Paul was at work, Jon was at football practice and the screaming girls were useless for anything except to watch Charlotte and Emily. The task of physically moving the dog from the yard and holding him during the drive fell by default to Austin. As it turned out, he really was the best man for the job.

"Aunt Shirley?" I was suddenly aware that Karen was saying something to me.

"What is it, Karen?"

"You're so white."

I took a deep breath and vowed to see this thing through without vomiting.

"Okay. Austin, get a towel off my bed . . . not a good one. Get an old towel, but a big one."

Consternation was written across Austin's forehead. He nodded slowly.

"Austin, I want you to cover Puppy John in the towel and bring him to the car."

"Yes ma'am."

My idea was that the towel would conceal the dog (which might actually comfort him) so I wouldn't see him. Sight unseen, I might be able to get to the vet without having to pull over and give in to the nausea that lurked just below my throat. I hurried to the car, opened the door for Austin then waddled back to the driver's side. I turned away deliberately while Austin was getting into the car. When I heard him shut the door, I figured the towel was probably draped over Puppy John and it would be safe to look. I turned the ignition's key, simultaneously chancing a look right.

What I wanted to do was thank Austin for being such a "stand-up guy," as Paul would say. I wanted to say how endearing his compassion was to my heart. I wanted to tell him I was proud of him for stepping up to the plate and being there for me. I wanted to give him an "atta-boy," but I didn't because what I espied was an uncharacteristically worried Austin and Puppy John, his macabre, panting, one-eyed self sitting happily on the towel that Austin had lovingly and gently laid *under* him. Snatching my head back to face the windshield, I was sure I heard my stomach beg my brain not to register the image that was now vividly imprinted in my mind: his good eye staring ahead, contrasting the loose eye which appeared to contemplate the towel stitching under him.

"Oh." I managed to croak, "I meant for you to cover the dog with the towel but, not to worry. I just won't look."

"You wanted me to what?"

I steeled myself behind the wheel. "It's okay, you did good, son."

"Mom?"

I instinctually turned, getting another eyeful of, well, *eyes*. My neck graciously jerked back to gaze at the road.

"Yes, Austin?"

"Mom, do you think he hurts?"

"I don't know, honey. It, umm, doesn't really look like he's hurting. But, *sheesh*, it seems like it would."

It got silent in the car except for the panting of smiling Puppy John.

"I just wish he'd quit smiling." I thought.

"Mom?"

Curses. Why did I keep turning toward them? I swallowed hard, wishing I had a pair of blinders.

"What is it, Oscie?"

"Are they going to cut his eye off?"

I was straining to hold it together now.

"I don't think I can talk to you about that right now, but I'm pretty sure they can put it back in the socket."

"For real?"

"I think so. The veterinarian will know what to do."

"Yeah, he'll know."

We had been to this vet only once, probably at a happier time. I drove the car into an empty spot. Austin cradled Puppy John, and I set about opening the door for him. The receptionist took the details and disappeared behind a door. In a matter of seconds, the veterinarian entered.

"Oh, man," He yelped, turning away. "What the ...?"

"We found him like this a little while ago." I explained.

"What did you do to him?"

"We brought him here. Can you put his eye back in the socket?

"No. I mean, how did he get this way?"

Standing my pregnant self there with my sad little boy and damaged dog, I couldn't believe that he was so accusing.

"I don't know, I . . . we have another dog who sometimes picks fights with him."

"THIS couldn't have happened like that. Someone would have to bash his head from behind."

"Doctor, I know no one did that." I answered defensively.

He seemed to soften a tiny bit.

"There's no way. It's been out too long."

"Could you try?" I begged.

He said an expletive and then, "Let me have him."

He called to someone in scrubs, "Come help with this."

I was sure we had come to the wrong place, but I was feeling pretty woozy now and needed to sit. Austin followed me to the seating area. We could hear the vet spout a swearword now and again, and I knew we wouldn't be back to this place. I walked outside and took a big breath. I couldn't seem to get the air all the way down into my lungs. I raised my arms and tried again. There. That was a good breath.

"Lord?" I whispered. "Please comfort that little fella, and don't let him be scared of the doctor. Soften the doctor, please. Amen."

When I returned to the sitting area, I saw Austin walking from the water fountain. He sat beside me. "...Mom? I don't think anybody did that to Puppy John."

"Of course nobody did." I whispered. "Mr. Vet just doesn't have a bedside manner. I hope he's better with animals than he is with people."

We heard the squeak of a door and the doctor emerged with Puppy John, seeming more subdued than before as he carried the poor dog over. The lids of Puppy John's eye were sewn together.

"I couldn't save the eye."

Austin silently gathered Puppy John into his arms.

"We didn't hurt this dog." I told him firmly.

The vet opened his mouth to say something then decided not to. He gave us some post-surgery care instructions and handed his receptionist my credit card. I couldn't wait to get away from him.

Puppy John healed faster than we expected, but every time I looked at his little Pekingese face, it made me feel a sting of sorrow for his losses: first, Mama Graham and now his eye.

Family life was one adventure after another but the blessings counted for so much more than the crises that challenged us. Still, it seemed we had to be ready for most anything.

Since we lived so far from our church, we couldn't be involved in everything, but we always participated in Christus Victor's Christmas Dinner Project. Paul signed us up to collect food for a family with six children. Since we had six children, he found it fitting. We liked the idea that the kids could help shop for the food and go with us when we took it to the church to be delivered. The local newspaper published an article I wrote to chronicle the events that this project wrought. It was edited and appeared in the 1995, July 31 Edition under the heading, "That's Life." A newspaper staff photographer came to our home and shot a picture of us all mashed and smiling in the Bronco's opened hatch. I recreate the article here:

My husband, Paul and I are extravagantly blessed with six children, and are often living examples of how the best laid plans can go awry. This happens Just when we are feeling smug over our skill in organizing a group. Thus begins my tale...

The week before Christmas our daughter, Sarah was to arrive by plane at 9:00 p.m. Since Paul was working until 9, going to the airport naturally became my responsibility.

Somehow I needed to coordinate a trip to the airport that would mesh with taking our sons, Jon and Austin to a church party that ended at 9 and not interfere too much with the limitations of having 1-year-old twins, Charlotte and Emily, out that late at night. Having my very helpful 10-year-old Elisabeth along would be my saving grace.

By 8:30 p.m. the boys were safely deposited at the party and the rest of us were at the airport 30 minutes early. Approaching the ticket counter, I asked about Sarah's flight.

The girl behind the counter said, "Oh, that plane is 45 minutes late. It wouldn't surprise me if it was as much as an hour late."

"This is still OK," I thought. "The boys will be catching a ride to my friend, Ginny's house after the party. I'll just take Elisabeth and the babies there, we can hang out with Ginny for half an hour, her daughter can bring them home with her then we can go get Sarah.

Thirty minutes passed at Ginny's house and I called the airline to see if the plane was indeed going to be an hour late.

"Can you tell me how much later flight number 545 is expected to be?" I asked the airline operator. To my horror, she responded, "Late? That plane arrived early at 8:50."

In the midst of rushing my brood back into the Bronco, I noticed the boys tumbling out of Ginny's daughter's car. I shouted for them to get in the Bronce, pronto.

Funny thing, the sense of smell. Years had passed since I quit the bad habit, yet the odor of cigarette smoke in my car was not to be mistaken. "WHO'S BEEN SMOKING?" I demanded.

"Well," Jon offered, "they did have a bonfire at the party."

When Jon is a father, he will understand how incriminating that answer was. I spent the drive sharing with them my dissertation on the evils of lying and smoking.

Halfway to the airport, Austin confirmed my suspicions by throwing up on his seat in the hatch, which he shared with most of a Christmas dinner to be delivered to a needy family the next day.

The phrase, "just when you thought things couldn't get any worse" applies here. Bearing right onto the airport exit, we heard a noise that sounded not unlike a boulder hitting the underbelly of the Bronco. At that moment, it became painfully obvious that nothing I was doing was motivating my vehicle forward. "There's a gas station." Elisabeth offered as we coasted near the pay phones in our Bronco and its spent drive shaft. Without going into much detail about the phone call to my husband to pick up a frightened Sarah and then rescue the rest of us or the call to the airline where I had a fruitless dialogue with an operator, I will say it was a frustrating period spent on the phone.

Just when it seemed like everything had gone wrong and God had bailed out on us, I was forced to recognize examples of His presence in this experience. He really was looking out for our safety: We lost the drive shaft on an exit ramp near a well-lit pay phone, not on the interstate at night halfway between St. Andrews and West Columbia.

Imagine how much worse it could have been, walking down the interstate for God knows how long lugging two babies, followed by a trail of two novice smokers one far more regretful than the other) and a 10-year-old girl still young enough to believe I could solve all our problems.

Oh, yes. And by the way, in spite of unimaginable odds, the Christmas dinner avoided peril and made its destiny to a very grateful family with, would you believe it, six kids.

By Shirley P. Graham
Columbia

A merry heart doeth good like a medicine.
Proverbs 17:22

Chapter Fourteen

Even though we were thrilled with the prospect of a new baby, Paul thought it prudent to sacrifice his mighty fertility.

"We are out of control." He cracked, yet his concern was certainly legitimate.

In November, I was eight months along when we drove to the urologist's office for Paul's vasectomy. This would be one of our most hysterically funny adventures, even by the standards of its victim, Paul. Who knew putting Paul under the knife would be so funny?

"Good morning," the doctor greeted us with his easy smile. He was a slim guy, maybe a runner. Totally relaxed, he reached for my hand and shook it, "I assume this is Mrs. Graham."

"My bride." Paul smiled.

"I ought to tell you that you will be in another room for the surgery," he explained to me.

"I will?" I asked.

"Yes, just during the prep and the actual surgery," he went on. "We'll bring you in when he's ready to be stitched up."

"Okay," I agreed. "Just point me in the right direction, and let me know where the bathroom is."

"Would you like a drink?" He offered.

"A Sprite would be great," I answered as he turned his attention to Paul.

"Have you been waiting long, Paul?"

"Not too long."

"Are any of my patients out there?"

"I don't know," Paul answered. "How would I know they were your patients?"

"My patients wear yellow tennis shoes."

Paul and I cracked up, letting the doctor's urologist joke break the ice. The doctor's career choice had easily cultivated an appreciation for its by-product: a breeding-ground for bathroom humor. He could have chosen to ignore the obvious, like the proverbial white elephant it was, or embrace it and enjoy the silly fun. His preference seemed the latter, although I had the feeling that Paul encouraged him. Even as the victim, Paul enjoyed jousting with his doctor in this genre of silliness. I know it sounds crazy, but there is something endearing about two brilliant men cutting up this way.

    A nurse brought me a cold can of Sprite and led me into a little room. Simultaneously, Paul was ushered into one across the hall where his powerfully fertile sperm would be re-routed on a benign path. We wiggled a goodbye with our fingers as the doors between us closed.

    "I'm sorry it's not a more comfortable chair," the nurse apologized, pointing to my seat.

    "That's okay," I smiled, gingerly resting my girth on the hard plastic surface.

    "It really doesn't take long," she consoled, pointing out a short stack of magazines and closing my door.

    Alone in the tiny room, I looked around at my surroundings: a refrigerator and a small counter with wire baskets of papers and a phone book. A Merck calendar was the closest thing to wall art that I could see. No designer had been in here. I set my Sprite atop a little table crammed beside me and picked up a worn copy of *Good Housekeeping* from back in the June that Austin and Sarah were born. Currently, it was November thirteen years later. I flipped to an article extolling the desserts of summer and read a couple of paragraphs before realizing I could hear Paul's voice across the hall. I bent my ear toward the closed door and heard three people laughing. As their talking began again, I was able to pick out a conversation going on between the assisting nurse and the doctor. Occasionally Paul snorted a little or made a short comment. I closed the *Good Housekeeping* and leaned toward the door as far as my belly would allow. This is what I heard, and I promise I am not making this up: Nurse: "What's this?"

    Doctor: "It's what you're going to be working with today."

I think I heard Paul chuckle.

Nurse: "Don't kid me, Doc, I'm serious."

Doctor, laughing: "I am serious, is it a problem?"

Nurse: "How am I supposed to work with this? Just look at how little this one is. I can barely see it"

Doctor: "It is - what it is."

Nurse: "Just what is that supposed to mean?"

"It depends on what you're saying 'is' is," he answered, injecting a paraphrased Bill Clinton quote. Their voices began to trail off. Paul mumbled something that made them all laugh again.

"Weird," I heard myself say. My mouth felt suddenly dry. I drowned it with a chug of Sprite which sparked a painful awareness of pressure building in the minimized capacity of my bladder. Morbid curiosity for the rest of this conversation, however intense, was not quite as powerful as my bladder's urge. I waddled down the corridor to the bathroom, feeling a pang of guilt, almost expecting someone to stop me and accuse me of eavesdropping. Hurrying back to my tiny prison cell, I pulled a pen out of my purse and began writing parts of the conversation I had heard. All I could find to write on was a folded crossword page of the newspaper. The *Good Housekeeping* magazine made a lousy lap pad. When this vasectomy was over, somebody would have some *"splainin"* to do.

The door opened. My pregnant frame, perched awkwardly on the hard chair startled an incoming office assistant. I must have looked like Tweedle-Dee, or maybe Tweedle-Dum.

"Oh," She exclaimed. "Sorry, I didn't realize someone was in here."

She yanked open the door of a little refrigerator and removed a box that looked like a pharmaceutical package.

"It's not much of a waiting area, is it?" She asked me sympathetically. "Are there even any magazines to read?"

I answered by pointing to the circa 1982 rags.

"I wonder if you could find out how much longer my husband will be in surgery.

"Hm-m. I can do that. Is he in there?"

She pointed across the hall. I nodded.

"I'll be right back." She excused herself awkwardly, squeezing past me in her exodus. In an instant, her little head poked back through the door. "They are stitching him up now." She offered. "The nurse will come get you when they are done. You can sit with your husband while they are cleaning him up." Her head disappeared as the door closed.

"Yeah," I thought, "maybe they should clean their mouths up, too."

Fifteen minutes later (it seemed like fifteen hours), the nurse came for me. Leading the way into the operating area, I could see Paul's head peeking through a mound of white sheets. He was still chuckling.

"Hey, Sweetie," he greeted me without any shame at all.

"I thought you were only getting local anesthesia," I answered.

"I did."

"Are you sure you don't have a laughing-gas leak in here?" This brought on another giddy display. Paul wasn't the only one in stitches.

"It was just funny," Paul laughed again. He was suffering hysteria, I was pretty sure.

"Is he okay?" I looked at the doctor.

"Mr. Graham is fine, the surgery went just fine."

I was amazed that he could sew stitches and bust a gut laughing at the same time.

"He's our favorite patient," the nurse added, doubling over, trying to stifle the giggles that expelled through her nostrils in staccato snorts. Between the three of them, it sounded like a herd of nursing piglets in there.

"Okay," I said, "will somebody please explain the conversation I heard during surgery?"

"You heard us?" The doctor asked.

"Clearly," I answered, reading aloud the dialogue reconstructed around my crossword puzzle.

They took it like juveniles, unable to tell me at first because of laughing fits. Between spasms, they explained that the conversation (which I didn't necessarily believe at first) was about their new, smaller surgical tools, not Paul's anatomy.

Paul wasn't feeling any pain when he left the clinic with instructions to stay in bed for the next few days. About halfway home the anesthetic began to wear off, so I hurried to Blockbuster for a few requested action movies to watch during his recovery and to the pharmacy for his pain meds, in that order.

Men. For the next couple of days, Paul was checked out in bed with ice packs, Tylenol 3, whatever I brought him to eat, and a background of Bruce Willis and Arnold Schwartzenagger lines. The kids stopped in to say "hi" from time to time, delighted that their dad on Tylenol 3's was more than just a little bit amusing.

Vasectomies are less invasive, require shorter recovery time, and have fewer complication risks than the birth control choices available to women. I could have had a tubal ligation or continued taking the pill except that Paul had promised to be *protection* of me. Although he joked about the procedure, I knew it wasn't really something he relished. He was just making the best of it. The reality was, he had humbled himself to go under the knife so I wouldn't have to. He was guided by his love and care for me.

Two are better than one, because they have a good reward for their toil. For if they fall, one will lift up his fellow. But woe to him who is alone when he falls and has not another to lift him up. Again, if two lie together, they keep warm, but how can one keep warm alone? And though a man might prevail against one who is alone, two will withstand him—a threefold cord is not quickly broken.
Ecclesiastes 4:9-12

Chapter Fifteen

Winter, 1995

I was glad when Jon passed his driver's license test. It was a special benefit since Paul was recovering from surgery and I, a roly-poly in the last stage of my pregnancy. Jon was proud to drive the white Lumina on errands or to his part-time job at Bo Jangle's Fried Chicken drive-thru. He didn't even mind chasing after its rolling hub caps. There was an art in knowing which turn was going to knock them out of their frames . . . again.

The front door opened late one afternoon, and I called from the kitchen, "Is that you, Jonboy?"

Charlotte and Emily sat coloring at their yellow plastic table in the corner. Moving the toddler furniture in here was a brilliant idea. It enabled me to keep a safe eye on them while I cooked. An additional perk was overhearing their two-year-old dialogue.

"Uh. Yes ma'am," Jon answered a little distractedly. I heard him knock softly on our closed bedroom door. In the same instant, all the crayons crashed onto the kitchen floor.

"Dad, can I come in?" Jon called lightly as the babies began to cry in unison.

"She say I a *dumb* cat," Charlotte cried hysterically. "I not."

Emily looked at Charlotte, a tiny fire blazing in her eyes.

"Chah- Lott not share cray-uns," Emily explained.

"Oh, great," I thought. "They are only two and

already calling each other names." Dumb cat. The origin of this particular slur was conceived from one of the few T.V. shows I allowed them to watch. In my head, I imagined Big Bird's voice claiming, *"Sesame Street has the smart cat seal of approval."*

However diabolical it may have been to construct such an insult, I had to give them credit because after all, how many two-year-olds know about antonyms?

"Shirl?" Paul called from the bedroom.

"Yeah," I grunted, "you need me?" I was crawling around on the floor with my big old belly, holding fists full of crayons. Gravity can be so cruel.

Paul sounded like he was laughing. "Come in here for a minute."

"Let me get off this floor," I said to myself.

"Mommy onna flurr," Emily spat. At two-years old, she really acted her age.

"It's *floor*, Emily," I corrected her for the zillionth time.

"No," She argued, "Flurr."

"Okay," I began, trying to explain logic to a two-year-old, "what's that?"

I pointed to the door.

"Durr," she quickly answered.

I laughed. She didn't.

"What about *store?*" I continued foolishly.

"It *sturr*," Emily explained soberly.

"Austin," I called, but he either didn't hear me or was pretending to be deaf.

"Lizard," I yelled up the stairs from my not-so-dainty position on the floor.

Elisabeth's response came in soft steps down the stairs. "Mom?"

"Hey," Gripping the counter, I pulled my heavy frame to a standing position, "Play with the babies while I go see about your daddy, will you?"

Elisabeth smiled, sitting comfortably at the tiny table.

"Bissa-bess color?" Emily asked.

"Yes, Mimi, and NO name-calling," I added, turning the pot handles away from the stove front, a child-proofing exercise that no longer required any more thought than breathing.

"Mommy sitting on a flurr," Emily informed Elisabeth.

I opened the bedroom door to Jon, standing beside the bed looking confused. Paul was shaking his head, a goofy, pain killer-induced grin spread across his teeth.

"Jon, tell your mom what you told me," He said. "Say it just like you did before."

"I just said that they built the poles at the bank too close to the car," Jon answered.

Paul guffawed.

I gave them both a blank stare. "I don't get it."

"Tell her," Paul prodded through his laughter, gasping for breath.

"You know those poles at the ATM?" Jon continued, "They should have built them *back* more."

I still didn't get it. Paul gave up on me and cut to the chase.

"He knocked the side mirror off the Lumina at the bank drive-up." Paul explained, lifting the fog.

It's got to be hard to be a sixteen-year-old boy. I applauded Jon's honesty. It must have been hard to admit his mistake. Not that he had actually blamed himself, of course. The bank's engineers should have had more sense than to *"build the poles so close to the car."*

The Lumina's defect that caused its hubcaps to fly off regularly would now have an additional affliction. Its side-view mirror would stubbornly defy all types of gluing for the rest of its life. This was the car that would be passed down to each new teen-age driver. It seemed somehow fitting that it would bear the battle scars of each young driver, and Jon was blazing the trail.

* * *

A few weeks later, my stomach was so tight you could bounce a quarter off it a couple of yardsticks high. Not that I would have engaged such an exercise. In the last days of pregnancy, everything becomes less and less amusing. The thing was, I wasn't sure if I was in the last days or weeks.

You would think, after so many children, that I could calculate a baby's due date. I tried to figure it out by subtracting two months and adding two weeks, or whatever that method was but I kept coming up with December 25th. Even when I used the little dial-a-baby thing at the O.B. office, the date always fell on Christmas. Doctor Freddie did not concur. Ultrasounds showed the wiggly little baby's entrance nearer to the fifteenth. I must have forgotten how to calculate. Over a nine month span, my brain had turned into oatmeal.

Still, my body did not betray me. All my vital signs were within normal ranges, and there was little to no edema present. A couple of weeks before Christmas, I woke up in the dark to contractions. I looked at the alarm-clock whose song Charlotte did not like. It blinked 4:30 a.m. The children would be up to dress for school in a couple of hours. I let my body relax through the contraction and wondered if this was the first or if I had slept through some of the smaller ones. When the contraction ended, I turned toward Paul. I had adapted to his snoring over the course of our marriage but he wasn't snoring now. He slept deeply, noiselessly, as I rolled onto my side and inched off the bed. He awoke anyway.

"Mornin', Sweetie." he mumbled. "Are you getting up?"

"I'm just potty-ing." I answered, hoping he could fall back to sleep. If this baby was coming soon, his rest would be important.

Paul drifted off to sleep again before I awkwardly stuffed my massive girth back under the covers. I took another look at the clock: 4:37 a.m. I was wide awake now, figuring out the new logistics that a birth would bring to this day. Another contraction rose up, so I noted the time: four-forty-five.

Paul was lying on his back, snoring now. I relaxed into the contraction. It was definitely stronger than Braxton-Hicks (false labor), but easy enough to handle. Paul was honking like a stuck goose now. Pressure peaked and the tension in my belly began to decline. The minute my uterine muscles loosened, I reached over and pinched Paul's nostrils together. He was breaking my eardrums. His breathing stopped momentarily as he opened his eyes and sputtered before sucking in a lung full of air. I let his nose loose, smiled at the confused look on his face, then watched as he fell back to sleep. I'd read an article somewhere about this method of temporarily interrupting a snorer, and I had resorted to implementing it on occasion. Paul had somewhat graciously become accustomed to it.

    I joined him in sleep for what felt like an instant before waking to a triangle of tensing muscles in my pelvic floor. This contraction had more bite than the others. I rode it out and looked at the time. It was 6:10. The children's alarm clocks would be going off in twenty minutes.

    "Paul." I whispered.

    "Huh?" His face was slack and he smelled like sleep.

    "I must be in labor."

    Paul's eyes popped open. "Really?" He smiled.

    "I'm pretty sure. I've had a few contractions so far. They stopped for a little while, but they're back now. The last one was about ten minutes ago."

    "Why didn't you wake me up?" Paul looked at the clock and picked up his watch on the bedside table. "Do you want me to time them?"

    "Yeah," I said. "Let's keep the kids out of school if this is it."

    We had a pre-arranged plan for Jon to follow us to the hospital with Austin and Elisabeth in the Bronco. A neighbor, Pam was at the ready to stay with Charlotte and Emily during the baby's birth.

    Paul timed a few pains before we decided it was real and dialed Dr. Freddie's answering service. We were disappointed to note that another doctor was on call for him, but since we had done this baby thing a few times, we weren't too worried. Paul woke the children then called Pam. We all dressed quickly and were on our way.

    Almost there, I listened sadly to the Lumina's blinker signaling right at our exit. I might as well admit that my contractions had stopped several miles back. Feeling foolish as my husband exited at the blue "H" sign, I knew I had to tell him. Paul checked the Bronco in the rear view mirror as we turned onto Highway 378, toward the hospital.

"What's happening?" He asked with anticipation.

"Nothing." I confessed, looking down at my bulge, trying to will it to contract.

"Nothing? Did they stop?"

I should have expected this familiar start-stop labor pattern. Austin was the only one of my babies who came fast with uniform labor, and that was probably only because of my castor oil and orange juice cocktail that preceded his entry. There were only two hours and forty minutes from the beginning of labor until Austin made his debut. Why I only tried the "cocktail" one time is a mystery, even to me.

I sighed, "Yeah. Let's get the kids some breakfast. Maybe my labor will crank up again."

"Sure." Paul turned on his left blinker for a whole block before pulling into the Bo Jangles across from the hospital. Jon took his lead and followed, parking beside us. The smiling faces of our excited children beamed through the windows. How I hated having to admit this was a false alarm. Being adaptable, however, was an uncommon gift they shared. Paul rolled down the window and explained that we had only struck fool's gold, but we'd buy some chicken biscuits anyway. Jon, Austin, and Elisabeth tumbled out, not nearly as disappointed as I had expected. Eating breakfast out during school hours was still a pretty good consolation prize.

We dropped the children off at their respective schools, Paul went to work and I spent the rest of the day moving around as much as possible.

The following day, labor came in truth. This time, we didn't take the children out of school but enlisted some back up drivers to get the children home and to the hospital, provided the baby was really serious. Daddy and Mother drove two and a half hours from Hartwell, Georgia, to help, and Ruthie met Paul and me at the hospital.

I already mentioned that Paul and I were comfortable enough with what was ahead, but the doctor on call didn't appreciate our confidence. In fact, the only time he showed up during my labor was right after we got settled in the labor room. "I'm Dr. Bullhead," (Not his real name but an apt one) he told us without any obvious interest in who *we* were, preferring the general information on my chart. He carelessly scanned over the scribbles on the clip board without bothering to smile or look directly at any of us. Ruthie shot me a look that showed her disgusted surprise at his rude behavior. "I'm going to order a Pit drip to get you started." Dr. Bullhead said to his clipboard.

"No, thanks," I declined, "I'll be laboring naturally."

He finally looked at me, personally offended by my presumption. He shook his head self-righteously without disturbing the bushy white hair on his face and head. "Yeah, I heard, but you don't want to do that," he answered me curtly. "You could be here for hours." I think he really meant that *he* could be there for hours.

"Really, I don't mind. Doctor Freddie already okayed it," I answered defensively.

I looked at Paul and noticed he was glaring bullets at Dr. Bullhead. A short laugh escaped his throat and he said, "Doc, we don't mind waiting and besides, I notice we're the only ones on the ward tonight." It was true. When we arrived, we had talked to the nurse about how quiet the halls seemed. She'd told us she had only been at work for a few minutes and the last delivery patient was taken to the maternity ward a couple of hours before her shift started.

Dr. Bullhead threw his hands in the air and stomped out. "Well then, call me if you need me," he growled, without a lot of sincerity and turned out of the room.

"Sheesh." I said.

Paul said a word more colorful than 'sheesh,' then added an additional comment about the doctor's character. Ruthie and I giggled in collective solidarity.

A few minutes later, the nurse walked in looking embarrassed. She read the contraction meter and took my vital signs. "You are doing great. The baby's heartbeat is good, labor's moving along."

"Yay," I answered. "We came here yesterday with false labor."

"This looks real," she said, then made a little frown and whispered, "I know you said you don't want Pitocin, but Doctor Bullhead sent me in here to tell you it is his medical opinion to hook you up to a drip."

"I sympathized with her middle-man position. "Tell

Dr. Happy Pants thanks, but no thanks," I replied.

". . . again." Paul added.

"I'm really sorry," the nurse reiterated, "I don't disagree with you, but you know I have to tell you anyway. I have to follow orders."

The nurse respected us and our choice to let the baby's birth occur on its own time and we respected her position, too. As labor progressed slowly through the night, the doctor's only interaction with us was through her. It wasn't a bad deal. She was much more pleasant than he. We would learn that Dr. Bullhead had a reputation for being, well, *bullheaded.* Each time we sent the nurse back with another refusal of induction his continued absence confirmed what we already knew: we were getting on his nerves. The feeling was mutual.

As the doctor left to do whatever doctors do when they are waiting for a womb to deliver a baby, Ruthie tried to familiarize herself with our video camera. As my contractions began to come harder and quicker, she decided I was better off with her holding my right hand. As Paul laid grip to my left hand, my forty-year-old uterus proved it remembered its *modus operandi.* The baby wasn't fooling around now.

"Pray me through this one," I pleaded with Paul and Ruthie. I closed my eyes and prayed for the baby's safety: "Lord?" I prayed silently through the contraction, "Lord, I give this little one over to You. Please bring this baby safely into the world with a blessing of Your love and grace."

The nurse hurried in. "I see the baby's head," she cried.

Paul started to smile. I couldn't return the favor, preferring to answer him with a sweaty, heaving, other-worldly groan.

"I called Dr. Bullhead," the nurse said to comfort me, but in her voice I heard an undercurrent of concern and irritation. "Don't push."

"I - can't – stop," I gasped as this child defied me for the first time, rushing to be born soon, hoping not to miss this interesting conflict on the outside.

The baby lifted its little red face into the light with

toothless jaws open wide to yell at its first day, "I'm nearly here and I'm mad, too."

Being busy as I was, I didn't see a smirking Dr. Bullhead saunter through the open door. Paul glared at him and contemplated two questions in his mind. One: "How much self-control had he at this moment?" and two: "Would losing it be worth going to jail?" I don't think Dr. Bullhead was intuitive enough to realize how close Paul was to choosing jail.

"I didn't think you needed me," he taunted. "Didn't you say you could handle this by yourselves?"

The nurse's panic was evident as her eyes darted frantically from the baby to the doctor to Paul, whose red face matched the baby's exactly. Paul's temperature had to be pretty close to 212°.

"She *didn't* need you until now," I heard Paul say through clenched teeth.

I responded with another push contraction, "UH-N-N-N-N-N-N-N-NN-N-MPH."

Paul's grip on me was a little firmer than necessary, and Ruthie's felt sweaty. I squeezed their hands and pushed with all my might.

"You're doing great," the nurse addressed me through the tension, trying desperately to help me focus.

I answered her with a noise not unlike the grunting of a weight lifter . . . from Mars. The nurse looked pleadingly at the doctor, and he finally took the helm.

"*Now* you need me," he growled, and I suddenly felt fright that the bitter hands of this arrogant, angry man would be the first human contact my precious baby felt.

"It's a boy," the nurse announced, relief brightening her face.

Paul allowed his protective posture to relax in the moment. A boy.

Dr. Bullhead handed the baby to the nurse and set about to cut the cord. He stopped abruptly, holding a pair of hemostats in mid-air, and addressed Paul.

"I guess *you* want to cut the cord, *Sir,*" He said sarcastically.

"No, *thanks,*" Paul answered, returning the sarcasm.

"He looks like a saggy little old man," I giggled as my new son upstaged the mean doctor.

Quickly, Ruthie countered my observation: "He's so beautiful."

Paul turned to us and smiled, tears welling up in his eyes. Distracted as we were by God's personal miracle in our lives, none of us noticed Doctor Bullhead preparing a hypodermic. He either hadn't read the list of preferences we had okayed with Dr. Freddie months before, or he was deliberately ignoring our wishes. He pointed the needle toward my thigh.

"Is that Pitocin?" I asked him. "I don't want it. I'll be breast feeding."

"You need this to stop bleeding."

Paul's posture changed suddenly. He seemed about seven feet tall.

"She says she doesn't want it," he intervened, daring the doctor to continue.

"Your wife needs this if you don't want her to bleed to death," he argued pompously.

"It's okay, Paul," I whispered to him weakly. I knew I didn't need the shot, but it probably wouldn't cause any damage either. I had given birth four times without it and knew nursing the baby would naturally contract my uterus. This guy intimidated me, which was obviously his intention, but Paul wasn't backing down.

"No, Sweetie, it's not necessary," Paul said to me, caressing my face, but still keeping a bead on Dr. Bullhead. This was a showdown.

"She doesn't want it." Undaunted, Paul spat the words, enunciating each consonant with confidence.

"Sir, I must warn you again that your wife could bleed to death, and I won't take that responsibility," Dr. Bullhead condescended.

Paul stared a hole through him. "I'll be happy to take full responsibility." He spoke quietly, but I sensed the volcano quaking underneath his words. Dr. Bullhead heard it, too.

"Suit yourself," he answered with false bravado and left, taking with him the negative energy he had brought into the room. I pictured him scurrying down the hall like a cockroach, looking over his shoulder.

The room was filled with peace now and the nurse handed Paul his freshly wrapped son.

"Eight-pounds, eight-ounces," she announced proudly.

Paul held our youngest Graham gently, saying, "Hey, buddy. Welcome."

He bent into me, and I reached for the baby.

"Here's Joseph," Paul said, calling his name for the first time as he presented our squirming little guy.

My eyes gathered Joseph in and gobbled him up.

"Hi, little Joseph-boy," I greeted him. "You better nurse before I bleed to death and all."

"You did great, Shirley," Ruthie added, kissing my cheek, "but I was afraid Doctor Bullhead was going to earn himself a beating."

"So was I," Joseph's daddy agreed.

Sons are a heritage from the Lord, children a reward from Him. Like arrows in the hands of a warrior are sons born in one's youth. Blessed is the man whose quiver is full of them.
Psalm 127:3-5

Chapter Sixteen

1995 - December 15

"Hey, little ham samwich." Paul cooed at his baby boy.

Joseph narrowed his fresh, new eyes. He liked this voice and already sought to identify with it.

"You want to help the daddy take a piece of Doctor Bullhead, buddy?"

Joseph blinked and made his lips into a tight, little Cheerio.

He was beautiful. Eight pounds and eight ounces of tiny masculinity, he seemed to be puffing his chest up from the start.

In just a couple of hours, Mother and Daddy arrived with Aunt Phyllis and all the children (except for Sarah who would be home the following weekend). Once inside the room, Jon, Austin and Elisabeth couldn't stop smiling and giggling over their new baby brother but Charlotte and Emily wore looks of total bewilderment. When Paul reached for them they lunged into his arms, clinging to his neck as though he were a big magnet. They lay their pretty heads on his shoulders in unison.

"Hey, knuckleheads." Paul teased them, "You have a brother."

Charlotte and Emily melded themselves more tightly into his sides. If water had gushed from the ceiling at that moment, Paul would have been completely wet except for two dry spots in the shape of two-year-old girls.

"Do you want to touch the baby, Charlotte and Emily?" I asked, offering them a ruddy little brother-in-a-blanket.

Simultaneously, they recoiled.

We finally persuaded Emily to put her tiny hand on Joseph's blanket. She complied and her hand surprised us by seeming massive beside Joseph's diminutive head. Charlotte shuddered, protecting her hand from this alien thing we called, 'brother.' Emily, having reached her limit of cooperation, jerked her hand off the baby.

Paul beamed nonetheless. He made a funny noise near

Charlotte and Emily's bellies. They bent their heads shyly, suppressing giggles and smiled as hard as possible without showing their teeth.

I gave Joseph to Jon, who handled him as gracefully as a seasoned father.

"Can I hold him?" Elisabeth asked suddenly.

"I want to, too." Austin added.

"Just hang on." I replied, "There will be lots of opportunities to hold this buddy."

Jon leaned his face into Joseph's wee forehead. He smiled and the braces on his front teeth sparkled with the light above. He slung his long, thick bangs aside but they fell right back in his eyes.

"Wanna play basketball, little guy? Wanna shoot a few hoops with your big brother?"

Joseph blinked his eyes, and seemed to thoughtfully consider Jon's proposal.

Weary, but filled with delight, I drank in the joy of this moment. Surrounded by people I loved, welcoming a beautiful, healthy baby into the fold, I wondered why God had been so extravagant. I could call to mind thousands of reasons why I didn't deserve His grace and yet, here He was showing exorbitant favor. In the midst of these lives that knew both failure and sadness, God had allowed the desire to love a houseful of children to live in the hearts of Paul and me. Then, He allowed us to find each other and set about to fulfill our wishes beyond our dreams. I learned something large about the heart of God that day. It is summed up in Psalm 37:4: *Delight yourself in the Lord and He will give you the desires of your heart.*

The first time I read that, I didn't know what to think. Couldn't it be dangerous to think such a lofty thing? Dare I trust my own judgment to assume that the desires of my heart might also be God's will for me? Will the Holy Spirit give me enough wisdom to know what the right desires are? What if I get it wrong? Does the World realize God wants to give us the desires of our hearts?

I tried to embrace God's desire from another perspective. What if He knows me better than I know myself? What if He is more aware of my desires and how they fit into His glorious plan than I?

If God had called Paul and me into a private meeting and asked, *"What would you like? What do you want?"* would we have said, "Oh, Lord, give us another fat, precious baby who looks just like Paul.""?

No, we probably wouldn't have realized we could. We probably would have let the practical, reasonable, limiting part of us answer something like,

"Lord, just help us to afford the ones we have and we will try to be satisfied with that. We wouldn't dare impose upon Your bounty by being greedy. You already blessed us and we know there are others who aren't so blessed."

But that would have been a prayer to a limited God. My God has no limits. He created me with His plan in Mind, and He *does* know me better than I know myself. Besides, His extravagance is drawn from the very riches in Heaven (Philippians 4:19). What a concept this was to wrap my brain around.

Through so many things, including the gift of Joseph, God was showing us the lavish generosity of a Father's love. He was stretching our limitations and fulfilling our secret wishes that seemed neither practical nor reasonable.

Paul relinquished Charlotte and Emily to Mother and Daddy as some noise was raised about returning the children home.

"Not yet," smiled the nurse, revealing a Polaroid camera, "…everybody, smile."

We smiled for Joseph's first family picture. He was one of us.

***

Joseph was truly his daddy's boy and I loved it. Charlotte and Emily preferred Paul's attention over mine most of the time and it didn't take long to see that Joseph's adoration for Paul was equally worshipful. I soon realized it was only my ability to produce milk that allowed me a turn holding Joseph. For months after birth, babies feel a physical sense of connected-ness to their mothers. Joseph, however, had transferred this whole psychological concept from his mother to his father. It was such a hoot to see how intensely he identified with him. Joseph was really a tiny Paul anyway. None of his features seemed to have been drawn from my gene pool. Maybe his belly-button, but that's all.

Jane said it best.

"Shirley," she had announced while holding Joseph for the first time, "I guess your gene pool had to run out sooner or later."

Glory to God in the highest heaven, and on earth peace to those on whom his favor rests.
Luke 2: 14

Chapter Seventeen

Since Joseph was healthy and I managed to avoid bleeding to death, we were free to return home the next day with our happy little Christmas bundle. Some of Paul's paternity leave had been eaten up when I had false labor, so it seemed like no time before he was back dispensing pharmaceuticals to the masses. There were masses of shoppers at Kmart, after all, since Christmas was almost here.

Joseph's birthday is December 15. The year he was born, Charlotte and Emily were two-and-a-half, which would have kept me pretty busy even if caring for them had been my only responsibility. It wasn't, though. Jon was driving age, so I was monitoring his activities as best I could. Austin had started making all the wrong friends, which kept me on alert for his safety. Elisabeth was a new middle school student with lots of friends, so there seemed to be an endless list of activities for her. Sarah had grounded herself in her life in Atlanta, so she didn't come on the weekends as much. Even though we expected her visits to decrease one day, we didn't expect it so soon. It sometimes felt like rejection.

Paul did every speck of Christmas shopping for our family that year. Working at the pharmacy at Kmart, he had the advantage of being on top of all the best sales. He also had a better sense than I of things the children would like, especially Elisabeth, which kind of hurt my maternal pride. For example, he came home from work one day with this revelation: "There's a boom box in the electronics department that goes on sale tomorrow."

I thought, *"So what?"* and patiently waited to hear where this idea was headed.

"I think Elisabeth would like it," He continued.

"You do?" I asked him. "Elisabeth? No kidding? Why?"

"He laughed and looked at me as though I'd sprouted a daisy on my head. The boom box would turn out to be just the thing she wanted. In spite of all the years I had raised Jon, Austin, and Elisabeth without him, he sometimes knew them better than I.

Anyway, I felt just fine relinquishing the sole responsibility of Christmas shopping to him in the *Year of the Babies*.

Lots of needs weren't being met by me around then. Whenever my children's hair looked shaggy (which seemed pretty often), I thought about the old adage, *the shoemaker's sons have no shoes*. I vowed to give them haircuts before the Candlelight service at church on Christmas Eve, my favorite event of the Season.

Before lunch on Christmas Eve, I perched Emily on the bathroom counter for her little hair cut. The flimsy patches of hair growing in on Emily and Charlotte's round little heads imitated male-pattern baldness. On occasion, it became necessary to trim their bangs right in the middle where hair grew into unfortunate points on their foreheads. Emily's tiny hand brushed her point into her right eye, then the left in a fruitless attempt to see past it. I wrapped a chair cloth around her and freed her from the obstruction with my comb.

My mother had bought the twins beautiful velvet Christmas jumpers with white blouses. I couldn't wait to dress them. Charlotte's outfit was red, Emma's green. Joseph would wear a flannel plaid one-piece romper. Once dressed, I knew I would wish I could hang all three babies on our tree.

Between the remaining haircuts, meals, diapers, and Lord knows how many other duties that day held, I was loading the dishwasher when Emily cried out with a hysterical "WAHHHH."

I dropped the silverware on the floor and headed in the direction of her scream. Her siblings and Paul appeared out of nowhere and we found Emily in the bedroom with a pair of bloody hair cutting shears. By now, Charlotte had started crying, too. Sometimes their double crying would start before we located the injured twin. That made it really hard to know who was hurt. Emily cried out again and big tears spilled down her trembling face. Paul picked her up as she held out her little thumb, missing half a thumb print.

My first thought was to take her to the hospital E.R. My second thought was an image of what the hospital E.R. probably looked like on Christmas Eve night. Paul was thinking the same thing. We reasoned that there wouldn't be any way to stitch Emily's thumb, so we covered it with antibiotic ointment and a big bandage. We actually made it to church, too. Emily didn't cry, but she wore a sober little face and let her daddy hold her throughout this service.

Charlotte gloried in her wholeness by flitting from one sibling's lap to another. We sat right in front of the choir, I holding ten-day-old Joseph in my arms. I usually sang with the sopranos, but Joseph's entry had interrupted my participation this year. I looked at this wonderful, beautiful sleeping baby, my heart so full I feared it might burst through my chest. Why had God shown us such extravagant favor?

The congregation began to sing softly as one candle lit another, and another. The song rose tenderly and the Holy Spirit embraced us lovingly: *"O, Holy Night… The stars are brightly shining. It is the night of our dear Savior's birth."*

I looked up as my eyes adjusted. My friend Jenny sat at the organ, tears streaming down her face. She saw me and turned away quickly.

After Luke 2 had been read in full, the congregation burst into a resounding *"Joy, to the World. The Lord is come!"*

A crowd of friends hovered near to get a glimpse of the baby Paul was now calling "Mini-me." It was a while before we could move outside the pew. Jenny finished playing the exit music and came near me. I hugged her. "You doing all right, my friend?" I asked her.

"The music moves me sometimes," She laughed, embarrassed. "My heart is just so full of Christmas." Jenny laughed again. "I looked out during the service and there you were holding a newborn babe." She smiled down at little Joseph and whispered, "It almost felt like I had been transferred to Bethlehem on Christmas Eve."

One day the angels came to present themselves before the LORD, and Satan also came with them. The LORD said to Satan, "Where have you come from?" Satan answered the LORD, "From roaming throughout the earth, going back and forth on it."
Job 1:8-9

Chapter Eighteen

1996: I have to admit there is a lot I have forgotten about the next few years. I do remember that Jon went on to graduate from high school and had too many girlfriends. He moved into and out of various abodes with a varied other graduated teens in varying levels of emancipation from home. Not having much inclination toward interior design, these young adults were usually willing to bring yet another renter into the fold. *The more the merrier* was the collective tone, plus, if two can live a cheaply as one, then several ought to be able to live even cheaper, right?

So many contributors to rent and utilities kept Jon and his room mates' monetary responsibility minuscule. That was so, as long as each dweller came through with his share of the costs, which didn't always happen, which explains why Jon moved around a lot during this, his initial period of adulthood. He was cute and funny, everybody loved him and every day held another opportunity for fun. He enrolled at Midland's Technical College, but continued to keep girls and partying above school obligations.

He'd return home from time to time, always hungry and sometimes with laundry. He still loved meeting his friends on the basketball court behind our house. Now and again, they lured Paul onto the court. I remember the day Paul hobbled into the house from a 'friendly' game with Jon and his friends.

"I think I might have hurt myself." He winced.

I laughed, not realizing he'd be "crippled up" as he referred to his condition over the next few days.

After his joints healed he told me,

"I've finally got to admit I can't do that anymore."

He was serious and refused their invitations from then on.

Attending Ridge View High School now, Austin was ever trying newer and riskier behavior. His art teachers encouraged his strong ability to draw. His acting ability was also encouraged, but Austin seemed disinterested in these two things that he used to love. Instead, his appetite was mostly for activities that took him right to the edge. I'd made it a point to know his friends and their parents, so it was pretty easy to keep tabs on him. Consequently, his indiscretions were easy to catch and he hated that. Every time he got in trouble, he'd say he wanted to go live with his father in Pensacola. I kept saying I would never consider it. Austin had become a handful and his father worked out of town a great deal of the time. Expecting him to suddenly fill the position of a full-time father to an at-risk teenage boy would be a bad choice for both of them. Worry and grief over Austin had created an aching emptiness in my heart but I continued to try new things to help him, to involve him in healthy activities. I got him on a soccer team and that was okay, but his heart wasn't in it. I was running out of ideas.

Sarah's involvement in school, sports and lessons kept her in Atlanta on many of her visitation weekends. Having inherited her daddy's innate ability to judge a person's character, Sarah was usually good at choosing friends. When she did come home, she sometimes brought a friend from school. Everyone enjoyed these times as they allowed us a glimpse into her 'other life' in Atlanta. More often than not, Paul drove to Atlanta to see her now. He would return home with photographs of Sarah on the basket ball court or softball field. Her life was busy and she seemed happy. Even though having divorced parents was a hardship, she had learned that being adaptable was her ace in the hole.

Elisabeth stayed pretty busy, too. She was playing violin with the middle school orchestra, taking parts in plays, participating in either softball or cheerleading. She was now taking an interest in soccer. Elisabeth seemed happy and well-adjusted, too. Despite her young age, she seemed to have a real understanding about working for the common good. I was hopeful that Elisabeth might be able to avoid the drama and difficulty that would typically accompany the teen years. Hope springs eternal.

Everyone in the family was bound by our collective love for the babies. Not one of us was above being a fool for their pleasure. I actually have videotape of Jon crawling into the clothes hamper solely because Charlotte and Emily asked him to. It is both sweet and amusing to see Jon folding his six-feet-one-inch frame into a fetal position inside the hamper. Cuter, still is seeing twin toddlers slam the wicker lid on his long-haired head and dance with glee.

Taking Charlotte, Emily and Joseph out during the day was truly like being a parade. People could hardly resist my supermarket cart overflowing with babies, however; Charlotte and Emily were still the main attraction. Strangers made over Joseph's shy sisters in matching outfits as though he was invisible. I imagined that if Joseph could talk he might be saying,

"Hey. I'm the baby. Look at me. I'm cute, too."

He was, too. White blonde hair had begun to sprout crazily all over his head. His eyes, so laser-blue, almost blinded you until he smiled and the crinkling of his eyelids provided shade. It was obvious the little buddy was just happy to be one of the bananas, which kept him grinning most of the time. If smiling was a sport, Joseph would have had an unbeatable smiling average.

Paul worked a lot of overtime now and worried about how much money we had to spend in order to live in such a large family. He brought it up sometimes when we were alone.

I awoke one morning to the alarm and turned to Paul's empty side of the bed. Before I had time to wonder where he was, I heard him say,

"Good morning."

I watched him walk from the desk across the room and push the button on the clock.

"Good morning." I said, sitting up in the bed. "Up already?"

Paul rubbed the back of his head.

"I got up about 4:30."

"What on Earth for?"

He pointed to the checkbook on the desk.

"Trying to dig up some money."

"Had you buried any?"

"No, but I should have."

"Are we in trouble?"

"Maybe."

"What if we sold the lake property?" I asked him, referring to the acre of land where the fishing trailer sat on Lake Wateree.

Paul said nothing.

"We hardly ever get out there in the summer or New Year's Eve or Fourth of July. Paul?"

"I plan for us to retire there." He answered quickly. "I don't want to give it up."

I didn't either, but I would have been willing to in order to lift this burden. We talked some about me going back to work but that wasn't really an option. After we considered the cost of three babies in day-care, we knew we wouldn't break even. Plus, I wouldn't want to leave the older kids home alone. Paul faced me and saw the worry etched between my eyebrows. His big hands reached for mine and he squeezed them. His hands were always so warm.

"It will be okay." He assured me. "I don't believe God sent us these children without a way to take care of them."

I smiled and felt the lines in my face soften. His faith was so attractive, so strong and so manly. It was one of the reasons I loved him.

Speaking of faith, we were still committed to being in church. We were back at Christus Victor almost an hour away. We had done some church 'shopping' and even joined a church near us for a time, but our hearts had remained at CVLC. We had returned. Austin was taking his Confirmation classes now and I was back, happily singing in the choir. Even Elisabeth sang in the choir sometimes. I loved seeing my family from my vantage point in the choir loft, spread across a whole pew, babies balanced on hips of varying heights.

Getting everyone in place wasn't the easiest job,

though. Thinking about this challenge prompted me to write a little article about it which ran in The Current, our monthly church newsletter. I share it here:

Dear Friends,

There's something that bothers me and I feel like I need to apologize or confess, or something. Here goes:

I brought the devil to church with me last Sunday. The truth is, I bring him along pretty often. Actually, he shows up at our house the night before. I know he is there because my good intentions start coming apart. I start thinking that I ought to lay out the children's clothes then I make a phone call or clean up something instead.

He's in my bedroom watching Saturday Night Live when I know I should be asleep. He nudges me when my husband asks, "Should I set the clock for seven or seven-thirty?"

"Seven-forty-five will be enough time." I answer. I can almost hear the devil chuckle when I say that.

I know he has spent the night when my eyes pop open in horror with the alarm clock loudly reprimanding my husband and me like it's been doing for thirty minutes. The devil always gets a big charge out of that moment.

You'd think it would satisfy him just to hang around the house while we all blunder about, blaming each other for being late or for having to go somewhere on this good morning for sleeping. He climbs into the car with us and reminds us that we are late again. Too late, in fact, to walk into Sunday School.

He even follows us into the Sanctuary and points out things to me, like that my son didn't iron his pants and I hate the shoes my daughter is wearing.

My mind sometimes wanders during Worship as I sit in the choir loft and I think about what I will make for lunch. Sometimes I give my kids a mean glare because I can tell they aren't keeping up in the Hymnal.

Somehow he manages to slip out of the choir loft and into the pew where my family sits, and I don't even miss him. He shows humorous things to my children and reminds them that if they just move their lips, I won't know they aren't really singing along.

I could go on. He does ride home with us and have dinner, but maybe he's been a guest at your table before and you already know how he can work an innocent situation into something negative.

I just want you to pray for me about next week. I'm going to try to make early preparations. I think it might help keep him away. It seems fair that I should prepare a place in my heart for worshiping God on Sunday. After all, I hear He is preparing a place for me ahead of time, too.

Your friend,
Shirley Graham

Then the LORD said to Cain, "Where is your brother Abel?"
"I don't know," he replied. "Am I my brother's keeper?"
Genesis 4:9

Chapter Nineteen

Spring 1997: I opened my eyes and flung an arm over to Paul's side of the bed. Empty. I must have been sleeping hard. I usually noticed when he got up. I ran my fingers over the knotted ropes of blue and purple behind my left leg. Joseph was over a year old, weaned, and now Paul was encouraging me to have a doctor look at my varicose veins. It was nice, knowing he worried about me, but I had put it off. I didn't notice as my husband stepped into our room with two mugs of coffee. His question caught me off guard: "Does your leg hurt?" He handed me my coffee. We had gotten pretty good at making each other's coffee the right shade and sweetness.

"Some. It's hot back here and throbs." I took the mug. "It always itches like crazy but it's okay."

"You know, I have some vacation days built up. I can take off work for you to recover," he said, reading my mind. "I think I can do a pretty good job being you for a few days."

"Then who's going to be you?"

"You can be me. I'll bring you some violent action movies to watch."

"You're too good to me," I smiled. "I don't deserve you."

"I know," he agreed, handing me the phone number."

"I'll call," I promised. "I wrote the doctor's name down in the kitchen the other day."

"Good. I've got to take good care of those pretty legs of yours."

"Thank you, but don't you think green, blue, and purple are pretty?"

He rolled his eyes.

The human heart is resilient. So much had happened since Joseph was born. The worst of it was that Austin had gone to live with his father in Pensacola. I continued to struggle with giving in to that. At fifteen years old, Austin was determined to find out who his father was. I'm sure he glamorized the prospect of living with him each time he was expected to do something he didn't want to do. As Austin fought against our values, it occurred to me that whatever he thought Paul and I stood for was the very thing he would rebel against. Striving to be a good example to him seemed to be the worst thing I could do to help him.

I didn't believe his father was up for the task. Plus, I thought if he really came and took him to Florida, Austin would miss being part of our family. I imagined either his father would tire of the responsibility or Austin would want to come home in a few weeks. I prayed for an answer but God was silent.

I had begun to fear leaving Austin alone. He had already run away from home more than once, and I cringed every time the phone rang. Would it be his school? A neighbor? The ring of a phone threatened to be another precursor to information I didn't want to process about the son I loved yet didn't know anymore.

Just before I was sure I had run out of ideas to turn Austin around, I had to make a trip to Walmart. Such errands were always such a hassle with three babies and a fifteen-year-old boy who seemed to hate me. We managed to get inside the store, and I strapped Joseph into the shopping cart seat. He pulled at the seat belt and whimpered a little. I handed him a little car from my jeans pocket. Good. He let himself get interested in it. I knew I had to hurry before he needed another distraction. I hauled Charlotte and Emily into the cart together.

"Stay seated," I insisted.

Charlotte's dimpled fingers pushed Emily over to give herself more room. Emily glared at her.

'I NOT," She told Charlotte.

As I pushed my toddler-stuffed cart, Austin followed several paces behind. I had to stop the cart two aisles over from what I needed because several boxes of merchandise waiting to be stacked blocked the way.

"Austin, I have to get over to that aisle, so I need you to push this cart around till I get back." I pointed just beyond us. "Charlotte and Emily will stay put, but you've got to watch that the baby doesn't get out. Can I count on you?"

Austin gave me an expressionless look.

"Come on, Austin, I need you. Will you answer me?"

"I will do it," he said evenly, avoiding the need to say, "yes, ma'am."

I sighed and hurried over to grab my merchandise. Hurrying back, I found Austin with the cart in the same spot where I had left him. He hadn't budged. I saw Charlotte and Emily, but Joseph, not quite two-years-old, wasn't in the seat.

"Where is he?"

"Who?" Austin asked innocently.

"The BABY, Austin, where is the BABY?"

"He wanted out," Austin explained, "So, I helped him get out."

"Where IS HE?" I begged.

"I don't know."

I would have to deal with Austin later. Right then I had to find my baby. I cursed the racks of clothes that obscured him.

"JOSEPH," I bellowed, caring not at all about the disturbance I was making. I snatched the cart from Austin. How could I trust him with the twins now? My heart was beating like a jungle drum, and hot tears streaked across my face. Gripping the handle, I raced past every aisle jerking my head up and down the shelved corridors.

"JOPIE. Where ARE you, Bubby?"

"Mommy," Emily pointed to our left.

"I see him," Charlotte finished.

I stopped in time to see Joseph smiling up at me from a rack of shoes. A lady wearing the store smock stood protectively beside him. "Thank you for looking out for him," I said to her as I scooped Joseph into my arms. I was crying openly now.

"Mommy ky-ing," Joseph added jovially. His sweet little voice was a balm to my soul.

We must have paid for the things I had gathered. We must have driven home. I don't remember talking to Austin. I felt deeply frustrated and grieved for the Austin I used to know. Where had he gone, and how was this new Austin's example going to affect his young siblings? How much worse might it get? What good was an ineffectual mother?

That night, Paul worked late. I put the little ones to bed and spilled my rejected heart into a little poem that asked questions about my boy, Austin. Where had that loving toddler gone? Where is the happy baby who once trusted me? What became of the giggles we shared when I pushed *him* through the store in a cart?

When Paul came home from work, I slipped a poem inside the pages of my Bible as a bookmark and shared the day's troubling incident. Paul looked down at the floor and shook his head.

"Sometimes," I confessed in a whisper, "I feel so tired, wrung out. I don't think I can wring anything else out of myself." My bottom lip began to quiver. "I'm scared, Paul. I'm scared of Austin being out of control, and I am scared of not feeling like I'm able to give him what he needs."

"It's not for lack of trying," Paul reassured me.

"I am scared of losing him, yet I wonder if it would help him to live with his father for a while. You know the old concept, *be careful what you wish for*. I can't imagine him being happy so far from life here. Maybe he would come back with a different attitude."

"Maybe." Paul was being a sounding board for me. As emotional as I was, that's the only thing I could handle from him.

"I've spent his whole life loving him, taking care of him, protecting him from harm."

"Yes, you have."

"He doesn't even know his father. He's only seen him a few times in his whole life"

"I know."

"I have never rejected him, but he is rejecting *me.*"

"It makes no sense."

I was crying again, sobbing. I thought I could actually feel my heart ripping inside my chest. "How can he hate me so much? He's been able to count on me his whole life. Not his father."

"I think this is about Austin, not you." Paul handed

me a box of tissues.

I blew my nose and took a deep breath. "I don't know what else to do," I confessed.

"What do you mean?" Paul asked, confused.

My voice was thin, strained, "Maybe I *should* let him move to Florida. Maybe his move would be short-lived."

Paul put his arms around my shoulders.

"It's your call, sweetie. I'll back you up whatever you want to do."

"It's not what I want to do. This is hard. I just want to do the right thing for him and the impressionable little ones. I can't seem to get a clear idea about what is best."

We went to sleep that night without a definite plan, but over a couple of weeks, I decided to take the risk. It was the only way I knew to put the ball in Austin's court. Surely, he would return home soon with a clearer understanding of his place in our family. Surely, he wouldn't be gone very long. I finally agreed to talk to Austin's father. He indicated that he would come for Austin the following weekend, although I really wasn't ready to make it final. When something unexpected came up and he postponed coming, I felt relieved. I hoped it wouldn't ever be convenient for him to include a teenage boy in his house.

Jesus continued: "There was a man who had two sons. The younger one said to his father, 'Father, give me my share of the estate.' So he divided his property between them. Not long after that, the younger son got together all he had, set off for a distant country.
Luke 15:11-32

Chapter Twenty

October 1997: Back when Paul and I first married, I learned about Via de Cristo (translated: Way of Christ). It is a Cursillo (Spanish for short course) weekend retreat sponsored by the Lutheran church.

Cursillo retreat origins are in Spanish-Catholic church. In 1949 the Spanish Civil War of 1936-1939 left behind more than 500,000 people dead and de-Christianization among many survivors. The young Christian men left to lead families were disheartened by this discouraging atmosphere. Some of these men, returning soldiers, attended and became encouraged by Cursillo through its Christian education, community and prayer. They returned home strengthened and fortified by the Holy Spirit to lead their families in Christ. Cursillo retreats are all about empowering Christian leaders. Eventually, Catholic churches in other countries held these retreats and they spread to other denominations. As other churches developed their own cursillo weekends, great efforts were made to keep its original format.

Denominations sponsoring cursillo do so retreat under different names. Catholics and Episcopalians kept the name and sponsor non-ecumenical Cursillo, Methodists sponsor ecumenical Walk to Emmaus. Other ecumenical cursillo retreats are called by the names, Chrysalis, TEC (Teens Encounter Christ), HEC (Handicapped Encounter Christ), Tres Dias, plus REC (Residents Encounter Christ) and Kairos (both prison cursillo ministries).

A number of our friends at Christus Victor had already made a Via de Cristo weekend and every one of them testified to the difference it had made in their life. Paul had enjoyed a wonderful pilgrim weekend early in our marriage and I couldn't wait to I get my turn. Until then, I had a few more years to nurse babies and change diapers.

With Joseph weaned, I had finally signed up for my pilgrim weekend. It was scheduled on the very weekend Austin's father had said he would come for him, so I went to the retreat not knowing whether I would be returning to a whole or fragmented family.

Via de Cristo weekends include a schedule of events and classes that keep the pilgrims busy throughout. I relished the novelty of not having any responsibility. It was a blessing to be shepherded from one activity to the next and just do what I was supposed to do. That in itself made it like a vacation. In some ways I felt like a child and that was so good for me. Years of caring for other people had faded my memories of the person I had been before I was Mom and a wife.

There were times when our small Pilgrim groups made posters of the Rollo (Spanish for *Talk*) we had just heard. I used to enjoy drawing back when my hands weren't busy all the time. It made me blush when one of my group members said,

"You draw it, Shirley, you are a good artist."

It surprised me to be so flattered. It was just a little thing, but such sweet encouragements throughout the weekend really strengthened my feelings of self-worth. The whole weekend was truly a retreat into God's loving care that wasn't without a good measure of humor. I recall finding a paraphrased scripture on the inside door of the bathroom stall that read: "Be still and go."

Looking back on that weekend, God's protection of me is so obvious. He showed me things to remind me of His love throughout every moment. I felt as fragile as a flawed piece of blown glass, already breaking within my weakest point, yet all around me were messages that said what I needed to know, *"Rest in Me," "You and Austin are Mine," "I'm God and I'm still in control."*

My Via de Cristo pilgrimage fortified me enough to face my return home. Austin's father had come, after all. Austin's room was left stripped of all the things he called his own except for a green terry bathrobe, one of his Christmas gifts from the past year. I remembered the story of Prodigal Son. A fine robe was among the gifts the father had given him when he returned home. The irony stabbed me like a knife in the heart.

The following Monday I prayed for enough strength to do what God had called me to. I wasn't feeling the strength. I heard from Ridge View High School that day. Someone from the office called to explain that I had to go there in person to formally withdraw Austin.

"You know I can't do this without You, God." I prayed. "Help me to lean into You."

Walking onto the school office, I was afraid to raise my voice much, lest the dam should break. It was so thin I was fairly whispering to the lady who addressed me at the front, "I'm here to withdraw my son, Austin."

"Okay." She smiled cautiously. "What grade?"

"Tenth." I whispered, and blinked back the tears that rose into my eyes.

"You need his home room teacher." She offered. "She's in her classroom."

She pointed down a short hallway, the end of which opened into the Art Room. Austin's art teacher, who was also his home room teacher, was digging around in the bottom of a supply closet when she heard me open the door. She spun around, embarrassed.

"Hello." She called.

I tried to smile, but my lips only made a tight little crack in my face. The sensation of a grapefruit in my throat was the only thing standing between my composure and the river of sorrow that threatened to spill over.

"Make me strong, Lord." I prayed silently.

"I'm Austin's mom." I whispered before realizing God had answered 'No' to my request. I began sob openly. She came toward me, arms outstretched.

"He moved to Florida." I tried valiantly to continue. "He went to live with his father."

"Sh-h, sh-h." She said, leading me over to a chair where I crumpled, giving in to the tears.

"I thought I could do this…" I apologized, "…without falling apart. They said I had to withdraw him in person."

"All right, then." Austin's teacher pulled a chair beside me. "Let me find out what has to be done and I will walk you through it."

I nodded my head and swallowed the grapefruit back in place.

She showed me some of Austin's work while I fought to restrain my emotions. It had been evident early on that the gift of art had been granted to Austin.

Somewhere between signing the necessary papers and driving home, I knew I had to find help. I had three babies, a young teenage daughter and a husband who needed me. I felt useless to them in my present condition. After about a week of broken hearted grieving, I called my family doctor for an appointment. After explaining my circumstances he wrote me a prescription for Prozac. A couple of weeks later my face remembered how to smile. I began to see humor here and there and realized God was working through the medicine. After a month I felt like I could handle my day-to-day responsibilities. After a year I began to wean myself off Prozac, but I am so grateful for the help it brought when I needed it.

He shall redeem their soul from deceit and violence: and precious shall their blood be in his sight.
Psalms 72:14

Chapter Twenty-One

Fall 1998: The following school year, Elisabeth was in ninth grade attending Ridge View High. Jon was living fairly close to the neighborhood. Paul and I bought a couple of retired desks from the School District for three dollars apiece. After scraping decades of old gum off, we washed the little desks with detergent and bleach and tried home-schooling Charlotte and Emily. It was fun watching them learn letters and numbers. An attitude of *I can do this* accompanied their every accomplishment. We were hooked.

We went back to the District Office to buy a little desk for Joseph. He was happy sitting with crayons and such as the girls carved newfound knowledge onto their writing tablets with giant red pencils. As a young girl, I had dreamed of being an elementary school teacher. God was encouraging me by fulfilling yet another desire of my heart. Once again, His timing was perfect. Now, more than ever, I needed something tangible to remind me I could be a capable, successful mother. Austin had been gone a long time now. His absence and disinterest in our family seemed proof of my failure. Wouldn't a good mother have come up with an antidote to his rebellion? These thoughts would have probably consumed me if I hadn't been blessed with the sweet, necessary distractions of the babies. We still called them *the babies*.

Paul worked a lot of overtime to cover our expenses and now we had child support to pay as well. He looked so weary some nights. I so wanted to help him.

Elisabeth was playing and taking violin lessons with the Ridge View High Orchestra. Her grades were still good, and she was playing on the soccer team. She seemed troubled, though – unlike her usual, happy self. Her best friends were exploring risky behaviors, and she didn't feel much in common with them anymore.

When Paul came home from work one night, I dished out his supper and sat down with him while he had country fried steak, rice and gravy, and collard greens with a big glass of sweet iced tea. This was one of his favorite meals with banana pudding for dessert. It was fun to watch this man eat.

"We could sell this house," I said.

Paul dug a hole in his rice under the pool of gravy, opened his mouth, and looked directly at me. He closed his mouth, paused then asked, "What for?"

"We could move to the lake. Elisabeth is the only one whose schooling we'd have to figure out. If Austin comes back, well, we can just cross that bridge if we get to it," I explained.

Paul's heaping spoon disappeared into the cave of his mouth. He chewed and swallowed while cutting a generous chunk of steak.

"What about Elisabeth?" He asked.

"I think she would be okay about it. Bless her heart, she always adapts well to whatever comes up. There must be something we can do to keep her at Ridge View if that's what she wants."

Paul chewed. "Hm-m," He said thoughtfully, "we could save enough money to build a house out there."

"You think?" I asked, surprised that he was readily considering this proposal.

"We could, yes."

"How long would we have to save?"

"I don't know. Maybe a year."

"Really. You aren't messing with me?"

"No, really, is this what you want?"

"Maybe."

So, this was how our move to Winnsboro began. We prayed about it and God kept a spark of pioneer spirit in us. The next step seemed to be to put the house up for sale. If it sold, then that would be a sign. Paul bought a book at the hardware store, *Vacation and Second Homes: 345 Designs*. We turned the pages and dreamed recklessly.

The house wasn't sold yet, but the idea of moving had taken hold. We started packing boxes away in order to enhance the space in our house. We rented a storage space and began filling it up with everything we could live without. After a long Saturday of packing and moving boxes and furniture into the storage, I went to the car to wait for Paul to lock it up. Several minutes later, I wondered why he was taking so long. I got out of the car and walked over to him. He just stood in front of the open storage area watching our furniture.

"What are you doing?" I asked him.

He turned to me. "By the time we pay for a year's worth of storage, we will have almost spent enough money to replace this stuff."

We both turned and looked at the chairs and side tables stacked to the ceiling.

"Do we have another option?" I asked.

"Let me think about it," Paul said.

We drove away with another plateful of food for thought. Monday we contacted a flea market nearby and rented a space. It turned out to be cheaper to put our things there and pay by the month than paying for storage cost. The next few weekends were spent putting price tags on our stuff and haggling with shoppers. The indoor flea market had a little grill where Charlotte, Emily, and Joseph bought corn dogs and Slushies with money they made on their own little flea market goods. Pretty soon, we were regulars and knew the names of the other regulars.

The most interesting thing about this venture was realizing we weren't emotionally attached to very many of our worldly goods. It was kind of exhilarating to slough off most of our belongings and still feel whole. An unexpected liberty replaced the fear of letting go, and I suddenly felt ridiculous for all the years I'd dragged this junk around.

We were sleeping at the lake now but I still showered at the house if I could manage the logistics. I knew I would sincerely miss my shower when the house sold. There was cleaning to do in the house after we moved everything out, so most weekdays, the little ones and I drove there after breakfast. I'd clean while they colored and played, then I'd shower and we'd pick Elisabeth up from school and head back to the lake.

Charlotte and Emily were wonderful tattle-tales for their brother. Being able to count on them to monitor Joseph's every breath was a sure thing. Since they had been *the babies* for two-and-a-half years, the girls loved the responsibility. This dynamic allowed me to steal a quick shower right before driving to Ridge View High for Elisabeth. Just before driving to get Elisabeth, I stepped into my nice, big shower on the afternoon of April 20, 1999. I thought about how much I was going to miss it. There was a contract on the house now, and it was just a short matter of time before the trailer would be our sole residence. I closed the sliding door, remembering how I had picked out the pattern at the glass store myself. I'd have to remember to buy a shower curtain for the trailer tub. I squeezed shampoo into my hand and worked it into my hair. Suds spilled over my forehead and smelled like berries. I wiped the shampoo out of my eyes and heard Joseph come into the bathroom.

"Hey, buddy-roe," I called out with my eyes closed. I had my face raised to the spray of water and soap ran in my eyes.

"Smi-oh, Mommy," I heard him say.

"What?" I answered, hoping he hadn't really asked me to smile.

"SMI-OH, MOMMY."

"No-o. No, Joseph!" I sputtered, my watery eyes blinking frantically. Through the wavy glass door, I could see Joseph holding my camera to his eyes. He faced me in a perfect photographer's stance. "No. You can't take pictures of people in the shower."

"But you weally can, Mommy. I just did."

I rushed through the rest of my shower and dressed hurriedly. Locating the now X-rated camera, I zipped it up in my pocketbook and looked at my watch. I still had about a-half-an-hour before Elisabeth's school let out. The phone rang. It was Paul.

"Don't Cindy and Silbino live in Littleton, Colorado," He asked. They had moved there a couple of years ago. Cindy had been successfully teaching her three sons at home for years now and recently advised me on some curriculum issues.

"Yeah, why?"

"Turn on the T.V.," he said.

"Okay," I said. "I'll call you back later. Love you."

I hung up and walked to the television in the middle of the great room floor. Charlotte, Emily, and Joseph sat in front of it in sleeping bags watching Little Bear. "Mommy's got to turn Little Bear off for a minute," I told them. They watched me change the channel without complaining. What I heard made my heart stop. Two young gunmen in trench coats had walked into Columbine High School in Littleton and opened fire on students and teachers. Thank God Cindy home-schooled her sons, but hadn't she told me Jeremy was taking a couple of college prep courses at a high school nearby? Was the name Columbine familiar? I would definitely be calling her soon. I watched the scene on T.V. in horror for a minute before my imagination took off on a tangent. I wondered how far-reaching this incident might be. Could Austin, Sarah, or Elisabeth be in danger at their respective schools? "We have to go get 'Lisabeth," I announced, more as an answer to my own thoughts than to my party of toddlers. I snatched up three little pairs of shoes and lifted Joseph into my arms. I used the hand I was holding Joseph with to add my pocketbook to the load. Charlotte and Emily followed me out the door that I didn't worry with locking.

Approaching the car line, I wished I had left earlier. It didn't take too long to get in line, but once there I wondered why I hadn't given any thought to being stuck. Panicked parents like me blocked my car from moving as I craned my neck to find my daughter. They had let school out early, no doubt because of the happenings in Colorado.

"Look for Lissy," I said to the children.

"I see Tracy," Charlotte offered, pointing a little finger toward the school entrance. I saw her, too, but Elisabeth wasn't with her. I thought about getting out of the car to find her myself, but I couldn't leave my toddlers in the car, and I might endanger them if I went inside the school.

I looked left and noticed a car driving up the embankment to the street. I would be willing to escape this blockage that way, too, if my teen-age daughter were in the car. The car in front of me moved forward about the same time Elisabeth approached the car.

"Hi, 'Li-bet." Joseph called as I opened the passengers' door for her. She flopped onto the seat, and I assessed the area for an exit. The car in front of me moved just enough for me to get past it and leave.

"Are you okay?" I asked her.

"Yes, ma'am, but all the teachers are freaking out."

"Did they say why?"

"Every one of my classes played CNN."

"Pretty frightening, wasn't it?"

"Yeah, but it was all the way in Colorado. It's not like we're affected by it."

I didn't argue with her innocent statement, although I knew Colorado's present horror would reach far beyond that state.

Elisabeth looked out the window. "I hate school."

I pulled into the driveway of our sub-division and shifted into park. I dashed up the steps and locked the front door without going inside. Back in the car, my racing heart rate began to beat normally as we got closer to the lake. I was happy to be taking my children away from civilization right now. There was nothing civilized about what happened today.

Austin in Pensacola and Sarah in Atlanta were safe and sound, thanks be to God. Cindy's boys were safe, thanks be to God. Columbine was not the school where Jeremy had been taking classes. When I called Cindy in Littleton, she was marveling over how many of her friends from all over the U.S. had checked on her by phone.

Security got a lot stiffer at schools everywhere after that day. Notes received from school addressed parental fears and made assurances that classrooms were being monitored carefully for safety. There were new guidelines about book bags and what was allowed inside them. There were new rules about what school kids were allowed to wear. Anybody wearing a trench coat was now eyed warily. The nation grieved and prayed for the abbreviated families we didn't know in Colorado and guiltily thanked God we weren't them.

The LORD had said to Abram, "Go from your country, your people and your father's household to the land I will show you."
Genesis 12:1

Chapter Twenty-Two

Spring 1999: Our house sold soon after the six of us crammed ourselves into the brown-and-beige, single-wide, circa 1969 trailer. I tried to get used to calling Lake Wateree "The River" like the locals did, but we had said it too long the other way. Living on a body of water, the front is the back and the back is the front. That is, the back doors usually face the road and the front doors face the lake, it's confusing at times. Out here, we had taken to calling the front the 'lake-side," the back the 'road-side.' The novelty of being in a new place occupied us for a while.

Paul drove Elisabeth to Ridge View in the mornings and I picked her up these last few weeks of school. We weren't sure what next year would hold, but we would play it by ear through the summer.

We had some lake neighbors. On one side was a vacation trailer where Raymond and Anne spent a number of weekends. Raymond was a sweet man with a love of laughter. Perhaps that's what initially attracted him to his wife, Anne, a delightful lady who broke into laughter frequently. Anne worked part-time at a funeral home, a perfect job for someone who made people feel good just by being around her. Raymond and Anne had known Paul's step-dad when he owned this property and always asked about him.

Just ahead of Raymond and Anne lived "Bug" and Carol. Bug managed mosquito control on the lake and was a volunteer fireman as well.

On the other side of us were Jerry and Ida. They had bought their house after Jerry retired from Frito-Lay not too long before we moved here. Their four grown children lived in North Carolina and visited often. It was heartening to see how close this family was. If Mr. Jerry needed a repair at his house, his boys immediately availed themselves to assist.

One of their sons had a boy and a girl, Jason and Jenna, about the ages of Charlotte and Emily. I was bringing in some groceries the first time we saw them riding bicycles down their grandparent's long driveway.

"Hey." I smiled at them. They stared back without smiling. Jason did a trick on his handlebars without taking his eyes off me.

"I'm Mrs. Graham." I continued to yammer.

"I have some kids about your age, I think." I smiled bigger.

They skidded under the carport at the end of their drive, set the bikes up on kick stands and stopped staring only after turning to run into the house.

Because they had a school holiday, Jason and Jenna were staying with Jerry and Ida for a few days. It took several more tries at conversation before they finally dropped their guards and said anything. Once the ice was broken and they met Charlotte, Emily and Joseph, there was a lot of visiting between the houses. The children swam in the lake and jumped for hours on the trampoline. Jason invented a trampoline game he called, "Rolly Balls of Doom."

One morning as I was feeding Gabby (our black & white Lhasa Apso), I glanced over at one of the trees. I had to do a double-take. It was completely loaded with soft blossoms. Mr. Jerry and Mrs. Ida were outside enjoying the weather, so I called to them,

"Good morning."

"Mornin'." they answered.

"Do you know what kind of tree this is?"

"That there's a pear tree." Mr. Jerry answered. "We got one over yonder." He pointed to the road side of his yard.

"Is it the fruit-yielding kind?"

"Sure it bears fruit. You won't get nothing but a pear off it, though." Mr. Jerry laughed at his little joke.

"Yes, but is it edible fruit?" I went on carelessly, setting myself up as a dumb city slicker."

"You can eat 'em if you want to."

"…they ain't nothin' but a mess, though." Mrs. Ida added. "I give all ours to th' fella what fixed the pump far us."

"Thanks for the info."

Several weeks later the blossoms had turned to tiny pears that slowly grew. When some of them began to fall to the ground, I gathered them up, added mature-sized ones off the tree and put them into a couple of paper grocery bags. There wasn't much room for anything additional in the trailer but I managed to find a few inches of unused space behind two leather chairs in the tight, little living room.

Two weeks later I remembered about them and thought I had better check on them. They looked pretty good as far as I could tell. Since I had never made anything with pears, I logged-on to the computer to see if pear recipes existed out in cyber-space. Turned out, I had done the right thing by putting them in paper bags for two weeks. Apparently, that's how to complete the ripening process. Another stroke of luck was that I just happened to have all the ingredients for pear/cranberry pies in my humble larder. Smelling those four pies bake made me feel connected to all the pioneer women in history. Why, we were living off the land, for goodness sakes.

Elisabeth still didn't seem herself. High school intimidated her. The greater population of the school was bigger and older than her. Some of Elisabeth's friends had made the transition along with taking new risks, something that didn't interest her at all. She didn't complain about moving to Winnsboro. She liked playing violin in the orchestra but complained about being the youngest player on the soccer team. She was on and off with some of her old friends. Now this Columbine incident was stirred up in the pot of her adolescent worries.

Her birthday was around the corner and I thought about giving her a party. Wateree State Park was exactly a mile from the trailer and Elisabeth loved camping. I asked her if she'd like a camp out birthday party and she jumped at the offer.

She made a short list of friends and we picked a date. Paul stayed the night with them and I brought Charlotte, Emily and Joseph home after the cupcakes and s'mores were eaten. Paul dragged in all the camping gear the next day and told me something he'd been in awe of the whole night,

"Those girls *never slept*. The campers around us complained about them all night."

"Why?" I asked.

"Aw-w, about two in the morning raccoons came out of the woods and sniffed around their tent. They were all hysterical over that."

"Um-m. I think I would have screamed." I said in their defense.

"…all night?" He asked.

"…if I had to go to the bathroom, yes."

"Women." He answered with a good-natured shake of the head. "I'm taking a nap."

The next week I picked Elisabeth up from school crying.

"I HATE that girl." She spat after closing the car door.

"What, honey?" I asked her. "What happened?"

She said the name of a girl whose name didn't ring a bell.

"She's making fun of me because we live in a trailer."

"That's stupid." I replied. "So what if you live in a trailer?"

"Mom. I hate her."

I held off on the value lesson I was thinking about. Right now Elisabeth just needed to vent over being hurt and ridiculed.

When we got home, she went to her room and dropped her book bag. Charlotte and Emily turned on their Abeka video kindergarten and Mrs. Bere's soft Florida accent filled the little trailer. Elisabeth walked into the kitchen where I was washing some potatoes for supper.

"Is there any tea?" She asked me.

"…half-a-pitcher in the refrigerator."

Elisabeth went to the cabinet and pulled out a glass.

"Mom, how long will we have to live here?"

"Your daddy said we could start looking for a builder in about a year."

We looked over at Joseph who was leaping from an armchair to a recliner. At three years old, he genuinely believed that with enough practice, he could teach himself to fly.

"I PIE-ing." He said in mid-air.

Elisabeth laughed in spite of her day. Charlotte held a fat, red pencil in her fist and glared at Joseph.

"I can't hear my teacher." She scolded him. "And, you CAN'T fly."

"I *can* pie." He said defensively.

"Shh-h." Emily added with a mean look.

Elisabeth took a small sip of tea. "I wish *I* could do school at home."

I'd been thinking it, too, but didn't expect to hear Elisabeth say it.

"You do?" I asked her. Surely her pain was talking for her. I wasn't sure I could take on another home school-er.

"I don't know." She answered. "I just wish we hadn't moved."

She had always been such a good sport. I longed for words that would be a comfort to her.

Want to plan something with Tracy this weekend.

"No." She answered, surprising me. "I don't want anybody to come here."

"Elisabeth, even Tracy? She's been here a million times already."

"…even Tracy." She raised her voice. "And I don't want to talk about this *anymore*."

I watched her leave the room but didn't believe for one minute that it wouldn't come up again.

Soon it did come up. Paul and I offered Elisabeth the option of being home schooled and she agreed to try it out. For a few weeks she seemed pretty happy. She was good at the self-discipline home school required and appeared to embrace the solitude and novelty of being her own boss. Into the second month, however she was showing frayed ends and the two of us were seriously getting on each other's nerves. By the third month I wondered which of us would be the first to crack because this arrangement just wasn't working out.

But let all who take refuge in you be glad; let them ever sing for joy. Spread your protection over them that those who love your name may rejoice in you.
Psalm 5:11

Chapter Twenty-Three

Summer 1999 officially arrived with the end of the school year. On his way to work, Paul would drop Elisabeth off at The Summit pool for swim team practice. The dark paneling and small windows in the trailer kitchen always made it feel like night in here. I twisted a plastic stick connected to the blinds and a dusty haze of morning light filtered into the room. Paul had made a pot of coffee before he left and it was still hot. I poured some into a red mug that announced the name of a prescription drug, a promotional gift left at the pharmacy by a drug rep. Paul knew I liked both red, and coffee, so he'd brought it home to me.

Joseph was always the first child up, then Emily. Charlotte was the last to rise, catching as many beauty winks as possible. Joseph perched hungrily on a stool at the small kitchen bar rubbing his sleepy eyes. Like his daddy, the boy loved his meals. I needed a shower this morning and hoped the three little ones would choose something quick for breakfast. I drew close, resting my elbows on the bar across from Joseph and cupped my chin in the heels of my hands.

"Want waffles, my bubby?"

"And thowup." Joseph answered.

I stood, confused. "What? Did you say, 'throw-up'?"

"Thowup. I like thowup on my waff-ohs."

"SYRUP." I translated. "OKAY, *syrup. Good.* Well, we don't have any syrup, but we have honey."

He looked disappointed, but nonetheless accepted my offer, "Oh, *wi-i-ite.*"

I took a frozen waffle brick out of the freezer package and popped it in the toaster. Emily shuffled in and climbed upon the stool beside Joseph.

"Hey, Pretty Face. Will you eat a waffle?"

"Mm-m hm-m, but just plain."

Emily tucked a couple of wild blonde curls behind her ear. "A plain waffle," indeed. It seemed she lived on air.

"How about if I spread some peanut butter on it?"

Emily shook her head vigorously.

"Syrup ... or honey?" I ventured.

"Plain."

Charlotte came into the kitchen yawning. A faded Disney Pocahontas beamed at me from the front of her night shirt.

"G' morning, Glory." I greeted her.

"Do we have my favorite cereal?" She answered.

She and Paul shared a love for *Smart Start*. I raised the box and she smiled. It would be another hour before swim practice was over. Elisabeth had been instructed to walk to the library near the pool and wait inside for me. We need to leave for the library in about forty-five minutes.

"Y'all eat and get dressed, now, while I jump in the shower." I told them while pouring milk over the flakes in Charlotte's bowl.

I showered and dressed, my hair was still wet when the phone rang.

"Hello?"

It was Paul.

"Shirl, everything's going to be okay, but listen." He began. "Jon and Elisabeth are at the hospital, but they are not hurt badly."

"Oh-okay." I answered, feeling panic rise in my chest. "What happened?"

"They were pulling out onto Two-Notch Road near Kentucky Fried Chicken. Somebody ran into them. That's a bad intersection."

"But Elisabeth was supposed to go to the library. What was she doing in Jon's car?"

"He saw her walking and picked her up. They had just dropped Jon's girlfriend, Laura off at work."

"Oh, no. Tell me where they are."

"Richland Memorial. They're in the emergency room, but they're okay, sounds like Elisabeth is pretty banged up. She's waiting for x-rays."

"I'm hanging up."

"Be careful Sweetie and don't forget the insurance card. Do you think you're okay?"

"I'll be okay, I just need to go - now. Love you."

"I love you, too." I heard him saying as I hung up the phone.

Cold droplets of water slid off my hair and clung to my shoulders. I shivered. At least I was clean and we were all dressed. Turning away from the phone, I assessed the situation. Having heard my side of the call, Charlotte, Emily and Joseph were looking right at me for direction.

"Let's go." I said, herding them out the door. "You can put your shoes on in the car."

I snapped Joseph's car seat belt while Charlotte and Emily buckled themselves. Thirty minutes later we found Jon sitting in a plastic chair outside Radiology, crying and apologizing for things beyond his control.

"I'm sorry." Tears made a path down Jonboy's cheeks. "I didn't mean to hurt her beautiful little face. Mom, she'll have a scar and it's my fault."

I hugged him. "She'll be okay, honey, we'll get her plastic surgery if she needs it. Where is she?"

"Back there" Jon pointed to the wall behind him then winced. His knee already had an ugly bruise brewing.

"You're hurt." I gasped. "You need an x-ray, too."

"I'm all right. Just please take care of Elisabeth. They'll let *you* go back with her."

I arranged the little ones on plastic chairs next to Jon.

"Stay with Jon." I told them before hurrying to the door leading to x-ray, "Your daddy is on his way."

They responded with collective silence.

A male tech met me at the door and guided me to a room where Elisabeth awaited her scan.

"She is a pleasant little thing." He smiled, opening a door.

I stepped inside and saw Elisabeth propped up with pillows in a transport bed. A thick, red crack had drawn itself across her forehead and dried blood was caked in her scalp. She was pulling at her hair.

"Don't lift your head." The tech reminded her.

Elisabeth settled back, opening her palm to show me

a fist full of long blonde hairs. Her head had impacted the wind shield, bending the glass with just enough elasticity to give a little before it broke. When her impression receded the glass tightened back up, snatching and slicing off random hairs in the process.

"Why is my hair falling out, Mom?" She asked.

"I don't know, Lizard, honey."

I started to hug her, thought better about it and kissed her cheek instead. She noticed my restraint and offered a disclaimer,

"It doesn't hurt much, Mom. Isn't that strange?"

"Have you had medication?"

An x-ray technician walked in before Elisabeth could answer.

"You must be Mom." The tech smiled. "This is one tough little girl you have here."

"I'm just praying her head is as hard as I have always thought."

"Ha." The tech laughed, going over to Elisabeth. "How are you feeling?"

"It doesn't hurt like I think it should."

"It's the shock. We'll let you have something for pain later. We need to make sure you're awake in case your symptoms suggest a concussion."

"Good." I said, concentrating on my daughter's eyes instead of the bright, distracting gash above them.

"Do you always have to aim for your head?" I asked her only half kidding.

She smiled, knowing I was talking about the two other scars she bore on her head. Both injuries had required stitches. Almost imperceptible now was a thin, vertical line of missing hair in her eyebrow paying tribute to a blow from a baseball bat swung by a Little League team mate. Paul had been with her at the ball field for that bloody scare. I saw it only after the stitches had been stitched and the dust had settled.

The other scar was hiding in her scalp, right under her occipital bone. She had earned that one at age five by falling backwards off a spring horse. I'd been in the Emergency room with her for those stitches. The blood that day had mixed with her light blonde hair and turned it pink. Elisabeth smiled up at me from her pillow, remembering.

"Is my hair pink?" She asked.

I brought her home with 27 stitches and babied her until she was herself again. Derm-abrasion surgery a year later would render her wound almost imperceptible. My best efforts never convinced Jon to get the x-ray he needed that day.

I cut Elisabeth some bangs to conceal the healing of her forehead. The consequences of that accident were small, considering how bad they could have been, and I still thank God for His mercy that day. This was only one time out of many that proved God's hand was resting on my children.

They devoted themselves to the apostles' teaching and to fellowship, to the breaking of bread and to prayer.
Acts 2:42

Chapter Twenty-Four

We had sort of been church shopping since moving to the lake. The drive to Christus Victor from Winnsboro was painfully longer than from Columbia. There were no Lutheran churches in Winnsboro, so we visited Lake Wateree Baptist Church which was the closest church. It didn't seem to fit the first Sunday we tried it, but over the years, we would visit often and come to love the congregation. I guess you could have called us regular visitors. We never missed their Vacation Bible School. VBS had truly become a yearly mission for this small church every summer as members poured their hearts and souls into reaching out to the community with the hands of Christ. In a county of mostly retired people, it was amazing how many children they could find every year.

The next church we visited was in Ridgeway about twenty minutes away. It was a small but beautiful, five-hundred-year-old Episcopal Mission church. We visited regularly for several months. Even though we loved it, it didn't fit our needs. Our four children made up about two-thirds of their non-adult Sunday School population. Since our children were home schooled and looked to church for a community of playmates, these small numbers proved to be too great a drawback.

I was browning a chicken breast in a frying pan for Paul when he got home from Camden Kmart pharmacy one Saturday night. His floating job took him to Kmart pharmacies all over S.C. and the Camden store was one of his favorites. I'd gotten used to hearing the names of some of the pharmacists and pharmacy technicians he worked with there.

Paul kissed me on the cheek as I seasoned his chicken with Cavendar's Greek seasoning and red wine vinegar. He disappeared into our bedroom, emerging a few minutes later wearing a pair of flannel jammie pants. He sat down at the small bar and watched me spread a thin smear of mayonnaise on a slice of sourdough bread. Swiss cheese and tomatoes would finish out Paul's chicken sandwich. It smelled pretty good in our little trailer.

"Want chips?" I asked.

"What kind?"

"Ridged ones."

"Don't we have plain ones?"

"Sorry."

"No thanks." He said. "Hey, I learned something today."

I set down his plate and looked at him.

"Give it up, baby."

As Paul used both hands to wrestle his sandwich off the paper plate he shared a conversation with me he'd had with one of his pharmacy technicians.

"Jackie told me there's a Lutheran Church on Mill Street in Camden. That's only about thirty-five minutes from here."

"Is that all? I thought Camden was more like an hour away." I replied, folding the potato chip bag and putting it away in the 'pantry.' The kitchen was small, but I had managed to find a corner wall and talked Paul into building some wire shelves there. I had fashioned a tacky curtain around it that actually went perfectly with the trailer's 1960's decor. Paul folded his eager lips around the big sandwich and chewed. His preference for thin chips over the ones with ridges was one of the few culinary preferences we didn't share.

"Well," he said, correcting himself and wiping at a blob of mayonnaise off the corner of his mouth, "it's about thirty-five minutes to K-mart from here. Mill Street's about fifteen minutes farther."

"Let's try it."

"What?"

"Let's go. How about tomorrow? Do you know when they hold services?"

"I looked it up in the phone book before I left work. There's a service at 8:15 and one at 11:00."

"That's a no-brainer then. Let's just go to 11:00 worship and try their Sunday School next week if we like it."

"Okay." Paul smiled and I didn't know if it was because I'd said yes or because he was enjoying his sandwich. "Have we got any tea?"

* * *

Sunday morning came and I got dressed before waking the children. My time always seemed to work out better in the mornings that way. We dressed the little sleepy heads and offered them cereal for breakfast. Gosh, they looked cute in their Sunday clothes. Paul made two mugs of coffee (blonde and sweet) and we all climbed into the car. Paul announced,

"We're going to try a Lutheran church in Camden today."

"Why?" Elisabeth asked.

I turned to look at her, thankful her face had healed from the wreck. Newly cut bangs hid the scar on her forehead. She was so pretty. I wished I could make her happier.

"Why not?" Her daddy asked rhetorically.

"Wie not?" Joseph parroted gleefully then laughed heartily at himself.

"Mini-me." Paul said to Joseph and they both laughed.

"Forty-two minutes." Paul beamed and parallel parked in front of St. Timothy's.

It was a medium size church with lots of big trees studded into the grounds. A traditional Lutheran red door adorned the entrance to the sanctuary. Block letters behind the glass of a brick marquis stated the facts, "Saint Timothy's Lutheran Church. Pastor Doctor Garry White."

We, a tight cluster of Grahams, made a path inside and received bulletins from a smiling greeter. Instead of sitting in our usual place up front, Paul and I shepherded the children into the first available pew we saw with enough seats. The familiar liturgy began and I realized how much I had missed it. Paul reached for my hand and folded his warm palm over it. We looked at each other and read each other's minds. By the time Pastor Doctor Garry White was halfway through with his sermon, the Graham family had found a home at St. Timothy's.

In his heart a man plans his course, but the Lord determines his steps.
Proverbs 16:9

Chapter Twenty-Five

Settling in with our new church was like snuggling up in a comfortable old housecoat. St. Timothy's overflowed with hospitality and we immediately felt like part of the family. We got involved in some activities, one of which was the Adult Progressive Dinner St. Tim's presents in December. The way it works is a few families host each course at their homes, starting with hors d'oeuvres, ending with dessert. Small groups of people drive to each home between the courses.

The main course was grilled Italian sausages at the Downey's house. Pastor Garry approached us and introduced us to Dave and Nita Vause, newly married and new members to St. Tim. We were about the same age. With his sandy hair and glasses, Dave reminded me of John Denver with a comic edge. He and Paul found an easy rapport while Nita and I sat on kitchen chairs and spilled our guts to one another starting at the beginning of our lives.

A smart blonde with a warm smile, Nita's posture was impeccably poised. Her straight shoulders reflected a childhood sprinkled with regular reminders from her Georgia mother to sit up straight and mind her manners. It didn't take crystal ball to predict that we would develop a sisterhood. Nita's affliction of getting so tickled she couldn't stop laughing was irresistibly contagious and in the next few months we would develop a lifelong friendship.

In addition to being a newlywed, Nita was also a widow, grieving a husband lost from pancreatic cancer the previous year. It was my good fortune to meet her when she was taking a hiatus from the work force. The grace of this timing allowed us time to get to know each other before she was lured back to the insurance business she knew so well.

Elisabeth's tenth grade home school year had lasted less than a semester. She started with a wonderful attitude but still wasn't much happier. She'd imagined the two of us would have more interaction, but it didn't turn out that way at all. Even though she did well to keep up with her lessons, she seemed miserable and the trailer was too small for even one person to be miserable.

Paul gave up traveling as a floater, got a raise in pay then took a permanent position at the Kmart Pharmacy in Camden. We found out that we could pay out-of-county tuition and enroll Elisabeth at Camden High School, so we did it right away. Paul scheduled his pharmacy hours around taking Elisabeth to school every morning which left me with only the afternoon pick-up. Camden had a soccer team that Elisabeth joined as soon as she could. It wasn't long before she made a number of friends who encouraged her to attend cheerleading try-outs for the following football season. Now Elisabeth was happy. The trailer was tolerable again, but she never invited new friends to visit until the house was built.

The day of cheerleader try-outs, I talked to the little ones as we drove to the school, "Elisabeth will be very sad if she didn't make the team." I explained. "Don't ask her if she made it, we'll just wait for her to say. We'll probably be able to tell if she made it or not before she gets in the car."

"I think she made it." Emily declared.

"Me, too." Charlotte agreed.

I stopped at the light beside Food Lion and Joseph studied the world outside the window. A young man crossed the street diagonally.

"Mommy." Joseph pointed at the man excitedly, "Wook. A hitchhike-ow."

Consternation etched a worry line on Joseph's face as he continued to watch the guy crossing the street.

"No, no, he's a bwue-bowd walkew." Joseph corrected himself but *bluebird walker* didn't seem right to him either. Another pained expression wrote itself across his tender brow.

"No," he shook his head in frustration, betrayed by the inadequacy of his three-year-old vocabulary. "What *is* he Mommy?"

I watched the man nearing the curb with no idea how to help Joseph then Charlotte shouted,

"He means a JAY walker, Mom."

"YES." Joseph agreed, the worry falling off his face. "I think THAT's wight."

We all broke into giggles that lasted until I turned right toward the school.

"Okay." I resumed a sober demeanor. "Remember to be very

gentle with Elisabeth."

"Why do you think she didn't get to be a cheer leader?" Emily asked in a defensive tone.

"I don't, honey, it's just that - she's new at that school. Sometimes they pick people they know. We just have to be ready, in case."

I parked the car, looked at the other moms waiting in cars then set my eyes on the door where Elisabeth would be emerging. Two pretty brown haired girls burst through the double doors squealing with joy, "I can't believe it." One of them exclaimed.

A mom in one of the cars smiled. No doubt one of the girls belonged in that car. I turned to the double doors again and one of them opened a crack. Elisabeth squeezed through the opening with her head down. She looked small and seemed to be wishing herself invisible. I wanted to cry. She walked sadly to the car and I heard myself moan, "Oh, honey."

Elisabeth climbed into the front seat like an elderly little woman, raised her small, sad face before breaking into a toothy grin. She spoke quietly, trying to conceal the joy bubbling up,

"I made it."

"You little bugger." I hugged her tightly as we all squealed over her victory, "Yipeee-e-e.

There be four things which are little upon the earth, but they are exceeding wise: The ants are a people not strong, yet they prepare their meat in the summer; The conies are but a feeble folk, yet make they their houses in the rocks; The locusts have no king, yet go they forth all of them by bands; The spider taketh hold with her hands, and is in kings' palaces.
Proverbs 30:24-28

Chapter Twenty-Six

The summer of 1998 passed without another major accident unless you count the bug on the ceiling in our tent that pooped on Paul and me when we went camping in Cherokee, North Carolina. (Who knew bugs could poop?) I'm pretty sure the bug was bunking with us in an attempt to either stay out of the rain or avoid the creepy caterpillar siege which had come en masse to this very park to become gorgeous butterflies soon. In their pre-butterfly bodies they, too, sought sanction from the unrelenting rain, so it shouldn't have surprised me to find one crawling on my neck during the night, but it did cause me to awaken screaming. Coincidentally, this was the same trip that prompted my vow to never to go camping again.

It seemed that insects were after me that 1998 Summer. In the kid's room, getting Joseph's shoes one morning I was more than just a little bit alarmed to find a furry, brown Wolf Spider between the pockets of a shoe bag I had hung on the wall. He boasted a span of about nine centimeters and I am not exaggerating. There he sat, *just chillin'* next to my innocent children's summer sandals. All my blood drained into my legs and paralyzed me for a second as I tried to decide how to approach this problem.

When I was able to speak, an odd little prayer tumbled out of my mouth, "Dear Lord God, Jesus in Heaven. Have mercy on our mortal souls."

I tiptoe-ran into the kitchen, grabbing a can of Raid from under the sink. Tiptoe-running back, I found the spider continuing his nap. I held the bug spray at a distance and pushed the button. A light mist of poison rose up before the weak sound of air told me the can was empty. The spider, irritated, waved at the small cloud of Raid with a furry arm and went back to meditating.

"What now," I wondered, *"a flyswatter?"*

"A SHOE." I answered myself aloud.

The spider rolled his googley eyes and I swear, he scoffed at me.

"GET ME ONE OF YOUR DADDY'S SHOES." I hollered to anyone in earshot.

Seconds later Charlotte, Emily and Joseph tiptoed toward me. Emily and Joseph each held one of Paul's flip-flops. Charlotte hung at the end of their three-person line, peeking around her siblings. Was she pondering Matthew 20:16: "So the last shall be first and the first last."? From the back of the line, if the need arose to retreat, she'd be the first in line.

"DON'T COME IN HERE."

I reached blindly into the hallway to grab an implement of death. Instead, my fingers closed around the flimsy weapons.

"Thank you, sweeties, but can you bring me a BIG SHOE, like, maybe Daddy's tennis shoe? Can you hurry?"

Charlotte ran to the end of the trailer, empowered by the realization that she could be the one to save the day.

At the sound of her returning footsteps, my open hand shot into the hall to accept the weight of Paul's sneaker. I breathed a short sigh of relief, gripping the shoe in both hands and taking my stance like a nervous batter. Bracing for the hit I noticed the shoe was trembling.

"How many guts would a creature like this spatter?" I wondered.

"Why don't you do it, Mom?" Emily's question broke my concentration.

"Okay, I'm going to." I answered and willed myself to swing the shoe.

When I opened my eyes, I was drawing the shoe away from a spot just beside the hairy arachnid who gave me a look that said, *"You're kidding me."* then, he rolled his eyes. Well, maybe he didn't roll his eyes, but it sure seemed like he did.

I shivered and tried again, this time with one eye open just a little bit. I managed to knock him onto the floor. I screamed, which caused a chain reaction of screaming in my by-standing children.

"MOM, HE'S RIGHT THERE." Charlotte informed me before leading her siblings in another new cacophony of B-movie grade screams.

"It's okay." I lied. "Go get me a cup."

Joseph stopped screeching just long enough to ask, "What for?"

"Just go do it." I answered.

"HURRY." I added, but there was actually no need to hurry as the spider seemed to find our excitement boring enough to yawn and inspect his fingernails there on the floor.

"Here." Emily said alerting me to the red Solo cup she was holding.

"Good." I took it from her and turned it over the wooly mammoth spider, prematurely sighing with relief.

I'd never heard the sound of spider fingernails scraping the walls of a plastic cup before, which brought on yet another wave of hysteria that sent the children running amok. Suddenly, Wolfie and I were alone together. I cringed, imagining him covering his giggling mouth with one of his legs and scratching the cup with all seven of the others.

As I squatted over the spider listening to the disconcerting scraping of his nails, I remembered a can of bug spray in the bathroom. I retrieved it, relieved to find it half full. The biggest spider I had ever seen died that day, but I think it was more from drowning than being poisoned. When his creepy arm waved one last time, the can was empty and the tip of my pointer-finger had a little circled arrow imprinted on it. I shuddered and slid him into a sandwich-size Ziploc (without touching him). We drove him to Ridge View High and showed him to the science teacher who merely pronounced him, "Impressive."

I tried to brighten the trailer up by painting the paneling mauve. It looked horrible. Square footage in the trailer seemed to diminish with every passing day. The old air conditioner gave out in July. We spent a week baking at night, despite wearing only our swim suits. The fans blowing hot wind on us made it feel like we were sleeping in a convection oven. I learned to love a cold shower.

When Paul had enough of our whining, he replaced our dead air conditioner with a really big one. The trailer was gloriously cool now but I was glad we weren't living next-door to Rick the Deck-Boy. Charlene wouldn't appreciate this. Turned out though, Paul was being a practical guy after all. The enormous, new a/c would be the right size for the house we would be building. Hooking it up to the trailer became the first real step in cementing our lake house dream and making the wait a little more tolerable.

With my blessing, Jon moved to Pensacola to get to know his father. He hadn't really been serious about school or work and the change would help him focus.

Paul and I had our feelers out for builders in the area. I set up an interview with a man named Wayne. Wayne and I sat at the picnic table on our deck that sunny day when I shared our building ideas with him. He had reminded me of a smaller Abraham Lincoln. I immediately liked this humble man who was recovering from a gunshot wound to his stomach. He had been handling a gun when it accidentally fired. His near death experience had changed him, he told me.

Paul's pharmacy hours kept him at work until 9:00 p.m. I didn't call him, opting to share the story of Wayne-the-builder when he came home.

"So, you have a good feeling about this guy?" Paul asked at the end of my story.

"I do. I really think you'd like him."

"Then he's the one."

"What? You don't want to meet him?"

"I trust you." Paul's eyes held an earnest love.

"…just like that?"

"Yeah, just like that." Paul answered. "If you say you like him, then I like him. Call him tomorrow and tell him to get started."

> *"I am the true vine, and my Father is the gardener. He cuts off every branch in me that bears no fruit, while every branch that does bear fruit he prunes so that it will be even more fruitful. You are already clean because of the word I have spoken to you. Remain in me and I will remain in you. No branch can bear fruit by itself; it must remain in the vine. Neither can you bear fruit unless you remain in me."*
> John 15:1-4

Chapter Twenty-Seven

Paul and I took our ideas to the architectural planner and soon afterward we owned a big roll of papers with pictures of our home visions. Paul hired a landscaping crew to pull up every pine tree on the lot and leave only hardwoods. He was off work the day they drove the big machines into the yard. It was a delight to watch our little section of the world change. I took advantage of Paul's day off by leaving the house to shop alone. It was always more efficient to shop without the company of my short people. Plus, my short people would much rather tromp around in the yard with Dad than be carted down grocery aisles.

When I returned, Paul and the kids met me at the car smiling sheepishly.

"Did the crew finish?" I asked.

"Yes," he replied, "but I've got to show you something."

"…something good?"

Paul laughed. "I wouldn't call it good, but it looks kind of funny."

I followed him toward the lake where he stopped in front of the pear tree.

"What? I don't see anything."

Paul walked around to the other side of the tree with our towheaded children trailing him.

"Look here."

I gaped at the other side of the pear tree which had been relieved of its branches all the way down to the trunk.

"Holy *Moly*, how'd that happen?"

"The guy driving the equipment just wasn't paying attention when he drove past it. He was real sorry."

"He amputated it. Does it need a tourniquet? Is it going to

die?"

"Probably, but we'll just let it go for now. Maybe it won't."

"Well. I guess we'll have to learn to live without pear pies."

Paul hung his head. "We'll just have to wait and see."

A week later, Wayne brought a crew out to start the foundation. That was exciting. It didn't look like I had expected. Instead of a solid concrete floor, the foundation was raised one wooden stilt at a time. It wasn't long before a small forest of stilts made a neat, square visible out the trailer's windows. It was really happening.

The sight of our stilted foundation kept us happy for a few weeks before we started wondering if that was all they were ever going to do. We made a call or two to Wayne, who assured us that we weren't forgotten. Fall came. Without a pregnancy or a nursing baby, I was back on duty for Christmas shopping now. Thanksgiving turned into Christmas and I thought about stringing Christmas lights from stilt to stilt.

Our Lhasa Apso, Gabby was acting weird. She kept coming home with one work glove. Mr. Jerry blew her cover when he revealed to us that she was stealing gloves around the neighborhood (The family is always the last to know.). The mystery of Gabby's strange glove fixation was solved on New Year's Eve when she crawled under the master bed and birthed three fat puppies. Three more were born right after midnight on New Years' Day.

The puppies proved to be an entertaining distraction, but I tried not to attach to them. I knew they were going to grow into adulthood. No matter how pitifully my children contorted their faces, I just couldn't agree to keep seven dogs. We still had a booth at the Flea Market and that's where we set up the "FREE PUPPIES" sign and before long we were back to being a one dog family.

I discovered the best coping tool for waiting out the house construction in home-focused magazines that I picked up on my grocery trips. Pretty soon I had a stack of magazines towering on my bedside table. I referred to them whenever I needed a shot of hope for the future and they fostered some creative flashes of designing genius.

Bedtime proved the best time to read my magazines, mainly because it was one of the only times I sat down. Paul and I had established a habit of reading together or doing crossword puzzles before going to sleep. He looked over at me from behind his copy of his John Grisham book, nodding toward the magazine I was holding.

"Do you need all of those?"

"Well, *yeah*." I answered, incredulous. "How else am I going to know what we need?"

"*All* of them? I mean, aren't they about four dollars apiece?"

"…a pittance." I answered, holding up my copy of Better Homes and running a finger over the colorful sticky-notes marking favorite pages. I neglected mentioning that some of them cost $6.50, maybe more. Paul retreated to his book. Emily's cat, Kit, breezed into the room and leaped on the bed.

"Where's Charlie?" Paul asked without looking up.

"He's tom-catting, I guess. I haven't seen him either."

Charlie, Charlotte's black-and-white cat sometimes disappeared for a couple of days.

"Hmm-m," Paul sighed, "my dogs are tired."

He shut the paperback and rolled over to turn his light out. A black-and-white book-mark poked out from the pages.

"Better put those dogs up. I'm ready to crash, too." I added, yawned and switched off my light. I pulled up the covers in the pitch-dark and snuggled against his back, threading my arm under his.

"Do you know what this is?" I asked.

"What *what* is."

"…old age." I said. It's creeping up on you."

Paul laughed, "I guess you do have a birthday coming up?"

"Yep, are you going to buy me a new house?"

"I'm working on it."

"Good night, Paul Graham. I love you."

"Good night, Shirley Graham. I love you, too."

"Don't ever leave me."

"I won't."

"And, don't ever die, Paul."

He chuckled. I'll never leave you, and I'll do whatever I can to hang around."

"…promise?"

"I've got a lot of people counting on me. I want to see them grow up."

"You think I'm going to grow up one day?"

"Probably not, Shirl, but that's okay."

Therefore the redeemed of the LORD shall return, and come with singing unto Zion; and everlasting joy shall be upon their head: they shall obtain gladness and joy; and sorrow and mourning shall flee away.
Isaiah 51:11:11

Chapter Twenty-Eight

I awoke late and didn't smell any coffee. Paul must have been running late for work. When I opened my eyes, Joseph's brilliant blue irises peered at me from his sweet baby-face.

"Mommy, I waked up."

"You're a big boy."

"I know." Joseph agreed, stretching a happy smile around his little white teeth. "Is daddy he-ow?"

"…no, buddy, he'll be home after lunchtime, though."

"Fits me wunch - now, Mommy."

"It will still be morning whether I fix breakfast or lunch, bubby. You got to play with your daddy yesterday, didn't you?"

Joseph nodded.

"Did you and your daddy work outside?"

I watched Joseph smile as his little head bobbed up and down. "Daddy's gunna make me a *tood*."

"Joseph." I sat up. "Don't say that."

"Why I not say, tood?"

"I don't know, I mean, I think you mean something else, but don't say that again until I figure out what it is."

Joseph looked sad. I changed the subject.

"Do you want some French toast?"

He nodded vigorously. Still sporting my night shirt, I soaked three pieces of bread in a milk-and-egg mixture. By the time the toast was cooked, all three children were up and ready for breakfast. I took advantage of this quiet moment to call Paul. He answered after several rings.

"Thank you for calling K Mart pharmacy."

"Hey, Paul, Joseph just told me that you were making

him a tood. "A tood," that's what he said. Please tell me what that means."

I could tell his hand was covering the mouthpiece, but heard him laughing anyway.

"I don't know." He lied.

"You must know. What IS A TOOD?"

"Okay." He relented. "Joseph's been asking me to make him one for a couple of days and I didn't have a clue, but I finally figured it out yesterday. He was trying to say, "sword.""

"Oh-h, a sword, the boy wants a *sword*. Next time you have these manly conversations you might want to bring me into the loop."

"You're right. I meant to, but it's funnier when you get to guess, too."

"Good point. I am relieved, though."

"I bet."

The phone rang again right after I put it in the cradle.

"Hey, Mom." Jon's voice was coming from Pensacola.

"Hey, hon, did you find a job?"

"Yes, ma'am, my dad helped me get a job as a transporter at West Florida Hospital."

"That's great. What does it entail, son?"

"I transport patients to x-ray or wherever they have tests."

"Do you like it?"

"I start next week, but yeah. I think I will like it, Mom."

I was glad he and his father were developing a close relationship. I hesitated before I asked,

"How's your brother? Does he seem all right?"

"Yes, I mean, you know, he's Austin. You should see how he and Uncle Mark get into it, though."

"…really? …how?"

"You'd think they hated each other."

"I guess they are a lot alike, really."

"Well. I'm not going to tell either one of them that."

I laughed.

"Do you need anything?"

"No, ma'am, I'm okay. I just wanted to say, "Hey" and tell you about my job."

"I'm happy for you, Jonboy. I miss you, but I think you are doing something you have to do."

"Yes, ma'am."

When I set the phone in the cradle and started picking up the children's plates I noticed that something smelled. It's probably a potato rotting on the row of shelves that I optimistically called a pantry. I walked down the hall toward the bathroom that doubled as a laundry room. Every room in the trailer had at least two functions. The smell intensified, maybe there was something rotting in there. I opened the lid of the washer and found it empty. I sniffed. It definitely stunk in there, but I could tell it wasn't the source.

"Mommy?"

I looked around and saw Charlotte.

"What's that gross smell?"

"I don't know. I'm trying to find it now."

"Our bedroom stinks."

"It does?" I walked out of the bathroom and into the bedroom where Charlotte, Emily and Joseph slept in a bunk bed. It had a single mattress on the top for Joseph and a double on the bottom for the twins. We knew this living arrangement was going to be a tight squeeze for everyone, but we'd be out of here in a year, right? The year was up months ago.

"Oh, man." I almost gagged from the odor. "How did y'all sleep in here?"

"It wasn't as bad last night." Emily said.

"Get dressed. It can't be healthy for you to be in here."

I scurried down the hall holding my breath. When I made it to the kitchen, I sucked in a lung full of new air. I had a bad feeling about this smell, but kept it to myself.

Two days later the odor was too terrible to stay inside. The children and I stayed gone all day and followed Paul home after the pharmacy closed. He changed into a pair of old jeans and a T-shirt and carried a flashlight outside. Scared of nothing, Paul crawled under the dank, dark trailer on his belly. A few feet away, the kids and I covered our noses from the stench.

"It looks like a cat,"

We took another step closer to each other.

"…and it looks like Charlie."

Paul backed out from under the trailer dragging a stiff Charlie. Even in the dark I could see big flat bugs scattering away from the little corpse. Charlotte ran inside and Emily's eyes filled with tears before following Charlotte; Joseph was close behind.

Paul dug a hole that night and we gave Charlie a loving burial. The children brought little chairs to Charlie's grave site in the following days. It became a prayer garden where they meditated and grieved at some point nearly every day.

As iron sharpens iron, so a man sharpens the countenance of his friend.
Proverbs 27:17

Chapter Twenty-Nine

Summer 1999 was filled with losses and gains, sometimes tied up together in the same package. Charlie's wasn't the only funeral we had to deal with when we lived in the trailer. The same week that Elisabeth was off at cheerleader camp, Paul, Charlotte, Emily, Joseph and I went to Jacksonville, FL to attend Aunt Jessie's funeral. My sweet aunt had been released from the crippling neck pain that had debilitated her for several years. Even as we celebrated her life and entrance into Heaven, it was painful to say goodbye to this giggling little woman who wore pink every day. In her honor that day, a number of us chose to wear pink over the traditional black. My brother, Dale and I both remembered Aunt Jessie with our eulogies and I sang *Precious Lord, Take My Hand.* My Uncle Charlie's face, wet with tears and the mournful cries of my Aunt Evelyn Ruth set the tone as we remembered her life.

Aunt Jessie and Daddy were born so close together they were in the same grade in school. Frequently, they were mistaken for twins. As a consequence, they were also good friends. My sister, two brothers and I had made the trip to Jacksonville, partly to stand in the gap for Daddy and Mother who would have been there if they could have. Parkinson's disease had robbed Daddy's physical abilities to the point that he could barely walk much less drive.

Despite the loss that had brought our family to Jacksonville, visiting with so many aunts, uncles and cousins made the trip feel like a reunion. After leaving the mausoleum where Aunt Jessie's cremains had been interred, we met again at a restaurant before heading out of town and spent an hour or so, moving around, visiting each table so as not to miss anyone.

At one point, Jeanne sat across from Uncle Charlie and Aunt Sadie.

"How's John doing?" Uncle Charlie asked in his characteristic nasal voice. The nasality is dear to me. It's a Peek trait that each of us possess to some degree. Uncle Charlie's candor was so refreshing to me. He was as public about his feelings as my

Daddy was private about his.

"Ophie told me that you and Dale were going to take him to the V.A. hospital for some tests." Aunt Sadie added.

"We did." Jeanne informed them, "I think I will need Dale to help me tell this story, though."

She called Dale over from the table where he was entertaining our *Yankee cousins* from Illinois.

"Dale, sit here by me and let's tell about Daddy's evaluations."

Dale chuckled and slid in beside Jeanne. "I think we can rest assured that Daddy's wit is still intact."

"See," Jeanne started, "Daddy had to answer a list of questions for the doctor. Some of the questions were the same, just worded differently. Some of his answers were supposed to indicate whether or not he was depressed. You know how dry-witted he is? Well, he got tired of answering the same questions and decided to have a little fun with the doctor."

Dale giggled in a high-pitch, like a little boy. "The doctor kept asking him, in differing ways, if he ever thought about death or killing himself. He was answering it for about the fifth time ..."

Dale started laughing too hard to continue so Jeanne finished, "The doctor said, "Mister Peek, do you ever have thoughts of suicide?"

"Daddy dead-panned, "Yes. Yes, I do"

Now, for the first time the doctor looked him in the eye and Daddy stared right back.

He said, "Mister Peek, can you talk about that a little bit?"

Daddy said, "I do have thoughts of suicide," He let his answer hang in the air for a couple of seconds then he added, "Not for myself, but for some other people."

The table exploded in laughter and Jeanne and Dale had to re-tell the story a few more times before everybody got to hear it.

Much too soon, the crowd of extended family began to disperse. Big hugs were exchanged along with email addresses and promises to get together soon. It was a good summer for traveling. Leaving Jacksonville, we took the long way home in order to stop in Pensacola for a couple of days to see Jon and Austin.

Paul and I also took the three little ones to Carowinds Theme Park on the border of the two Carolinas that summer. I remember vividly because I learned a hard lesson: *Grown people are prone to motion sickness from the Teacup Ride that makes a backward circle.* Yeah. I'll never do that again.

Upon our return home I checked my email and found an email invitation from my cousin, Kenny to participate in an ongoing email chat invented by daddy's baby sister, my Aunt Helen Marie. The chat included my cousins, Joyce, Charlene, Kenny, Bonnie, Hollie and an occasional cameo appearance by Uncle Charlie. WORDS, as it was called, hailed from Illinois, Pennsylvania, Georgia, and now South Carolina. This ingenious plan Aunt Helen Marie had come up with was sort of like an exclusive chat room open twenty-four hours a day, so no pressure; i.e., it's not necessary for everyone to be on the computer at the same time to be part of the conversation. All our email addresses were listed in the address bar, so instead of answering with the *reply* button, we hit *reply all.* Over a few weeks my cousins became as dear to me as my best friends. Most of us managed to check in with WORDS at least every few days, which allowed glimpses into each other's daily joys and struggles.

Mr. Branham's irregular habit of sending crews out to Winnsboro was finally resulting in a house that was almost finished and we were crawling impatiently toward completion. The trailer seemed to lose square footage every day. Every night when I bathed the children, the floor felt a little more like it was caving in. If we stayed much longer, the bathtub would surely drop to the ground with my babies in it. The "year" we planned to dwell there would soon be two years.

As old and little as the trailer was, I was thankful that it didn't deter company. Silbino and Cindy with two of their three handsome boys, Tony and Teddy, came down from Colorado to visit Cindy's parents in the fall. As a lovely consequence, they drove to the lake and spent a wonderful day with us, too. It was a beautiful day for laughing and talking. Cindy walked through the yard with the children and me, pointing out tomatillo plants that grew wild and solving the mystery of what those little green tomato-looking things were. She also showed me how to find fresh dill to season and garnish my culinary creations. I remember saying, "You mean spices grow right in my back yard?"

"Dill is used as a spice," Cindy reminded me without looking at me like I was crazy, "but it's a weed. You know? 'Dill: *WEED*?'"

She certainly made a good point. We grilled chicken breasts

outside with fresh dill and grieved when we had to wave goodbye. Colorado was a long way away and another visit soon was not likely.

"Hurry back, watch for deer." We chanted as their van backed out of the lot.

"Watch fow dee-oh" Joseph agreed, not really understanding why. The sun glinted off his white-blonde hair making it sparkle like diamonds. Paul laid his hand on Joseph's little shoulder draped with the white super-guy cape I had made him. I'd finally given up trying to convince the little fellow humans couldn't fly. He was so sure he'd learn if only he practiced hard enough.

"Next time we'll visit you in your new house." Cindy sang out the passing car window.

We walked inside sensing the flotsam of their absence as well as their lingering warmth. The trailer felt momentarily cavernous with just the six of us and we wandered around looking for something to do. The collective mood was somber as we wished that our friends lived closer.

When the insurance company paid for the injuries Elisabeth sustained in the accident she'd had with Jon, Paul took her car shopping. She was still on sabbatical from having friends over but nonetheless happy to be at Camden High and working part-time at Domino's Pizza. Cheerleader practice kept her busy through the summer, navigating the country roads back and forth to Camden in her new red car.

The red Pontiac Sunfire Elisabeth chose for herself seemed an indulgent first car for a sixteen-year-old, but Paul and I had talked about it a lot beforehand. Truly, she had suffered with injuries and rarely had she complained. We agreed that her situation was unique, in that she lived so far from her school. We also agreed that she was trustworthy and we both felt like she had a real appreciation for the blessings in her life. Elisabeth had always had a strong work ethic and a value system deeply rooted in what was right. She was a lot more responsible than I remembered being at her age. Still and yet, I couldn't watch her drive away without sending a prayer for safety down the road along beside her.

And as Moses lifted up the serpent in the wilderness, even so must the Son of man be lifted up: That whosoever believeth in him should not perish, but have eternal life. For God so loved the world that He gave His only begotten Son, that whosoever believeth in him should not perish, but have everlasting life. For God sent not his son into the world to condemn the world; but that the world through him might be saved. He that believeth on him is not condemned: but he that believeth not is condemned already, because he hath not believed in the name of the only begotten Son of God.
John 3:14-18

Chapter Thirty

Before we knew it, the summer heat had stepped aside, making room for the crisp nights of Fall and Winter, 1999. Charlotte and Emily started first grade and we found a home school support group in Camden. This was something pretty exciting because it brought us into weekly communion with other home-school families. Charlotte and Emily were drawn instantly to a pretty little brown-haired girl named Lauren. Their friendship soon resulted in sleep-over's. The sleep-over's resulted in getting to know Lauren's family, which became a special blessing to all of us.

Lauren's parents, Barry and Angie, were raising two girls, Lauren and Lindsay. Angie was also pregnant with their third daughter, Leah. Angie led American Girls Club, one of the home-school clubs offered by our support group, based on the American Girls dolls and the rich American history that came with them.

The first time I saw Angie was at a home-school mom's dinner at San Jose Mexican Restaurant. I couldn't believe how beautiful she was. It didn't take long to find out that her beauty was rooted inside the Christ-like love that lived in her heart. Even heavy with a child, Angie was petite. Her long, blonde hair danced around her pretty face and her smile was genuine. I wanted to know her better, despite the fact that I felt like a toad beside her.

I met her husband, Barry later when the home-school kids gathered in a room of Camden First Baptist Church for standardized testing. He had been asked to pray for the children who were testing. Charlotte and Emily were already seated in desks and I stood holding Joseph's little hand on the opposite side of the big room from Barry. As parents and younger siblings encircled the test-ready children, we all bowed and Barry began his prayer. What he did in the next moment convicted me for the rest of my life.

"Lord?" Barry's voice was strong but humble. "I just love you so much."

I remember opening my eyes and looking at this man. I couldn't recall ever hearing anyone tell Our Creator they just flat-out loved Him. What's more, I wondered how I got into my forties without starting my every prayer with those words. What if my own children had never said they loved me? I knew it would break my heart. I was immediately persuaded by Barry's shameless love to change my prayer life. It was as though God had lifted a veil and gently shown me direction.

Barry's simple confession of love to Our Father so impacted my heart, I didn't hear the rest of his prayer. I was concentrating on my own silent prayer,

"Heavenly Father, I love you, too. Thank you for allowing me to hear Your servant, Barry's dear prayer. It opens my eyes to how I have neglected You. I love You, Lord, I love You so much."

Winter came alongside a growing longing to move into the house that looked pretty complete from the outside. Paul and I had picked white siding and dark green shutters. The color sample read *Charleston Green*, and it was so dark it looked black. The deck that faced the lake was finished, except for the railing, but that didn't stop us from climbing a ladder to walk through the inside when Paul was home. We would wander happily around up there, imagining where the walls would be and what modifications were necessary.

Most mornings, Elisabeth would leave for school about the same time Paul left for work. When they were gone, I would start waking the children for school. The first lesson of the day was Bible study. Joseph wasn't in school yet, but he was allowed to watch the Bible lesson with his sisters while having breakfast.

When Joseph came into the World, he was already focused on being big. He was a diligent observer who imitated what he studied with fierce confidence. His spirituality was awakening and he started asking deep questions. Tired of being excluded from Communion at Church, he wanted to know what he had to do to participate. I promised to ask Pastor Garry if he could take his Communion Instructions early, which he eventually did.

One morning as they ended a Bible class on videotape, Joseph brought me his paper plate garnished with cheese toast crusts.

I took it and turned the plate over so the crusts would fall in the disposal.

"Thank you, Moncchichi."

"Mommy," he said quietly, "I want to ask Jesus to come in my heart."

I stopped what I was doing and knelt, looking into his beautiful eyes. Charlotte and Emily's Math teacher explained a number line from the T.V.

"Let's go to your room."

I let him lead me down the hall and we sat alone in the room he shared with his twin sisters. Of course he was young, but surely I was not in authority to say he was too young for God to lay this burden on his heart. This was God's business.

I didn't want to get the Sinner's Prayer wrong, so I employed an "A-B-C" method I'd learned in the Baptist church to guide us through his prayer.

A: Admit that we sin and can't save ourselves.
B: Believe Jesus died on the Cross to save us from our sin.
C: Confess that Jesus is the Son of God.

"Joseph?" I began, "Pray and tell God you know that you sin."

Joseph closed his eyes and said the words,

"I sin. I'm sorry to do wrong things."

It seemed that his lisp and trouble with the letter "R" wasn't as pronounced as usual.

"That's right, Sweetie. Now, tell Him you know Jesus died to save you from the punishment of sin."

"He did."

"That's right, but tell *God* that you know."

"God, I know Jesus died to help me. ...On the Cross."

"Now you say out loud that Jesus is Lord."

"Jesus *is* Lord."

"Okay, Joseph. Watch Jesus work in your life now. There is no telling how He is going to use you, but you can be sure He will use you for something good."

"Are you sure?"

"I believe it with all of my heart. We will live with Him in Heaven one day."

Joseph looked thoughtful then smiled. "Thank you, Mommy."

"I am so proud of you, Joseph. God has some important work for you."

"What is it?"

"We don't know yet. He will reveal it to you just a little bit at a time. All you have to do is trust and obey Him." I kissed his smooth cheek and hugged him close to me. How I loved this little man, and how I loved God for knowing we needed him in our family.

"Mommy?"

"Mm-m hm-m?"

"I like it when you call me, "Puddin'.""

"Thank you, Puddin'.

"I don't want Charlotte and Emily to say, "Puddin'" to me, but you can."

"I am honored, sweet boy."

Hear my prayer, LORD;
let my cry for help come to you.
Do not hide your face from me
when I am in distress.
Turn your ear to me;
when I call, answer me quickly.
Psalm 102

Chapter Thirty-One

Spring 2000 brought Austin and Sarah's graduations which were on the same day, in two different states. Our friend, Phyllis, one of the pharmacy techs Paul worked with at Kmart stayed with the children at the trailer. Meanwhile, Paul attended Sarah's graduation in Atlanta and I drove my parents and Jon to Pensacola to attend Austin's graduation at the Civic Center. Only God could have given me the strength to endure this weekend.

En route, Daddy repetitiously gave me directions and Mother was a wreck long before we had the flat tire in Evergreen, AL. Daddy took the lead in trying to unscrew lug nuts that seemed welded to the wheel. An Alabama highway patrolman happened upon us and stopped long enough to chew Jon out for letting his grandfather change the tire. Jon would have never disrespected his Papaw. Daddy was used to being in charge and Jon was only being respectful.

The patrolman used a tool from his car to loosen the lug nuts and left Jon to finish the job. Hot wind blew on us from the cars whizzing past as Jon got the tire changed. Just before arriving in Pensacola I called my dear friend, Hilda for advice on where to find a real tire.

We made it to Austin's graduation a little early despite all the difficulty and I found a place for my kin and me amidst my ex-husband and in-laws. We sat in the arena awaiting the pomp and circumstance that would bring about a new chapter in Austin's life and I noticed Jon humming. What a blessing to have him by my side. I closed my eyes and let my thoughts drift back to a day when Austin was in Kindergarten and told me he would be the graduating class of 2000. This day seemed so far away back then; I could have never imagined all the things that would bring us to this moment.

I chuckled and Jon stopped humming. "What's so funny, Mom?"

"I just figured out what you were humming. …how very appropriate."

Jon smiled, not having consciously picked out just the right song to hum. As he resumed the melody I closed my eyes again and reviewed the words in my mind while we waited.

Love you forever and forever
Love you with all my heart,
Love you whenever we're together,
Love you when we're apart...

Driving home the following day, I cried all the way to Alabama, pulling myself together to buy Paul a lottery ticket at the state line. I loved my parents but Mother didn't understand what I was going through and Daddy was slipping so much that he couldn't help me anymore. It seemed that my nerves were hanging outside my skin like broken electrical live-wires. After I dropped all my passengers off, I called Paul.

"I just wanted to hear your voice." I told him.

"Was it terrible?"

"Is hell terrible?"

"I'm sorry, Sweetie, but I'm here. I'm here, Baby, and you're almost home."

> *Just as a body, though one, has many parts, but all its many parts form one body, so it is with Christ. For we were all baptized by one Spirit so as to form one body whether Jews or Gentiles, slave or free – and we were all give the one Spirit to drink. Even so, the body is not made up of one part but of many.*
> *Corinthians 12:12-14*

Chapter Thirty-Two

On the heels of Wateree Baptist's Vacation Bible School 2000, the finishing touches were being put on our new lake house. As fast as we could, we emptied the trailer and moved our things inside. Paul made arrangements to have our trailer moved off the property. He was home from work the day it was removed. Giddily, we watched a giant truck haul the empty shell we had lived in for two years down Dutchman Lane. Emily was doing her *Crazy-leg Dance,* and Joseph twirled in circles. Elisabeth waved.

"Chah-chah?" Paul's voice distracted me from the trailer's departure and I looked away from it to see my little girl leaning against her daddy. Tears streamed down Charlotte's cheeks.

"You're crying?" I asked in disbelief.

"Well," Charlotte slid the back of her hand across her cheek, "it was our house."

"Do you want me to tell them to bring it back?" Paul asked in jest.

Charlotte smiled shyly. "No-o-o."

The sun bore down as the month of July continued to fill up. Charlotte and Emily's birthday was on the 20th and we began to plan a tea party. After sending out the invitations we left town, all packed to meet Jeanne and Scott's. Our families were meeting at Christian Family Living Retreat Center in Topsail Island, NC, for a weekend retreat hosted and sponsored by the priestly order of Marianists.

Paul and I drove the younger children up to the beautiful beach front and a day later Sarah and Elisabeth joined us. Unfortunately, timing of the vacation proved inconvenient for Jon and Austin. We missed them and wished they were with us the whole week. It was more fun and more meaningful than we could have imagined.

We loved being with Jeanne and Scott's family and getting to know several other families with kids of all ages. The week was filled with many planned events. Each camper was also assigned a cubby-hole and a secret pal. All week, we were to tuck little gifts into the cubby of our respective secret pal, things like funny gifts, notes of encouragement and cheerful messages.

Two families at a time were responsible for the meal preparation, which gave us all another chance to get to know each other. In addition, there were nightly games of board games for the kids and party games for the adults. One of the adult games I recall playing was Two Truths and a Lie. Another night we shared the unique stories of how we had fallen in love with our spouses.

At the week's end, each couple would have an opportunity to renew marriage vows. A final closing ceremony would include a crazy talent show, and the secret pals were to be revealed to all.

There was plenty of time for families to enjoy the gorgeous beach alone or play together on the sandy grounds. Now and again, some of the adults and older kids pulled together an impromptu game of volleyball. Even as I write this, I long to take another vacation to CFL.

Still, no vacation is ever perfect and conflict appeared about mid-week. Every day the families gathered together in the Chapel for a Homily and Holy Communion. As the only non-Catholic family in attendance, we respected the Catholic tradition that excluded us from sharing the Sacrament of the Communion meal, but it began to annoy Paul. That's what I thought, that he was merely annoyed, but I began to realize that he was both disturbed about this practice of exclusion and deeply longed for some resolution. I didn't know just how troubled he was until we met with Father Ted at Paul's request.

CFL Retreat Center is built like a two-story motel. By merely stepping outside one's door onto the balcony, its U-shape allows each unit a fabulous view of the ocean. It was on a low-traffic area of our balcony that Father Ted intimated to Paul the Church's stand on trans-substantiation and consubstantiation. As Paul and I talked with Father Ted, I was alarmed to see tears of frustration brimming in Paul's eyes. Father Ted must have been surprised as well because he suddenly seemed out of his element and suggested that we continue our conversation in private with some of the other on-grounds clergy.

Several minutes later, Father Ted had assembled the whole

Marianist group into the same room where the adults usually played party games. There, Paul poured out his pain. I was moved to hear the earnest longing of my beautiful man's heart. His contention was that the *whole* family of believers in Christ should share in the Sacrament. He didn't find any logic or compassion in closed Communion. He understood the doctrine, but with the passion of Martin Luther, he believed it to be in error.

When he finished, we looked around at the faces in the circle where we sat and discovered that Paul wasn't the only one who was moved. It was quiet, then one by one the priests, brothers and nuns around us began to share their thoughts about closed Communion. We were surprised to find that so many of them shared our feelings. One of the brothers explained to us that the American Catholic Church receives protocol directly from the Vatican, although many priests in the United States would prefer open Communion. Before our little conference ended, we were assured that most priests wouldn't refuse Communion to anyone who presented himself to the Altar to receive bread and wine. Paul and I didn't wish to break any rules, however and agreed that we would exclude ourselves from taking The Host. It was enough to have been heard by this loving company of clergy who cared.

For he will command his angels concerning you to guard you in all your ways. On their hands they will bear you up lest you strike your foot against a stone. You will tread on the lion and the adder, the young lion and the serpent you will trample underfoot.
Psalm 91:11-14

Chapter Thirty-Three

July 2000: What fun it was to take the two flights of steps that led to the front door of our new house. Paul walked behind me,

"My dogs are tired."

We trudged up to the deck and I opened the door.

"Enter, Counselor. Thy bed awaiteth thee."

Paul stumbled in. "A pox upon me, m'lady. My legs have become as those of an elephant."

I laughed and we drug our suitcases into the new bedroom. Paul set his in the big walk-in closet before turning back to survey our room.

"I want to get bedroom furniture for this room, but I know we can't do it this paycheck."

"Be patient, darlin'. We can fill this house up one thing at a time."

"I know, but I am impatient. Man, my legs are heavy. I must have hurt myself playing volleyball this week."

Our family slept soundly that night. We were tired but felt blessed by the blessing of being together in the newness of our new house. I was the first one awake the next morning. I started some coffee and heard Paul call me.

"Hey, Shirl."

I went back in our room. Paul was still lying in bed, on his back.

"Look at my leg."

The closer I got to him, the wider my mouth dropped open. His knee was bright red with red streaks radiating from it.

"What the hay?" I asked. "Streaks are not good."

"No, they aren't. How am I going to work like this?"

"You're NOT." I answered, alarmed that he would even consider doing anything before seeing a doctor.

We had been seeing doctors in a Camden practice, a husband and wife. Mrs. Dr. Gill was wonderful with our shy youngsters and Paul had developed a comfortable rapport with Mr. Dr. Gill. I left Elisabeth with the children and drove Paul to see him.

Paul wore shorts because, frankly, long pants wouldn't fit over his swollen calf. He limped into the office and we were quickly ushered into a room. When Dr. Gilstrap entered Paul's room he made little effort to cloak the shock on his face.

"THAT looks infected."

Paul joked, "Do you reckon, Doc?"

"You've got to go to the hospital." Dr. Gilstrap came closer and examined the redness. "Where is the wound?"

"I think there's a little opening right there by my kneecap." Paul rubbed the place with his thumb. "Hard to see, the swelling has mostly obscured it."

"When did it happen?"

"I'm not sure. It couldn't have been much more than a superficial cut. Maybe I fell on a seashell or something when I was playing volleyball. We just got in from the beach last night."

"So you've been on vacation?"

"Yeah …in North Carolina."

"Is this the best ploy you could come up with to keep from going back to work?"

Paul chuckled.

"Let your wife drive you over to Kershaw County hospital. I'll make a call and do the paperwork needed to get you in a room. You're going to need some I.V. antibiotics. I'll be by tonight to check on you."

"Thanks, doc." Paul hobbled off the examining table and we headed to the hospital just a few blocks away.

No time was wasted getting Paul into a room with an I.V. dripping antibiotics into him. I left him there just long enough to drive home and pack his bag. Leaving Elisabeth in charge of her young siblings again, I drove back to Kershaw Hospital in Camden.

Paul was propped up in bed when I pushed his door open.

"Greetings, dahling. Look at what I've brought you."

I raised the crossword puzzle from Sunday's newspaper and Paul smiled.

"Nice. I thought about that right after you left."

"Why, you know we've always been tele-psychotic, Sugar."

"Is that what we are?"

"Well, yeah."

I handed him the crossword and stepped out of my flip-flops. Before I could crawl under the sheet and assume our crossword puzzle position, he was already spelling *ominous* into the little boxes. I scanned the *DOWN* list.

"Seven down is *sated*. Did anything exciting happen after I left?"

Paul wrote *sated* in the blocks and answered me simultaneously.

"I gave some blood to the vampire-guy from phlebotomy. Dr. Gilstrap stopped in and told me it's an official staph infection, but I kind of figured it was."

"At least it's not Flesh-Eating Bacteria. Your thumb's in my way."

Paul wrote *nebulous* before repositioning his fingers.

"Actually, Flesh-Eating Bacteria is a staph infection gone wild."

"Serious?"

"It can be."

"How do you know all this stuff?"

Paul chuckled modestly while filling in another word.

"I must have read it somewhere."

I stayed as long as I thought it was reasonable to be away from the children then drove back home to the Boonies. I wanted to call Paul when I got home and say I was home safely like I used to make him do when we were dating, but I didn't want to risk waking him.

I woke to Tuesday. There was shopping to do and I wanted to see a watermelon the children said was in their daddy's garden. Slipping into my flip-flops, I felt thankful we lived in the country where I could check the garden in my pajamas. I walked into the yard, making a conscious lookout for snakes. Paul could spot one a mile away, but the camouflage God had painted on snakes could fool me easily. I stepped gingerly past the rows of eggplant, tomatoes, cucumbers, squash, Crowder peas and peppers, gasping when I beheld an enormous watermelon sprawled out on the edge of Paul's garden. Immediately, I remembered the cover of a *Good Housekeeping* magazine with a watermelon carved like a basket. I sent up a thank-you prayer for this garden gift from God's bounty. It had grown just in time to become a perfect tea party centerpiece on Saturday. Since I was already praying, I reminded God that it would be nice to have Paul home for the party.

    God, in His wisdom, didn't grant me a *yes* to that prayer. Paul stayed in the hospital all that week and I became solely responsible for the whole tea party. I was able to pull it off with the help of Elisabeth and Joseph who dressed as proper waiters in black pants and white shirts and poured lots of tea. Elisabeth was my right arm that week, filling in as a mini-mom while the Windstar and I made several trips between Winnsboro and Camden. The busy-ness didn't stop me from worrying about Paul through the tasks. A fifth antibiotic was administered before his infection began to respond. I wouldn't even entertain thoughts of what would have been the next treatment if the antibiotics failed. It could have been amputation.

The Lord will rescue me from evil attack and will bring me safely to His Heavenly Kingdom. To Him be the glory forever and ever. Amen.
2 Timothy 4:18

Chapter Thirty-Four

It was Fall and the 2001 school year had cranked up. Paul and I had settled on using the Bob Jones satellite home school curriculum. A satellite system had been installed and Paul was responsible for videotaping the classes for K-5 and Third Grades. Joseph was so proud to be starting school. Our friends, Barry and Angie were also trying this system out for their home school kids. We had already talked about the possibility of letting the girls share a school day together from time to time.

Paul turned fifty-one on August 8th, bringing September 16, Elisabeth's sixteenth birthday just around the corner. She had settled in so easily at Camden High School. Her grades were good, she had friends and played soccer in addition to being on the cheerleading squad. I thought it was high time she started having friends over again. A surprise birthday party would be a great way to have all her friends over at once.

Occasionally, we'd hear strains of music from Karaoke Charlie under the pavilion at the Wateree Bait Shop across the lake. I loved to do karaoke but Paul never had given it a shot until this one night. Under the shelter with four of our children rollicking around eating hot dogs, Paul said, "You always sing the song, *Crazy* for me. Tonight I'm going to sing a song to you."

I smiled at his sweet idea, not really thinking he'd carry it out. He always said he was tone-deaf and that was pretty much true, although it hadn't ever stopped him from singing the hymns in church. I forgot about this comment after a while.

Elisabeth was big into country music during that time and she'd graced the microphone a couple times with popular country songs.

While I whistled for Elisabeth's performance with my two-pinkie whistle, Paul walked right up to the microphone. I watched him speak a few words to Karaoke Charlie then the music started. Paul locked eyes with me and his toneless voice rang out the sweetest rendition of, *Blue Eyes Crying in the Rain* I had ever heard. By the time he sat down beside me, tears of love and gratitude were leaking trails down my cheeks.

When September arrived, school was going strong at our house. Charlotte and Emily began challenging themselves to rise ridiculously early just to see how soon they could finish their lessons.

Paul was at work one morning and the kids were about halfway finished with school, even though it was still morning. I was making tuna salad for an early lunch when the phone rang. It was Paul.

"Hello?"

"Shirl, turn on the T.V. A plane just flew into the World Trade Center.

"A plane?"

Just turn it on, you won't believe this."

Charlotte and Emily were sitting on the couch watching their classroom tape on the VCR in our great room.

"Hey, girls, excuse me please, I'm going to flip on the news for a minute."

"Mom, we are almost done." Emily whined.

"Just hang on, your daddy said I need to see this." I adjusted the video equipment and got the television on the screen.

As the newscasters conversed, a tape played of a plane plowing into one of the Twin Towers in New York. What we learned over time was that a series of coordinated suicide attacks had been launched by al-Qaeda on the United States that September 11, 2001 morning. Nineteen members of al-Qaeda had hijacked four commercial passenger jet airliners, intentionally crashing two of them into the Twin Towers of the World Trade Center in New York City. Everyone on board and many others working in the buildings died in this horror. Both buildings collapsed within two hours, destroying nearby buildings and damaging others.

"Mom?" I heard Joseph's voice beside me and only then did I realize I had been standing in front of the television for several minutes, just shaking my head in total disbelief.

"Just a minute, sweetie."

The newscaster's voice suddenly raised an octave, "We are getting reports ... reports of yet *another* plane ... another commercial plane ... with passengers, aimed at the Pentagon ... yes, that's right, heading toward the Pentagon at this moment."

"We have to pray." I said aloud.

Gathering the children around me on the couch we held hands.

"Lord, Jesus, be with the people on that plane. Save them, Lord, I don't know what to pray. Only You know what is going on right now. I ask for Your peace, let the people on the plane feel Your presence. Let them feel Your might, Lord and not be afraid."

Our attention was again drawn to the news report. Instead of subsiding, this terrible abomination escalated as the hijackers crashed the third airliner into the Pentagon in Arlington, Virginia, just outside Washington, D.C. A fourth plane crashed into a field near Shanksville in rural Pennsylvania after some of its passengers and flight crew attempted to retake control of the plane, which the hijackers had redirected toward Washington, D.C. There were no survivors from any of the flights. As a result of the attacks 2,973 victims and the 19 hijackers died. The overwhelming majority of casualties were civilians, including nationals of over 90 countries.

The repercussions of this terrorist attack would affect the United States on many levels. Besides the obvious airport security changes that would now be implemented, the fact that America had been attacked on our own turf was very personal. The United States, under the leadership of George W. Bush responded to the attacks by launching the *War on Terrorism*. It invaded Afghanistan to depose the Taliban, who had harbored al-Qaeda terrorists. The United States also enacted the *USA Patriot Act*. Many other countries also strengthened their anti-terrorism legislation and expanded law enforcement powers. Some American stock exchanges stayed closed for the rest of the week following the attack and posted enormous losses upon reopening, especially in the airline and insurance industries. The destruction of billions of dollars worth of office space caused serious damage to the economy of Lower Manhattan.

The images of smoke pouring out of the holes in the World Trade Center were engraved in granite on our memories from the tapes that played over and over on TV for months afterward.

Our security at home felt shaky as well. Emily sometimes had nightmares and would wake up nervously repeating the name, "bin Laden, bin Laden." I stopped letting the children check the mail now. Anthrax threats were on the rise and Post Offices around the U.S. were carefully inspecting all mail. As a result, the Post Office required new guidelines for the mailing of packages.

The whole world grieved with Americans. Support and sympathy came in from countries all around the globe. It seemed so crazy that we, the country usually responsible for aiding other countries in distress, would be attacked. The violence served no other purpose but to invoke terror. This was too illogical a concept to embrace. By October, the new atmosphere of fear had settled over the nation.

Every year, especially since I had researched its origins, Halloween was a celebration I preferred to ignore. In the wake of September 11, 2001, I was hardly alone in my discomfort this October. Everyone's concern for safety was heightened this year.

Jon turned twenty-two on October twenty-ninth so I called him while my home school-ers did their lessons that morning.

"Hello, twenty-two-year-old son. Happy birthday."
"Thanks, Mom. I'm getting old, aren't I?"
"Pshaw. I called to tell you the story of your birth."
"Mom, you really don't have to do that this year."
"I don't mind at all."
Jon groaned.
"Well, I have told you before, I think, that I carried you in my body for nine months."
"Yes, ma'am"

Jon made a tired noise.

"And I found myself on the threshold of Hell after thirty-four-and-a-half hours of labor."

"MOM. PLEASE."

"Just to bring your nine-pound self into the World."

"MOM. Nobody believes it was thirty-seven-and-a-half hours."

"Quite honestly, Son, it was probably closer to thirty-eight, but how are you going to celebrate?"

I'm going out with some friends."

"Friends who remain anonymous, or do they have names?"

"Mom."

"Okay. Just be careful. You are the only twenty-two year old boy I've got."

"I'll be careful, Mom."

"Watch for deer."

He chuckled.

"I'll watch for deer."

"I'm going to have dinner and a little party here on Halloween."

"I already have plans to go to a party."

"I figured you probably did, but I thought I'd ask. I love you, Jonboy."

"I love you, too, Mom."

I hung up and went online to a website I had read about in the newspaper. There I found some cool recipes for Fall that included a beef stew cooked inside a pumpkin. I gathered construction paper, crayons, scissors and colored pencils so Charlotte, Emily and Joseph could make invitations to our Fall Festival. We invited our neighbors to celebrate Autumn on October 31. The Pumpkin Beef Stew was truly delicious and turned out to be a yearly tradition.

Another surprise was the pear tree which had blossomed heartily in the Spring and now bore pears on its long-limbed side and even a few on the naked side! Little branch nubs reached out from the trunk with an occasional limb offering fruit much too high to pick. If the pears on that side managed to ripen and fall before the crows picked them to death maybe we'd even enjoy eating some of them! At any rate, we were amazed as well as delighted that it had somehow overcome the damage it had endured.

    Wateree Baptist Church began a tradition that year as well. Even though we lived in what was mostly an area of retired people there was also a handful of children in varying age groups who were members of Wateree Baptist. A hay ride for these neighborhood kids was put together by my friend, Brenda. A little while after our dinner a truck with a hay-strewn trailer behind it rolled up to our house. Brenda came bouncing up to the door with her two kids, dressed in costume, asking for a few more riders. Charlotte, Emily and Joseph complied happily. By bedtime that night, we had managed to fill the evening before All Saint's Day with enough wholesome fun to tire Charlotte, Emily and Joseph plumb out.

    Our nightly devotions began with a chapter in the Bible. We were working through the Old Testament, which was pretty slow-going but I figured we had plenty of time. Some of those chapters were pretty long. Occasionally, the children took turns reading a chapter or part of one. After the reading, we took turns saying our prayers out loud. Joseph's prayer usually sounded like this:

    "God, bless eb-body in the World, and ... and bless eb-body in the World.

    <long pause>

    Bless eb-body in the World..."

    And so on. We were all very patient.

    Devotions included Charlotte, Emily, Joseph and me. Elisabeth was usually there and sometimes Paul, when he didn't work until 9:00 p.m. After Devotions either Paul or I would read to the children. When Paul worked late, I'd read a chapter in one of the Narnia books. When he was home, he took a turn reading to them. Ever since they had hit the bookstands, Paul's reading was from a chapter of the Harry Potter series. A movie version of the first book came out in theaters on November 16 that year and the Graham family was front row and center.

    Joseph's sixth birthday in 2001 came just before the Sunday morning of our Christmas Cantata at St Timothy's. After Paul had agreed to my suggestion to bestow Joseph's gift in the form of a birthday puppy, we made a plan to let him pick out his new *best friend*. Paul drove and we brought Elisabeth, Charlotte and Emily along for this momentous family event. Everyone was excited. Even on a general day, Joseph was so smiley that I used to tell people the corners of his mouth touched at the back of his head; but on this day of days, I am pretty sure they overlapped.

  The last "almost there." was uttered in the parking lot of Kershaw County Animal Shelter as we ushered the happy honoree inside. We soon found ourselves in a corridor with kennels on either side, surrounded by a grand orchestra of yipping and woofing. It was a child's fantasy, and each of us was caught up in the utterly timeless music of puppy love.

  Driven by the momentum of a sudden, specific instinct, Joseph began to run, ignoring every cage, right and left. Arriving at the very last cage, he gazed at five or six round little fur-balls rolling and tripping over one another in a single sibling entity of varying browns.

  "That's him." Joseph announced, jubilant as an archeologist uncovering the Holy Grail. As though he expected him to be there all along, Joseph pointed to the drabbest of the browns; a little fatty who could have one day made a perfect stray.

  "Joseph." I tried to explain, "There are other puppies you haven't even seen yet. How can you be sure?"

  "I AM sure." Joseph proclaimed, "I want *him*."

  "But," I continued, following the advice of the shelter keeper, "these over here are called Shelties, and they make really good pets. Don't you want to take a look?"

  Reluctantly, Joseph lumbered over to the Sheltie cage. "Look at that one, Joseph." I urged, "I think he's smiling at you."

  Unimpressed, Joseph smiled politely and leaned back toward the roiling mound of brown puppies. For a millisecond I thought about employing the girls as reinforcements, but it would have been fruitless. Fluttering obliviously from one puppy kennel to the next, Elisabeth, Charlotte and Emily were completely caught up in the Romance and Joy of All Things Puppy. I chanced a look at Paul, hoping for some support, but all I could read in his eyes was satisfaction over his beloved little boy who constantly amused us. 'Mini-me,' his little clone who looked more like Paul than Paul himself, was in love with a little brown puppy. The pride in Paul's eyes matched up nicely with the smile on his lips and I was pretty sure we weren't going to bring a healthy Sheltie home.

"I still want Chocolate Bar." Joseph spoke firmly, his expression turned serious.

"Chocolate Bar?" I asked.

Joseph pinned his bright blue eyes on mine.

"That's his name," he informed me resolutely, "Chocolate Bar."

The puppy's color reminded me of dead leaves on a sunless day, or maybe thin gravy over stale bread, but sweet, rich chocolate seemed a bit of a stretch. Still, though, having a name pretty well sealed the deal. I gave up. It was Joseph's birthday. If the idea was to let him pick, then I must surrender to the cause.

The shelter was cleverly designed so that we had to walk through the kitty section en route to the check-out desk. All the cutest kittens were allowed to roam free, no doubt, because of suckers like us. The cages were about shoulder height, making it very easy for a lively gray and white feline puff to race up to us and jump squarely on our shoulders. Weighing approximately minus two ounces, this natural salesman pounced on Paul's and then my shoulders right away. He was the prettiest kitten I had ever seen. I swear I am not kidding when I say he kissed my cheek before moving to the next person. Irresistible? You bet. I imagined some of the more theatrical kittens singing, *It's a Hard Luck Life* in the background. So, what were we going to do now, leave him at the kitty orphanage? I didn't think so. By the time we got to the office area, we'd all been properly smitten by the kitten. By the time we got to the car he suddenly had the name, Frankie.

We didn't know it yet, but these two small creatures would work their way into the fabric of our lives and teach us something holy.

But you will not leave in haste or go in flight; for the LORD will go before you, the God of Israel will be your rear guard.
Isaiah 52:12

Chapter Thirty-Five

Paul drove us away from the civilization of Camden into the woodsy nature of Winnsboro. Living there had made some changes in us. When we lived in the city, we used to leave our guests with this departing blessing,

"Bye. Love you. Be careful. Call us when you get there. Hurry back to see us."

Now, even Joseph added, "Watch for deer," although he had no idea why.

Joseph learned by observing and mimicking the behavior of his family. Being the last of seven children probably left him feeling like he had eight parents sometimes. He constantly reached to keep up, which left precious little time for frivolities like asking, "Why?" He was, as I have stated before, just so happy to be one of the bananas and trusted us all.

My friend Amy had recently confirmed this when she met me at the door of Joseph's Sunday school class recently. She smiled and dimples transformed her pretty countenance into a little girl's face.

"I got to teach Joseph's Sunday School class this morning." She sparkled.

"Did you have fun?" I asked, suddenly jealous of her lucky break.

"I always have fun teaching Sunday School." She assured me. "I asked them to tell me where they live."

"Oh, dear. What did my Joseph tell you?"

"He was so proud." Amy giggled. He said, "I live in The Boonies.'"

How many times had he heard us say that before he took it for a fact? Kids are so literal. I had taught him and his sisters a little jingle with our address in the words. He might have sung it for Amy if he'd only known that where one *lives* is also his *address*. We laughed, but I was nonetheless alerted that Joseph was old enough to understand a new concept. I shuddered, thinking of my sunny boy of joy getting lost and being asked where he lived. How many Boonies could there be in the United States alone?

Paul looked tired as he drove the green Windstar under the house and shifted into park. Small animals and humans spilled out of the car squealing and chattering. Alone in the car, I could finally speak quietly and still be heard.

"Hey. That was fun, Paul Graham." I almost whispered. "Thanks for going along with the puppy idea."

"*Going along?* It might have been your idea, but I've got a dog in this fight, too." He answered.

I loved his colorful Southern language style, although it sounded rote and mechanical right now. Paul smiled without much heart and pushed the driver's door open. I couldn't tell if he was mad or just tired these days. He reminded me of those clowns at the circus whose weary expressions reveal terrible pain under face paint. It made me tired to be with him sometimes, and I found myself napping just to be doing something with him. It did no good to ask him if he was depressed. That only seemed to irritate him all the more.

I gathered up all the jackets left behind before I got out of the car. My burden of children's outer wraps was light, but awkward. I looked ahead and my breath caught in my throat as the setting sun lit up the western end of the lake, reflecting fabulous colors of turquoise and pumpkin. Every single day it displayed a brand-new, stunning sight to behold. It was too wonderful to keep to myself. I looked for Paul and found him at the foot of the steps, already observing this glorious sky.

"Look, Paul."

"I see."

It's so pretty."

"Remember?" He asked me. "I wanted this house to face that direction."

"Thanks for that." I said sincerely.

He reached for my bundle of coats and moved aside so that I could go up first.

"Why do you always do that?" I asked.

"What?"

"You know, why do you always make me lead the way?"

"Protection." He had answered stoically. "I've got your back. If you fall, I can catch you."

Such a gentleman. Tired as he was, I knew he would catch

me, indeed, no matter how much adrenalin it required. I wondered who had taught him manners, but before I could ask this, Charlotte threw the front door open.

"Mom and Dad, can we put Chocolate Bar and Frankie in an empty drawer with blankets and pillows?"

"And keep the T.V. on so they won't get lonely?" Joseph added from behind her as the puppy did free-style air-swimming in his arms.

"Or," Emily called from inside, "can we take turns letting them sleep with each of us in our beds?"

"I'm sleeping with Frankie." Claimed Elisabeth who gleefully slid a string of red yarn across the floor in front of the little gray puff.

"We'll take all that under advisement." Paul answered, dodging their requests, "Just show them around and let them get used to us for now."

"Give them some food …and remember," I added, "the puppy really belongs to Joseph."

"We know." Charlotte and Emily said in unison. The timing twin's share is no myth.

We lingered on the landing observing the children through the glass of the French doors. Happy, excited children are such a blessing to watch.

"If I died right now, they wouldn't remember me." Paul said aloud, but I don't think he meant to.

"Stop saying that."

He had said this several times over the years and I hated the sound of it.

"It's true."

"It's not true. Even the buddy will be six tomorrow. Even *he* would have memories."

"Not many."

"Stop it, Paul. That's not going to happen, but if it did, God forbid, I would make sure they knew you."

Paul chuckled.

"Besides, I asked you early on not to ever leave me or die."

"I can only promise I won't ever leave you."

I put my fingers in my ears, "La, la, la, la, la. No more talk. Let's go have a birthday party."

"That's a good idea."

We finished our climb to the door.

The children didn't acknowledge our entrance. Paul went to our bedroom. Starting supper was what I had planned to do, but decided to join him instead. He was lying across the bed on his stomach, so I followed his lead treating it as a completely normal occurrence, which it was becoming.

"Are you *wo' out* already, Counselor?"

He grinned as if I'd caught him with his hand in a cookie jar.

"I only worked four hours, but I do feel worthless."

I giggled, "Maybe you're *lethargy-boy*."

"I *am.*" He used up a waning store of his energy by smiling and closing his eyes.

"Well, I'll be *lethargy-girl* with you later, but first I have to make the birthday dinner."

"What did the buddy pick this time?"

"Since Domino's is too far away to deliver, we're having home-made pizza."

"The boy loves pizza like his daddy."

"Yes he does." I agreed. "Take a nap and I'll wake you when it's ready."

Paul didn't answer, but fell softly to sleep.

O Lord thou hast searched me and known me. Thou knowest my down-sitting and mine up-rising, Thou understandest my thought afar off.
Psalm 139:1-2

Chapter Thirty-Six

The alarm clock went off like it did every Sunday. Pushing the snooze button, Paul croaked, "Time to make the doughnuts!"

I laughed. This memory is important to me because when I recalled it later, it made me realize he must have been okay at the start of the day. We got up and began our routine of getting ready for church.

Blow drying my hair at the bathroom mirror, I caught a glimpse of Paul in my peripheral field. He had stepped out of the shower with his towel wrapped around him and just stood there, watching me. I turned toward my husband, who looked at me with an odd half-smile that ten years of marriage didn't help me to read. I turned off the dryer and smiled back with a question on my face. "You okay?" I asked. He vaguely nodded, but continued to stand there. I turned the dryer back on. There was much to do. It would soon be time to head to church forty-five minutes away. Eight-year-old Charlotte & Emily would need help with their hair and little Joseph required a lot of help getting ready. Paul had been cast to narrate the Christmas Cantata, and Elisabeth and I were to sing Handel's Messiah with the choir, plus Elisabeth had a violin part. Running late as we were prone, wouldn't do on this day.

"Is there something I can take this morning?" I asked my pharmacist husband as I rushed to pull up my stockings. "My throat is still a little sore."

"Yes." Paul answered, offering no suggestions. He was a man of few words these days, but his answer was incomplete, and it sure didn't give me any guidance. I chalked his indifference up as a clue he was mad about something, but we didn't have time to discuss it now. I decided to ignore whatever was eating him and finish getting ready.

Paul's attitude irritated me. It seemed he acted like this a lot lately. If I did stop to question him about my offense, it would take me an hour to pull it out of him. Nine out of ten times it would turn out he had misinterpreted something I'd said or done. Why couldn't he just tell me his complaints sooner, or when it was more convenient? I always wished he could communicate more easily, but doesn't every wife bear the burden of that wish? Just the night before, we had been sitting on opposite sides of our bed together wrapping gifts for our seven children. They would all be here in less than a week to celebrate Christmas with us. This kind of necessary preparation always took us a while to complete, and it would have made the task more interesting if Paul had been willing to talk a little. There was a time when we would have been cutting up, really enjoying this kind of thing. We had been instantly drawn to each other's humor from the start and we had carried it into our marriage. Unfortunately, my attempts to engage him in conversation were falling flat. In frustration, I'd given up and wrapped the gifts silently, as though I were alone, just like him. Finally, I offered a rhetorical question, dripping with sarcasm. "Isn't this fun?" I spat.

Looking up from his wrapping paper with an answer filled with genuine sweetness, Paul smiled and responded, "Yeah, it really is!"

Even though his response was more evidence of our communication problem, I couldn't help feeling humbled by his innocent perspective. As I had focused bitterly on the task at hand, Paul had been concentrating on the gentle blessings. It made me stop and think. Another Christmas. God had given us seven healthy children and allowed us enough to give to them from His bountiful provision. Even though half of them were grown, we would all be together this Christmas. How many years had it been since we celebrated Christmas as a whole family?

Now, here we were on this Sunday morning with Paul seeming vaguely offended and I, wondering what was going on in his head. Paul had progressed to his underwear and shirt, and now sat on the edge of the bed, wearily dangling his socks over his knees. His head was bent down as though he were trying to work up enough strength to put on the socks. As much as I wanted to avoid a discussion, my heart went out to him. Reluctantly, I sat beside him and spoke quietly, but firmly, "Paul, you've *got* to tell me what's wrong."

He turned his head and gave me that strange look again without answering. Something empty in his eyes that hadn't been there before told me that he *couldn't* answer me.

I stood, backing away from him and toward the phone

without losing eye contact. "I'm going to call an ambulance, Paul. Something is wrong, okay?"

Under normal circumstances, he would have objected to an ambulance for any reason, but he only continued to stare with that half-smile.

The smartest man I had ever known couldn't speak. Wasn't it ironic that his role that morning at church was to narrate?

Let us therefore come boldly unto the throne of grace, that we may obtain mercy, and find grace to help in time of need.
Hebrews 4:16

Chapter Thirty-Seven

The luxury of calling 911 hadn't been available to us out in the country just a few weeks previously. The paramedic station had just been set up in our little town. I felt thankful for God's grace in the timing of whatever we were experiencing and thought about it as my fingers punched in "9-1-1." I felt confirmed that God was near and still in control. The only choice was yielding to His guidance.

My eyes stayed locked on Paul's as an EMS dispatcher logged in my information, assuring me an ambulance was on its way. I hung up the phone, still holding Paul's child-like gaze and returned a quick smile. It was bizarre. How could I be managing something this frightful on the phone while exchanging a cordial smile with my husband? The efficiency part of me was running in high gear. I looked away from Paul long enough to dial our next door neighbor's number. I might need some extra muscles getting Paul to the driveway. Living in a house built on stilts thirteen feet off the ground, I knew I shouldn't try to get my 200-pound husband down the steps by myself. Time would likely be of the essence, so I wanted to make sure Paul was ready and waiting when the ambulance arrived.

"Hello?" Mrs. Ida answered.

"Mrs. Ida," I responded in staccato, using my might to control my voice, "Paul can't talk. I think he is having a stroke. I called 911. They are sending an ambulance."

"Here." She said quickly, her voice reflecting worry, "Talk to Jerry."

I repeated the message to Jerry and asked him if he would help me get Paul downstairs.

"I'm comin' right now." He answered.

I took Paul's socks from his hands and slid them over his feet then I looked around for his pants. He was still watching me absently. There was a knock on the bedroom door.

"Who is it?" I called gently.

"It's Elisabeth, Mom, Can I come in?"

I walked to the door and opened it a crack

"Elisabeth, your daddy is…" then I wondered what to say. "…not well."

"What's wrong?" She asked.

"I'm not sure, honey. He can't talk. Maybe it is a stroke, but I called an ambulance."

"What do you want me to do, Mom?"

"I want you to finish getting the little ones ready and take them to church. I don't want them to be frightened. They will feel safer in their routine among what's familiar. I'll ride with your daddy to the hospital and leave a message at church for you. Papa Rod and Grandma Millie will be at church, too, so find them and sit with them."

"Okay, Mom, I love you." Elisabeth looked straight at me with her bright-blue eyes and I wondered how I could be thinking how pretty she was at such a time as this.

"I love you, too, honey. Thank you."

Someone knocked at the outside French doors on the lake side.

"That's Mr. Jerry." I informed her. "Let him in while I find your daddy's clothes."

As Jerry entered the house, I found Paul's pants on the bed and helped him get them on. I wasn't doing quite all the work, he was able to help by pushing his foot through the leg hole.

"I love you, Paul. You're going to be okay."

Paul looked at me serenely and nodded his head.

"Shirley?" I heard Jerry call from outside my bedroom door.

I fastened the button on Paul's waistband and let Jerry in. His wife, Ida and neighbors, Raymond and Anne soon followed, with (Bug) close behind.

Jerry was retired from Frito-Lay. Having supported Ida and their four children by driving big trucks, Mr. Jerry still carried a muscular frame built up by daily doses of heavy lifting. He tried to talk to Paul, "What's goin' on, Paul?"

Paul looked into his face with no expression.

I got a pair of Paul's house slippers on him and Jerry led him out the door, supporting Paul's big arm and calling him "buddy." Not very much older than Paul, it seemed funny to see him in such a fatherly role as he kept Paul steady, walking gingerly down those miles of wooden steps. Ironically, the tears brimming in his eyes made his muscles seem yet bigger to me.

Having instructed Elisabeth to drive Charlotte, Emily and Joseph to the church, I felt comfortable knowing they would all be in the bosom of our trusted St Timothy's church family and that Paul would be safe in everyone's prayers.

I listened for a siren, but the only noise outside was the chirping of morning birds.

"They should be here now." I complained, although I had no idea how long it had been since I called. It seemed like hours.

"I called them again." Bug answered, "They said they were on their way."

Eternities passed waiting for the EMT's. Finally, it rolled into our driveway. I guided Paul into the EMS van and stayed beside him while he performed the telltale brain function tasks for the paramedic. Paul was able to follow her commands and even verbalize these four responses: "yes, no, up," and "down."

"Can you raise your hands in front of you, Mr. Graham?" The lady paramedic asked as she began the battery of tests. Paul obeyed and we observed a tiny discrepancy. One hand was ever so slightly lower than the other.

Due to its location, Paul would be airlifted to Providence Hospital fifteen miles away.

"I'm sorry." The paramedic apologized to me, "You can't ride with Mr. Graham."

I started to tell her I was panicked and would get lost, but Raymond must have noted my anxiety. He seemed to appear from nowhere and spoke right up.

"I'll drive your van and the others can follow us."

My fists uncurled and I realized my palms hurt from the pressure of my fingernails digging into them.

"Thank you." I sighed gratefully, turning my attention to Paul. He looked in my eyes but I had no sense of whether my words registered or not.

"I will be there soon after you arrive." I promised, squeezing his warm hands and kissing him on the cheek. "I love you."

I hated leaving him, but felt the helicopter would have him at Providence long before we could make it by car.

Relieved, knowing I wouldn't have to rely on my limited sense of direction, I climbed into the passenger side of my car. Raymond turned the key in the green Windstar van's ignition and we left the professionals to take care of Paul.

The best place to land the helicopter seemed to be Wateree Baptist Church a block away, but after our departure, the plan was modified to land it beside the Winnsboro I-77 interstate exit about fifteen minutes away. Paul rode to it in the ambulance. The actual hospital wasn't much more than ten minutes by car from this exit.

Driving down I-77, Raymond was quiet as I made a couple of phone calls on my cell phone. Paul's step-dad, Rod and his wife, Millie, were already getting ready to drive from their home in Chapin to be at our church for the Cantata. I wanted to let them know what was going on but ask them to stay on the course in order to be with our frightened, worried children at the church.

Since Ruthie lived in Chapin also, her phone number had the same prefix as Rod and Millie's. My fingers automatically dialed Ruthie's number instead of Rod's. I didn't realize what I had done until I heard Ruthie's husband, Warren say, "Hello?"

"Uh, Warren?"

"Yes?"

"This is Shirley. I meant to call Rod and Millie, but I should tell you that Paul is having a stroke."

"A stroke?"

"I think so. That's what it seems like."

"Oh, Lord."

I started to ask him to tell Ruthie, but he was already calling her to the phone.

"Ruthie," I heard him say, "Get on the phone, Shirley says Paul's having a stroke."

"What?" I heard Ruthie say before grabbing the phone.

"Shirley, what's going on?" Ruthie asked then listened with shock to the rushed details of our morning. She dropped what she was doing and left right away to be with me at the hospital. My neighbors, Jerry, Ida and Ann, Raymond's wife were already at Providence. I will always believe God guided my fingers onto the so-called *wrong* numbers that morning. He knew I would find His comfort and calmness in my childhood friend.

After calling Ruthie, I made another call, this time to Brad, one of our choir directors, asking him to look out for the children. Then, I cupped my hands in my lap, praying silently,

"Lord, I don't know what to pray so please pour me out and fill me up with Your Holy Spirit. Allow the Holy Spirit, Who knows what to pray, speak for Paul in my stead."

Allowing the Spirit of God to fill my being, I spent the whole rest of the trip in submission to His prayers for Paul. A peace and calm fell over me like morning dew. I am sure Raymond knew I was praying, because even though he is usually full of uplifting words, he expressed his sensitivity and kindness by making no effort to console me with conversation.

Proverbs 25:20 says, *Singing cheerful songs to someone with a heavy heart is like taking someone's coat in cold weather or pouring vinegar into a wound.*

What a blessing it was to be with someone intuitive enough to live out this proverbial wisdom. The comfort I took in his silence was enormous.

Arriving at the hospital before Paul's ambulance came unnerved me. There must have been a change in transporting Paul. *"But why?"* I wondered, "Had something gone wrong? Had Paul taken a turn for the worse?"

Looking up and seeing Ruthie coming through the entrance, I actually felt some of the tension fall from my face. Ruthie hugged me as I updated her.

"I hear something." She said suddenly, and I heard it, too. It was the *blat-blat-blat* of a propeller guiding the helicopter down onto the landing pad I had seen on the way in.

"Thank God." I cried, hurrying stupidly to wait right outside the landing strip as though I could do something to help. With the wind blowing hair in my face, the EMT's emerged, looking at me like I was crazy. I was quickly ushered out of harm's way as my husband was carried through the door on a stretcher.

Ann, Ida and Jerry had arrived during my foolish heroics and sat together in a row of waiting room chairs. A nurse suggested that I take a seat and they moved over to welcome me, but I couldn't sit. Adrenaline reigned in my veins and I needed to be next to Paul. Hospital policy was keeping me away from him. There were endless channels of paperwork that required my signature, our insurance card, things that seemed far less important than my presence beside Paul. In the waiting room, my neighbors and Ruthie watched me pace back and forth, their eyes darting left and right like the eyes of cat clocks. Ruthie didn't ask me to sit.

Finally, a nurse I hadn't seen yet walked down the hall and asked for me. I jumped to attention and followed her to a small room. Paul lay on a wheeled hospital cot. It was so quiet. Everything in the room was chrome or white. It was kind of ethereal.

"Hey, Sweetie." I whispered, but Paul didn't answer. He just looked absently into my face. "I love you." I offered.

He just watched me then closed his eyes. Was he hurting? I took his hand in both of mine and squeezed it, silently calling on God for help. I yearned to soothe Paul. Instinctively, just as I had sung it countless times to my restless babies, I began to sing, *Away in a manger, no crib for a bed...*

After a while, the hospital staff determined that Paul needed to be at a facility more accommodated to serve his needs. Providence Hospital was the closest hospital to us but it specialized in heart problems. It seemed like precious time was being wasted but really, God was making a way. I suspected the staff knew more about Paul's condition than they were letting on.

Ruthie and I drove to Lexington Hospital to wait for Paul's arrival in the ambulance. There were three hospitals where they could have sent him. The grace in being at Lexington was that the brain surgeon God would use to save Paul's life just happened to be there that morning.

Sitting in the Emergency Room, Ruthie and I had no idea which direction the ambulance would be coming. Gazing mindlessly out the glassed walls, Ruthie, suddenly exclaimed, "Look, Shirley, there's Paul."

Sure enough, I turned in time to see him being wheeled out of the ambulance.

"Does he see us? Ruthie asked, because he was looking directly in my eyes.

"He's looking at me." I said in wonder and then he was gone. "But, he can't possibly see us from that distance. Plus, I think these windows are tinted."

How did he know where to find me? The connection I felt to him was vivid and intense, yet, he told me later he remembered nothing about the whole morning. He didn't even remember waking up. He must have showered and dressed on auto-pilot, functioning by rote.

Ruthie and I stayed in a room with Paul until he was moved to the radiology floor for a look at his brain. Later, I was called out to talk to Doctor Samuel, Paul's neurosurgeon who looked like a movie star. As she talked to me, a finger of her tiny, life-saving hand pointed to a film showing the inside of Paul's head.

"Do you see this?" She asked, "It's bleeding in your husband's brain. Only, I don't think he's having a stroke. Do you see how round and contained the bleeding area is?" She went on, "It looks like a tumor to me. I think your husband has a tumor that has begun to rupture."

Kindly and gently, she waited for the information to sink in. A few seconds passed and I felt clear and focused. Looking from the film into her face, I asked stoically, "Can you remove it?"

"Yes" she quickly answered.

"Dr. Samuel," I began, "My husband and I have seven children. We need him."

Her confidence was just the comfort I needed. "I will take care of your husband, Mrs. Graham," she promised, "but we have to wait until we can reduce the swelling in his brain."

"I will be praying for you." I answered.

For we are God's handiwork, created in Christ Jesus to do good works, which God prepared in advance for us to do.
Ephesians 2:10

Chapter Thirty-Eight

Date: Lexington Hospital, West Columbia, South Carolina

Hospital time runs different from the time outside it. Hours and minutes are measured by visiting hours and shift changes. A doctor's explanation that an operation should take six hours alters hospital time even more. Noon no longer means mealtime if someone you love is in surgery. It's just a continuation of nervous small talk and moving over to make room for a new waiting visitor. Days and weeks melt together and have no sequence. I still can't remember where some of the incidents of that week fit.

Lexington Hospital's ICU waiting room quickly became my home. I dozed in the chairs off and on and learned to make the coffee. The Pink Ladies went home at 5:00 p.m., so I started answering the phone calls. *ICU waiting room - just a minute. Is there any family here for so-and-so? You have a call.*

Throughout this week, the Face of Jesus became quite common to me, disguised as friends and strangers. My church family proved my instincts right and stepped in to care for my children. Before week's end, twenty-four-year-old Jon and twenty-one-year-old Austin arrived from Pensacola, Florida and twenty-one-year-old Sarah drove down from Nashville, Tennessee. Between St. Timothy's and Wateree Baptist down the street, dinners and casseroles were flowing into our home in my absence. Our trash was being emptied and our children and pets were being loved, fed and comforted.

Back at the ICU waiting room, I was still wearing the red dress I had donned for church, but it was now Monday. I received Paul's visitors. His old football buddies came, worried about him, seeking any information. Getting to know these strapping men and seeing the bond they shared with one another was a precious thing to behold. Some were coaches, some military heroes, yet each one was reduced to helpless frustration by his inability to lift a fallen comrade. It was easy to see that any one of these men would willingly die for another.

Paul's pharmacy and attorney friends filed in. They were so used to giving counsel to patients and clients, yet Paul's cohorts had no advice to offer this situation. These brilliant pharmacists, technical assistants and lawyers only had questions. Our friend, Bill would only shake his head in disbelief that his wise friend and mentor lay in peril. Talking to Paul's friends, I became more and more aware of how much an example Paul provided them.

He was so reasonable and fair. His faith was unshakable. His face conveyed serenity and kindness. He loved babies and felt a personal responsibility for women alone. If the occasion arose, however, Paul was quick to call on the power that rumbled beneath the surface of his demeanor. I thought of his courage to defend the pharmacy techs from irate customers. He wouldn't waffle if someone was out of line.

"You'll have to stop talking to my employee like that or I will call security," he was known to say without raising his voice. Recipients of this message could tell he just might actually leap over the counter and stop them himself. I knew no one on this Earth who could make him tremble. Paul saw himself as a protector; it was his calling. His familiar mantra, "I am protection of you," echoed in my mind.

Yet here we sat, warriors for Paul's welfare, in a room where we were ready to do the battle we had no skills to do. Self-control as we waited was the only outlet for our nervous energy. As ineptitude gnawed away at our hearts we drew patience from our prayers and each other.

Unable to do anything for Paul, his friends sought to attend to me instead. I felt humbled by their service, and recognized it would be unkind for me to refuse their offerings. In reality, I was in great need their offerings. I had tried to ignore it, but I thought I had pneumonia. My throat was raspy now and a rattle vibrated in my chest. I had planned to will some high C notes out of my throat for the cantata but that seemed a month ago. I called my doctor's office Monday morning and tried to explain my situation to the receptionist; that I couldn't leave to be seen by the doctor, but needed some kind of coughing aid.

"Is this Shirley Graham the home school mother?" The receptionist asked.

"Well, yes. Who is this?"

"Shirley, this is Melonie from your support group."

I'd just met Melonie the week before at a home school support group meeting. I remember her saying she only worked at the office a few hours a week if they needed her. Again, I sensed the wonder of God's perfect timing over situations and people. Wherever I turned He was leaving an autograph, signed with His provision and grace.

Thanks to our information network of home school mothers Melonie was already aware of our family's plight. Between Melonie and Paul's pharmacist friends, I had expert identity references vouching for my need. It wasn't long before I held a pharmacy bag filled with prescriptions of antibiotics and cough medicine for *Shirley Graham*.

Elisabeth had gone to my email account and made sure my cousins knew what was happening. I drew strength from all the prayers being lifted for Paul's recovery.

Other friends seemed to have a psychic knowledge of other things I needed. Pastor Garry handed me a bank envelope filled with one dollar bills. "I know you won't leave." He said to me, "You might feel like eating sometime, and the cafeteria isn't open all night. You'll need these for the snack machines."

Then he held out a little zippered bag of toiletries, lovingly packed by his wife.

"Teresa sent this and told me to tell you she is praying for all of you."

I looked in the bag with a sudden surge of joy. Nothing else I could think of would have made a more thoughtful gesture.

"How in the world did she know?" I queried.

I had finally admitted to myself that the odoriferous cloud following me around was actually me. I smelled. Until this experience, I didn't know what crazy things the body does when reacting to stress, like producing a strong odor. Teresa's little bath-in-a-bag enabled me to shampoo and bathe from a sink in the restroom across the hall. I welcomed it as a daily luxury.

Others simply called and asked. "Can I bring you something?" Jennifer, my choir director told me over the phone. "I'm coming to sit with you. Is there anything I can bring?"

"Clothes." I quickly responded. "…and a pair of shoes that aren't heels."

Susan, Jennifer's mother-in-law, packed me a bag that Jennifer picked up on the way. Susan's clothes were a perfect fit.

My brother, Dale walked in after driving three hours from Hartwell, Georgia. He and Ruthie stayed up at night with me. Meanwhile, Paul's condition seemed to worsen.

"Why isn't Dr. Samuel doing something?" I wondered in the small hours of morning. "If he's getting worse, doesn't that mean the drugs aren't countering the swelling in his brain?"

He couldn't talk at all now and his right arm and leg had ceased to function. He seemed deeply depressed. I kept a close watch on the time. When visiting hours arrived, I eased in behind him in the bed and wrapped my arms around him. I'd fall asleep instantly, sleeping long past visiting hours. Mercifully, most of the night staff overlooked this infraction of the rules. It was the only time I slept soundly.

When I returned to the waiting room, I had visitors. Allyson and Heather (daughters of our dentist and Sunday School teacher, Dr. Hal and his wife, Sylvia) were home from college. During this sweet family's visit, Allyson and Heather offered to stay with Charlotte, Emily and Joseph at our house. Their offering of help included taking the children to participate in a caroling event and party, one of our church's Christmas traditions. More important, it would allow them to spend the night at home.

Eight-year-old Charlotte and Emily and Joseph, just-turned-six, had been lovingly shepherded into the home of my friends Nancy and Tom from church. Monday, they brought the children to see Paul. Tiptoeing timidly into his room, they positioned themselves on either side of his hospital bed, not knowing what to do. Paul's face began to contort and he cried. I don't know what he was thinking, because he never remembered any of this. The children hugged him. Unable to imagine what was going on in their young minds, I had no words of advice or comfort to impart. I just knew it would be wrong to refuse them the right to be a part of whatever was happening to our family. Paul's surgery was scheduled for Tuesday. How much of their father, if any of him, would be left waiting for them on Wednesday?

After their visit, Nancy met Allyson and Heather at the church with the children. The timing of this festivity was healthy. What the children had just witnessed had been grave. It seemed logical to me that a familiar activity would help to remind them that continuity remained in their young world.

When Sarah arrived from Atlanta, she and Elisabeth went in to see Paul together. I hugged them both. "I'm so glad you are here."

They smiled, but their mannerisms registered nervousness and discomfort.

"Your daddy can't talk," I gently began, leading them past the nurse's station, "…so we shouldn't ask him questions. Questions seem to stress him."

Our older daughters both nodded their pretty heads, trying to understand, yet not quite daring to believe me. We tiptoed into Paul's room and Sarah spoke first, struggling to camouflage her fright with a wooden smile.

"Hey, Dad." Her face looked so small, too young to be filled such worry. She fished around nervously for conversation.

Paul looked at her painfully, absently. Sarah and Elisabeth covered their shock with plastic pleasantries, yet their eyes were plagued with denial.

"I love you, Daddy." Sarah added in a high-pitched voice, fighting back the scream that trembled just below the surface of her nerves.

"How are you? Can I do something for you? Do you want anything?" Sarah timidly ventured, immediately regretting her questions. The very thing she was trying not to do was her first response. Tears filled the rims of Paul's eyes and made paths down his cheeks. He listlessly hung his head.

"It's okay," I whispered to Sarah, "…he'd probably like you to hug him."

Elisabeth waited her turn as Sarah tenderly wrapped her arms around her dad's big shoulders. She backed away from this unfamiliar man so Elisabeth could step forward. Obediently, Elisabeth leaned into his neck, this stranger's neck, leaving some distance for fear of hurting him. Paul just cried silently. His working arm failed to squeeze his little girls. His other arm lay heavily at his side. Could this really be the same muscular arms that had lifted these gleeful girls high above his shoulders, tossing them splashing into Lake Wateree? Lost deeply in the lonely forest of Paul's dark new reality we were nothing but a blur to him now. I pictured his brain's command center sparking madly in an effort to light the neurons that instantly fizzled out like wet firecrackers.

"Maybe we should go." I whispered to them. They readily agreed, relieved to cast off their necessary pretense.

"Bye, Dad." Sarah waved as she smiled one last staged smile accompanied by sincere words. "I love you."

"I love you, Daddy." Elisabeth mouthed, quickly turning out the door. Her smile faded quickly as she stepped out of her daddy's ugly dream. As much as they wanted to be near their big, strong daddy, they were anxious to leave this fragile one. It was too disturbing to process the terrible witness of this visit.

Walking my shell-shocked daughters down ICU's corridor I felt their faces reflected in two broken halves of my heart. They looked like two lovely, walking mannequins except for their darting, jungle eyes, that seemed ready to run or fight.

I kissed them goodbye and watched them walk mechanically, out the double doors. I covered my face with hands that smelled like hospital air. Could I have made that easier for them? Should I have told them not to visit their daddy? How many more awful decisions would I be expected to make?

"God?" My heart called out, "…are You still there?"

He was. I felt Him in my heart, but I didn't sense His

offers of advice at the moment. I scrubbed the tears out of my eyes and took a big breath. Turning into I.C.U.'s waiting room (my own little makeshift home), I was surprised to see Gary Smallen looking up at me from the little desk just inside the door. He fitted the phone in its cradle.

"You know, the coffee's pretty good in here." He mentioned to me, as though we had already been in the middle of conversation. I laughed, suddenly relieved to find him sitting there writing phone messages to the family victims of Intensive Care Purgatory.

"It ought to be." I answered, "I made it fresh not too long ago."

"Nice job." he said, raising his Styrofoam cup in honor to my coffee skills.

"Where is your Pink Lady dress?" I asked, referring to the uniform of the mostly retired volunteers who usually manned the desk.

"The Pink Lady clocked out without telling me where to find my size."

"Too bad." I rued. "The hat that goes with it would really set off your eyes.

"I'm not kidding." Gary started his story.

"I step in here right when the clock's striking 5:00 p.m. and this wiry little grey-haired lady slaps a message pad in my hand and starts barking orders about how to answer this phone. Scares me to death. It's time to go home and she's out of here like a shot. I find myself in this chair here afraid to make a phone faux pas. Where do they find these women? Are they retired prison guards?"

I giggled despite the hard situation I'd just come from. Gary must have spent at least the past fifteen minutes planning this greeting.

"I don't know, Gary, but thanks for coming here."

He stood up and hugged me.

"What's the latest on my friend?" He asked, becoming serious.

"I gotta tell you," I began, "I don't understand why he has to wait until tomorrow for the surgery. He can't talk anymore, his arm and leg aren't functioning, and he just cries."

"Do they know what the bleeding is about?"

"It's a tumor, she thinks, and it's ruptured. Something about the bleeding in his brain. It's filling the communication centers that tell his body what to do. The speech part and the part that controls motor skills, something like that. There's swelling, too and I think that frightens me most of all."

Gary scratched the top of his head and looked at the floor. There was a band around his head where he had worn a baseball cap all day. As a high school football coach, the hat was a necessary part of his daily uniform. His habit of removing it indoors reflected his manners. Like Paul, Gary was a gentleman.

"Why, though?" He asked, looking at me. "Paul is the healthiest one of us. I mean, he takes better care of himself than anyone. What would cause a tumor?"

"I don't know, Gary, but I can tell you that he had a melanoma spot once before. His mama told me over and over to make sure he wore sun screen every day."

"But, that's *skin* cancer, isn't it?" He reasoned.

"Yeah," I replied grimly, "unless it should metastasis."

Gary looked away, beyond and past the hospital. His eyes were focused on a time long ago when the skin of their teen age bodies was Kevlar and youth was forever.

"I remember," he started thickly, "When we would go to Myrtle Beach in the summers. Did Paul ever tell you?"

I nodded and Gary continued.

"We went so many times that all we had to do was to sprinkle a little bit of sand on the hood of the car because it knew the way."

We forced smiles over the old joke they shared.

Gary's smile evaporated while he stood there wishing he could go back and change the course of history somehow.

"Paul's back would turn absolutely purple from sunburn."

"We didn't know how bad a thing sunburn could be." I reminded him.

"We didn't know." He repeated trying in vain to absolve himself. "We were kids."

"Do you want to see him, Gary?"

"I'm not immediate family." He reminded me.
"You're not his brother-in-Christ?"
"Well, yeah."
"That's right." I said, but with visiting hours three hours away, we settled in a couple of chairs instead. I drank a cup of tea, trying to melt a stubborn chill, while Gary entertained me with adventure stories that he and Paul had survived. He needed to talk and I needed to listen, to learn about a time when I had no claim on Paul. Back when his character and personality were still forming. I realized I was getting tired when Gary said he needed to go home. His sweet wife, Lynda would have late supper waiting for him and she'd be anxious to hear an update on Paul.

Alone again, I opened the travel bag Nancy had brought earlier when the little ones were here. I was grateful to find that she had packed a neck pillow and a travel blanket. A little coughing fit reminded me to make another cup of tea to calm my inflamed bronchial tubes before turning out the light. Getting comfortable in my chair, I rested my heels on the travel bag and opened my Bible to John 11. I read,

So the sisters [Mary and Martha] sent word to Him saying, "Lord, behold, he whom you love is sick." But when Jesus heard this, He said, "This sickness is not to end in death, but for the glory of God, so that the Son of God may be glorified by it.

The intensity of the Holy Spirit's presence in the passage called me to claim Lazarus' foreboding resurrection for my Paul. I drifted off to sleep with thanks on my lips. Slipping in and out of sleep, I dreamed about God's massive hands cupped together like an old Allstate Insurance commercial. Instead of a little house, His hands held an operating room with Paul in the middle on a Gurney. He was anaesthetized and Doctor Samuel was performing his brain surgery. The surgery attendants were calm, Dr. Samuel was calm, and nothing in God's great hand was going on without His knowledge. I knew with certainty that Paul's death was not what this trouble was about. Just like with Lazarus, God had something else in mind. My job would be to hang on for the ride and trust Him more than ever before.

* * *

I awoke to thumping noises in the room with me. Opening my eyes a sliver I saw two human shapes bumbling into the dark room dragging suitcase shapes. Jon and Austin had just arrived from Pensacola in the middle of the night. It felt so good to hug my boys whom I hadn't seen for too many months. Do sons ever stop looking taller with each visit?

I reached up to hug them hard and relayed a current update on their step-dad.

"Do you want some tea?"

Exhausted, they both declined. The drive from Pensacola to Columbia is a long one. My big boys fell asleep in an instant, their long bodies folded into capital N's on the stiff chairs. Despite the sober reality of Paul's condition, the room was kindled in warmth. I willed myself to stay awake so I could watch Jon and Austin's lanky bodies sleep.

I was on the threshold sleeping again when a lady wearing scrubs came inside the dimly lit room to ask where a different waiting room was located. I started to answer that I was the wrong person to inquire for directions, when it occurred to me that I knew her.

"Oh, my goodness." I exclaimed. "You are Marie, aren't you? I'm Shirley Graham, I mean, I was Thornton then."

I stumbled along. "My Austin was the second baby born at The Birthing Center. You were my nurse-midwife." I pointed to a big lump on the other side of the room. "There's Austin now."

It had been twenty years since we had talked, but Marie remembered us.

"Shirley." We embraced and she sat beside me. "You framed a quote for me."

"That's right. Robert Frost. *A baby is God's opinion that the world should go on.*"

We giggled like little girls, then settled back to catch up a bit.

A hospital nurse now, Marie had just gotten off work. She was looking for someone on a different floor but ended up the I.C.U. waiting room by mistake. Noting the dark circles under my eyes, Marie wanted to know why we were in this waiting room. After I explained, she shared the story of her cancer treatment and surviving sixteen years before. Looking at her beautiful, healthy glow, hope filled me. She had been so encouraging during my pregnancy and childbirth with Austin in the midst of my separation and divorce from his father. I wondered if God had guided her here to encourage me again. If God *had* sent her it sure wasn't because I could tell her how to find her way around this hospital.

Slipping off to sleep again, I pondered over the timing of this reunion. Why had she shown up just after Austin arrived, his first visit in three years? Was that a confirmation of Divine orchestration? If so, then how could I ignore the fact that she had survived cancer? Had God sent her to give hope for Paul's survival? I *felt* comforted and hopeful.

Resting in the glow that God had visited me through Marie, I claimed Proverbs 3:5-6 which instructs us to:

Trust in the Lord with all your heart and lean not on your own understanding, in all things acknowledge Him and He will direct your paths.

It was a blessing not having to lean on my own understanding. I had none. Acknowledging Him in all the details was a great relief over trying to figure any of this out. I drifted off to sleep again, knowing Paul's death was not as close as it ought to have seemed.

This is the confidence we have in approaching God: that if we ask anything according to His will, He hears us. And if we know that He hears us – whatever we ask – we know that we have what we asked,
1 John 5:14-15

Chapter Thirty-Nine

I have always loved my brother, Dale, five years older than I. His life always seemed full of fun and adventure. Married to Sally since he was nineteen and she, eighteen, they personified real family to me. As their family grew, they always seemed to approach the crises in their lives with solidarity, tenacity and humor. God had given them four beautiful sons who were almost all grown now. Dale's trade as a general contractor and electrician allowed him to use the gift of perfectionism he inherited from Daddy. Among her many skills, Sally was a great cook who could turn dried beans and cornmeal into a feast fit for company.

Even though Dale and Sally made life look easy they were no strangers to struggles. Zeb, their third son who was born very prematurely teetered between life and death for the first three months of his life. It was during this time that Dale, a cradle Christian, really learned to talk to Jesus and truly know Him as his Friend. The Lord gave their family a testimony as they fairly lived at the hospital fighting for tiny Zeb's life.

After God took them through that fire, it was hard for Dale and Sally to keep what He'd taught them to themselves. This is why I shouldn't have been surprised to see Dale walk through the waiting room door the next night; or to learn that, with Sally's blessing, he planned to stay there with me as long as I needed him. He knew that his presence, just the loving act of sitting and listening quietly to me, was the most extravagant gift.

Our parents were in Georgia. Daddy's battle with the larceny of Parkinson's Disease confined him and Mother. The cruel symptoms had already violated Daddy's once-famous long-legged gait and replaced it with a metal wheelchair. I knew Dale had come, in part, to stand in the gap for them. That week he became a different kind of friend to me. No matter how close you are to a person, sitting up all night in a hospital waiting room brings the relationship to a deeper level of love. We talked about Paul coming home, and I frankly broached the issue of Paul's condition. Dale was ready to install an elevator in our house-on-stilts.

It was all so surreal. Previous business Paul and I had done at this very hospital had resulted in bringing beautiful babies home, yet here we sat, making arrangements to bring their broken daddy home. How different, now, were our plans for returning home from this place.

Sitting in that waiting room, reading in my Bible and praying God kept blessing me with the knowledge that Paul's death was not what this situation was about. And although I knew he wouldn't die, I didn't believe he would ever be the same physically or mentally. I fully expected him to go home in a permanent wheelchair. Little did I know that Paul's will and my extravagant God were much stronger than my limited speculation.

> *After he had said this he went on to tell them, "Our friend Lazarus has fallen asleep; but I am going there to wake him up." His disciples replied, Lord, if he sleeps he will get better." Jesus had been speaking of his death, but his disciples thought he meant natural sleep. So then he told them plainly, "Lazarus is dead and for your sake I am glad I was not there, so that you may believe. But let us go to him." Then Thomas (also known as Didymus) said to the rest of the disciples, "Let us also go that we may die with him."*
> *John 11:11-16*

Chapter Forty

It was Tuesday. This was our third day in ICU and Paul's brain surgery was about to happen. During the past days Paul had received each one of our children from his bed in ICU. Each one seemed shell shocked; not sure what to do or what to say to him. His arm didn't work, he couldn't talk. The unspoken truth was that these visits were necessary in case there wasn't another chance.

As Paul was being rolled into surgery, Pastor Garry was right there beside me. He continued to exhibit an uncanny ability to show up at just the right time and I will ever be thankful to his wife, Teresa for sacrificing him so graciously.

"Now let's go down to the cafeteria and get you something to eat." He urged, but hunger for food had become an emotion from another lifetime ago. I did, however, hunger to be in prayer, standing in the gap for Paul.

"No." I resisted. "I need to go to the Chapel."

A smile lit his face, "I know just where it is."

"Really?" I asked him doubtfully. He, Dale and I had already been lost dozens of times in the hospital corridors, seeking the cafeteria or drink machines.

"Really." He answered with unshaken confidence, proudly leading us directly to the Chapel.

Entering the quiet sanction of the Chapel, we found ourselves a spiritual part of the reverence there. Pastor Garry knelt with me at the altar rail. We bowed our heads, pleading with God to spare Paul's life and health. I had never wanted anything more earnestly.

"Lord Jesus." I began, "I don't know where to start. You know the need in my heart far better than I. Pour all the self out of me. Fill me instead with Your Holy Spirit. Let the Spirit pray through me for my husband."

I closed my eyes, submitting to the power of the Holy Ghost, Who pled my case. There is no way to describe the wonderful immersion of peace I felt. Wholly swept up in prayer, Pastor Garry's voice in my ear gave me a little start and I realized he had been turning pages in the Altar Bible in front of us.

"Read this, Shirley."

Looking up, I could see that he had turned the altar Bible to Psalm 118. I read:

O give thanks unto the Lord; for He is good: His mercy endureth forever. Let Israel now say that His mercy endureth forever. Let the house of Aaron now say, that His mercy endureth forever. Let them now that fear the Lord say, that His mercy endureth forever. I called upon the Lord in distress; the Lord answered me and set me in a large place. The Lord is on my side; I will not fear. What can a man do to me? The Lord taketh my part with them that help me; therefore I shall see my desire upon them that hate me, It is better to trust in the Lord than to put confidence in man, It is better to trust in the Lord than to put confidence in princes. All nations compassed me about; yea, they compassed me about: but in the name of the Lord, I will destroy them. They compassed me about, yea, they compassed me about, but in the name of the Lord I will destroy them. They compassed me about like bees; they are quenched as the fire of thorns; for in the name of the Lord I will destroy them. Thou hast thrust sore at me that I might fall: but the Lord helped me. The Lord is my strength and song, and is become my salvation. The voice of rejoicing and salvation is in the tabernacles of the righteous, the right hand of the Lord doeth valiantly. The right hand of the Lord is exalted; the right hand of the Lord doeth valiantly. I shall not die but live and declare the works of the Lord. The Lord hast chastened me sore; but He hath not given me over to death. Open me to the gates of righteousness: I will go into them and I will praise the Lord; This gate of the Lord, into which the righteous shall enter. I will praise Thee for Thou hast heard me and art become my salvation. The stone which the builders refused is to become the head stone of the corner. This is the Lord's doing, it is marvelous in our eyes. This is the day which the Lord hath made; we will rejoice and be glad in it. Save now, I beseech Thee, O Lord: O Lord, I beseech Thee, send now prosperity. Blessed be he who cometh in the name of the Lord: we have blessed you out of the house of the Lord. God is the Lord which hath shewed us light; bind the sacrifice with cords, even unto the horns of the altar. Thou art my God and I will praise Thee: Thou art my God and I will exalt Thee. O give thanks unto the Lord; for He is good: for His mercy endureth forever.

    I bowed my head once more, silently breathing the Lord's Prayer on Paul's behalf. During His ministry here, this is the only prayer Jesus left to us. I figured He must have had a good reason for that.

    Following my lead, Pastor stood and turned to leave the Altar. The pews had sure filled up during the time we'd been praying. My eyes adjusted to the light and I recognized the parishioners as my friends. Among them was Marilyn Crosby who had been a fellow charter member of Christus Victor Lutheran. Marilyn and Paul had served together on the Christus Victor Counsel, she and I had sung together in the choir. She had been a mentor for me, serving together on Via de Cristo Cursillo retreats. Marilyn was formerly an accountant who had been called into the ministry. She was close to graduation from the Lutheran Seminary in Columbia, South Carolina.

    I reached into my cluster of friends to embrace each one, then, sat down beside Marilyn. Everyone drew close to hear my whispered update on Paul.

    When I finished, Marilyn gathered my cold hands into the warmth of hers. My fingers were stiff and I realized I had been clutching them together in the hollow of my lap. Even still, I felt God's perfect peace, in and around me as Marilyn's compassion drew the chill out.

    "Look at me, Shirley." Marilyn said, her bright eyes searching mine, "I want you to remember something."

    "Yeah, Okay." I answered, not sure why she sounded so grave and urgent.

    "Don't miss all of the *little* miracles while you are waiting for the *big* one."

    I stared at her, taking it in.

    "That's it." She concluded. "Miracles are all around you. Be aware of them."

    "Yes. Thank you, Marilyn." I agreed, taking note of all the

perfect timing, people and situations God had orchestrated around this crisis. "They truly are."

> *"Lord,"* Martha said to Jesus, *"if you had been here, my brother would not have died. But I know that even now, God will give you whatever you ask."*
> John 11:21-22

Chapter Forty-One

Pastor Garry finally had supporters in his campaign to feed me. Paul's step-dad, Rod and Millie had arrived, but I regret that can't remember all the others. I succumbed to a bottle of orange juice, but that was the best I could do before hurrying back to the surgical waiting room.

Nita was the first person I saw waiting. She smiled and stood, emanating feminine business radiance in her work clothes. My beautiful best friend, Ruthie sat beside her, somehow able to feel my emotions inside her own heart; just as she had been doing for nearly forty years. Too bad this was what it took to get two of my favorite people close enough to meet each other. I squeezed between them.

"It's supposed to take five hours." I told them.

"They told us." Ruthie said.

"Who?" I asked.

"A nurse came out a few minutes ago and asked who was here for Paul. She told us to tell you everything was going well."

I winced. "I knew I shouldn't have gone to the cafeteria."

"She said she'd be back." Nita added.

I put my purse on the floor beside Nita's as a little figure in scrubs stepped inside the waiting room. I thought it must be the nurse again, so I stood up. The figure said, "Mrs. Graham?"

It was Doctor Samuel. I grabbed both mine and Nita's purses and rushed over to her.

"He's great." Dr. Samuel told me happily. "He did very well."

"You're done?" I asked, "It's over? It didn't take as long as you thought."

"No. It didn't." She agreed.

"Is it gone?" I asked her.

"Most of it. There are some residual cells remaining, but a few radiation treatments will destroy them. I will explain it all when I meet with you later, but I just wanted to let you know how well your husband did. You should be proud of him."

"I am."

Nita and Ruthie giggled behind me.

I turned to look at them, "What?"

"My purse." Nita made a little snort and giggled again, "Can I have it back?"

* * *

Paul stayed in recovery for what seemed like hours, during which time Doctor Samuel showered and changed clothes. I was to meet her in a small conference office for the specific details of the surgery and Paul's condition. She said I could bring whomever I liked. My entourage included my children as well as Ruthie, Nita, Pastor Garry, Marilyn, Dale, Danny, Rod, Millie and others. The little room was packed, yet more chairs were being dragged in.

Doctor Samuel was nonplused and 'poised' didn't even begin to describe her. She wore a soft cashmere sweater over a nice pair of dress pants. She'd even taken the time to add earrings and a matching necklace. To pass this tiny woman on the street, one would never have guessed she had just dug a tumor the size of a golf ball out of my husband's skull.

She confirmed that the tumor had indeed ruptured and then went on to explain the brain bleed and its effect on Paul's behavior. Most of us had already heard a briefing on this part. Maybe she was stalling.

"Has a biopsy been done on the tumor?" I asked at the first break in her monologue.

"The tumor is cancer." She replied quickly, relieved to get her mouth shut of the bitter words. "We don't know what kind of cancer yet."

She gave us a synopsis of different kinds of cancers and their different personalities. Who knew? Not me. I always thought cancer was all the same and just grew in different places. I thought the location determined the type. Wouldn't cancer in the lung, for example, be lung cancer? Apparently not.

"Since your husband had a documented melanoma lesion removed, we will probably find the tumor was melanoma. She paused and looked at me, inviting my question.

"But, it's gone now, right?"

Dr. Samuel looked straight in my eyes. "The tumor or the cancer?"

I was confused. "Well, both."

"Not both." She took a breath. The rest of us were holding ours.

"I don't understand."

"Your husband had a skin lesion removed previously and the margins appeared to be clear."

"That's right."

"But you see, there must have been at least one cell that got away. It only takes one. With melanoma, one cell can travel to another place and metastasis occurs."

I felt my eyebrows wrinkle while concentrating on her words.

"Melanoma travels through the blood." She explained. The cell used his bloodstream as a vehicle to end up in his brain."

"I think I get it," I said, "but you removed the tumor, so it's gone, right?"

"The tumor in his brain is gone, save for the residual remains which we will treat with radiation. I must tell you that there is probably another tumor in another organ."

"Why?" I asked, shaking my head against such an awful prophesy.

"Melanoma is like that. We will do something called a PET scan that looks at his whole body. It will identify any other lesions."

"So," I made little fists in my lap, "He'll have surgery or radiation on the other tumor. Is it over then?"

"He will still have melanoma, if that is what it is."

"So," I tried again, the reality of it turning to bile as I

said it, "What I think you are saying is that we will just keep cutting chunks out of my husband until finally there is nothing left to cut."

Maybe she was tired, she seemed to crack. She seemed indignant to my question and began delivering an analogy about two men who were both given six months to live. One man accepted it and took a vacation. He did all the things he always wanted to do. The other man planted a garden. After six months, the first man died, but the second one was still living. I tried to follow the meaning, but the metaphor just didn't comfort me. I didn't need a lesson in walking on the sunny side; I just wanted to know the truth.

She changed gears and described our next course of action. I listened quietly but I didn't want to hear her anymore. There would be another doctor; Trip, she called him. Doctor Trip, highly respected, regarded by many as the best doctor in his field, a good friend of hers. He would be Paul's oncologist. The room felt small, stuffy. I wanted to get away from her, to scream. I was crushing one of Ruthie's hands with both of mine, but she hung on to me anyway. The last time she'd held my hand this tight I'd been pushing Joseph into the world.

I didn't realize it at the moment, but my family had just entered a sub-culture that would teach us more about cancer than we had ever wanted to know. The family of a cancer victim is victimized, too. In a sense, the whole family has contracted the disease by proxy. I don't mean in the literal sense, as though cancer were contagious, but in a very real way nonetheless. In the coming months I found myself referring to Paul's appointments in first person plurals. "When is *our* appointment with the oncologist?" "*We* have a PET scan scheduled." If Paul was being called to bear this burden, then I wanted to carry some of it. That promise I made, *"... in sickness and health,"* was being put to the test.

As our friends and relatives filed out of the little conference room, I returned to my personal cocoon in the I.C.U. waiting room. Strange, how comfortable a straight-back chair becomes when it's the closest point to a loved one. I poured hot water from the coffee machine into a Styrofoam cup. The tea bag in the bottom rolled around as it became saturated. A few bubbles floated up as leaves stained the water into tea.

I thought about the wedding in Cana, Jesus' first miracle, turning water into wine. I wondered if this is how it looked with the wine coloring the water. Who had been there, who had seen it happen? Who would know how it had looked? Clear water filtered through the bag and strained out reddish-brown swirls. I stirred it with my plastic spoon and reached into a little basket for sugar packets.

"Lord?" I whispered in my heart, "Give my Paul a miracle."

I looked around the waiting room. There was my new friend, a young man named Pete, sound asleep in his chair a respectable distance away from mine. We waiters respected what little privacy was here among us in the I.C.U. waiting area. Pete was probably in his early thirties; his wife was lying in a room around the corner. He loved her. They had small children. Yesterday an aneurysm had ruptured in her head and ruined a lot of their plans.

Margie's chair was empty but for her brown sweater that awaited her return. She was probably across the hall in the bathroom washing her face. Small comforts. Margie's son had flown through a windshield on the way home from college last week. Eddie, I think she had said.

"You are the Great Physician." I whispered to my Creator, "Give us all miracles."

While he was still speaking to her, messengers arrived from Jarius' home with the message "Your daughter is dead. There is no use in troubling the Teacher now" But Jesus ignored their comments and said to Jarius, "Don't be afraid. Just trust me" Then Jesus stopped the crowd and wouldn't let anyone go with him, except for Peter and James and John. When they came to the home of the synagogue leader, Jesus saw the commotion and weeping and wailing. He went inside and spoke to the people, "Why all this weeping and commotion?" He asked. "The child isn't dead, she's only asleep." The crowd laughed at him, but he told them all to go outside. Then he took the child's father and mother and his three disciples into the room where the girl was lying. Holding her hand he said, "Get up, little girl."And the girl, who was 12 years old, immediately stood up and walked around. Her parents were absolutely overwhelmed. Jesus commanded them not to tell anyone what had happened and he told them to give her something to eat.
Mark 5:35-43

Chapter Forty-Two

Your husband is awake, Mrs. Graham.

I opened one eye and focused on the smiling face of an I.C.U. nurse. Opening the other eye, I smiled back, surmising that she wouldn't be smiling if it was bad news.

"He wants to see you."

"He's talking?" I was standing now, tossing my travel blanket into my chair. My cell phone rang.

"He's talking and he says he's hungry." She added as her scrubs disappeared out the door. "Come on back when you can."

"You bet." I followed her, fumbling for my phone without slowing my pace.

"Hello?"

"Shirley? It's Phil."

"Phil. Come on over here. Paul is awake and the nurse said he's talking. He told her he was hungry."

"I'm coming." I heard him say as I hung up. I was already out in the hall facing the double doors that would open to my answered prayer.

Paul was sitting up in bed when I arrived. He sported a faded hospital gown which matched smartly with his thick, gauze turban. I gave him a smile that broke into laughter when he smiled back at me.

"Hey, honey." I gushed, surprised that my voice now seemed possessed by Minnie Mouse.

"Hey, sweetie." Paul answered. I laughed again and hugged him. Something beeped and I figured out I was sitting on one of his tubes.

"You're back."

"I am?"

I hugged him again, the machine beeped.

I wasn't sure of him. I fished for a while, keeping the conversation simple before deciding how much of Paul was really here.

"I love you so much."

"I love you, too, sweetie."

"How do you feel?"

"Okay."

"The nurse says you're hungry?"

"Yes. I am."

We looked at each other. "Do you know what happened?"

"Not everything. Just what I was told. Doctor Samuel said I had surgery."

"She's pretty, isn't she?"

Before he could answer, someone knocked. Shadow-boxing behind the curtain soon produced Pastor Garry between a split of panels. He stepped through laughing at himself but stopped laughing when he saw Paul.

"You're a sight for sore eyes, my friend." Pastor Garry's arms hugged us both at once. He stepped back. "I left a bunch of your visitors in the waiting room."

"Who?" I asked.

"Phil-somebody, Gary-something, Charles-,"

"Paul's *brothers*." I offered. "You know, Phil Graham, Charles Graham, the others…" I winked at Paul.

"Would you like to see them, or do you want to wait a while?"

"Now's good." Paul grinned. "Bring those knuckleheads in."

He sounded like my Paul. How could this be?

Pastor Garry left and returned with part of Dentsville High School's 1967 football team and their mentor, Coach Richardson. Phil came in first. His right arm hugged Paul as his left hand set a Zesto's four-piece chicken basket in his lap.

"I heard Garnto was hungry." Phil explained, pretending his cheeks weren't wet with tears. Paul was already pulling the grease spotted cardboard platter out, spilling over with what is most assuredly the best fried chicken in the world.

"Good choice." Paul said biting into a perfect breast.

The Greek word, *phileo* would adequately describe the joyous atmosphere there in Paul's room; a fallen brother, raised up as the witnesses watched him eat Zesto's. Big grown men, laughing and slapping each other was the righteous response to what God had granted us: a miracle. A flat-out, modern day, Lazarus-style miracle.

Rod, Paul's dad, stepped through the veil of curtains and hugged his greasy boy, back from an abyss. He wrapped a bear-hug around each of the grown boys surrounding Paul's bed. He knew them well. A couple of decades ago, these guys had consumed his groceries and made all manner of noise in his house.

The curtain parted again. Jaws dropped in unison as the beautiful Doctor Samuel waded gracefully into the testosterone-filled room.

"…these your friends, Mr. Graham?"

"Brothers." Mark answered quickly.

"Oh, yes." Dr. Samuel played along. "Big family."

"I'm his dad." Rod reacted.

"I really am his brother." Paul's brother, Danny defended himself.

Pastor Garry bowed, "His minister, and brother in Christ."

"I get the picture." Doctor Samuel said smugly, then

to Paul, "How are you feeling, big guy?"

"I'm good." Paul nodded his gauzy head. "I feel pretty good. Except for this head dress that keeps slipping around. Can we get rid of this thing?"

"Sorry." She apologized. "That has to stay. She noted the fried chicken bone-yard. "Did you eat this?"

"I was hungry." Paul explained. The room erupted in muffled laughter. "Is it okay?"

"If you're not nauseated, it's fine. Can you tell me what year it is?"

"Two-thousand-one."

"Who's the president?"

"George Bush."

"W. or H.W?" Rod intoned from the peanut gallery.

"Pay no attention to the man beside the curtain." Dr. Samuel advised Paul.

He nodded.

"Do you know where you are?"

"This is a hospital. Lexington?"

"Right. Mr. Graham, you are an amazing man."

"Thank you."

"You know what? I can't do anything about it tonight, but I don't think you need to be on this floor very long."

"Great."

"Trip… Dr. Trip, will be in later tonight. You'll like him. I think you can go to the recovery floor if he agrees that it's okay. In the meantime, let your "brothers" go somewhere else and drink a few beers in your honor. We're all proud of you."

She turned and it seemed the curtain parted itself for her as Paul's visitors began falling all over themselves to prove they knew their manners.

In her absence, the room fell silent. Paul looked up at the envious eyes of his visitors.

"Bo." Phil said in awe, "That was your *brain surgeon?*"

Paul smiled and nodded sheepishly.

"You know?" Frankie stepped forward, rubbing his scalp, "I think I've got a pain right here in my brain. Could you get her back in here?"

He cried with a loud voice, Lazarus, come forth. And he that was dead came forth. Then many of the Jews which came to Mary, and had seen the things which Jesus did, believed on him. But some of them went their ways to the Pharisees, and told them what things Jesus had done.
John 11:43-46

Chapter Forty-Three

Paul's guests left before anybody complained about their joyful reception over his resurrection. Soon after their departure, a scratchy intercom announcement advised us that visiting hours were over. I, however, hid quietly under the covers and rested my cheek against my husband's smooth back. I breathed him in, loving his scent and thanking God for this glorious moment.

"Be glorified in this, Jesus." I prayed.

Paul and I slept so soundly amid the beeping machines. In that place between reality and dreams, I drifted back to the dawn of our love when my apartment in Lexington had been only a couple of blocks from Paul's job at Kroger Pharmacy.

***

Way back in the spring of our romance, after we had finally admitted our feelings for each other, Paul would sometimes stop in after work to eat the supper I had saved for him. He'd come to my door smelling of cologne, his leather jacket and that other lovely essence. He'd hug me then plant a mighty kiss on my lips. At my little table, he would pull off his tie before digging in. He always raved over anything I had cooked, singing its praises as he dined. When my apartment door closed behind him and he left for home, I watched him through my blinds whispering, "I love you, Paul Graham."

I always loved when he left his tie hanging on the back of a chair. I would put my face into the fabric and breathe in Eau de Paul. I'd go to sleep those nights, his tie near my face, on my pillow.

***

    Striving for invisibility in I.C.U. had become my stealthy habit. When visiting hours ended, I just couldn't bear to leave my husband. Had *my* health been in peril I'd sure want Paul beside me. The day nurses were less tolerant of my disobedience to this rule, but I'm pretty sure most of the night nurses knew I remained with Paul and slept. Some would even slip in to get Paul's vital signs and smile at the sight of me hiding behind his broad back. Only one night nurse had ever made an issue of my disregard of this rule. After having napped with Paul I would finally return to my nest in the waiting room, keeping a close eye on my watch, unwilling to miss the visiting allowed every two or three hours.

    I felt no appetite for physical food, only eating to pacify friends who insisted I ought to, yet I was starving for Spiritual food. My Bible fed my needs. I loved my Life Application Study Bible. Paul had bought it after our friends, Larry and Tammy showed us theirs. It was a New International Version (NIV), which made it an easy read, but the thing that made it so different for me was its Life Application feature. Included in the commentary at the bottom of each page were suggestions of how each passage applied to daily life. I now read my Bible for the sheer pleasure of it. Sitting there in that waiting room, reading and praying, it was almost as though I was outside myself. The image I envision is devoid of time or space. Although separated from Paul that week, I felt close to him when I went to the Lord. I dozed in the waiting room, waking just minutes before visiting hours began. The weight of my Bible rested comfortably in my lap like a heavy quilt. I lifted it, setting it carefully in the seat I was vacating. I found my purse under the chair, slung it over my shoulder and walked across the hall, grateful the bathroom was for just one person. The little room offered enough privacy for a person to curse, pray, cry, brush teeth or shampoo hair at the sink. The door closed itself behind me and I hung one strap of my purse on a hook. Digging out my toothbrush and toothpaste, I turned to the mirror and leaned in. "What's coming next?" I wondered aloud and was glad my reflection didn't have an answer. I wasn't sure I really wanted to know. I brushed my teeth and washed my face. I didn't look great, but at least I was clean. I entered I.C.U. through the double doors and waved at a couple of nurses whose names had become familiar to me. How many shift changes had we seen by now? Paul was asleep when I entered. Dr. Samuel stood beside his bed reading a clipboard listing his vital signs over the past few hours. She turned to me and smiled.

"I hear he gave them a hard time last night."

"What happened?" I asked, surprised.

"He insisted that the cap under his dressing be removed or he'd do it himself."

"He was sleeping when I saw him." I said, defending him.

"Sometimes patients become agitated after trauma to the brain. He's taking steroids to minimize swelling as he heals. Steroids can also foster agitation. He's doing great, though." She began waking him and I buried an urge to stop her.

"You feeling okay today, Mr. Graham?"

Paul's eyes opened and he pulled himself up to a sitting position. "G'mornin'."

Dr. Samuel was wearing street clothes without pockets, so I marveled when she magically produced a penlight out of thin air.

"Follow my light." She commanded.

Paul's eyes shifted left, right, up and down. It there was anything amiss in his responses, I sure couldn't see it. She clicked off the light and I forgot to watch where she put it away. She looked at Paul's head dressing.

"I heard you were giving my night staff a hard time."

"This skull cap thing kept sliding off my head. I couldn't get anybody to take it off me."

"The cap has to stay. Those orders are mine."

She lifted the white gauze encircling the plastic cap and made an imperceptible adjustment; to pacify Paul, I assumed.

"I'll get someone to re-dress the gauze before you go to another floor but the cap stays on your head."

Paul said nothing.

"How many skin lesions have been removed?" She asked.

Paul and I spoke simultaneously.

"Two." He said as I said, "One.".

"Two or one?" She asked, looking back and forth from Paul to me.

I started to repeat, "One", but Paul was already saying, "Two" again.

Her eyes shifted to me for comment.

"I... think he's counting Tuesday's surgery." I explained, figuring the cranial surgery caused his confusion.

"No." Paul said with resolution, "Two."

"Two?" I questioned him. "I only knew about the one you had removed before Joseph was born, and now this one."

Paul nodded his head, contending. "Two."

I wondered why he hadn't told me about this. I would learn that there had been another one before we dated. I thought about His mom and how many times she had made me promise to put sun screen on him. Had she known?

"Pathology has confirmed another tumor in your lung." She said to Paul, and I wondered if his heart dropped like mine just had.

"It's in the middle lobe. Dr. Trip will set you up with a surgeon after you recover from this."

Paul nodded in earnest acceptance. Leaden silence hung between us.

"Is it ... how big is it?" I stuttered in a small voice that clanged through the density of quiet like a gong.

"It's about the same size as the one we excised in his brain." She addressed me, crediting us with her surgery. She turned back to Paul, changing the subject. "I'm hoping to get you out of here and down to another floor so you can go home soon. You could probably go home now, but the hospital won't let me discharge you straight from ICU."

I nodded, answering with a mildly responsive, "Okay." All this good news, bad news was hard to keep up with.

I wasn't really listening to her. I was trying to remember the day Paul showed me the big hole Dr. Chow had cut and stitched around the dark mole he removed. Why hadn't he told me it was his *second* melanoma?

Dr. Samuel turned, adding, "You keep making me look good, Big Guy." then she slipped out through the curtain.

Back in the waiting room, it occurred to me that I'd be moving soon, too. I started organizing my personal things for transit and hoped my new waiting room nest would be as accommodating as this one. Before late afternoon, Paul's new room was issued with a surprise awaiting me there. Right beside his bed was my own personal bed. Taking a real shower would be my first piece of business. Dressing in the bathroom after a glorious shower, I heard conversation. I raked a brush through my clean, wet hair and opened the door. Pastor Ron had stopped in with greetings from Christus Victor and a giant poster. A green and red cross made from thumb prints adorned the center. Get-well wishes from our friends were written all around it in green or red ink. Reading the personal wishes brought tears to my eyes.

"That was sweet." I told Paul after Pastor Ron left.

"Yeah." Paul answered. He sat up in bed, hands folded in his lap like he wasn't sure what he was supposed to be doing. He looked peaceful but tired. The bandage on his head had been re-dressed and made him look like one of the Three Wise Men, but I didn't say it. His sense of humor was absent and I didn't want to stress him.

"Are you thirsty?" I asked.

"No," was all he said.

"Do you mind if I walk down the hall in search of a Coca-Cola?"

Paul shook his head.

I had only walked a few feet when I noticed Gary Smallen carrying his hat and wandering the corridors, too.

"Psst." I hissed and his head twisted toward me. "…you looking for the Grahams?"

"Yeah. I went up to ICU and they told me Paul Graham wasn't there. I was too scared to ask why they had moved him."

I giggled, dropping a coin into the Coke machine.

"Good news brings him to this floor." I reassured Gary.

A can of Coke clunked out and I freed it from its confines. We walked toward Paul's room.

"That's great." Gary smiled, then, "Hey, Shirley, how are *you* after all of this?"

"Exhilarated." I answered, smiling back at him, "Happy. Thankful."

I stopped in the hall and looked at him.

"You know what, though, Gary?"

He waited.

"My heart is so full of joy over Paul's successful surgery and yet …"

I hesitated, hating both the truth and uncertainty of what I was going to say.

"I also realize that life as we have known it has changed forever."

> *Jesus performed many other signs in the presence of his disciples, which are not recorded in this book. But these are written that you may believe that Jesus is the Messiah, the Son of God, and that by believing you may have life in his name.*
> *John 20:30*

Chapter Forty-Four

Friday morning's light cast tiny rays through the blinds, breaking up the room's dimness. The door to Paul's room swooshed open with a new shift nurse who floated in on silent feet.

"Good morning." I heard myself greet her.

Paul opened his mouth to receive her thermometer.

"Good morning." With the thermometer in place, she began wrapping the blood pressure cuff around Paul's upper arm.

I studied his face, trying in vain to read his mind, wondering how much of my husband was left in the wake of brain surgery. He seemed articulate enough, which was a miracle in itself.

The nurse's extraction of the thermometer put an abrupt end to his silence, "I'm ready to go home."

"Well, Mr. Graham, normally I'd be discouraging you from such thoughts, but rumor has it that you're going home today."

My heart began to race, transforming my new joy into both thrill and panic. I was proud of my hunky husband's sheer will to get back to business but shuddered at the responsibility that would entail. Could I handle whatever his needs might require?

"So, is his doctor really ready to release him?"

The nurse un-wrapped the sphygmomanometer from Paul's arm and answered, "That's what they are saying. Dr. Samuel ought to be in pretty soon. She's already started her rounds on this floor."

I giggled in Paul's direction, awed over the brazen healing God had just performed.

"Good." He smiled and his eyes crinkled the way I knew so well.

Amazingly, the nurse's prediction turned out to be accurate. Dr. Samuel arrived smiling her movie star smile and gave Paul the okay to return home. She seemed pretty proud of herself and I thought Paul's healing must still be making her look pretty good. We left the hospital with instructions to visit Dr. Samuel's office and to see oncologist Dr. Trip the following week. I pulled the Windstar up to the hospital entrance where Paul's tall frame filled up a wheelchair. I was hoping he wouldn't insist on driving. Maybe it wouldn't come up if I stayed behind the wheel. A male transporter ferried him into the passenger seat and Paul sat silent.

I smiled stupidly but I was nervous, unsure if I really knew this post-surgery husband.

"We dodged a pretty big bullet, Counselor." I fished, pretending confidence.

"I could have driven."

"Oh, I know, honey, but I'm okay." I turned on the right blinker.

"It's left." Paul stated.

"Um. No, I think it's right."

"Left."

I didn't feel like arguing with someone whose head had just been cracked open and dissected, so I turned left. If we had to turn around when the mistake became obvious, so be it.

It was only a few feet before I realized Paul had been right about left. I knew that my dyslexic sense of direction was legendary but it humbled me painfully to realize I couldn't even trust it against a newly kneaded brain.

"Oh, man. You're right"

Paul didn't answer. I knew he was thinking he could have driven better. I turned onto I-26 and we drove silently for a few miles. I was concentrating so hard on the road. Maybe if I made perfect road decisions the rest of the way home it would make up for my mistake. I wanted to do this job right. If I was being called to serve as Paul caretaker I wanted to be the best one available. I relaxed my muscles deliberately and thought, "No pressure."

Paul didn't initiate any conversation as our wheels rolled out of West Columbia into Columbia. I managed to exit where I was supposed to on I-77 and finally spoke,

"I still can't believe brain surgery only kept us in the hospital for five days."

It was only December 20th. We'd lived a month's worth of events in those five days.

"Three," Paul corrected, "from the actual surgery."

He wasn't being cocky. He was testing his intellectual abilities, making sure he was all there.

I giggled over my nerves.

"Three." I emphasized the word with a nod of conviction.

"We'll have Christmas at home. When is our appointment with the oncologist?"

Paul kept his eyes on the road, driving vicariously, "It's written in our discharge papers."

I exited at the second Winnsboro sign and finished his thought, "Okay, we'll look at what they gave us when we get home."

"Us, we and our" had replaced "I, you, my and your" during this hospital stay. We had promised oneness to each other in our marriage vows, yet making good on being two, yet one in sickness and health almost became an entity of its own. Our marriage took on another dimension. A new depth of love and trust took roots in our single, shared heart. Even though our whole family suffered some degree of this affliction of cancer, the physical sacrifice always fell on Paul's strong body. Claiming the cancer in plural was an unconscious response, a verbal effort in sharing Paul's burden, and he didn't fight it. His acquiescence was the only thing hinting that he couldn't bear this alone.

I turned right after the Volunteer Fire Department. The woodsy terrain lining the right side of our road gave me a thrill and I swallowed an excited squeal that bubbled up in my throat. We were coming home. Everything familiar rose up to greet us as I drove under the stilted house Paul and I had designed together. I put the van in park and met Paul as his car door shut. I couldn't stop smiling. Paul was *walking* up the stairs to the door. He wasn't being carried or wheeled home; he was walking with his own able legs. He'd been made whole. My heart resounded, *"God is so good."*

"KNOCK, KNOCK." Paul said loudly, stepping through the French doors of home.

"DADDY." Sarah's surprised greeting rang out like a chiming bell as the rest of our seven children poured into the room. Sarah's eyes were moist and she reluctantly stepped aside to give the others a turn at welcoming Dad back home. No one was quite sure how hard to squeeze him.

A panicked thought rushed through my head. The shopping I'd planned to finish up this week was spent mostly in the ICU waiting room. Sarah was the hardest one of my children to buy presents for, and her shopping was the least finished. I made a mental note to send Jon and Elisabeth into Camden with a credit card. What a blessing it was to have all our children home on this day of days.

"Do you want to sit, Paul?"

Paul gave me a gentle smile, "Maybe I'll sit right here on the couch."

He gingerly wove a trail around the narrow opening leading to the Daddy Spot on the light tan, leather sectional we had ordered without measuring first. It was huge, never fitting anywhere we had tried to impose it, but very comfortable. Creatures of habit, Charlotte, Emily and Joseph instantly assumed their usual couch positions, leaning into their daddy's center of gravity. This was such a familiar scene to me. To date, Paul was halfway through Harry Potter, reading a chapter to the children before devotions every night. A ripple of joy swelled my heart. He *would* finish reading the book to them after all.

Chocolate Bar's puppy bed sat in a corner of the room. Something didn't look right. He was there in the bed but his fur looked matted and dull. My breath caught when I noticed he was barely moving.

"What's wrong with the puppy?"

The big kids shrugged in unison. My next question took on a higher pitch of alarm.

"How long has he looked like this?"

Sarah responded, "I didn't think he looked too good, either, but I don't know what puppies are supposed to look like."

"He's sick." I told them and went for the phone.

I caught the vet's office right before closing and they agreed to see Chocolate Bar. Jon and Sarah drove the poor little thing to the vet and left him overnight. When I called the following day, the vet told me we could pick Chocolate Bar up. She had given him fluids and although he looked some better, he still didn't have much of an appetite. He'd managed to eat a little, though and it appeared good health was on his horizon. Still, when Austin picked him up, the vet told him to call her if something didn't look just right.

Then our mouth was filled with laughter, and our tongue with shouts of joy; then they said among the nations, "The Lord has done great things for them.
Psalm 126:2

Chapter Forty-Five

The gauzy days that preceded Sunday, December 21, 2001 were cold. Powdery snow fell on Winnsboro Friday night. Saturday my insides froze as Paul insisted on going outside to throw snowballs with the kids. I held my breath with each icy, wooden step he descended, dutifully taking pictures and praying through the lens that he wouldn't lose his balance. God was characteristically gracious. Tiny Frankie, the cat was such a source of entertainment for us that he could have looked just right in a tuxedo and cane. It was easy to tell he thought he was bulletproof and could jump like nothing I have ever seen. Michele and Monica, Paul's sisters, had sent us a Honey Baked turkey breast. It came in a foil bag that we left on the kitchen counter long enough for Frankie to smell it. In a flash, he made such a leap to the empty bag I was sure he had wings. When we pulled the reluctant kitty out of the bag, his fur was matted with turkey juice, his eye was greased shut and his little tongue reached crazily beyond his nose.

Paul was eating well, too, thanks largely to the steroids he was taking and the wonderful casseroles that continued to pour in from three churches and numerous friends and relatives. He seemed quieter than usual, yet peaceful. It wasn't unusual to see him tear up anytime the subject of conversation centered on our loved ones who rallied 'round us. He didn't talk about it much, but I suppose he was like me, feeling humbled and enormously thankful for the thick blanket of grace surrounding us. We were getting into bed that Saturday night when Paul said,

"What time do you want to get up in the morning?"

Was he serious? Did he really feel well enough to get up and dress in the morning, drive into Camden and worship? Was it practical or safe, a single week after our nightmare began, only five days after having an evil golf ball of cancer pulled out of his head?

"For church, you mean?"

"Yeah."

"For real?"

Paul looked a little irritated. "I really want to go."

"Me, too, but is it too soon?"

"I don't know, but I want to go."

"Okay, then, let's go."

I turned off the bedside light and shuddered under my covers. Not only because the road conditions would be dangerous tomorrow after the snow melted and re-froze, but because I had no doubt that Paul's intention did not include sitting in the passenger seat.

I slept lightly, hearing every breath and movement Paul made. My eyelids snapped open when dawn broke and I was ready to roll. Fight-or-flight mode kept a stubborn hold on me. I rolled over and watched my wonderful man breathe. How I loved his nose, so straight and neat, his eyebrows so perfect, so serene. I lay back down, unable to resist the urge to thread my arms through his so I could feel his weight and strength. I loved the smell of him. I rested my head on his smooth shoulder, thankful for my olfactory system.

"Mornin'." I whispered into his neck.

He stirred, gave me a groggy, "Mornin'." His eyes trailed a path across the bed and landed on the alarm clock.

"Paul, are you still sure about going to church?"

"You bet." He rolled onto the edge of the bed and sat up slowly. "My mama *born* me ready."

"Be that as it may, this is just about where we were this time last Sunday. I'll appreciate it if you can reduce the drama this week."

He stood and limped toward the shower, willing his creaking joints to awaken.

"I'll take that under advisement." He smiled, adjusted the water and closed the shower door.

I held my breath and lifted a silent prayer indicative of the fretful caretaker I had recently become. "Don't let him slip and fall, Lord."

Fortunately, I'd showered before bedtime last night after whispering instructions in the ears of my children to keep an eye on their daddy. I dressed quickly and began the task of waking my peeps.

As Paul turned the key in the ignition later, my heart skipped a beat as I feigned calm collected-ness on the outside. If he suspected that I was whistling in the graveyard, he never let on.

I'm not sure I breathed much on the way to Camden. Paul

drove just fine, but I found it hard to relax my stomach muscles until we parked in front of the Sanctuary. Paul parallel parked the van perfectly. The children ran ahead, scattering across St. Tim's snow-spotted lawn toward Sunday School. Elisabeth intercepted Joseph's little fist as he raced by her.

"I'll take Joseph to his class, Mom and Dad." She called before disappearing with him behind the red double doors.

We were late. It was our bad habit, being late. Paul had fought for punctuality as best he could in the beginning, but finally adjusted to being late whenever we all went somewhere. He joked that we attended the 9:45 Sunday School class, although the class started at 9:30.

Paul pulled the red Lutheran door open for me and we stepped inside. He walked half-a-pace ahead of me down the hall to our room.

"Paul?" I hastened, trying to keep up.

Instead of answering, he looked straight ahead like he was being drawn by an invisible force.

He was so intense, I was suddenly afraid he might do something inappropriate; just what, I couldn't say. He turned the doorknob to our class and fairly kicked the door open.

"Paul." I started to gasp but it was too late. We stood exposed in the open doorway to the somber, then incredulous faces of our friends. One by one they began to smile, stand and clap, prompting the tears that streamed down all our faces. God had brought a real Lazarus into Saint Timothy's Lutheran Church, physical proof of His miraculous healing power. We embraced each other then celebrated thanks to our mighty Savior in a hand-held prayer-circle.

To everything there is a season, and a time to every purpose under the heaven: A time to be born, and a time to die; a time to plant, and a time to pluck up that which was planted; A time to kill, and a time to heal; A time to break down, and a time to build up. A time to weep, And a time to laugh; a time to mourn, and a time to dance.
Ecclesiastes 3:1-4

Chapter Forty-Six

Chocolate Bar was looking awful. He moved like he was aged, not like a lively new puppy. Austin drove him back to the vet who received him with knitted brows, then called me at home.

"Mrs. Graham, won't he eat at all?"

"...or drink" I said sadly. "Yet he vomits. He's so pitiful."

She whispered to Austin that he could leave the puppy. He exited, looking back at her as she stroked Chocolate Bar's tiny head.

"You worry about getting your husband well and I'll call when I find something." She said to into the phone.

* * *

Our house felt like a train station with kids of all sizes coming and going. Every member of our family was home, my husband was alive, recovering and it was almost time to celebrate the birth of the Christ-child. Paul was quieter than usual and prone to thankful tears but I couldn't remember a more loving Christmas together.

Before we knew it, the big kids were gone again and our days began to resemble a new normal.

That's when the vet called.

"I stayed up most of the night doing research. I'm finally able to pinpoint Chocolate Bar's condition." She began. "It's called mega-esophagus."

"What does it mean?"

"For some reason, his esophagus is too big. A birth defect. When he tries to ingest anything, it kind of pools and he can't swallow."

"Can it be corrected?"

"No, that's the thing. We can operate and insert a stomach tube so he could get nourishment, but even that wouldn't be a guarantee that he'd live long."

Under normal circumstances, this decision would have fallen on Paul, but because of the cancer and surgery, I quickly took charge.

"The stomach tube might not even be an answer then, is that right?"

"I'm sorry. Yes, that's right."

"Doctor," I whispered into the mouthpiece, "I want you to put the poor little thing to sleep."

"Are you sure you don't want to see him first?"

"I am sure. If I make this decision, then my people won't have to. I know it's the right thing. They are all too fragile right now."

"I agree, Mrs. Graham."

And so it happened that Chocolate Bar was no more. Paul and I gathered our youngest four children on the couch. I explained Chocolate Bar's situation while Paul's warm hand covered mine. We wept.

* * *

Over the next few weeks, frequent visitors made the long drive to our house bearing gifts of food, service or other helpful fare. I remember coming home to two grocery bags sitting on chairs outside our front door. Where they came from was a mystery for two years until a dear lady named Jakie confessed that she had left them. A group of women from St. Tim's came to the door one morning with mops and cleaners, intent on making our house sparkle (which they did). Amy sent a basket filled with household consumables, like paper towels, toilet tissue and aluminum foil. Another ladies group brought an envelope filled with money collected for us at their last meeting. This altruism humbled me so deeply. Christ was using these precious acts of benevolence to teach me new ways to show His love. Like Mary preparing for God's son, I treasured all these things in my heart.

In the midst of the love I felt, a nagging worry about

the cancer lurking in Paul's lung tormented me. The oncologist had said we might be interested in contacting Duke University's doctors. There was a procedure being done there that had turned melanoma victims into survivors. It involved making a vaccine for the patient from the actual cancerous tumor.

"Sign me up." Paul had told Doctor Trip, but that had been weeks ago. Now that Christmas had passed along with New Year's Eve. I knew Duke hadn't sent a word because I had called the oncologist several times now. The news was always the same, *"We are still waiting for Duke to send word."*

Paul seemed much too patient. I wasn't sure if his complacency was due to the trauma of his surgery, the medicine he was taking or maybe just thankful satisfaction for life but I found myself being seized by a rising need to rally for him.

With Paul napping and Charlotte, Emily and Joseph busy with their home school assignments, I took advantage of an opportunity to call the doctor's office. This time I would insist on an answer. I tiptoed into the room we called *the school room* and dialed Dr. Trip's office. I looked absently at the border of cursive alphabet letters Paul and I had hung, partly for decoration and partly for function. This room was supposed to have been a garage except for the hundred-year-flood plain that required us to build the house on stilts. During construction it became evident that a room was more practical than the intended garage. The desktop computer was in here, along with a couple of children's desks, the school records and consumables. I leaned my head against a window pane and listened to the phone ring.

"Lexington Oncology Associates."

"This is Shirley Graham, Paul Graham's wife. May I please speak with Dr. Trip's nurse?"

"One moment."

Pressing the phone to my ear, Barry Manilow sang to me about the ruination of Copacabana Lola's sanity. This was the first time I had noticed that the upbeat tempo was a sorry contradiction to the tragic story.

"Mrs. Graham?" A woman's voice mercifully

stopped Barry before he could finish the last *Copacabana* chorus."

"Yes?" I answered as the song continued to play stubbornly in my head. Poor Lola.

"This is Dr. Trip's nurse. We're at lunch right now, but is there something I can help you with?"

"I hope so. My husband has a tumor in his lung."

"Yes, ma'am, I talked to you earlier today. We still don't have any word from Duke on that."

"Will you give me the phone number so I can call them?"

"Oh. They don't do that. The contact has to be made through us."

"Will you please call them, then?"

"I'm sorry, but I don't have the authority."

"But, you see, we've been waiting since last month. If they are not going to accept Paul as a candidate in the program, then we need to be doing something else about this tumor in his lung."

"Yes ma'am, I know, but we still have to wait to hear from them."

"What if they don't call? Listen," my composure was falling away, "what I am hearing you say is that you don't have the authority to call Duke, but I know *someone* there does. My husband and I still have four children to raise and the youngest one is barely six years old. I'm begging you to make this call because it might be the thing that saves my kids from growing up without their daddy." I realized I was putting a lot of pressure on her, but I didn't care. I felt sure she had more resources to save Paul than I did. Her voice was trembling and I knew I had made her cry.

"Okay, Mrs. Graham. Let me see what I can do and I'll be right back in touch."

"Thank you." I squeaked, I was also crying. "Thank you, God bless you."

She called back in less than half-an-hour.

"Mrs. Graham?" She said gently, "I just got off the phone with the people at Duke and they told me your husband had been rejected a while back; they didn't seem to know why we weren't contacted. Maybe it slipped through the cracks because of the holidays."

"Wow. Thank you so much. At least we know what to do now. Will you make sure Dr. Trip knows to schedule my husband for lung surgery just as soon as possible?"

"I sure will, Mrs. Graham. I'll make sure he knows right away."

I slipped into our bedroom and rested carefully beside Paul. His warm hand found mine.

"Hey." He smiled.

"Hey." I went ahead and got it over with. "I finally got the answer from Duke. They said you're not a candidate for the vaccine."

"Sons-o-guns."

"I'm sorry."

"Did they say why?"

"No."

"Damn."

"We know what we have to do now, though."

"True. I hate to think about getting sliced open, but if that's what it takes to see my children grow up, I'm there." We held hands quietly for several minutes before he spoke again. "Did you know, they have to cut through muscle and bone to excise a lung? It's supposed to be worse than heart surgery."

"We'll get through this. God's hand is on you."

"Yes, it is."

The wind composed a plain but lovely melody through the chimes outside our window.

"I love you, Paul Graham."

"I love you, too, Shirley Graham."

We both closed our eyes.

"Shirl?" Paul said after a moment.

"Hmm?"

"I know you saved my life."

"Somebody had to marry you. You were a good catch."

"No. I mean you really saved my life. If you hadn't called for help, I know I wouldn't be here now."

"What else would I have done?"

"I guess what I mean to say is, thank you."

The Lord himself goes before you and will be with you; he will never leave you nor forsake you. Do not be afraid; do not be discouraged.
Deuteronomy 31:8

Chapter Forty-Seven

Paul's lung surgery was scheduled and he only had to wait for it a couple of weeks. It turned out to be an eventful couple of weeks, though. Our new kitten, Frankie, was losing the hair on one of his ears and it wasn't too long before Kit and Gabby had tiny bald spots, too. Once I realized it was ringworm, the children were also infected. I even found a spot on myself then *really* panicked when a spot showed up on Paul.

Between Paul's cancer and this fungus, I was feeling overcome by the forces of germs, yet Paul remained nonplused. The fungicide prescription didn't work as fast as I had hoped. Out of frustration, I came close to deciding that the animals were going to have to go, but right before Paul's surgery date, our ringworm finally showed signs of healing.

The night before Paul's lung operation, I slipped under the covers beside him. He was reading The Notebook by Nicholas Sparks. I scooted over to his side and rested my head on his shoulder. The scent of soap rose off his skin as I read the writing on the page he was reading. He moved it out of my range of vision, looked over at me and smiled.

"You'll like this."

"Looks like you're close to the end."

Paul flipped through the last ten or twelve pages left to read.

"I might finish tonight."

Maybe he would, but I could usually count on him to fall asleep in the middle of a chapter; the book falling inch by inch in staccato stages to his belly. He'd always wake up when his grip gave completely out and look to see if I was watching. I don't know why he was so embarrassed to find me watching him succumb to his circadian rhythms

A groan was my reply to his usual precursor, "I wasn't sleeping."

The clock said 10:12pm. Something was keeping him awake. Maybe he really would finish the last chapter. Was this book causing Paul's uncharacteristic insomnia or was hunger or anxiety bringing it on? Pre-surgical fasting had left him with an empty stomach for tomorrow's excision of his lung's middle lobe.

A fountain pen lay on top of the daily crossword puzzle between us. Paul had already zipped through three-quarters of the answers. I'm sure he could have completed it without me, but this little bedtime ritual was something we shared. I picked up the puzzle and squinted at its list of *down* clues, stopping at number 57; "Thing: *Latin*". I followed the number trail to "57" and started filling in R, E, T. The pen started skipping before I finished writing the E, so I adjusted, turning the pen point toward gravity and drew circular scribbles in the margins. Paul knew this law term, which told me he must have quit the puzzle before getting very far into the 50's. I finished the 'T' and heard his book shut.

"Hey. Paul." I watched a tear roll down his cheek.

He swallowed. "This is good. You have to read it."

"...but, you're crying."

He nodded. "You need to read it."

"Okay." I watched him roll over and turn out the light. I embraced him from behind, lacing my arm under his. My words broke through the quiet darkness and floated up before falling on his ear.

"I love you, Paul Graham."

"I love you, too, sweetie."

"Let's go kill some cancer tomorrow."

"If you're waiting on me, you're backing up."

I closed my eyes and whispered a thank-you prayer for the love God had put in our hearts for each other.

My recurring nightmare during this period was that roaches, mice and spiders of all sizes were everywhere I looked. These nocturnal dramas always depicted me as sole exterminator, alone in my awareness of what impending danger these vermin posed. Rarely was I fast enough to make much of a difference and my weapon was always ineffective. Whether I was using odd tools like Paul's flip-flop or a can of hair spray, the infestations kept coming. I tried in vain to keep up. Battling the little beasts, I dreamt muscles in the back of my neck twisted and pulsed with pain. Wiped out, I'd wake from these episodes before dawn, realizing the headache I dreamt was real.

I surreptitiously slipped out of bed and gratefully swallowed the migraine medicine. My spot was still warm when I slid back between the sheets and Paul slept soundly. Although the pills usually did a wonderful job masking the pain, Paul always seemed to know I was fighting a headache, anyway.

The alarm clock was set to music. Paul had the volume cranked up loud enough to rule out the possibility of going back to sleep. We passed each other in the bathroom and Paul put his hand on my arm, "Do you have a headache?"

"I'm okay."

He pointed to the trash can where the triptan's blister packaging was barely visible.

"It's almost gone." I assured him.

I'd almost forgotten about the remaining pain. I'd woken with last night's Alpha Course at church on my mind. In our small group, Kristy had asked to pray for Paul's healing. She had laid her pretty hands on his shoulders and prayed the sweetest prayer. After petitioning Heaven on Paul's behalf, she told us that her hands had felt hot and drawn to him. She asked Paul if he had felt the heat.

We finished getting ready without much conversation. The children were probably still asleep in the beds of their home school friends. The only disruption they would have this week would be visiting and having school with their best buddies. Hopefully, this would circumvent some of the worry they would have about Paul.

"Ready?" Paul asked me, but maybe he was asking himself.

When I turned to him, he was standing, arms opened. My arms encircled him as he bent into me and lay his head on my shoulder.

"I wish you didn't have to do this." My eyes felt moist.

"I do, too, but I'm also glad I have a way to fight it."

I noticed we called the devil *"this"* and *"it,"* rather than to use his medical name, "cancer."

"Lord, Jesus?" I buried my face in Paul's neck. "Please protect my husband, Paul Graham. Bring him to health and make him whole quickly."

"Amen." Paul closed and picked up our bags

Following him down the steps to the car, we set out to the hospital to do battle with Satan himself, but thanks to Our Deliverer, we were not alone. He'd sent angels at every turn.

* * *

    We checked in and I was directed to a special waiting area while Paul was being prepped. I was surprised and touched by the presence of at least a dozen of our precious friends already there. By the comfortable way they held their Styrofoam coffee cups, one might have thought they had been there for hours. I joined them but my visit was brief. A young woman popped in after about twenty-minutes advising me to return to pre-op if I wanted to see Paul before surgery.

    Instead of the dread and worry I expected to greet me behind the privacy drapes of Paul's cubicle I heard quiet laughter. Paul lay smiling on his Gurney, surrounded by the familiar faces of nurses Mitzi and Deborah, friends from Christus Victor Lutheran. When another voice, also familiar from CVLC, said, "Hello." I recognized Dr. Oliver peeking out from under his anesthesiologist cap.

    Clearly, God had been just ahead of us, dropping calling cards so we'd know He was blazing this trail for us.

It's better to take refuge in the Lord than to trust in man. It is better to take refuge in the Lord than to trust in princes.
Psalm 118:6-9

Chapter Forty-Eight

The surgeon's work was finished and Paul had been moved to the Recovery room. Our band of friends waiting in the surgical floor waiting room received the good news jubilantly. The other wait-ers had filed out in celebration and I followed a nurse's directions to the recovery room where Paul was still sleeping. En route, I met Paul's best friend, Phil, coming down the corridor wearing a tense expression.

In the early days of our marriage, Paul and I had rented The Great Santini video. When we watched it together I was taken aback by how much Robert Duvall reminded me of Phil. It wasn't that he looked like him, but their voices and mannerisms were strikingly similar. When I remarked about this to Paul, he smiled.

"I wondered how long it would take you to notice."

I greeted Phil halfway down the hall. Grabbing his arm, I gushed, "He did great, Phil. Come with me to the recovery room."

"It's over?" Phil's expression didn't change. He had worried long and hard and didn't yet trust the hope I offered.

"It's over, and the surgery took less time than expected."

Phil's eyebrows remained pinched together. "Did they say the cancer is all gone?"

"That's my understanding."

In my excitement over Paul's victory, I gripped Phil's arm and it seemed to make him uncomfortable. I released his arm and pulled open the drape Paul lay behind. A nurse attended to him, checking vitals. I whispered,

"I thought he'd be awake."

The nurse turned,

"He's beginning to come out of it."

I walked closer so I could better see his face. He was so pale. The nurse seemed to read my mind.

"His color will return quickly. He just needs to warm up some. They keep that O.R. so cold."

I looked over at Phil. His similarly pallid complexion told me he hadn't bargained on being so close yet. I felt sorry for him and wished I had been more intuitive than to drag him in here. I put my warm hand on Paul's cold forehead and fought an urge to recoil.

"Where will he go from here?"

"He'll go to another floor. Probably ICU for tonight." Paul's eyes fluttered briefly.

"Hey, buddy." I said softly, but he was already out again.

"It might be a while." The nurse explained. "There's no place for you to sit in here."

Since the recovery room was so lacking in hospitality Phil and I decided to go to the cafeteria and drink coffee from paper cups.

"He's going to do fine." I said to Phil, hoping to ease the tension etched around his eyes.

"Shirley," he began and I suddenly felt worried.

Phil had a fierce respect for Paul. So much so that I had to wonder if he really thought I belonged with him. In Phil's estimation, I don't think anyone would have measured up. I didn't necessarily disagree, but in my heart, I knew no one could love Paul more than I. He continued,

"This is the second operation the man has had on a major organ. Don't get me wrong, Paul Graham is the strongest human being I know, but this *melanoma*; that's a formidable opponent."

"Phil, I know, but we saw a miracle when Paul recovered from that brain surgery. I don't know what God is doing, but I know He's in it somewhere. I can't *not* trust Him." Then I added, "Paul feels it, too."

Phil's bottom lip trembled. "I'm praying for him. I can't imagine…" He shook his head.

"I'm going to keep on praying for him."

"That's the best thing you can do."

"Shirley…" He paused. Phil's habit of addressing me before he made a comment was personal but there was something a little intimidating about it, too. He had been in the military when he was pretty young, then joined the National Guard. In between being a weekend warrior, Phil coached high school football.

Like Paul and Fran, Phil and his wife, Barbara had started out as high school sweet-hearts, marrying soon after graduation. Besides being a stunning beauty, Barbara taught school. She and Phil sometimes worked at the same school.

Paul and Fran and Phil and Barbara became a foursome; they were best married-couple friends. When their children came several years later, the four adults added *Aunt* or *Uncle* before their names. Consequently, Paul and Fran's divorce in the 90's was a break-up that fundamentally affected both families. If I seemed like an outsider to Phil and Barbara I could certainly understand.

"Shirley," Phil went on, "you know about the water-skiing accident that gave Paul..."

He paused here, considering the right words,

"...his *particular* gait."

It was a question but not knowing how much of their history I was privy to, it must have seemed safer to make it sound like a statement. I nodded. Paul did have that little hitch in his walk that lent a deliberate confidence to his pace. Kind of cool, like a dancer's walk.

"Did you know he was in a full leg cast for months? "

"He told me that story."

"He should have gone to medical school." I heard irritation in Phil's voice. "No one was more qualified than Paul Graham."

"He told me they didn't accept him. That's how he ended up in Pharmacy, right?"

"Yes," He grimaced and rotated his head from side to side. "But it's so much more than that. He ... he had every qualification. Paul didn't have the *right socio-economic criteria.*" Phil over-enunciated the syllables. "The university already had their quota of white boys in the program. That's why he got turned down.

Phil set his coffee on the Formica table-top and continued the litany of insults Paul had endured.

"Do you know he was turned down from the Air Force, too? He had every qualification. He was in R.O.T.C.

and should have joined the military as an officer. The medic who gave him an evaluation said he was unfit for the rigors of military. *Unfit.*"

I was beginning to understand why he was reciting these injustices to Paul. Every blow Paul took to the chin was a personal affront to Phil, and he hadn't come to any terms with them yet.

I nodded, "He told me that medic told him he'd be in a wheelchair before he was forty. He said that had made him mad."

"Made ME mad, Shirley. Any one of those things would have crushed a lesser man, yet I've seen Paul Graham rise up from the ashes over and over. I *know* how strong the man is, I've seen the evidence, but this cancer, these surgeries ... I don't feel good about any of it. I ..."

Phil's voice failed. He looked down into his cup, the coffee, cold now. I watched his fingers flex and close around it as though strangling Paul's cancer with his bare hands.

"He doesn't deserve this. He's never smoked a cigarette and here he is today having a lung removed. It's not fair."

"Phil, the only thing we can do right now is trust God to be in control. He was in control when He allowed Paul to go through those fires, and He'll be in control tomorrow."

"I know, but it's hard for me, Shirley. It's just hard."

We were quiet for a moment before Phil slid his chair back and stood. "I need to get back to work."

I nodded, "Thanks for being here. It meant a lot to me."

"You tell Paul Graham ... you tell him I love him," Phil blinked and swallowed, "and I'm going to be praying for him."

"He knows that, Phil, but I'll make sure he hears it from me."

With Phil gone, I found myself alone. Not sure where I belonged now, I wandered over to the nurse's station to find out. A dark-haired nurse on the other side of the station busily entered information into a log book. I watched the whorl of her crown gently vibrating over her work and wondered if the thick hospital smell lingered on her when she went home every day. I imagined it did.

She finally looked up, giving me an audience. I told her who I was waiting for and she pointed down the hall to Paul's room. She started to go back to her work but stopped,

"Hey, is your name Shirley?"

I nodded.

"Somebody left this note."

She handed me a scrap of paper with, "Nita is here" scratched across it.

"Thanks." I scurried to Paul's room and found him asleep. Nita sat beside him reading a book she'd brought.

"Hey." She whispered.

"Hey. How long have you been here?" I hugged her around the neck.

"Long enough to hear Paul's life story."

I looked at him sleeping and felt jealous for missing his post-surgical ramblings.

"Did he talk crazy?"

"Not at all."

"Serious? Tell me."

"He told me about his childhood."

"Are you sure he was lucid?"

"I doubted it at first, but, yes. It was kind of like he needed to get it off his chest."

"What on Earth did he say"

"He said y'all were the "imposter family." She quieted a giggle bubbling up. "… And that his birth name was really Joseph Paul Fournier, which I already knew. He said when his mom married Rod they started calling him by Graham and that's how people knew him. When he was eighteen, the Selective Service required him to either use his legal name or change it legally, so he hyphenated his last name to Fournier-Graham."

"That's all completely true." I smiled, absently folding the little paper with the scribbling, "Nita is here" into a tight little stick.

"I knew it was," she agreed, "it was almost like a confession. I mean, I just listened, but I felt like I ought to give him Absolution afterward." She giggled.

"Was he was supposed to be moving around and

talking?"

"I didn't think so. I tried to get him to go back to sleep, but he wouldn't. Now and again, he'd drift off to sleep, but he'd keep waking up, talking. He told me what it was like growing up over there by where Columbia Mall is now."

"Nita, I'm sorry I missed it, but I'm so glad you were here."

"I thought the same, Sweetie."

I looked at Paul sleeping soundly.

"He doesn't look like he'll be waking up any time soon."

"I think you're right." Nita stood and smoothed the wrinkles out of her dress pants. "I'm going to head back to work, can I bring you anything?"

"I can't think of anything. Paul will be here in intensive care tonight."

I leaned in and lowered my voice, "How weird is it that he has a roommate?"

This time, Paul's procedure had been conducted in a hospital that had been around a long time. It wasn't as plush as Lexington Hospital and the floors seemed understaffed. What's more, Paul's roommate was a paraplegic man around thirty who had a number of needs.

Earlier, when I had tiptoed in the room to see if Paul had come from recovery yet, this young man complained to me that he'd been calling a nurse for hours. The odor of urine was awful and I wondered why his needs weren't being met. It took me several minutes of walking the halls on my healthy legs to find a nurse who seemed at all interested in supplying his requests, much less in cleaning him up. I didn't want to ignore him, too, but attending to someone besides Paul wasn't something I had anticipated. I guarded myself against taking on any more responsibility, yet felt torn between two patients.

"I thought Intensive Care rooms were private, too." Nita whispered back. "Do you have your cell phone?"

I nodded.

Nita hugged me, "Promise you'll call me if you need anything here?"

"Okay. Hey, I'm changing the spelling of Nita to N-

E-E-D-A. I didn't realize I had to be needy in order to see you so often."

"Ha-ha." Nita said it without expression. "You think I haven't heard *that* before?"

A bright smile flashed across her face as her heels clicked toward the door.

Paul's roommate called out to her as she passed through his section of the room,

"Hey. Will you bring me another pillow?"

Nita's voice was kind, "I'm on my way past the nurse's station right now and I'll let someone know for you."

I settled into the chair Nita had vacated to watch Paul sleep. He was so pale. I didn't know yet how fragile this lung extraction had made him. When he awakened I would realize the surgery had left him without enough strength to raise his body into a sitting position. In the following days he would be moved to a private room on another floor. The top section of the bed would be raised so he could breathe better, but gravity would always pull him back down. Even with his morphine drip, there was just no way to make him comfortable for very long.

After Paul was moved to a post surgical floor, I would learn how to help the nurse slide him back up using towels or sheets under his body. It was heartbreaking to watch my big strong Paul bear such pain and weakness. As Phil said in later days, Paul had been *filleted*. Certainly, that's how it appeared when his bandage was removed. An incision around his ribs opened slightly for thick drainage tubes. On his discharge day my presence in his room during the tube removal was flatly refused. But I could still hear him yell from way down the hall.

Paul's hospital stay was longer than it had been for his brain surgery. I was so glad to get him out of there. I learned what it means for the patient when a hospital is understaffed. It's got to be terribly frustrating for the nurses on staff.

A hospital is like a little planet, operating in the same Solar System as Earth. It's not bound by Earth's constraints of time; both night and day co-exist cooperatively, according to each patient's situation. While it may be run by mortals for mortals, there remains a tangible atmosphere of Heavenly proportions. This ethereal Presence serves to remind us we are mere vessels through which God works His ultimate purpose. It is a comfort and a guide. It must be the Holy Spirit.

    We bade goodbye to the Planet of Hospital as hastily as possible. Paul didn't ask to drive the car. I drove in silence. Any effort to assert conversation would have been downright cruel. I was glad I had decided to leave the children with their friends while settling Paul in at home. There didn't seem to be a good reason for them to see their daddy in this condition.

    I took the turn onto our street gently. The crunch of gravel under the wheels cued Paul to open his eyes and brace for the long walk up two flights of steps. By the time we made it into our house, Paul was spent.

    The first wrong thing we tried was putting Paul in our bed. It was too flat. His recliner (a.k.a. the "daddy chair") became his sickbed and it was there that his recovery began. Since I'd learned to sleep in hospital waiting room chairs, finding my place of rest beside him in the leather straight-back chair was a breeze. The living room became our new bedroom until Paul could stretch out again.

    Frankie, the kitten, slept as much as Paul during this time. Since Frankie was practically weightless, Paul didn't mind having him perch right on top of his surgical wound. Strange bedfellows were they, albeit precious to the sight.

    Frankie was adored by everyone in our family with the exception of Kit. It had never occurred to Kit that her status as Alpha cat would ever be disturbed, yet this invader, this playful puff of grey and white energy was really getting on her nerves. She would sometimes look at us with disdain as if to say, *"Whatever possessed you to bring this little rat here?"*

    Kit was now six years old. I'd made her an exclusive indoor kitty after Paul pulled Charlie's body out from under the trailer a couple of years before. She had already started getting fat and I didn't want her to meet the same fate to which her more agile brother had succumbed.

    A few days after we returned home, Paul complained

that his legs felt heavy and tired but didn't hurt or have any overt redness. He followed the medical instructions for returning home, yet he wasn't improving. On the contrary, he was exhausted for hours from the smallest activity. Walking to the mailbox knocked the starch out of him for the rest of the day. Something didn't seem right.

Wednesday, he called the surgeon's office for advice. Since classic symptoms for blood clotting were absent, the surgeon was not alarmed. By Friday, it was worse so Paul called his oncology office from the phone in our bedroom.

"I know I have an appointment on Monday," I heard Paul saying on the phone, "but I'm going in the wrong direction. No, there isn't any redness and they don't really hurt, but they feel heavy. Okay. No fever, no. Okay, well if you're not worried then I'm not either."

I heard the phone hit its cradle with a little more force than usual. They didn't know him like I did. Paul Graham took the blows of life on the chin and only complained if there was a really good reason. Now he was mad and there was no way he would beg for attention.

I ventured into the bedroom with him.

"You want to go to the emergency room?"

His legs may not have been red, but his face sure was.

"Oh, hell, no. Two medical experts have deemed me fine, so I'll just wait until Monday." He seethed.

Together, we spent an eternal weekend. Monday finally rolled in and I couldn't wait to drive Paul to Dr. Trip's office. The doctor took one look at Paul and lost all expression. He sent us immediately to the hospital for an ultrasound on his legs.

Back to Planet Hospital. We were getting so accustomed to the drill. I drove Paul to the nearest entrance and he was wheeled inside. I parked the car and almost ran inside. I'd remembered to pack a few things for both of us in case we ended up staying, which I expected. This time, Frank and Martha Bernhardt from church had taken the children into their home and were prepared to keep them through the week if necessary. Our kids were really getting to know our church family like… well, like family.

I found Paul looking less than amused, filling out

insurance forms.

"Is this your wife, Mr. Graham?"

Paul nodded.

"We can get you on back to radiology while she finishes this up."

Paul handed me his clipboard and I wrote quickly, eager to follow him to Radiology. Instead, I was told to stay in the waiting room this time. I sat in my chair thinking a million thoughts, feeling all kinds of feelings. I went through a little checklist of our blessings:

-The children were safe with people we trusted.

-We had made it through the weekend without a trip to the Emergency Room.

-The car was parked and Paul's problem was being assessed.

-The forms were filled out.

Those points made me feel relieved, yet if Paul had blood clots, he could die. If he didn't, then what *was* wrong? How would I manage if he was gone? Had we changed our wills since we moved? I didn't think so. If he died, would I have to give up home schooling? Would we have to move? Where would we go?

I was distracted by a television nearby. Regis and Kathy Lee had a chef demonstrating a guacamole recipe on their show.

So, you're saying if you leave an avocado seed in the dip, it keeps the guacamole from turning brown?

That's right, Kathy. And there's an easy way to get the seed out, too. Just stick a fork in it and turn, the seed pops right out.

It's funny, the things I remember. I have used those tips again and again since that day.

I was called to attention when I heard, "Paul Graham? Is there someone here for Mr. Graham?"

I followed the voice to an orderly who brought me to my husband, lying on a Gurney in the hallway, waiting to be placed in a hospital room. Replacing the dull, emotionless expression he had worn since Friday's phone call to the doctors was a relaxed smile. He reached out to take my cold hand in his warm one.

"Do we know what's going on?"

"The ultrasound showed bi-lateral blood clots." Paul said. "Both legs."

"Oh, no. Are you kidding me?" My heart banged around inside my chest. "What will we have to do? Will there be surgery? How will they get them out?"

"I'm wondering the same things, Shirl."

I can do all things through Christ Who strengthens me.
Philippians 4:13

Chapter Forty-Nine

Before Paul had time to warm up the bed Dr. Trip appeared at his bedside,
"You understand you have blood clots in both legs?"
"That's what I heard." Paul replied. "I knew something wasn't right."
"I'm sorry we didn't get you in Friday, Paul. Waiting was the wrong call."
I gave myself a turn in the conversation,
"One thing I can tell you about Paul is that he's not a complainer. If he says he's uncomfortable, he's already hurting pretty badly."
"I've made a note of that," Dr. Trip said humbly. "And now we need to get you straightened out so you can go back home."
Paul smiled,
"Sounds like a good plan."
"We're going to put you on the blood thinner, Coumadin unless you prefer a different one."
Just where was that accent from? I'd have to remember to ask him. Dr. Trip treated Paul as a medical colleague and respected his opinion, especially in the area of medicine. Paul concurred about Coumadin.
"As soon as we can get it set up, I want you to have a Greenfield IVC filter inserted."
"Okay." Paul nodded. Dr. Trip continued.
"The filter is placed endovascular-ly," he noted my consternation and added, "meaning it's inserted via a blood vessel."
"Like his jugular vein?" I asked.
"Exactly. It can also be placed via the femoral vein in the groin. They do it by guiding a catheter into the IVD using fluoroscopic guidance. The procedure is only slightly invasive and pretty quick.
"That sounds good." Paul replied. "Then I can start

weaning off the Coumadin."

Dr. Trip's smile fell, revealing he disagreed with this suggestion, but decided not to bring it up just yet.

"Paul, why don't you just drop by the office right after we get you released from here?"

"On our way out?" I asked.

"Yeah, you know our office is just behind the hospital. We need to decide on Chemo- options and I know you live pretty far from here. Maybe it'll save you a trip. Plus, I want you to meet my practitioner, Imogene. I was lucky enough to talk her into coming to work with us over there and I believe you're both going to like her."

Paul nodded.

"Do you need to ask me anything before I go?" Dr. Trip added, looking from Paul to me.

Paul shook his hand.

"I think you covered it, Doc."

Besides being considered the best oncologist in town, Dr. Trip was a very personable guy. He had plenty of the intellect with none of the lofty, *holier-than-thou* aura some doctors carry. I especially liked the way he listened to us without interrupting. As he left Paul's room, I suddenly felt as though he'd taken my security blanket with him. I looked at Paul, suddenly panicked,

"You have blood clots."

"I know."

"You could have died."

"It's true."

"Paul. What if you do?"

He laughed uncomfortably.

"I mean it. What should I do if you die?"

"Do?"

"I mean, would I go to work? Do we have a plan?"

"You'd be fine. I trust you. That's why I picked you."

"I appreciate that, but specifically, what would you advise me to do? Would I have to stop home schooling? Sell the house?"

I couldn't believe I was talking to him like this. I guess the reality of his mortality was beginning to soak in.

"You wouldn't have to quit home schooling. Or go to

work. Or sell the house."

"Okay." My eyes darted from Paul to random things in the room. I took a deep breath, walked to the other side of his bed, climbed in and scooted up next to him.

"You promised not to leave me. Please don't die."

"I'm trying not to." Paul held up a section of newspaper and a pen. "Want to share a crossword puzzle?"

I nodded and snuggled up beside my man to work on a crossword puzzle. This would be enough for right now.

* * *

During surgery, an assessment of Paul's jugular as well as his femoral veins was done. A decision was made to place the Greenfield Filter in his groin area. The insertion procedure was over soon after it began and it wasn't long before we were packing up to leave the hospital.

Dr. Trip's reception area was almost always full. Nurses and other staff fluttered behind a sliding glass window that remained open, attending to charts and greeting patients by name like old friends. A low water fountain sat, pretty much ignored, on one side of the reception area. We sat against the wall, Paul reading a book, I, a magazine that barely captured my attention. Stealing a look over the pages, I noticed that most of the patients seated in the waiting room had someone with them. Some shared whispered conversations and others sat in silence. Turbans and lap blankets made it easy to determine which ones were the patients. One or two bolder ladies in the room sported bare scalps except for thin layers of soft fuzz.

The door opened, revealing a jeans-and-scrubs clad figure holding a clipboard. She looked at us expectantly,

"Paul Graham?"

I felt guilty being called back so quickly and fought an urge to remind the nurse that there were others ahead of us. Sicker and suffering folks. We didn't really belong here anyway, did we?

We followed her to a room.

"I'm Juanita." She smiled easily. I guessed her to be about twenty-four. "Dr. Trip won't be long at all."

Inside the room, she dragged a stool next to Paul. He

stepped up to sit on the crisp, paper-covered "bed" and opened his book. He wore the maroon University of South Carolina Alumni sweatshirt I had given him last Christmas. I smiled, noting how nicely his broad shoulders filled it up.

Juanita turned to write something on Paul's chart and I whispered in his ear,

"You're pretty handsome for a guy who's supposed to be sick."

About that time, Dr. Trip walked in, took a look at Paul's sweatshirt and shook his head disgustedly.

"A Gamecock? No-o-o. I know you didn't wear that in *here*."

"I had to back my boys, Doc. You've got way too much orange in here."

Paul was referring to the many displays of Clemson University memorabilia that decorated the room.

"You can't be serious. I was just thinking that I needed to *add* a little more orange."

They were shaking hands when Dr. Trip noticed Paul's book.

"You like Greg Iles." Dr. Trip stated his observation.

"He's pretty good." Paul picked up his book.

"Yeah." Dr. Trip answered. "I've read most of his."

He set Paul's chart on the counter beside me and I instinctively read the first few lines, "Paul Graham, pleasant looking 52-year-old man, pharmacist ..."

"Paul, I've been looking into the Coumadin situation and I don't feel good about you stopping it."

"How long do you think I'll need to take it."

I grabbed my purse and dug around for a pen and notepad.

"I'm thinking you'll need to be on it for a while, maybe continuously."

"So, why did I have this Greenfield filter procedure?" Paul's tone held an undercurrent of irritation.

"To keep you safe in case you threw a clot."

"Am I safe?"

"I think so, but I like to err on the side of caution."

Paul fell silent, but I knew from his expression that he'd be bringing up the Coumadin subject again someday.

I continued scribbling the doctor's comments on a small notepad.

"The other thing I want to talk to you about is the drug, Interferon."

"You want me to take it?"

"I don't think it would hurt. You know, it's supposed to stop the growth and spread of cancer cells."

"Okay." Paul concurred.

"Would you mind giving yourself a shot twice a day?"

Paul was nonplused.

"No."

I stepped forward, "Dr. Trip, couldn't I learn to give Paul the shots?"

"Yep. Whatever works best."

Paul gave me a surprised look. I hated getting shots, I hated seeing needles go into somebody and yet, I couldn't bear the idea of Paul having to give a shot to himself. He was already going through so many painful procedures. Doing the injections was one small thing I knew I could do for him.

Dr. Trip explained that the injections would go into the subcutaneous tissue of Paul's stomach. It sounded awful, but I was determined to see this through. While Dr. Trip instructed me, Juanita stepped out and returned a moment later with Paul's prescription and another lady. She was short, in her forties, and wore her straight, blonde hair with fluffy bangs and cropped close at the neck.

"Oh, good." Dr. Trip smiled, "I get to introduce you to Imogene."

As Imogene stuck her hand out to shake Paul's then mine, Dr. Trip told us how long they had known each other and how proud he was to have her on staff. Little did I know it then, but this little woman's insightful instruction would soon be one of the greatest gifts anyone would ever give me.

***

While Paul was checking himself out, I stood behind him reading a poem taped to the counter,

"What Cancer Cannot Do."

"Cancer is so limited.

It cannot cripple love, It cannot shatter hope, It cannot corrode faith, It cannot eat away peace, It cannot kill friendship, It cannot silence courage, It cannot invade the soul, It cannot reduce eternal life, It cannot destroy confidence, It cannot shut out memories, It cannot quench the spirit, It cannot lessen the power of the Resurrection.

Though the physical body may be destroyed by disease, the spirit can remain triumphant. If disease has invaded your body, refuse to let it touch your spirit. Your body can be severely afflicted, and you may have a struggle. But if you keep trusting God's love, your spirit will remain strong.

Why must I bear this pain? I cannot tell; I only know my Lord does all things well. And so I trust in God, my all in all. For He will bring me through, whatever befall.

Our greatest enemy is not disease, but despair."
--Author unknown

The entire law is summed up in a single command: Love your neighbor as yourself.
Galatians 5:14

Chapter Fifty

Paul began willing himself to recover quicker than he was supposed to. Frankie the cat slept alone more and more often.

Looking for Paul one day, I found him outside holding his sides and wincing in pain. It took me a minute to find my voice.

"What are you doing?"

"I'm putting these plywood squares under the house."Paul caught his breath. I don't like it exposed."

"But, Paul, can't you wait a while? I don't think you're supposed to be lifting your arms over your head yet."

"Why do you think that?"

"I thought I remembered the doctor saying it."

"I don't remember anything like that."

This business of hearing something different would become a pesky problem for us. I made myself a mental note to check the little writing pad I had archived this information on. He would want to see it before he could believe the doctor has said this.

Paul's habit became dressing every morning, limping down the steps and cutting big squares of particle board into smaller squares that he could lift. Then, he'd climb on top of a picnic table to nail the boards to the underside of the house. Before long, Mr. Jerry began showing up with his own hammer.

"Hi, Mr. Jerry." I greeted him the first time he came to help. "If I'd known you were here, I'd have brought you some tea, too." I handed Paul his thermal cup filled with iced tea.

"I don't need none." He answered. "Me 'n Ida just had us some lunch."

"I see you are aiding and abetting my husband in doing what he's not supposed to be doing yet."

"Well, there probably ain't nothing we can do to stop him. Jerry winked, causing the chain reaction of Paul's smile. He knew an ally when he saw one.

"I reckon I couldn't a' set over at the house watchin' when I knew I could he'p him."

"All right." I turned to go inside. "I'm going back in to finish the children's lessons. Y'all holler if you need anything."

The job began to move along much quicker. Together with Mr. Jerry's help, they were able to manage larger pieces of plywood. Sometimes I would still hear Mr. Jerry banging away long after Paul came in to lie down and hold his throbbing side. I don't know if his efforts helped or hurt his recovery but six months later he looked as good as new, albeit a filet scar running around his ribs. Sooner than I imagined possible, he'd gone back to work, part-time at first, then full-time.

The internet had provided a beautiful connection to friends and family as well as a rich resource for information on cancer. My regular updates on Paul's progress to our email chains at St. Timothy's, Christus Victor, our Camden Home Educator Support Group, "WORDSville" and the Via de Cristo prayer request chain often resulted in more than verbal encouragement. Every now and then, we'd find God working through a personal email or a phone call from someone who had read Paul's update and just happened to have helpful, current information on some cutting-edge technology.

One update I sent out told of the residual tumor matter left in Paul's brain. This remaining cancer was yet to be addressed and we were putting it off. The only radiation treatment we were aware of was *whole-brain radiation* which we knew would result in immediate cognitive degeneration. Paul's internet research had rendered us a small bit of information on something called Gamma Knife Radiation. The article we found told of a facility using this process somewhere in Virginia. It suggested three or four others, but their location wasn't mentioned. I was pretty excited to have found this piece of information and told of it in my update.

Moments after I clicked *"send"* the phone rang.

"Hello, Shirley? This is Pastor Ron from Christus Victor Lutheran."

"Hey. I just sent an update out."

"Yes, I know, that's why I'm calling. I have a friend who actually works at a Gamma Knife facility."

"No kidding? Oh, that's wonderful. Where is your friend's location?"

"Well, that's just it, Shirley. She works right here in Columbia. There's a Gamma Knife Center inside Richland Memorial Hospital."

> *"But I will restore you to health and heal your wounds,"*
> *Declares the LORD.*
> *Jeremiah 30:17*

Chapter Fifty-One

By the end of May, hundreds of blossoms clung to the pear tree and life began to feel more predictable and routine; so much so that we were once again comfortable making commitments. I was singing again in choir and Paul went back to his position on the church council. We even signed up to serve on the Alpha team at church on Thursdays. Alpha was much more than fun, it fed our souls and it was great being able to give something back again. We learned that the funny thing about giving blessings back was we always ended up getting them all over ourselves in the process.

As Paul drove our family to church one Sunday morning I sat in the front passenger seat finishing my make-up. The little mirror on the back of my sun visor served as a reasonable enough vanity area. I was so happy to relax now with Paul behind the wheel although I remained aware we still had an issue of something foreign left in his brain. His Gamma Knife treatment was scheduled for the following day and we would soon find out if Paul's cancer was going to respond to it. If not, then Whole Brain radiation was the next step and with it, immediate cognitive damage. Whole Brain radiation would be a last ditch effort.

Mascara brush poised mid-air, I turned to ask Paul what time he had to start fasting for the procedure tomorrow, but something weird caught my attention.

"What's that?" I said instead, pointing to a scraggly dog-looking animal at the top of an embankment on the left.

"Coyote." Paul answered without hesitation.

"Naw. Really. What *was* that?"

"Coyote." Paul repeated, less patient than before.

"No way. A coyote in South Carolina?"

"Look," Paul chuckled, "I can't explain it, I'm just telling you what it was."

Later that afternoon, lunch dishes put away and Sunday naps behind us, the weather would lure us outside.

We liked to take the children for bike rides at the State Park just a mile past our house. After collecting all the bikes from all around the yard and piling them in the trailer, Paul hitched up the Bronco and we drove to the Park.

Paul parked near the little camp store where five or six Park Rangers congregated.

"Hey. I bet they could explain that coyote we saw this morning." I said and jumped out to ask.

They turned to me as I approached,

"Excuse me."

I felt like an alien intruding on their man-talk.

"I have a question." I said, (realizing as I spoke that Joseph must have gotten his, *"I have a guestion"* phrase from me).

"All right. Shoot." One of the men replied with great tolerance.

"My husband and I thought we saw a coyote this morning. I was just wondering if there had been any coyote spottings around here."

They all looked away from me, stealing uncomfortably glances from each other.

"Well." One of them took off his hat, revealing a perfectly groomed head of red hair. "You probably did."

He rubbed his forehead and replaced his hat.

"There's a theory that coyotes have migrated here from North Carolina."

A different ranger spoke up, "Yeah, and there are rumors that some of them were transplanted here on purpose to keep the deer population down."

I stepped back.

"Ma'am," the redhead spoke, "nobody's real sure where they came from. We just know we've had reports of people seeing them."

"So, what *other* animals might I be surprised to see out here besides foxes and raccoons? So far the most exotic animal I've seen was a huge bobcat."

"Don't say you heard me say it, but there are some residents who swear they have seen brown bears." The other ranger added ominously.

I swallowed, thanked them for their information,

wishing now I hadn't asked. Some things are better left unknown.

* * *

On the way to the Gamma Knife center at Richland hospital, Paul and I discussed two Zesto's locations and which one we would visit to celebrate the completion of this first treatment and the end of his fast. Our prospective lunch was easy to talk about and gave us a nice distraction from the unknown we faced. We walked down a hospital corridor leading to door on the left. The words, "Gamma Knife Clinic" in block letters alerted Paul to open the door. I stepped inside as he followed.

"Good morning."

The voice belonged to a short-haired woman who reminded me of my friend, Jane.

"I'm Debbie and this is Teresa."

Teresa looked up from her coffee and wiggled her fingers at us.

"I'm going to guess you are Paul."

"That's me." Paul approached their station and Debbie handed him a paper to fill out.

"I'm Mrs. Paul." I added, "Don't throw me back."

"Welcome to the Gamma Knife Clinic." Debbie handed Paul a pen bearing the name of a drug.

"I know." She apologized. "There's paperwork for everything. Sorry."

She handed Paul a clipboard with all the papers he had to fill out and ushered us into Paul's "room." It was a cubicle cordoned off by sliding curtains. It looked kind of like the sectioned areas of a hospital Emergency Room.

It was here that he did the paperwork and waited together for instructions. After a while, we'd meet the Radiologist, technicians would apply Lanacaine to spots on his forehead and scalp and a metal halo would be bolted to his head. I grimaced for him as he insisted that it really wasn't all that bad to have the heavy metal apparatus fastened to his skull with screws. I'm sure he was lying, but was always trying to protect me, even to the point of trying to protect me from worrying about him.

Gamma Knife technology is fascinating. "The "blades" of the Gamma Knife® are beams of gamma radiation programmed to target the lesion at the point where they intersect. A single treatment session draws 201 beams of gamma radiation together to converge on the lesion in its exact proportions. Exposure is brief and only the tissue being treated receives a significant radiation dose, while the surrounding tissue remains unharmed. If the cancer responds to the radiation (and sometimes it doesn't), the lesions slowly decrease in size and dissolve.

I had brought a book and some home school work to occupy my time as I waited in Paul's prep room but it was hard to concentrate on anything, considering there was a miraculous machine down the hall shooting 201 low radiation laser gamma rays into my husband's brain while he listened to loud music. The only thing I could focus on was talking to Jesus and gleefully envisioning Paul's vile enemy shriveling up like a salted slug on a summer sidewalk.

His treatment complete, Paul was returned to the room for observation. The halo was unbolted and an injection of steroids offset any swelling the radiation had incited. The halo's screws left deep, red indentations on Paul's forehead and scalp. Even though the technicians cleaned them up with a solution-soaked cotton ball before we left, they continued to ooze a little blood for several hours.

For Paul it seemed a small price to pay for what could be an opportunity to watch our kids grow up. Thanks be to God for this brilliant technology that not only gave us hope, but allowed my husband's wonderful intellect to be preserved.

I could always expect Paul to have a bodacious appetite after the Gamma Knife for two reasons; one, he would be breaking a fast and two, the steroid shot would kick his hunger up ten or twenty notches. We drove directly to West Columbia for fried chicken and once again, Zesto's did not disappoint us.

Steroids aren't all fun, though. They have a reputation for making people cranky and Paul wasn't immune to this side-effect. His patience took a hit from it, he couldn't sleep at night. Plus, it gave a distinct roundness to his face that he hated. It also seemed kind of creepy to note that while steroids assist healing and reduce swelling, no one really knows exactly why.

Paul had regular P.E.T. scans to determine metastasis in his body, but for his head, cross-sectioned M.R.I. and C.A.T. scans were required. The progress, if any, of the radiation treatments on his cancer was studied by the radiologist. We left the clinic and got back to our lives, pretending not to think about what the results were.

***

Some spring days it was just impossible for my kids and me to stay inside. I looked forward to winding down the school year and enjoying the summer that hinted at it's coming from time to time.

"Let's take a walk." I suggested after the children and I finished a lunch of tuna salad sandwiches and tomato soup.

"Yay!" Their collective reply resonated in tandem with the ringing phone. I grabbed the earpiece off the wall.

"Hello?"

"Hey, Hon. Is this my bride?"

"Yes, handsome. What are you doing bothering me in the middle of the day?"

"I just heard from Dr. Trip's office."

Since his words had just caused my heart to stop beating, I said nothing and waited tensely for Paul's message of life or death.

"The cancer in my brain responded to the radiation and is shrinking."

"Thank God." I cried, "Thanks be to God, Paul. I am so happy."

"I'm busy here in the pharmacy, I've got to go, but I had to share that with you."

"I love you so much, Paul."

"I love you, too, Shirl."

I met the kids outside and tried to share our good news in terms they could grasp. I don't know if they understood anything except that we should be happy because Daddy's news had been about something good, and that seemed to be enough.

Out in the yard, our first agenda was to find a big stick to fight off all the bears and coyotes. Charlotte had already spotted a nice, straight stick before I walked outside and we crossed the road to check it out. It was perfect for bear fighting. I took in two lungs full of sweet, spring air and blew it all out with a sigh of relief. The sky radiated its bright blue beauty and I was so happy. My Paul was going to be okay. Thanks be to God.

The children and I walked past our next-door neighbor's house and Emily pointed to the next house.

"Mom, look. Someone's moving in that house."

Sure enough, I saw a slim, young man in work clothes, coming out from beside the little blue house that had been empty. Paul and I had seen him with a smallish woman the week before. I thought they must be newlyweds. I waved. He waved back. We walked down his dirt drive as he approached us.

"Hey." I stuck out my hand, "I'm Shirley and these are my little ones, Charlotte, Emily and Joseph."

I immediately regretted my words, forgetting that the girls had recently told me they hated being called, *little*. "*It makes us sound like babies.*" They had complained.

"How do you do? I'm Mike." Mike said, with a hint of North Carolina in his speech. I shook his hand. "My wife, Barbara and I are renovating this house. We're going to be your neighbors.'

"Terrific. I answered. "Can we meet her?"

"She's not here now, but we'll both be back tomorrow and probably every day after that for a long time. Right now, I have to go back to my work because I'm pouring concrete and concrete waits for no man.

"Hear, hear." I agreed, "Then carry on and welcome, it's so good to meet you."

I made a point to bake them a loaf of bread and visit the following day. Sure enough, Barbara was there, working alongside her husband. Barbara was a tiny little thing whose short, blonde cut framed her pretty face. I was surprised to learn they weren't newlyweds after all, but my own age with two daughters as old as my older kids. I was further amazed to learn that Mike had retired from the Air Force and Barbara was an accountant. What's more, Mike and Barbara were also grandparents to three adorable grandchildren.

"We hope to have this work far enough along by July the Fourth to have a little party." Barbara informed me the day I met her. "We'll let you know as we get closer to the deadline."

"Wonderful." I answered, so happy to have peers nearby.

Our neighborhood was made up of retirees a good bit older than Paul and me. Barbara intimated to me later in our friendship that the night before I brought the bread, she had been lamenting in her prayers about being stuck out in the Boonies, lonely for friendship. She said she had prayed that God would send her a friend then the children and I showed up. I would learn over time that God had actually sent Barbara and Mike as a gift to *me*.

* * *

Marie, one of our beautiful friends from St. Timothy's passed away that year. One of Marie's favorite things was the Women of Faith conference and several women from our church were attending the Charlotte, North Carolina conference in Marie's honor. I had attended one a few years before and convinced Nita that she didn't want to miss this one. At the last minute, I learned the church had additional tickets available, so I invited my new friend, Barbara.

Nita, Barbara and I rode to Charlotte together and shared a motel room. We slept little and spent our waking moments laughing. It was surprising to me that three new friends could mix together so easily, but such are the relationships God orchestrates. The conference was wonderful. We laughed and cried and laughed and cried. For women, laughing and crying are our emotional barometers for the quality of just about anything.

By the time we got back home, we had developed a firm sisterhood. Barbara and Nita were two people who became my prayer partners and I have come to cherish our Christ-centered kinship more and more through the years. Having friends who pray with me is an indescribable blessing.

A few days later, Paul was working late and I was in the kitchen making soap. My kitchen smelled like a mix of peppermint and lime, which didn't really blend all that well. The children were in bed, trying to force themselves to stay awake until their daddy came home and I was enjoying this rare moment of quiet when the phone rang. I grabbed a kitchen towel off the counter and wiped my minty hands.

"Hello?"

"Hi, Shirley. It's Tim."

My baby brother was calling from Atlanta.

"Hey. Is everything okay?"

This question had become the precursor to every phone call Since Paul's initial hospital trip.

"Not really." He paused and I heard him swallow. "I'm calling to tell you I have cancer. It's in my throat."

If I ascend up into heaven, thou art there; if I make my bed in hell, behold, thou art there.
Psalm 139:8

Chapter Fifty-Two

My brain was actively denying that Tim had really said, "...cancer in my throat." It took me a couple of seconds to register that I had heard him correctly. I opened my mouth to say something but my vocabulary had unexpectedly shut down. I tried to swallow but my mouth was suddenly too dry. Tim continued,

"I don't want you to tell anyone, because I'm not ready to share this with anyone but immediate family."

"Okay." I managed to croak out. "What kind of cancer?"

"Squamous cell... it usually doesn't come back if the treatments get rid of it. I'm scheduled for surgery after the Peek reunion in Atlanta."

"Surgery to do what?"

"To remove as much as possible, I guess. Initially it's a tonsillectomy. Believe me I'm not sure about a lot of things. I ask a lot of questions, but every time the doctors answer me it's like I'm trying to take a sip of water from a fire hose."

"Don't make me laugh, I don't want to laugh."

"Laughing is what we know, Shirley. I'm scared as hell, but if I don't find a little levity somewhere, I won't be able to do this."

"You'll do this with God's help. The fire hose was a great analogy."

"Thanks."

Tim, I'm going to tell you how Paul and I remember what is said at those doctor visits.

"Okay."

"Before the doctor's appointments we make a list of our questions on a note pad. When we ask each question, we write down every answer. It's okay to ask about the spelling of a word or to say, *"Slow down."* Paul and I have learned that if we don't write it, we can't remember everything. Sometimes we even hear different things. It's like you say, it's just too much information. Writing it helps."

"Okay. I'll write that down."

"I'd laugh at that if I weren't in shock right now. Who knows so far?"

"...about you being in shock?"

"No, Smart Aleck."

"I told Dale. I'm calling Jeanne after we hang up. Mother and Daddy don't know. I'm not going to tell them just yet."

Daddy's Parkinson's disease was taking a physical toll on him and Mother was an overwhelmed caretaker. We had all taken to protecting them as best we could. It suddenly hit me that Tim and Helen's three-year-old daughter would have to be told, too.

"Oh, man. What about Natalie?"

Tim took a quick breath.

"I talked to Father Ramer about that."

The reference to his Episcopal priest made me think about Tim's participation in choir. Would he be able to sing after this?

"Father Ramer told me I'd need to relate it to her on three-year-old terms. I pulled her onto my lap yesterday and said, "You know, Daddy's going to have an operation soon because I'm sick. I have to get something removed from my throat that doesn't belong there.""

Tim paused and chuckled,

"She said, "Daddy, you know how birds get things caught in their throats? Sometimes they have to get them out, too, and then they're just fine.""

"Wow. That's an insightful little girl."

"Isn't she amazing?"

I could tell he was smiling as he spoke."

"She's going to be just fine, Tim."

"I think so."

"So, how did you find it?"

"We were going to Sea Side, Florida for a few days and I thought I'd go to the doctor before we left town. My left lymph node was swollen and I figured I must be coming down with something. A filled prescription of antibiotics seemed like a good thing to pack. The medicine didn't help me, though. When we came home, I called the doctor who referred me to an ENT doctor. A needle aspiration determined cancer."

"Squamous cell."

"Right."

"Ruthie had squamous cell removed from her hand."

"Really?"

"Yeah. She's fine now."

"That's good to know."

"Paul's going to want to talk to you when I tell him."

"I was hoping he would."

"Tim, I love you, and I want you to be assured that I will pray for you unceasingly."

"Thank you, Shirley." His voice was cracking.

"Do you know what Paul always says?"

"What's that?"

"He says, "God is in the miracle business, and Paul Graham is living proof.""

"It's true."

"I love you, little brother." I told my six-feet-two sibling.

"I love you, Shirley."

For where two or three are gathered together in my name, there am I in the midst of them.
Matthew 18:20

Chapter Fifty-Three

The 2002 Peek Reunion was hosted in June by my sister, Jeanne and her husband, Scott. It had been so many years since I'd seen my cousins I wondered how I could possibly recognize them. Most of the guests stayed in a nearby motel, and I remember standing beside Paul as he checked us in.

"Look." I whispered to Charlotte, Emily and Joseph, "Look around you. We could be related to some of the people in here without even knowing."

The main festivities were held in the expansive hospitality of Jeanne and Scott's Atlanta home. Dale had driven Mother and Daddy to Atlanta from Hartwell. Daddy used his wheelchair all the time now. His siblings, Charlie, Evelyn Ruth and Helen Marie also made it to the reunion. My cousin, Bonnie brought t-shirts emblazoned with "Peek Family Reunion" on the front with a fruit and nut tree alongside it. The tree was a brainchild of my cousin, Kenny to imply that *"the fruits and nuts don't fall too far from the family tree."*

Peek Olympic Events included a three-legged race that Jeanne and I lost together. Winners of the events were rewarded with construction paper medals artistically created by some of my nieces.

It was so wonderful to be together and pure joy to hear our Aunts and Uncles tell historical tales. Some of those stories may have even been accurate. We shared the history later in emails between us. A number of new email addresses were added to "Wordsville" (our cousin-blog-thing) and we took delight in getting to know one another online. "Wordsville" was soon changed to Kuzinville once the emails began to come out en force. Now, we would hail from the North, South, East and West coasts of America and much of the country in between.

Our Uncle Charlie, Daddy's brother, made an occasional cameo appearance in Kuzinville via his son, Ken's computer. Uncle Charlie and his wife, Aunt Sadie, who always wore their hearts outside of their chests, made it clear they loved us shamelessly. They also made methodical calls to us, their nieces and nephews. We were on a schedule with one of us getting our turn as it came up on their list. The cousins among us who were suffering would get additional calls at other crucial times.

Uncle Charlie was actually fighting lung cancer himself and yet his voice always had a way of making me feel safe and sure. I heard a familiarity there that took me way back into my childhood. I also heard the tones of my father's voice coming through the words Uncle Charlie spoke, which was a special comfort now that Parkinson's was stealing Daddy's mind. This familial acquaintanceship probably resonated in the ears of my siblings and cousins, too.

By contrast, the bond of brotherhood Paul found with Uncle Charlie was based, not in genetics and memories but in the power of loving each other through their cancer battles. It was never necessary for me to be on the extension for Paul and Uncle Charlie to carry on long conversations. If Paul got to the phone first, I might not get to talk at all. Their mutual respect was the kind I imagined to be shared by soldiers who had survived war. Now that the reunion was over and Tim's cancer was common knowledge he, too hunkered down in the foxhole along with Paul and Uncle Charlie.

I set my alarm clock for thirty minutes before Tim's surgery in Atlanta was scheduled. I turned it off, rolled off the bed onto my knees and spent another thirty minutes begging God to cure my brother. I remember that Paul woke up and looked alarmed when he saw me kneeling beside the bed, then he was quiet because he knew why I was praying. Had the prayers been visible going up in our bedroom it would have looked like a lovely thick fog.

As Paul and I prayed, a series of events unfolded in Atlanta that resulted in a change of plans for Tim. When his tonsils were removed, it was discovered that the cancer had spread to the base of his tongue. The plan to remove as much of the cancer as possible was nixed due to the compromise it would put on Tim's ability to swallow. A last minute decision was made to try a different approach. Tim's chemotherapy and radiation would start right away. He would have an operation to install a feeding tube directly into his stomach so that he could nourish himself when the treatments disabled him from eating normally. In addition, he had to have any necessary dental work and cleaning done immediately, before the radiation began. This would minimize the potential damage radiation might do to his teeth and jaw. Tim wouldn't be able to talk for months and the radiation would even permanently destroy the growth of his facial hair.

Tim remained brave as his cancer treatments loomed in the future, but there was yet more to bear. He called us on the eve of his first chemotherapy and radiation treatment and I answered the phone.

"Hey, Tim."

"Hi, how is everybody?"

"We're good. Are you ready for tomorrow?"

"Well, as our daddy says, "I'm as ready as I'll ever be."

"I keep forgetting to ask you what your recovery time is estimated to be. How soon will you have to go back to work?"

Tim chuckled at the irony, "I guess it doesn't matter. They called me in and fired me today."

"Oh, my goodness. Tim, is that how you're rewarded for all your years of service?"

That was my first thought. But to the company's credit, I'll have a severance package that includes 18 months of health coverage."

I remember the day he really couldn't eat anymore. Paul and I had come to Atlanta with Charlotte, Emily and Joseph to visit and give him a few '*attaboys.*' On our last day there, Uncle Charlie and Aunt Sadie met us at a buffet restaurant, along with my cousin, Charlene. We stayed at our long table through at least one shift change. Uncle Charlie's and Paul's stories of cancer-survival encouraged Tim that day and strengthened the bond between the three.

The young cousins behaved like the children they were, getting in and out of their seats and visiting the bathroom every few minutes. Charlene and I sat across from each other behaving more like rivaling siblings than cousins. Now and again we'd catch each other eye-balling Tim's plate. Gracing it in golden crispness was the most beautiful fried chicken breast you have ever seen. We had been watching Tim for at least half-an-hour now, which was plenty of time to figure out that he wasn't fooling anyone into believing he would be able to eat it. Every now and then he'd position his knife and fork as though he might really do it, then he'd set the utensils back down on the table. He was listening to Uncle Charlie and

Paul's war stories but it was easy to see he was thinking about the chicken, too. Finally, Charlene queried in my direction,

"Do you think he's going to eat that, Shirley?"

I managed to scrape up enough remaining macaroni and cheese off my plate to cover half my spoon.

"He might need some help, Chah."

"Why, I was just thinking that he might want a little help." Charlene dead-panned.

Tim smiled and began to cut it in half.

"It really would be a shame to waste it now, don't you think?"

"Tim?" Charlene smiled sweetly, "I don't mind helping you finish that if you need me to."

"... I still have a little room left, too." I added. "Plus, you're my brother. I feel a duty."

Tim set equal halves on each of our plates.

"*Bon appétit.*" He suggested with a smile.

Fried chicken is a nearly holy thing in the Peek family. Wasting a piece would be akin to breaking one of the Ten Commandments.

Even though we giggled as we polished off Tim's chicken, we couldn't pretend we didn't feel the unsettling gravity of this moment. As much as we needed this light-hearted fellowship we knew in our hearts everybody was scared and clung to the hem of Jesus' garment.

Leaving the restaurant before our individual families drove back to our respective homes, hugs all around were in order. I watched as Uncle Charlie hugged Tim, then Paul. Embracing Paul, Uncle Charlie made a noise that indicated he was crying. The adults drew close to them and we shared tears in a collective hug. There we stood in that strip mall parking lot, a big huddle of grown people sniffling and dripping shamelessly. I felt Jesus right in the center of us.

"I'm praying for you boys." Uncle Charlie's voice cracked and the divine presence of the Holy Spirit bound us firmly.

> *Is any one of you in trouble? He should pray. Is anyone happy? Let him sing songs of praise. Is any one of you sick? He should call the elders of the church to pray over him and anoint him with oil in the name of the Lord. And the prayer offered in faith will make the sick person well; the Lord will raise him up. If he has sinned, he will be forgiven. Therefore confess your sins to each other and pray for each other so that you may be healed. The prayer of a righteous man is powerful and effective.*
> *James 5:13-16*

Chapter Fifty-Four

Somebody had taken a close-up picture of, Tim "The Grill Man" Peek eating a hot dog at the reunion and it ended up getting posted on Kuzinville. Instead of deleting it I forwarded it to myself now and then. During the nearly four months Tim was unable to talk and eat, this photograph inspired me to visualize his healing when I prayed.

I couldn't imagine being unable to talk, but not being able to eat was completely inconceivable. Treatments began around August and by September a chalk board became his primary mode of communication. The radiation and chemotherapy wiped him out. A boy likes to lean on his daddy when he's weak, yet his daddy's strength had already seeped largely into the unholy monster that was Parkinson's disease. Still, Tim's memories of Daddy's will and tolerance sustained him. Meditating on Daddy's three-month recovery from injuries sustained in the big car accident of 1969, Tim persevered bravely.

In July Tim would turn 45 and I wanted so much to celebrate him. It was hard. My foundation of hope was often darkened by an inky puddle of "what if?"

Recognizing all too well that it might be the last birthday gift I'd ever send Tim I gave a whole lot of thought to what might be just the right thing. What I ended up sending him was sort of like a party-in-a-box. The hardest part about finding items to fill Tim's birthday party box was that it couldn't have any food treats inside. How do you have a party without sweets? Daily pondering over this question finally resulted in a finished product that I took to the Post Office.

My face was graced with wet eyes and a great, big smile as I handed it to the postal worker. These are a few of the things the box held: party hats, confetti, balloons, horns, a toy that played, "Happy Birthday To You" and a plastic jar of goo.

Not surprisingly, Tim and Natalie's favorite of the treasures was the goo. Its understandable appeal was that when you poked air in it with your fingers it made the universal sounds of gas passing. Tim and Natalie communicated with it gleefully using the language of laughter and shared hours of unbridled juvenile merriment. Who really needs good taste or maturity when it's your birthday?

After the noise lost its amusement for Helen, she suggested that they call to thank me. It might seem impossible, but Tim really used to call us sometimes, Helen on the extension, serving as his mouthpiece. Their patient, cooperative method of communicating was one of the most loving things I have ever witnessed. They must have shared a heart in order for Helen to be so intuitive about what Tim's response would have been, had he been able to speak. He began referring to Helen and Natalie as, "my angels."

The encouragement of his cousins in Kuzinville also fortified Tim throughout his ordeal. By Halloween he could talk some but it was pretty painful. In November his lymph nodes were removed to see if cancer was gone. The verdict? No traces - cancer-free. Thanks be to God.

TIM'S COMMENT:

Thanksgiving 2002 I was finally able to eat. It was vegetable soup. The only thing left was to get rid of the stomach feeding tube which wasn't until January of 2003. My goal was to eat on my own without the feeding tube.

As far as losing my job the day before I started chemo and radiation, at the time I surely didn't feel that it was a blessing. In fact for several weeks afterwards I did my best to find any kind of a job at Coca-Cola including appealing to the CEO, Doug Daft. No luck. However, the blessing was that with my severance package that included healthcare for 18 months, I was able to not worry about going back to work (which, knowing me I would have) and just concentrate on getting through the therapies and getting well. That is where I felt that God was looking out for me. I was able to support my family even though I could not work and lift that worry off my mind. I also had great healthcare insurance that provided me with basically everything I needed including delivering cases of Ensure (which if I never see another can of the stuff will be too soon....) to my door to keep sustenance in my body.

Tim learned that prayer works. He also learned to let people help him; to depend on others. Uncle Charlie's strong spirit carried him as well. Tim used Kuzinville as a way to make his situation public which not only gave him a communication outlet but a huge cheering section. Between Tim and Helen, regular updates on Tim's progress inspired us as well and reminded us to pray. God was certainly listening to His Peek children praying.

Love is patient, love is kind. It does not envy, it does not boast, it is not proud. It does not dishonor others, it is not self-seeking, it is not easily angered, it keeps no record of wrongs. Love does not delight in evil but rejoiced with the truth. It always protects, always trusts, always hopes, always perseveres. Love never fails.
1 Corinthians 13:4-8

Chapter Fifty-Five

As far as Paul's condition, he and I had gratefully, joyfully fallen into a pattern of normalcy. He was feeling well and worked twelve hour days with regularity. Of course, we understood the melanoma would always be a potential show stopper if it took up residence in one of Paul's organs, but for now, life was as predictable as it gets in a family as big as ours. We'd become bigger fans of the Health Food stores and read everything we could get our hands on regarding alternative cancer treatments. Dr. Trip encouraged us to be pro-active in Paul's recovery.

Joseph's American Boy History Club had planned a camping trip that he and his daddy were excited about. Paul had ordered a new sleeping bag and a special backpack just for the occasion. Sometime just after plans were being made, Paul was scheduled for a routine visit to Dr. Samuel, the brain surgeon. Paul had worn one of his many University of South Carolina hats and Dr. Samuel felt obligated to comment.

"Are you a Gamecock fan, Mr. Graham?"

"Yep. Those are my boys."

"I've never been able to follow football." Dr. Samuel apologized. "My daughter gets aggravated with me because I still don't get it."

I laughed, "I think you're okay, doctor. Surely you get extra points for being a brain surgeon."

Doctor Samuel pulled out some films from Paul's last CT scan and addressed Paul.

"We've got some more work to do, big guy."

We studied the films and she showed us a tumor, not quite as big as the last one she had removed. This one required another surgery.

Paul pulled his pocket calendar out of his back pocket and I went for mine in my purse. I guess we knew the drill by now. Dr. Samuel told Paul the next date she would have available and Paul said something that made me love him more but shocked me, too.

"I don't want to have the surgery until after my camping trip with my son."

Dr. Samuel nodded. "Okay, when's that?"

Paul flipped the pages of his calendar as nonchalantly as if they were planning a lunch date.

"I work here," he turned a page, "how about here?" Paul raised his little book so she could note his open date. She checked her own calendar and penned in Paul's surgery date.

Paul and Joseph did go on that camping trip and had a grand time. When Paul's surgery came shortly afterward, I waited with our blessed throng of friends in the waiting room. I'll never forget how Doctor Samuel looked when she came out of surgery to tell me,

"I opened your husband's head and the tumor almost jumped right into my hand."

That's when a voice from Paul's waiting group piped up,

"We *prayed* that tumor out."

The Gamma Knife Treatments had been our best friend and the residual cancer in Paul's brain continued to respond well to this method of radiation. By now, though, Paul had been treated four times and we were on a first name basis with the neurologists, nurses and technicians who ran the Gamma Knife Clinic. Unfortunately, the M.R.I.'s Paul got at three month intervals continued to show small, yet regular tumors.

As his treatments became routine, Paul, enjoying his new lease on life, was more determined than ever to make every minute count. The cancer had given him a new perspective on everyday things and he started surprising me by bringing flowers home. One day he even apologized to me for always leaving me with the burden of disciplining the children and promised to share some of that responsibility. He began pursuing activities just for the two of us. One night when he wasn't able to sleep he booked a May cruise for us online. Neither of us had ever been on a cruise. It was sweeter than ever to be married to him and I thanked God for saving him.

By October I was making daily trips to the pear tree to fill grocery bags with the green fruits. The floor in the large room we used for an office/school room was knee-deep in bulging brown bags and I knew I'd have to do something about it soon. I'd never canned anything before but it seemed like the only reasonable thing to do with the pears, there were just so many of them! I figured Nita, being from Georgia and all, might be able to help. My aunts from Georgia were always canning, or rather, "putting up" produce. Nita had admitted to a life-long love affair with pears, so I'd been bringing Ziploc bags of pears to church for her on Sundays. Surely she'd know how to help.

"Hey, Nita!"

"Well hello!" She replied. "You sound like life is good!"

"My cup of life is overflowing." I answered. "In fact, it's overflowing with pears at the moment. Listen, didn't you tell me you knew how to can stuff?"

"No." Nita snorted before laughing out loud. "You got me mixed up with my aunts."

"Yeah," I sighed. "My aunts from Georgia are Mason Jar Queens, too. The genes must skip a generation."

"I'll tell you what, though." Nita offered. "If you find someone who can walk us through the canning process, I'll help you."

"That sounds like a good deal. I'll get back to you after some research."

I paced around the house for a few minutes trying to remember if I knew of anybody nearby who had ever mentioned canning fruit and vegetables. Who was I kidding? This was the Boonies. Hardly anybody I knew lived nearby. I decided to take my chances and call Barbara. I had no idea if she knew canning, but at least she lived nearby. Turned out, her mom was an experienced canner and she thought she remembered most of the process. So it came to be that the three of us, Nita, Barbara and I, congregated in my kitchen early on October 31 to can all those pears. We three blondes began the day with the bright ambition of being done in a few hours. Paul came home from work around 4:00 pm and found us still in the kitchen peeling, paring, and boiling pears. There were pears cooking in three giant pots on the stove, bubbling in a mammoth turkey roaster on the counter. Even still, grocery bags full of pears stood in menacing rows awaiting preparation. We were punch-drunk and fell into a laughing heap when we realized Nita was gingerly trying to cut up a scalding pear straight out of the boiling water.

After we recovered Paul asked, "Why don't you just run them through that juicer?"

It was brilliant. Run the scalding pears through the juicer then combine the juice with the pulp that had been separated from it. Voila! Pear butter in a fraction of the time it would have taken to do it manually! Exhausted, we finally finished around 7:00 pm with an amazing 137 jars of pears or pear butter gracing my kitchen counter. And this wasn't the end of pears. The tree continued to proliferate. There would be no more canning of pears after this fiasco, however, as Nita, Barbara and I shared canned pears with family and friends, the little tree bore fruit enough for Pear Crisp desserts any time we wanted. Other friends would come in from Camden to pick our pears and there were still plenty of birds and who-knows-what feasting at will. The harvest from this damaged little tree seemed impossibly huge. The only explanation that made sense was this. When the big piece of equipment accidentally sliced off half its branches, the little tree must have thought it had been pruned!

Do not be anxious about anything, but in everything, by prayer and petition, with thanksgiving, present your requests to God. And the peace of God, which transcends all understanding, will guard your hearts and minds in Christ Jesus.
Philippians 4:6

Chapter Fifty-Six

Paul and I awoke to the alarm clock playing that, 'song' Charlotte didn't like. He squinted at it and pressed the button on top.

"Sorry."

"That's all right, hon. We've got a big day ahead."

It was Monday morning and Paul had the day off work. Yesterday's newspaper crossword lay unfinished between us. Right before falling off to sleep the night before, he said we had gone without bedroom furniture long enough. We had lived in the house for two years now. Paul was ready to replace what we had sold at the Flea Market before moving into the trailer. The plan was to go to downtown and pick out a bed. We'd looked at a lot of them over the past several months in store circulars and magazines always choosing the same cherry finished, sleigh bed style furniture.

Paul started the coffee. Joseph sensed he was up and Paul's leg immediately became a Joseph magnet.

"Hey, Daddy." Joseph was wrapped tightly around Paul's leg. "Good moanin'"

"Good mornin', bubby." Paul picked up his little man and they shared a hug accompanied by cave-man noises. Joseph was getting so tall.

"Daddy, I want to ask you a guestion."

"What 'guestion' do you have for me this morning?" Paul replied, knowing full well what Joseph would ask because he asked this question every day.

"Aw you goin' to woak today?"

Joseph's R's were still a challenge to his speech, but we all loved it. The sink in this new house had a water purifier feature. To hear Joseph ask for, "p-yow wataw" hadn't lost an ounce of its cute appeal.

"Well, let me see..." Paul feigned consternation. "Oh, yeah. I don't go in today."

"Weally?" Joseph's voice went up an octave. "We can wowk outside?"

Paul laughed and set Joseph on the floor. Joseph wrapped around Paul's leg.

"I wove you, Daddy."

"I love you, too, Jopus."

"Can you make me something in your wowk-shop?"

"Maybe after we get back, but we are going into town today. How about I make you some breakfast?"

"Awight, and we can wowk later?"

"Maybe, buddy."

Almost dressed, I tied my tennis shoes then tiptoed out of the bedroom. I wore a big old smile. A long, angular bar separating the kitchen from the living and dining areas was the only semblance of a wall in this part of the house. I sat down soundlessly in a dining room chair, hoping my presence wouldn't interrupt their precious conversation. Raising Jon, Austin and Elisabeth had been lonely business. I used to long every day to be married to a daddy like Paul, so I didn't begrudge a millisecond of the time and fun the children had with Paul. In fact, I basked in it.

Emily swept past the length of the bar. She was grinning so hard her face looked like three cracks and a nose in the middle. She stopped long enough to 'shh' me with a finger to her lips. Hanging by Emily's embrace, poor Kit gave me a tolerant look that said, "This is my life. I do what I have to."

Emily jumped out from behind the bar, her blonde curls bouncing crazily around her head.

"BOO." She said to her Daddy and brother.

Joseph laughed and Paul pretended to be startled.

"Good mornin,' Mi. You almost made me drop this milk."

"She didn't scare me." Joseph interjected, defending his manliness.

Emily giggled, resembling a happy little mouse.

"I knew you didn't see me."

To Kit's relief, Emily put her down. Emily hugged her daddy around his waist as Kit took this opportunity to make a dash to hide under the bed. Paul lifted Emily off her feet. She looked a little like Kit hanging there in Paul's embrace.

"Mm-m-m, M-M-Mmph." Paul said, squeezing her.

"DAA- dee." Emily protested unconvincingly.

"Can I squeeze a giggle out of you?" He asked.

"NO, DADDY."

"I bet I can." Paul squeezed Emily three quick times in the middle of her *"No, Daddy."* It made her sound like, *No-ho Da-ha-dee-hee.*

Emily leaned back laughing as Paul's big arms caught and supported her.

"I *thought* I could squeeze a giggle out of you."

Charlotte rounded the corner of the bar, her walk had a slow little sway. She gave me a sidelong glance that seemed to say, *those nutty kids* and smiled with her lips together.

She made a slow ascent onto one of the bar stools facing the kitchen. Paul saw her and set Emily's feet on the floor.

"Well, good morning, Chah-Chah." He crept toward her menacingly.

Charlotte answered his greeting in a high pitch, barely suppressing a squeal.

"Hay, Daddy."

"Can I squeeze a giggle out of you this morning?"

Emily and Joseph jumped up and down.

"No-o-o-o-o." Charlotte answered.

"I bet I can."

Charlotte's lost control of her smile and revealed front teeth.

"No-o-o-o." She insisted, but Paul already had his big arms around her. The next thing that came out of her was a high-pitched,

"Ho-ho-ho-ho-hee-hee-ha-ha."

Eventually, everyone was hugged, fed, dressed, buckled up and riding off in what felt like an adventure. First stop was downtown Columbia, an area called The Vista where many of the train stops had been renovated into upscale restaurants. We weren't here to eat, however. Paul pulled our Windstar Van into a parking place between the furniture store and River Runner canoe Outdoor Center.

"Yook, Daddy." Joseph's eyes were like silver dollars. "Boats."

"Daddy wants to look at those, too, buddy." Paul answered then he turned to me,

"I've never canoed down the Congaree Swamp before."

His comment was met with a blank expression from me, "Me either."

"Let's do that sometime." Paul said brightly.

"Heh-heh. Maybe we could." I replied, hoping secretly that I never inhabited a canoe stirring the snaky, crocodile-rich waters of the Congaree.

We exited, some of us tumbling, out of the van. Knowing that my children insisted on visiting every bathroom in any structure we ever entered, I should have taken them right to the bathroom, but I didn't. It wasn't until we had traveled deep into the furniture store with a floor salesman that the first child's bladder urges prompted him to utter the words,

"Mom, I gotta go potty."

"Okay." I said, relenting to what now was *three* whining voices.

The salesman was talking to Paul in earnest about dovetailed drawers and such when I excused myself to them for directions. It seemed like hours later when the last pair of little hands was scrubbed and dried and I set out with my duckling entourage to find the rest of our party. We located Paul on the opposite side of the cash register from the salesman. Joseph ran ahead of us and wrapped himself around Paul's leg like a human twist-tie. Paul looked up from a brochure he was reading.

"I picked it out." He said, and I laughed, thinking he was kidding about picking it out without me. "Do you want to see it?"

"Well, YEAH."

"It's right over here." Paul led me to a bedroom display while the salesman diligently filled out forms in triplicate.

A cherry wardrobe/entertainment center towered over a large, ornate chest-of-drawers on the left side of the display. Catty-cornered on the right side a hulking bed sprawled ominously, audaciously, flaunting leaf and scroll carvings and giant claw feet. All I could think was that it was HUGE.

"Oh." I replied brightly, forcing myself to speak without revealing the shock I felt. "This is the one you want?"

"This is it. I like it."

Now, I knew Paul Graham pretty well. It wasn't his habit to be selfish or insist on his way about much of anything. Quite the contrary. He was the guy who would offer the best bite of his gourmet delight to me so he could watch me enjoy it. He drove the Bronco so I could drive the better car. He went along with any crazy decorating idea I had for our house.

"It's just paint." I recalled him saying of my most recent wall texturing project. *If it turns out a disaster, we know where they sell more paint."*

I really hadn't minded sleeping on the mattress and box springs but it had really bothered Paul. He was kind of embarrassed about it, even though the rest of the furniture had been replaced. It was at that moment that I knew I wouldn't disagree with Paul's choice. I knew that his happiness was my joy. I had almost lost him and God had brought him back, if Paul wanted 20,000 pounds of furniture to sleep on, then so be it. In spite of myself and despite the miracles of healing we had witnessed, I wondered, *"Will it be on this bed that Paul takes his last rest?"*

The sight of his sparkling eyes as they surveyed the bedroom suite made me smile. Well, it *was* a sleigh bed, and we *had* agreed on that, but imposing as it was, it didn't seem big enough to hold the king-size mattress we already owned.

Paul walked over to the chest-of-drawers, opened the top drawer and looked inside.

"It's really made well."

"Sure seems solid." I agreed. "Is this a *king-size* display?"

The wardrobe's door-knocker lion-head pulls locked in on me and glared with four menacing eyes.

"It's a queen."

"Oh. Do you feel pretty sure the king-size is going to fit in our room?"

"Sure, it will, but there's one piece that isn't displayed."

"Small piece?" I asked, hopefully.

"...the bedside table. He's ordering it, now."

"Well, that's good." The lion-heads seemed to approve. "As it is said, so it is done."

Charlotte, Emily, Joseph, Paul and I continued our adventure next door at the River Runner. Paul showed us a red canoe he had visited before and somehow, it had been paid for and strapped to the top of our car before we left. That Congaree Swamp trip was beginning to look less like the pipe dream I hoped it was.

We followed up with a buffet feast at Golden Palace Chinese. The waiter left four fortune cookies on the little tray that held the check.

"Wead mine, daddy, wead mine." Joseph begged.

Paul adjusted his glasses and read Joseph's fortune between his fingers.

"A light heart carries you through the hard times."

"Oh." Joseph replied. "What did it mean?"

"It means you're going to be just fine because you have a happy heart."

Joseph smiled. Emily waved her little paper strip in the air.

"Listen to mine. 'All the effort you are making will ultimately pay off.'"

"Nice one, Mi." Paul said and I agreed. "Let's hear Chah's fortune."

Charlotte leaned into the table and shifted in her seat. Situated just right, she read,

"Change is happening in your life, so go with the flow." That's really a dumb fortune. What's yours, Daddy?"

Paul slid the paper out of his cookie and read the tiny

words through the bottom of his lenses,

"Advice is like kissing, it costs nothing and is pleasant to do."

"That's funny." Joseph deemed amid everyone's laughter.

"Okay. Paul said, "One more fortune, Mama? What does yours say?"

"Mine's not as exciting as your Daddy's. It says, "Allow compassion to guide your decisions"''

"Hear, hear." Paul clinked his tea glass to mine. "I think you already do that."

We left the restaurant sated, finished up some business at Best Buy and Sear's and ended our adventure at Food Lion for groceries. The van was now weighed down leaving only space enough for Elisabeth's little body to sit when school was out. We set off to pick her up when Paul answered a call from his cell phone. I hated to admit how much it still alarmed me to hear the phone ring. Paul pulled off to the side and answered it.

"Hello?"

My insides jelled as I strained to hear the caller. Paul's face went serious.

"Okay. Okay. Yes. I'll be ready as soon as you are. Just let me know. Thank you."

Paul pressed the hang-up key.

"Something's wrong." I said.

Paul nodded.

"The last PET scan... it looks like another metastasis."

"Where?"

"My adrenal gland."

Paul laid his forehead on the steering wheel and I put my hand on his shoulder.

"Oh, Paul. We're going to deal with this, honey."

Paul nodded without raising his head off the wheel.

"God has brought you through worse surgeries. We'll get through it."

Paul raised his head and I was surprised to see his eyes were dry. He took my hand in his and rubbed my thumbs.

"Yes, we will." He whispered.

Taking a big breath, he turned the ignition and exhaled, driving to Camden High School to pick up Elisabeth. Carrying on in the midst of these problems seemed so bizarre, but what else could we do?

Even during Paul's emotional distress and the cancer showing up in new places, our lives often seemed so regular. Staying busy meeting the needs of our family was a blessing in that way. We'd still go places together, joke around like we used to and count on each other for basic things when it seemed like we should have been having nervous breakdowns. Looking back, I realize we were being granted a portion of what the Bible calls *peace that passes understanding.*

Even now, with this news of another awful surgery, we kept our evening plans to visit friends. Ann and Carlos Anrrich from our old neighborhood had invited Paul and me to their house for dessert and espresso. After getting all four of the children home and instructing Elisabeth on their supper, Paul and I headed out to Columbia once again.

Ann and Carlos were gracious with a generous air of relaxation. Carlos used his nursing degree at the clinic on campus at the University of South Carolina. His family was from Cuba, but he had lived in the states since he was a teen. Carlos played guitar, bringing his warm, tenor voice alongside chords that floated effortlessly from his fingers.

Ann's pretty laughter added joy to her lightness. She was an artist with a special flair for turning a canvas into a page from a fantasy storybook. The subjects for much of the art that adorned her walls were the beautiful Anrrich daughters, Mariel and Sarah and various cats and dogs. We met for the first time at the pool, back when I was pregnant with twins and requisitioned Ann to paint a watercolor for us of Sarah and Elisabeth. It didn't take us long to become good friends.

Soon after we arrived for dessert, we sat out in their screened porch and told them about the impending surgery. We talked about it for a little while, Carlos adding encouraging tidbits from his medical background. Ann was the first to change the subject,

"Does anybody want to go in the house? I'm about

ready to make the espresso and cut the torte."

We followed Ann into the kitchen and watched her as she loaded the espresso pot and turned on the stove.

When Carlos mentioned kayaking, Paul's interest was immediately sparked.

"Yeah, Ann and I go down to the Congaree Swamp and float in kayaks or sometimes canoes. I like the canoe ride better."

"I've always wanted to do that." Paul piped in.

Ann joined in, "You'll have to come along with us the next time we go."

"Um. Excuse me, y'all, but isn't the Congaree Swamp where people go to get bitten by rattlesnakes and eaten by crocodiles?"

"Nah." Carlos grinned wickedly, "You can always outrun them."

I shivered and Ann's laughter tinkled in the air like a wind chime,

"C'mon, Shirley. Be tough."

Talk of this crazy adventure continued and I realized that my opinion had been overridden by the lunatics in my company. Against my better judgment, I agreed to go along with the idea, secretly hoping it would be forgotten.

Paul's new surgery would soon be scheduled and yet we were behaving as though the cancer had never come, or that it was a thing of the past. Our attitude was of having risen above it. Somehow, that made me smile. Somehow, talking about this wild nature trip was one way cancer hadn't defeated us.

* * *

I was busy washing dishes when I heard the radio announcer offer a dinner for two at Key West seafood grill near Dutch Square Mall for the best joke.

"What the hay?" I thought, and dialed up the radio station number.

I was surprised when my call was answered so quickly and a deep, yet lively voice requested that I identify myself.

"This is Shirley Graham." I answered in a tinny voice

that echoed through my own radio speaker.

"Have you got a good joke for us this morning?"

"Sure." I answered, channeling my Georgia relatives for an exaggerated Southern accent. "Do y'all know why mah hand, is jis' like a lem-mon pie?"

"No, Shirley." The announcer asked with a slight undertone in his voice that said he wasn't too sure if the accent was pretend. "Why is your hand like a lemon pie?"

"Why, don'tcha know? That's 'cause it has *mah rang* (meringue) on it."

Awful, I know, but I won the two dinners."

The day before the adrenal extraction, our home school friends, Barry and Angie gathered our children into their home. All three of the Ogburn daughters, Lauren, Lindsay & Leah were in home school now. Lauren was Charlotte and Emily's best friend. I was thankful to have them safely sleeping there. Later in the morning they would all begin a home school day without being disrupted by what Paul and I had to do. I hoped that surrounding them with a sense of fun and change would distract them from any anxiety over their daddy's surgery.

This time around, the procedure used by the surgeon was laparoscopic adrenalectomy. This minimally invasive surgery promised a shorter hospital stay, decreased postoperative pain, improved recovery times, and better cosmetic results. Paul and I looked forward to a quick, almost painless recovery and a ride home soon after. What we weren't counting on was Nita's gift and what it would bring.

I hadn't long been in Paul's hospital room when there was a little knock on the door. We both looked up and saw a stack of white bags enter ahead of Nita's smiling face.

"Hay." She greeted us with an earful of her Georgia roots.

"Hay, hon." I grabbed the door to keep it from slamming on her.

"I guess I should have asked if Paul was allowed to eat anything before I brought this. Are you even ready to eat, Paul?"

"I'm great." Paul answered, unconcerned with whatever the regulations might be about eating.

"Bring it on. My mama born me ready."

"He's feisty when he kills cancer, ain't he?" I asked Nita.

"He's feisty most all the time, I think."

The white paper bags Nita pulled fried chicken out of made the whole room sound and smell crispy and good.

"I stood in line forever, so I really don't have time to visit. Everybody in Columbia must go there for lunch."

"What does that tell you?" I asked rhetorically.

She began setting up Paul's stainless steel roller tray: a cardboard tray of chicken and fries in the middle, iced tea on the right and slaw just to the left. Her mama had trained her right. Paul dug in making short work of the meal as Nita and I chatted. When I moved to discard his chicken graveyard I heard Nita say,

"Are you okay, Paul?"

He didn't look too good. His face was turning green and he had his hand on his abdomen. Minutes later, he started moaning,

"Oh-h-h." He uttered and I could see he was trying to lean forward.

I ran out into the hall, spotted a nurse and motioned for her to come to Paul's room.

"My husband." I began, "Something's wrong."

She rushed in as Paul's moans cranked up another decibel. "OH-H-H."

Nita turned toward me, "I hate to leave, Shirley, but I have to get back to the office."

"I know, Nita, it's okay."

"I'll call you after work."

As Nita exited, another nurse stepped in, immediately noticing the discarded food containers.

"Did he eat this?" She pointed to Nita's post-surgery gift.

"Yes." I answered sheepishly

"*That's* what's wrong."

What we learned that day was that Paul wasn't going to die, although he might have felt like it. For laparoscopic surgery, the abdomen is pumped with air and therein lies the rub. Typically, the patient is only allowed a liquid post-surgical diet until the air dissipates in about twelve hours. Instead of a liquid fast, Paul had put grease, raw cabbage and the like on his stomach.

Nita regretted her kindly intentioned benevolent deed. Paul ended up staying one day longer than anticipated at the hospital, but that was the only harm done, although Paul reminded her numerous times afterward that she had tried to kill him.

For I know the plans I have for you, declares the LORD, Plans to prosper you and not to harm you, plans to give you hope and a future. Then you will call upon me and come and pray to me, and I will listen to you.
Jeremiah 29:11-12

Chapter Fifty-Seven

Once more, we returned home from the hospital and picked up our routine. Elisabeth, Charlotte and Emily hovered at their daddy's bedside like little overbearing mothers, taking lunch orders and leaving get well pictures on his bedside table. Joseph's daddy-ministry involved sitting on the bed beside his daddy. He enjoyed being a boy, but he wanted to be a man like his daddy more than anything

Jon had been living in Pensacola, working with his father at an open M.R.I. facility for a couple of years. He and Austin had even shared a living arrangement for a while, which gave me a small window into Austin's life as well. Jon had been seeing a beautiful girl named Darcie, but things weren't working out between them. Lately, he had been calling, talking about moving back to South Carolina. I'd looked into some school programs for him and checked out job availability Columbia hospitals. I looked forward to the day he'd be moving home.

The phone rang right as I climbed in the bed. It was Jon. I was just about to launch into sharing some of my great job and school information when he stopped me.

"Mom, I called to tell you that you are going to be a grandmother."

I tried to absorb his words. Why had he sprung it on me like this, so flippantly? It made me mad, but I willed some control before I spoke.

"Jon. First of all, I am proud of you and Darcie for not considering abortion. But secondly, I realize already that I will never know that baby."

"Mom, you will."

"I know you, son. You'll stay in Pensacola and you should. You're not the kind of guy who will let your child grow up without you. For me, though, the distance factor will limit my ability to be involved, and I'm going to hate it. In spite of that, I need you to know I am thankful that you are having this baby."

"I know, Mom, and I know this puts you in a terrible position as far as telling Charlotte, Emily and Joseph. Now, you're going to have to talk to them about things you probably aren't ready to discuss."

"Oh. Yeah. Well, I'll deal with that. I know this was a hard call for you to make. I'm praying for you. Do the right thing."

Paul had been getting ready for bed as I talked to Jon. It wasn't too hard for him to figure out what the call was about, so we just looked at each other after I put the phone in the cradle.

"You okay?" He asked.

"Yeah." I sat cross-legged on the bed and looked at my hands. "I'll be okay as soon as I get my head wrapped around this new plan."

"I know you were happy about Jon coming back home."

"Yeah… oh, well."

"I know you love babies."

"Yes, I do. That's something we share, isn't it, Counselor?"

"Yes ma'am"

Paul turned out the light and put his big arms around me.

"You never know what's around the corner." I said into his shoulder.

"Nope. We still don't really know."

Paul had no idea how much truth he'd just spoken.

In May, Paul and I set out on our cruise. He had booked us on a smoke-free Caribbean cruise-liner that made stops in St. Croix, Virgin Islands and Nassau. Despite the Trans-Derm Scope patches stuck behind our earlobes, Paul was sick throughout the cruise. We managed to get to a couple of the shows, but Paul spent a large portion of the cruise nauseated, asleep in our cabin. He didn't miss the dining table, thanks to steroids and the man's sheer will, but he clearly wasn't himself.

When the ship docked in St. Croix, Paul wanted to go off sightseeing, just him and me. It was unsettling, my husband me walking around in a foreign country with the cancer that insisted on being our unwelcome companion. I went along with just about anything Paul wanted to do at this stage, understanding these could be his last opportunities.

We walked up and down steep streets, mostly looking at the shops from the outside. When the day's heat drew the moisture out of us, we stepped inside a little store and bought a couple of orange sodas for an unknown amount of foreign currency. Much to my relief, we started back toward the ship and I began to feel hope that we wouldn't get lost and left behind to become street people of the island. Then, I saw a shop window display of linen clothing and towels.

"Do you mind stopping inside?" I asked my quiet husband.

"If you're waiting on me, you're backing-up."

It was still good to hear him sounding like my old friend, even though I knew he was trying really hard to be himself. We held hands and stepped inside the friendly little linen shop. Two smiling ladies ran the store, one was from the States. Paul and I looked at stacks of crisply ironed linen napkins and meticulously smocked baby clothes. Hanging from a small rod, I found a line of beautiful, little, white linen christening gowns. My breath caught when I read the sales ticket, "$15.00."

"Is this right? I asked Paul, "Fifteen American dollars?"

"That's what it looks like."

Sure enough, the price was right and I was thrilled to buy this beautiful garment for my new grand baby's Baptism.

Back on the ship, Paul seemed to be going through the motions of getting through the cruise. I wondered if he felt like that old song, *Is That All There Is?* One thing I worried about was that he might fall into despair as he sometimes did, but my worries were unfounded. In retrospect, I think that the cruise was really his gift to me.

We returned home with pictures of our trip and trinkets for the children. Some of the pictures were sad. One, a standard cruise portrait of Paul and me all dressed to the nines, was the saddest to me. I'm wearing a strained smile as Paul stands beside me, not smiling at all, his face splotched and bloated from the steroids.

Now that we were home, Paul dragged himself to work part-time. I was gift-wrapping the baby's christening gown for Darcie's upcoming baby shower when he limped through the door after work one afternoon.

"Hey, Hon, why are you walking like that?"

Paul dropped into a chair and rubbed his ankle.

"When I was leaving the parking lot in Camden, I shut the door on my leg."

"How did you manage that?"

He pulled up his pant leg, revealing a jagged slice of broken skin.

"You know how you get in the car and close the door? You just kind of do it in one fluid motion, climb in, sit down, pull your legs in and shut the door."

"Yeah."

"I guess I closed the door before my legs were in all the way."

Paul's confession sent a chill down my spine. It sounded to me like his extremities weren't registering his brain's commands. We looked at each other, both wondering silently what might be blocking the messages.

The following Sunday, as we dressed for church, I noticed Paul's shirt buttons weren't in the right holes. He laughed and started working on them. As we descended the steps to the car, I said,

"Hey, Hon, your buttons still don't look just right."

He looked down at his shirt, three buttonholes off. He fiddled with them a little without seeming to care. I held my breath as Paul drove us to church and I determined to call his doctor the next morning. Paul's driving was terrible and I didn't start breathing normally until he parked and we walked away from the car. I shuddered, looking behind me at the lazy way the van was parked.

We'd missed Sunday School. Going into the Narthex I thought about re-doing Paul's buttons before we stepped into the Sanctuary, but didn't. I'd already told him two times.

A third reminder might irritate him. Besides, maybe it wasn't my place to protect him that way. It might make him think I was emasculating him.

Paul looked unsteady as I looped my hand through his right arm. We stopped at Nita and Dave's pew and hugged them. Nita said,

"Do y'all want to go eat Chinese food after church?"

"I won't turn down a meal." Paul answered a little too loudly.

"We'll meet you after church." I whispered and we continued to our usual seat, second front pew from the end closest to the aisle, on the left side by the piano.

Charlotte and Emily slid down the pew first, Joseph following closely. Emily sat down and pushed Joseph away from her. Joseph gave her a hurt look. I sat next to him and put my arm around him. Paul sat on my right and pulled my hand into the safety of his warm hand. At least this felt normal, I loved our hand-holding ritual.

I hadn't sung in the choir for a few weeks, using the excuse that I'd missed choir practice the week before. Really, I felt like I needed to be on this pew keeping an eye on Paul and the children. It was a task that needed to be done and I was really the only one who could do it now. Elisabeth slipped in between Charlotte and Emily and the service began.

Paul lasted through the Liturgy and the Children's Sermon. The little ones left for Children's Church where they would color and hear a lesson on the Scripture of the day. Early into Pastor Garry's sermon, Paul began to nod off. As long as he wasn't snoring, I wouldn't wake him. Lately he'd fallen asleep in Sunday school, too. I looked at his shirt buttons and wondered how many people had noticed.

"Lord, have mercy." I silently prayed.

After church we met Nita and Dave at a Chinese restaurant in Camden. It was located in a large strip mall, the only business open on a Sunday. Even though Paul had acres of room to park, the Windstar was angled awkwardly over two car spaces. Nita met me walking into the restaurant and I whispered for her take a gander at Paul's parking job.

"Did you see his buttons?" I added.

"Yes, I wondered what that was all about."

"He's not right." I crossed my arms against a sudden chill. "Something new must be in his head."

"I'm sorry, Honey." Nita said, briefly hugging me with one arm. "I know this is awful for you."

I knew Nita really did know all about what I was going through. She'd been widowed before she and Dave met, having lost her husband, Vonn to pancreatic cancer.

When we finished the meal, Dave offered to pay the tab but Paul wouldn't let him. They stood at the register for an inordinately long time as Paul made error after error on his check. Dave was patient and kind to his friend, but it was obvious something was terribly wrong. Paul didn't resist when I asked if he'd mind me driving home. Once home, he went straight to bed and slept for a couple of hours.

Monday rolled in and with it I found myself working diligently to finish up the school year. Charlotte and Emily sat with me at the dining room table as I drilled them on the steps of long division.

Paul, quiet and bored, wandered from one room to another. He was too bored to do anything productive enough to lift his mood.

I watched Charlotte and Emily as the division light went on in their heads. It made me so happy to see them grasp a concept. Paul was in the computer room where he had been playing Solitaire on the computer. He must have gotten tired of playing solitaire, because he came out of there and walked past us at the table. Just before he got to the threshold of our bedroom door, he fell backwards and hit the floor. BANG. I was on my knees in an instant, leaning over him as Charlotte and Emily's voices chorused, "Daddy."

Paul lay on his back, his eyes pinned on mine.

"Hey. What happened?"

"I don't know. My legs just stopped working. They just buckled under."

"Can you move?"

"Yeah, I think so."

Well, don't, I mean, not yet."

"Okay."

Do your toes and fingers move?"

He wiggled both sets of digits.

"Yeah."

"Paul, I don't think you should get up yet. Let me call Dr. Trip's office and see what we ought to do."

"Okay." I walked to our bedroom, picking up a remote phone and a pillow off the bed. I held the phone up to my ear with my shoulder and helped Paul put the pillow between his head and the hardwood floor.

"Mommy, what was that?" Joseph walked out of his bedroom holding his pencil and work book.

"Daddy fell." Emily whispered. Her eyes were as big as saucers.

About that time I heard voice of Dr. Trip's receptionist.

"Hi, this is Shirley Graham, my husband is a patient of Dr. Trip's and he just fell."

"He fell?"

"Yes."

Did you help him up?

"No, I wasn't sure I should until I talked to someone there. He's had tumors in his brain and I thought he might be having a seizure or something."

"Well help him up."

"Okay. Will you hold on?"

Paul rolled onto his side and got up mostly without my help. When he stood, I pulled a kitchen chair under him and he sat in it.

Back on the phone I said, "Hello?"

"I'm here."

"I want to schedule an appointment for my husband as soon as possible."

We were at Dr. Trip's office bright and early the next morning. He gave Paul an order to get a CT scan that we took over to Lexington Hospital.

The results told us what we already suspected. More tumors had grown in Paul's brain. We would be visiting the Gamma Knife Clinic as soon as possible. In the meantime, Paul would be forbidden to drive, due to the threat of a possible seizure. He didn't take the news gladly.

On the day of our Gamma Knife appointment, we

went in early, feeling familiar with our surroundings, ready to get the show on the road. After all, this would be Paul's fifth radiation, we knew the drill. This time, though it seemed to be taking longer than usual for the staff to set Paul up. One of the technicians stopped in the cubicle where we waited with news that the doctor wanted to see us. Fifteen minutes later we found ourselves sitting across from a very anxious neurologist who had always seemed so calm before.

"Mr. Graham, this is your last CT scan. He held the dark and nebulous film aloft. I've called you in here because I want to make sure you are aware of the details."

Paul nodded thoughtfully.

"You've already had *four Gamma treatments.*"

"I understand." Paul replied.

"I don't think I can advise you to do this again."

"What's the problem with getting a fifth treatment?" Paul asked.

The doctor held the film against the light.

"Do you see the tumors here?"

Paul and I leaned forward and squinted to see the tumors.

"Now, do you see this area near the tumors, right here? That's *necrosis.*"

Paul didn't flinch. I was trying to remember what *necrosis* was. Wasn't that a medical term for *rot?* If it was, Paul certainly didn't seem rattled. The doctor continued,

"This necrosis occurred because of multiple irradiations from treatments on this area. Now we are faced with radiating this area again."

"Do it. I will assume all the responsibility." Paul answered serenely. "It worked before and I don't see any reason why it wouldn't work again. Besides, I don't have another option."

"Mr. Graham, here's what you don't understand. These are unchartered waters. We've never administered more than four Gamma Knife treatments to a patient."

"Then I'll be the first." Paul replied resolutely.

The doctor looked at my husband intensely.

"Okay, Mr. Graham. This will be your call."

As I waited for Paul in the cubicle, I thought about

the doctor's message, *"We've never administered a fifth Gamma Knife treatment."*

I knew what he meant. Either the first one or two did the trick, or the patient died. No one had ever lived long enough to need a fifth one.

"What are You doing, Lord? You've kept healing him. Are you going to keep on?"

On the way home after the procedure, we stopped for a few groceries at Kroger. Standing together in the line to check out, an older gentleman and his wife waited behind us. I don't know what Paul thought the man had implied, but the next thing I knew, Paul was livid. I looked on helplessly as he angrily shouted harsh words to this unsuspecting gentleman. Vainly, I asked Paul to calm down. He responded by storming out of the door into the parking lot. I turned to the couple in apology,

"I'm sorry. My husband just had a procedure; he had radiation in his brain. This isn't really him."

The man mumbled something and I turned to the bewildered cashier.

"I'll be back for my purchases."

I ran to the door guessing the catalyst for Paul's defensive behavior had been the steroid shot they always gave him after the Gamma Knife treatment. Through the glass of the double doors, I could see he was almost to *Moovies,* a video rental store across the parking lot. I changed my mind about chasing him, went back for my two bags of groceries and carried them to the car.

Parking in the Moovies lot, I watched him moving methodically from one video display to another. I felt like the owner of an alligator off its leash.

"Dear Father." I whispered, *"Who has my husband become, and what am I supposed to do with him?"*

As my prayer hung in the air, God gave me an understanding that He wouldn't be giving us another miraculous healing this time. Paul was dying. He rented his video and came to the car as though he expected me to be there. On the way home, he was calmer, but still justified his actions toward the man.

Paul didn't indicate that he sensed the same

understanding God had given me. I let him lead the way. Sometimes he'd seem to know, like when we left the younger children with Elisabeth and took a short drive down the road to dump the week's trash. I didn't say anything when he got into the driver's seat and drove us down the main road leading to the dump site. About halfway there, he began to talk.

"I couldn't sleep again last night." He'd told me, lips trembling.

Let's park the car, Paul. Talk to me, Honey."

A boat launching park appeared on the left. He pulled the Bronco into a parking place and tried to kill the engine. It chugged and spat for a while, fighting to continue running. Paul had bought this vehicle used and pieced it together the whole time he'd owned it. It had long ago stopped being reliable (Paul had been stranded more than once) yet he insisted on driving it, leaving me to drive our newer car. For as long as I'd known, the air conditioner only worked if the car was moving. Paul took great pride in the number of years he'd coaxed the Bronco along.

"I woke up last night and researched my condition on the internet." He looked down. "I've finally come to terms with the fact that this cancer will end me sooner or later."

He closed his eyes and rested his forehead on the steering wheel. Everything in me longed to encourage him, to tell him it wasn't true, to offer hope that he would be with us much, much longer, but I forced my lips to stay still. Paul needed to hear himself say these words aloud. Listening with my mouth closed was the most loving thing to do for him now. I felt honored that he trusted me to hear his confession and wished I knew a way to give him absolution. I squeezed his warm hand, suddenly aware it had been a long time since I'd begged him, "Never leave me, never die."

The time was coming to let him leave me, to let him die. We wept, holding each other in the very car where we'd shared that first kiss. We embraced, bathing each other in a Baptism of sweet yet bitter tears.

"I love you, Paul. I always will."

"I love you, Shirl."

Other times Paul seemed to think he was bulletproof.

He'd refuse to wear sun screen and talk about the future as though the cancer was non-existent. He'd get unhappy and frustrated but transferred his feelings on something besides the cancer, usually me. Arguments arose because of his belief that I could make him happy if only I wanted to.

Now that he was home on medical leave he would usually refuse to let me engage him in conversation. Then, finally he'd accuse me in some way,

"You're not even attracted to me anymore."

"I'm not attracted to anyone BUT you. I love you." I would say, "How have I ever behaved otherwise? I'm here beside you, Paul. I'm not going anywhere."

He never had an answer that made sense to me. In fact, once he told me,

"If you ever showed me that you love me, my life would be perfect."

"Perfect?" I thought, although I was too shocked to speak it aloud. Cancerous tumors showed up in his body with alarming regularity and yet, he thought *I* could make his life *perfect*? Just what did he think I was holding out on him?

Paul began to get confused in other ways. There were things he couldn't do anymore. Home schooling one morning, Charlotte came into the kitchen asking me for help with a fifth grade math problem.

"I'm right in the middle of getting our lunch ready, Charlotte, I told her, "Can you get your daddy to help you?"

As I ran about, completing the lunch task, I happened to pass by the bedroom door. Glancing in, I saw Paul sitting in a chair, Charlotte's math book open on his lap. Charlotte stood beside him, sweetly, respectfully, patiently watching him study the page. Minutes later, she was at my side in the kitchen, whispering, "Mom?"

I turned off the water in the sink and turned to her.

"Daddy can't help me." She explained quietly with a note of unmistakable fright in her voice. "He said he doesn't understand it."

It frightened me, too. Paul had always been as comfortable doing math as he was breathing. Like most everything else, it came easily to him. So easily, in fact that he hadn't started out well when helping the older children back when they were in school. I remembered him going over math problems with them.

"Just look." He would tell them, "It's easy."

I remember the defeat on their faces as they must have thought, "If it is easy, I must not be very smart."

Paul never meant any harm, of course, he just couldn't relate. Naturally, I had talked to him those many years ago about how I thought he might adjust his tutoring conversation, and he had been thankful for the insight. He replaced his words, "Look, it's easy" with "I know this is complicated, but you'll get it."

Now, he had trouble counting change, specific trouble. What I mean is that he couldn't count by certain numbers. In the pharmacy, since he couldn't count pills by three's, he substituted counting by two's or five's.

He was tormented by doubt and despair in his mind, body and soul. Satan was right on his heels, rushing to devour him for he knew his time was short. Paul believed him when the devil tried to convince him that no one loved him. His words still ring in my ears,

"I feel like, if I fell off the face of the Earth, no one would miss me. No one would care."

One hard day when despair brought Paul to this awful place, I told him,

"I would miss you. I would care. I chose you out of all the men in the world. You were the only one I wanted and you are still the only one I want. Besides that," I continued, "Everyone you've ever known, and some people you don't, pray for you daily. Plus, you've never gone to the hospital once without an entourage."

He still wouldn't look up. I spent hours just being with him, trying to encourage his spirit. Nothing seemed to lift the fog suffocating both of us.

Feeling desperate, I dialed Pastor Garry's cell phone number.

"Hi, Pastor. How are you?"

"I'm great, Shirley, how are you?"

"Good, good. Listen, didn't you tell me you might be coming out here to visit today?"

"Yes, I did, Shirley, but I'll probably have to plan it

for another time."

"Oh, that's okay. I know you're busy, I mean, I'm disappointed, but we'll live."

"Are you sure? I can manipulate my schedule if you need me to."

"Oh, no, no. It's fine. We'll look forward to seeing you another time. It's okay."

"All right then, you take care."

"Thanks, Pastor, you, too."

I hung up and felt all the air leave my lungs. I wished he had been able to sense that I was lying my head off. I picked up the phone and hit re-dial.

"Hello?"

"Um, yeah, Pastor? It's Shirley again. I do hate to pressure you like this, but can you please come over? It's Paul, he's just so depressed. I can't help him but I think he would respond to you."

"Of course, Shirley. Can you give me about 45 minutes?"

"That would be wonderful, wonderful. Thank you so much… and hey."

"What is it?"

"You don't have to mention that I called you, okay?"

"I won't, Shirley. See you soon."

In less than forty-five minutes, Pastor Garry's car rolled down our driveway. I closed my eyes and whispered, *"Thank you, Jesus."*

Paul walked from room to room wearing his brown plaid bathrobe, looking for something that would hold his interest for more than fifteen minutes. So far he hadn't found anything. When Pastor Garry's tires crunched in the gravel driveway, Paul stopped pacing and looked out the window to see who was coming. I admit I'd been avoiding conversation with him. He knew it and it only made him more certain that I didn't love him. So far, I hadn't come up with a better way to get my tasks done than to ignore him some of the time. This morning Paul's needs took priority over school, but I couldn't put the children off any longer.

Pastor Garry smiled outside the glass French doors out front. God bless him. Paul opened the door,

"Pastor Garry?"

They man-hugged and Pastor said, "I was just in the neighborhood."

Then he laughed his head off because we lived so far out in the woods and his inferior sense of direction was famous. He required a deliberate plan and a map when he ventured beyond the familiar.

Paul's mouth made a thin crack in his face and I even saw a few of his front teeth. I was relieved to see him smile, even if he had to force it.

"Can I fix you a glass of tea?"

"Yes, Shirley, that would be great."

"Paul?"

"Yeah. I'll drink one." Paul's voice held no emotion.

Pastor looked in Paul's eyes, "How are you, my friend?"

"I can't complain." Paul lied.

"Would it do any good anyway?"

"Probably not."

Pastor Garry laughed again and put a hand on Paul's shoulder. Paul didn't laugh. I put straws in the tea and carried a glass in each hand. My chirpy pretense felt like a pathetic effort to balance Paul's despair, but I couldn't stop myself from infusing polite, Pollyanna-ish pleasantries.

"Do y'all want to drink these out on the porch?" I smiled in happy contrast to my real desire to run away.

Pastor Garry turned to Paul for an answer.

"That would be okay." Paul answered, again without enthusiasm.

I carried teas outside to the little bistro table facing the shoreline. Paul and Pastor arranged themselves in two tall chairs and looked out on the lake. It seemed that sunlight had strewn diamonds across the surface of the river.

"What a magnificent view." Pastor Garry lifted the glass to his mouth.

Paul scanned the surface of the river in agreement, but didn't speak.

"If you boys would excuse me," I reached for the doorknob. "I have to go be the schoolmarm."

"Duty calls." Pastor called, excusing me. Paul said

nothing but scratched a scaly spot on his head that never completely healed.

Inside the house I checked on Charlotte, Emily and Joseph then put some ground beef in a pot. I'd transform it into spaghetti sauce before supper. Paul and Pastor Garry had been outside for about an hour while I'd been inside. I washed my hands and dried them quickly on a kitchen towel then turned the handle on the front door.

"You're back." Pastor Garry leaned forward to greet me. "Just in time."

"What am I in time for?"

Paul pulled a chair out for me.

"Pastor Garry gave me this necklace." Paul lifted a pendant off his chest and I read,

"St. Benedict. Who was he?"

"I was just telling Paul. You have heard me talk about visiting a monastery from time to time."

"Yeah." I replied, "...the Monkery?"

Pastor laughed his big laugh.

"That's right. Well, I actually *belong* to the Benedictine order."

"...How? I mean, we're Lutherans. Is it a Lutheran monastery or something?"

"No, it's just a monastery that welcomes others who are not necessarily Catholic. The largest numbers of Benedictines are Catholic, but there are also some within the Anglican community and occasionally within other Christian denominations as well, for example, within the Lutheran Church."

"Women, too?"

"Women, too. All Benedictine monks and nuns who have not been ordained are members of the laity among the Christian faithful. Only those Benedictine monks who have been ordained as deacons or priests are also members of the Catholic Church clergy."

"That is very cool, Pastor Garry. You're a bona fide Lutheran monk."

"I am."

"So what did St. Benedict do to get canonized by the church?"

While Paul examined the pendant between his thumb and forefinger, Pastor continued.

"He was protected by God. I know two stories about his protection. In the first, Benedict went away by himself to live as a holy hermit. He was discovered by a group of monks who prevailed upon him to become their spiritual leader. His regime soon became too much for the lukewarm monks so they plotted to poison him. Gregory recounts the tale of Benedict's rescue; when he made the Sign of the Cross over the pitcher of poisoned wine, it broke into many pieces. Thereafter he left the undisciplined monks."

"What's the other miracle?" I scooted forward in my seat..

"There were more than these, but these are two that exemplify God's protection of him."

"Oh. Okay. Please continue."

"In this story, Florentinus, a priest of a nearby church, became consumed with burning jealousy over Benedict's popularity. Blinded by this envy, he sends a poisoned loaf of bread to Benedict. However, Benedict knows it is poisoned. He asks his pet crow, or raven, who got bread every day from Benedict, to take the bread away and put it where no one could find it. The raven did so, after some protest, and returned three hours later for his usual treat.

"Wow." I said and wondered silently what this would mean to Paul. He was always the one to say he was "protection of" other people. Surely, it would comfort him to remember that God Almighty was protection of Paul.

We prayed together and after Pastor Garry left, I had this sudden desire to throw Paul a party. It was a crazy, impractical idea. We were broke. We had a ton of debt. Paul was constantly worried about the bills, but this burden to give him a party only intensified.

Finally, I prayed about it,

"Lord, if this is YOU wanting to give Paul a party then make a way for me."

I went to the pantry for two big cans of tomatoes. My mind wandered (or so I thought it did),

"I could buy the party fare in increments with each visit to the grocery store. I could stash a little at a time."

I opened the tomatoes and poured them into a pot over the nearly thawed ground beef. As was my habit, I had pre-cooked the meat in bulk then frozen it in zip lock bags. This made quick preparation for meals like spaghetti, tacos hamburger stroganoff and chili. I went to the freezer and got out a package of chopped onions and bell peppers.

"…Chili." I said quietly to myself, stirring the frozen vegetables into the potential sauce. We had a freezer in the laundry room. Storing big bricks of ground beef and pinto beans in the freezer would be a covert way to cook for a crowd ahead of time. Even with Paul on medical leave, I didn't think he'd notice. Ice cream was the only real reason I could think of that he ever opened the freezer.

"Are You doing this, Lord? If You aren't, please make me stop thinking about it."

He didn't stop me. I poured a can of mushrooms into the sauce and followed it with a splash of red wine. Stirring the orange-red concoction, I breathed the spicy steam into my nostrils. I got a big pot out of the cabinet and put hot water in it for pasta. When I set it on the stove, a lone bubble rose from the sauce letting me know it was almost hot enough to boil. I turned it down to medium-low, wondering if Barbara and Mike had room in their garage for a growing stockpile of drinks.

> *...when their sorrow was turned to joy and their mourning into a day of celebration.*
> *Esther 9-22*

Chapter Fifty-Eight

God really was bearing down on me with this party idea. Paul's actual birthday, August 8, rolled around. To throw him off, we did a little family celebration with cake, ice cream and gifts. As long as no one *told* Paul about his surprise party planned two weeks later, it seemed I might pull this off. I delivered a load of drinks to Mike and Barbara's garage every return home from the grocery store. Our freezer was nearly full with frozen bricks of ground beef and beans.

Now that Paul's medical leave kept him home, I didn't have enough privacy to send invitations. Surreptitiously, I called Gary Smallen, Pastor Garry, Paul's brother, Danny, his law friend, Melvin and the people who worked with Paul at the Pharmacy.

To the question, "What should we bring?" I answered,

"Frito's, sour cream or cheddar cheese."

Because of the secret nature of the party, I hadn't asked for R.S.V.P.'s. As a consequence, had no idea how many people to expect. I figured I could add meat or beans to my giant crock-pot as people showed up.

Friday before the party, Paul had an appointment with Doctor Trip. Toward the end of his appointment, he asked about getting his driving privileges back.

"There's a C.E. (Continuing Education) seminar at the fairgrounds that I'm signed up for. I'll need your approval to drive there." Paul said this with some irritation.

"Sure." Replied, Dr. Trip without hesitating. "Go to your C.E."

Dr. Trip's words returned a happy sparkle to Paul's face. I couldn't help but smile. The timing on this was so perfect. The C.E. seminar was scheduled for tomorrow, the same day as the party. There would be time to decorate after he left.

I'd kept my plan from the younger children so far, but the older children knew. Jon and Austin wouldn't be coming from Pensacola, but Sarah was expected to be home in time for supper. Elisabeth had already helped me in some of the preliminary preparations. We would wait until Saturday morning to tell the little ones, right after their daddy was on his way to Columbia for the seminar.

We returned home and Sarah had already arrived. She had come about thirty minutes after Elisabeth returned from school. I prepared some linguini with Greek seasoning, grilled salmon and steamed asparagus for supper. We dined inside, listening to Sarah catch us up on her current news. Catching up was necessary now that she wasn't home every other weekend as when she was younger.

At bedtime I crawled in bed with the crossword puzzle as Paul undressed.

"I'll be glad to drive to that C.E." He said.

I stared with intensity at the crossword puzzle and tried to act nonchalant.

"Yeah, do you remember how to drive, Counselor?"

Paul gave me a little grin. Man, it was good to see that grin.

"My mama born me to drive."

I smiled, imagining myself decorating and cooking as soon as he was gone. Paul walked to his side of the bed and I braced myself for him to sit. A permanent affliction from the skiing accident in his twenties was, when he sat, his knees gave out right before his bottom hit the seat. The bed rocked for a second as Paul climbed under the covers and picked up a section of the newspaper.

"It's supposed to rain tomorrow."

"Really?" I asked, my heart sinking.

"...Eighty percent chance. That's pretty high. You seem disappointed, do you have plans tomorrow?"

"What? Oh. Not many." I lied. "I'm just thinking about you having to drive to the fairgrounds for that C.E."

"Baby, I'm a big boy. I can drive in the rain."

"I know." I quickly changed the subject. "Is this a Law C.E. or a Pharmacy C.E.?"

"...Pharmacy." Paul turned the newspaper page over and folded it into a manageable size.

"Anything interesting?"

"Maybe." He picked up a brochure from his side table and read aloud,

Cancer Prevention: Separating Fact From Folklore. Interesting or not, I'll still get six credit hours for it."

"Will that satisfy what you need for this year?"

"Yeah. It should."

I handed him the crossword puzzle and pen. He settled in and immediately filled in some blocks. I watched as his eyes fluttered and his hand dropped slowly. Jerking, when his hand fell, he woke, turning quickly to see if I had caught him falling asleep.

"I was just resting." He slurred and I giggled.

He put the puzzle down and turned off his light. He couldn't see me grinning about tomorrow in the darkness.

"'night, Shirl."

"Good night, sweet Principal."

As usual, Paul was asleep before his eyes had time to fully close. I lay there beside him in the night, listening to him breathe, thinking about the doe I had hit a few weeks back in the Windstar.

I had just come off the interstate onto the long country road that led to the longer country road that led to our country street. I could see her face in my headlights, just ahead to the right. She was in my path before my foot reached the brake. If she was trying to commit suicide, her timing couldn't have been more impeccable. She caught the left headlight and ran, falling to the other side of the road. My fingers trembled as I called Paul on my cell phone. I felt so alone out there. His voice would be a comfort.

"Hey, Paul? I just hit a deer. I'm okay I just wanted to call you."

"Did you kill it?"

"I don't know. Hold on."

I backed the car up to where the deer lay and heard a raucous rustling in the grass. The night was too black to see, but it sounded like she was running into the woods. I remember hearing a hunter tell me once that deer run from pain. That's why hunters take dogs along to find the animals after they are shot.

"Paul?"

"Hm-m?"

"I ... she ... ran away, I think. Do you think maybe she's okay?"

"Maybe. Come home, Sweetie, there's nothing you can do."

He had such a lovely habit of saying just the right thing to me when I was undone.

These days I hardly knew what to expect from him. After receiving radiation and steroids, he would sometimes get frustrated or angry toward people who clearly had no malice toward him.

Paul made a small gasp that halted my musing abruptly. He rolled toward me like a ninja, closed his fist and held it mere inches from my face.

"NO. PAUL! IT'S JUST ME. I'M YOUR WIFE. IT'S SHIRLEY. PAUL, PLEASE, DON'T!"

He froze over me, his fist still held aloft, willing himself to think.

His fingers splayed open in conscious defiance of his instinct to attack, then he lay back, breathing heavily,

"I thought it was you."

"WHAT was me?"

"The pain. I guess I was dreaming, but it was so real."

He laid a palm against his left rib.

"Right here, it hurt so badly, like I was being stabbed. I thought somebody was doing it to me. I just wanted it to stop. I've never dreamt pain like that. *I'm sorry.*"

I was shaken, but so was he. I was so glad I hadn't gone to sleep yet. Thank God, he had come back to himself.

"You thought I was stabbing you? I wouldn't ever hurt you, Paul."

"I feel terrible. I'm so sorry. I wouldn't hurt you, either, but it was so real."

"You're okay now?"

"Yeah, yes, I am." He rubbed his side.

"Is the pain still there?"

"No." He rolled over and held me, burying his head

into my neck. "I'm so sorry."

"It wasn't you, Honey."

"I could have hurt you."

"It's okay, Darlin', you didn't hurt me."

We fell asleep like that, holding on to each other.

Weeping may endure for a night, but joy comes in the morning.
Psalm 30:5b

Chapter Fifty-Nine

I pretended to be asleep when Paul got up the next morning. The Seminar was on the outskirts of Columbia and he had to arrive pretty early. As soon as I heard the front door close my eyelids snapped open. I stayed still until the Bronco's engine roared and I heard tires roll over the gravel driveway. Jumping out of bed, I ran to the kitchen and started throwing huge cans of tomatoes, beans and frozen bricks of cooked meat into my giant turkey roaster. Morning coffee would have to wait. Beyond the French doors facing lakeside, the sun was casting glittery confetti over the water's surface. Joseph appeared brightly, already dressed to go outside.

"Hey, Mommy."

"Get over here and hug me, little Mister."

He bounded up to tackle me with arms wide open. I intercepted him before his exuberance knocked me down. We shared a mighty squeezing then I looked into his brilliant eyes.

"Hey, Bubby. I've got a surprise to tell you about. We are going to have a party."

"Weally?" His whole head smiled.

Emily stumbled in holding a tolerant Kit.

"We're having a party." Joseph told her excitedly.

"Now?" Emily asked, sharing Kit's less than amused expression.

"I don't really know." I told them honestly. "I don't know who all might come or what time they will arrive, I just know we are going to celebrate your daddy's birthday."

"It's not his birthday." Emily spoke in a monotone. "Plus, he's not even here."

"It's a surprise, Em, that's part of the fun. When he gets home from his meeting this afternoon, his friends will be here."

"Oh." Emily released her cat prisoner who slunk masterfully under my bed, simultaneously avoiding Joseph who continued to bounce happily throughout the house, singing,

"We're gonna have a par-tee, we're gonna have a par-tee."

It wasn't long before the others were up and everyone began bustling about. I started coffee and hurried outside with tape, rolls of streamers and a sign that said, "Happy Birthday, Paul." In minutes Mrs. Ida and her daughter-in-law, Melissa walked over to make a welcome offer to help. I unloaded the decorations and ran back upstairs to start another giant pot of chili on the stove. If no one showed up for this party, we were going to have chili for years to come.

Elisabeth drove her car to the marina for ice and Sarah made a short run in the van to Mike and Barbara's house. They helped her load up the colorful wall of drinks I'd erected in their garage. Mr. Jerry walked over hauling the most gigantic cooler I had ever seen.

"We got this up Sam's Wholesale. Hit didn't cost but about $75.00. Y'all kin use it if y' want."

Mr. Jerry set the massive cooler in the shade under the house. Sarah and Elisabeth employed Joseph to help them ice the drinks. He was thrilled to have an important job.

By noon a few people had arrived, but by 4:00pm, our lawn was littered thickly with Paul's friends, family and co-workers past and present. The Bronco's front end came into view as Paul drove to the house.

"Here he is."

The first group in Paul's sight was a circle of old football friends. Coach Richardson, Phil, Gary, Charles, Frankie and Mark nursed cool beers in the gentle August heat. Pastor Garry leaned forward from the queue of lawn chairs where he sat with most of our Sunday School class. Dale and Sally waved with practiced nonchalance. They had come from Hartwell, GA., were staying for the rest of the weekend and would join us for worship at St. Tim's tomorrow.

Paul's head leaned uncertainly out his open window, his eyebrows knitted together in confusion. He pulled the

Bronco onto our grass then walked toward his people. He looked quite Ernest Hemingway-esque in the light, raw silk shirt and white linen pants I had bought him. He needed them now that the steroids had caused his weight to climb a size. He'd said he didn't want them at first, but finally had to admit they fit and he looked great in them. I met him halfway, put a Corona in his hand and hugged him simultaneously.

"Happy birthday, Sugar."

"My birthday? Wasn't that a couple of weeks ago?"

"Yes, but these guys were all tardy. Makes your birthday last longer."

"Good trick." He chuckled, passing hugs around.

"Hey, Bud." Paul man-hugged his baby brother, Danny who had driven down from Charlotte, NC.

His middle brother, Steve followed,

"Happy birthday, brother. You're getting old."

Paul and Steve embraced.

"That's my plan. I'm trying to get as old as I can."

I looked out across the lake, my cheek muscles hurting from the permanent smile on my face. Frank's son, Hunter bounced along the water in a Jet Ski under a cloudless sky the color of Paul's eyes. Rain didn't seem a likely threat.

The Anrrich's were our last guests to leave. Ann, Carlos, Dale, Sally, Paul and I sat on the lake side deck in tall chairs, laughing and enjoying each other.

"Oh, I wanted to mention to you, Paul, we're planning a little canoe trip down the Congaree River in a couple of weeks."

Paul perked up,

"I'd like to go."

"Y'all have a real good time with the snakes and crocodiles." I smiled.

"Aww, c'mon Shirley. We do it all the time." Ann chided. "It's fun."

It didn't sound fun to me. I'd go along with it because Paul wanted to do it, but I could not look forward to this venture.

It was dark when Paul and I waved goodbye to the Anrrich's, our arms draped around each other's waists.

"WATCH FOR DEER." Joseph called out, finally understanding why, now that he'd seen the Windstar's damage.

We walked to the house, still laughing about how secretly the party had gone off. We counted up the guests and were astonished to conclude there had been just under ninety visitors who dropped by today, thanks to word-of-mouth invitations only. There would have been more, but we learned later that rain had poured all around our lake house, missing us entirely. Rain in Camden, the town of Winnsboro, and Columbia kept some of our friends away. I believed with certainty that this party was by God's design. Surely, Paul couldn't despair now. Surely, he could rest in this lovely proof of being beloved by so many.

It was pretty late and we were pretty tired. Happy, but tired. Dale and Sally went off to sleep in Elisabeth's room and Elisabeth slept in Joseph's other bunk. Paul and I got ready for bed.

I love it when a job comes together. A golden glow seemed to permeate the room and fill up my heart until Paul said,

"Why did all those people come here anyway?"

I laughed, thinking he was kidding.

"Aren't you going to answer me?"

"Yeah, Hon, they came for you." I answered, my mouth suddenly turning dry. "Because you are a well-loved man."

"Humph." He said, walking to the closet in his shirt and underwear. "I'm sure that's not the only reason they came."

"Do you think they all had a hankering for chili?" I tried vainly to make a joke.

"Maybe." Paul sat on the bed and looked defeated.

I was stunned. In his wildest imagination, how could he make his party out to be a farce? He hung his head.

"…Honey?" I moved over beside him. "What's wrong?"

"I just feel like no one cares, like you don't love me."

"You're wrong. I love you like crazy."

"Then why don't you ever act like it?"

"Paul, do you know how illogical you sound right now? You just spent the day with people who go as far back as your childhood with you. Eighty-eight of your friends were here today celebrating the fact that you'd been born."

He wouldn't look up. I could tell he was crying. I hugged him. He didn't yield, but I still wouldn't let him go.

"I want to pray with you, Paul."

"Okay."

"Lord, God, Creator of the Universe, Creator of Paul, of me, of everything, I love You. Please draw close to us."

I could feel Paul's muscles relaxing."

"Forgive us, Lord, from our sins. Put your healing hand on Paul and remind him he is precious to you."

Miraculously, Paul seemed almost limp from the peace that came over him.

"Make him understand that he is precious to me, too. Let him feel Your presence, light and love. Heal him in the Name of Jesus. Amen."

I opened my eyes. Paul's eyes were still closed.

"Lord?" Paul's voice was husky. "Help me. Help me with the abandonment issues that hound me."

I could barely believe I was hearing Paul admit he had abandonment issues. He'd never even been able to entertain the possibility before, yet, he was admitting it to God. He continued,

"I believe You can help me, Lord. Amen."

Admitting to his Creator what he'd always considered to be weakness Paul was finally free to rest in Him. He relaxed. I could see it in his posture first, as though God had blown breath into him. When he lifted his head and I looked into the clear blue eyes of the man I loved, I knew God had shaken the devil off his back the instant Paul submitted to His Almighty power.

I smiled, "Honey. You ... you look different."

"I feel better. Thank you."

I giggled, feeling almost giddy, having witnessed this amazing phenomenon.

"We have to remember this, Paul. We have to pray anytime you are hurting like that."

Paul nodded humbly, undressed and lay down to

sleep with the gift of peace God had sent.

    "Thank You, God." I whispered in my heart. "Thank You for bringing my husband back to himself. You are wonderful. Thank You for this party today. Thank You for the guidance You sent me. It was a great idea, Lord. Thank you for the ones who came, please bless each one. Thank You for prayer, thank You for leading us into prayer tonight. Please help me to remember. Thank You for Paul's confession, please grant his request and heal this broken place in his heart. I love You, Lord. I love You."

    I must have fallen asleep during my prayer because the next thing I knew, morning had broken.

* * *

    From this time on, I did pray with Paul when dark clouds of despair began their descent. It was the only thing that soothed him, and it always soothed him. That was the amazing thing; that it always worked. How many times had I prayed for God to show me a way to comfort Paul? This was His beautiful answer. This manifestation of His comfort for Paul was one of the most enormous ways God drew close to us. He opened me up to be a vessel of His encouragement for Paul as his life ebbed. God's presence drawing in had nothing to do with anything I did right, though. He came close to us only because we needed Him. He came because of our need, that's all. His love was magnified in our need. I couldn't help wondering, though. What if we had understood the mighty power of God through the prayers of a husband and wife from the start? How much stronger would our marriage be if we had always prayed like this? Even though I sensed that the responsibility of raising our family would soon fall solely on my shoulders, I couldn't spend much time worrying about it. The daily responsibilities held as much worry as I could handle.

> *More than that we rejoice in our sufferings, knowing that suffering produces endurance, and endurance produces character, and character produces hope.*
> *Romans 5:3-4*

Chapter Sixty

Paul's medical leave continued but he was a lot happier now that his driving privileges were reinstated. His driving still made me nervous, although, I didn't begrudge his occasional trips to town. He had figured out that I wouldn't let the children ride with him anymore, and he didn't begrudge me that, either.

I was loading molasses into the bread maker Paul had bought me for Christmas when the phone rang.

"Hi, Shirl."

He sounded happy.

"Hey, Sweetie. Are you in jail? Do I need to come make bail for you?"

"No arrest yet. I'm at the hardware store."

"I can't believe you went to the hardware store without me. That's our best date place."

"I thought I'd call before I head home and make sure you didn't need anything from the store."

"You are so sweet. I do need some honey. I just used the last drop making you a loaf of bread."

"That's all?"

Yeah, but you don't really have to stop. It's not urgent or anything."

"Okay, Sweetie, I'll see you in a little bit.

"I love you."

"I love you, too."

These days, I never knew which Paul I was going to get from moment to moment, but it was so nice when the old Paul showed up. I hung up, determined to keep this joy in my heart as long as I could.

A roast simmered in the Crock-Pot. I took a can of LeSueur peas out of the pantry and a saucepan from the cabinet. When Paul walked in laden with bags from Lowe's and Food Lion supper was almost ready.

"Hey." I greeted him and turned back to the peas on the stove.

Instead of replying to my greeting, Paul sneaked up and hugged me from behind.

"Are you trying to kiss the cook?" I laughed.

"I love you."

I turned to him, still holding the serving spoon I'd been using to stir the peas.

"I love you, too, Darlin'.

Paul handed me a colorful bouquet of flowers he'd bought at the grocery store. I gushed,

"Oh, my goodness."

I couldn't believe he'd brought flowers. This wasn't a usual practice. We were both so practical, but he'd broken tradition. What was he thinking?

"I'm charmed, Paul. They are beautiful."

"I wanted you to know I appreciate you." He looked embarrassed, like a young man on his first date.

"I know I don't tell you that enough, but I realize all you do for our family, especially me."

"Paul, I don't do anything I don't want to do."

"I know I don't make it easy for you sometimes, and I haven't been much help to you lately."

"You do a lot." I objected. "I couldn't do what you do.

Paul held up his hand, he wasn't done yet.

"Shirley, I'm going to start helping you more. I also want to say I'm sorry for putting the burden of disciplining the children on you through our whole marriage. I'm going to try to change that, too. I promise, I'm also going to start demanding that they respect you more."

I was stunned. I didn't know he recognized this dynamic I had come to accept over the years. My eyes leaked and I wrapped my arms around him. We stood there in the kitchen rocking in our embrace.

"Thank you, Paul. I love you so much."

I believed him, but my heart broke because I didn't think he would have much time to carry out this new plan.

The weekend arrived and along with it came the swamp trip I so dreaded. These days, I determined myself to go along with Paul's wishes as much as possible. An undertone of foreboding that these could be his last chances hummed constantly in my ear. I exercised reaction formation and willed myself to pretend it would be a blast to creep along the water dodging its life-threatening denizens.

We woke early. Paul dressed and went outside to tie down his white kayak and the red canoe he had bought from the River Runner. I wasn't convinced that this water venture was child-friendly, but my opinion was out-numbered by all my fellow swamp people. I dressed the children and myself in the most snake-proof attire I could come up with and it wasn't long before we were on Interstate 77.

Carlos and Ann were already at the swamp when we arrived and so was another woman who was already floating around gaily in her kayak. We tumbled out of the Bronco, and squished around on the damp red clay that made up this launching area. Ann called out introductions and we waved at the kayak-er who smiled largely while making figure eights, I assumed, to beat away the predators underneath her.

As far as launches go, this one looked pretty rustic. I was pretty sure I was going to fall off the "launch," a slimy, mossy, red clay cliff that hung ominously over our canoe. Giggling from utter fear, I somehow managed to wobble in and steady myself in my seat on the far end facing other end. Paul got in last with Joseph and Charlotte between us in the middle.

"Turn the other way." Everyone said at once, and I realized in horror that they were addressing me. If I turned around in my seat, it would mean I'd be leading us out.

"Then I ought to change seats with Paul. I'm not particularly strong." I explained shrilly.

My objections were met with unwelcome *attagirls* from the entire group. I don't know why they were so confident in me. I certainly didn't mean to emanate reliance.

Bound like burritos in our life vests, I took up my oars. My only comfort being out on the water was that the sooner we got started, the sooner we'd get to the end of our journey. Ann quietly pointed out a snake hanging off a tree branch pretending to be a string of the Spanish moss surrounding it. We rowed to the other side to avoid it but I suspected there were snakes on that side as well.

With Paul rowing along and me at the other end of the canoe, the current was manageable. In fact, it really was beautiful, as the sunlight filtered pin-light lasers through the leaves and Spanish moss. If not for the fear of my abbreviated family slipping under the murky death water, it might have felt peaceful. I was also beginning to get distracted by what seemed to be a change in the current. Rowing was becoming a bit of a task. The children between us were completely silent, struck mute by sheer terror and mortification. Indeed, I wasn't the only Pollyanna here.

The canoe took a sharp turn to the left and I began to row furiously.

"Hey, Paul." I called to him from behind me. "Which side should I be rowing on? We're about to crash into the bank."

"I don't know."

Alarmed, by his answer, I contorted my burrito-body so I could see him, noting with great panic that the reason for what seemed like an increased current was because I was the only rower.

"You'll be fine." He added tiredly, adjusting his Panama Jack hat to block the sunlight on his face as he lay napping.

"I ... can't." I said, paddling hard as I could on the right side. I imagined a family reunion of rattlesnakes dripping off the branches ahead and bearing large appetites for the bucket of Kentucky Fried Graham's being unwittingly catered right to them. Our discarded bones would be duly consumed by whatever crocodiles meandered nearby. No one would ever know we'd been there at all.

I thought about dropping the oar, covering my face and letting the canoe have its way with us, but my image of the snake party caused a little used section of my brain to spark fireworks. Cerebral cells and neurons screamed loudly from that dark and dusty place inside my head to say, "It's only a few inches deep!"

The message registered just short of our sliding under a thick canopy of Spanish moss that undoubtedly camouflaged spiders the size of Paul's hand. I sort of screamed and yanked the oar out of the water on the right and rammed it into the soft sand on the left. Using every corpuscle in my body, I pushed the canoe away from the bank to the comparable safety of the middle stream.

"Oh cool." Carlos cheered guiltily. "I wasn't sure you were going to make it there. Heh, heh."

Before I had a chance to tell him how funny he was (not), Carlos suddenly lost his balance and turned over in his little vessel. He splashed around frantically in the shallow water, scrambling frightfully back in his kayak. His breath came out in a series of short shrieks.

"ANN." I called.

"He's okay." Came her aloof reply, although clearly twinged with an undertone of worry. "Cah-los is just real scared of snakes."

"He's in very good company." I assured her, watching as Carlos righted himself and sighed deeply.

It seemed like a pretty good opportunity to bring up the idea of going home. I was willing to be the biggest wiener, so I said,

"How long did y'all want to canoe out here?"

Carlos answered first, "I've had about enough."

Ann's musical voice floated across the water, "I was just thinking it might be good to dock, too."

"Mommy," came Charlotte's wise yet nasal reply, "I really want to go.'

"Me, too." Emily and Joseph whined in unison.

Paul yawned and stretched from the back of the canoe. "Are we stopping?"

One by one, we pulled our vessels to the eroded bank that looked like a small cliff. It was the sweetest thing I had seen for hours. Disembarking, we smashed around on the edge of the water and climbed the slippery embankment. Wet clay stuck to our arms, legs and clothes like fat, pink slugs.

Paul didn't look good. He'd been completely out of character on this icky ride. He always took the lead and protected us, but today he had checked out, leaving me to handle it all. Carlos talked to him as though Paul were himself, but the truth was, he was listening to Paul as a nurse, initiating conversation for the purpose of evaluating his answers. Paul was exhausted out of the boat. All of us were. We worked together to pull the canoes and kayaks out of the water and over the sticky soil. It was a short walk to our cars, but it was blazing hot now and the job of hoisting the boats atop the cars awaited us. Paul sat down on a rock.

"Hey, Sweetie." I said quietly rubbing Paul's back. "Tell me if I should worry about you."

Paul sighed. "I don't think so. I just need to sit here a minute."

"I'm going to get the canoes loaded, all right?" I said optimistically.

Paul closed his eyes and nodded.

Ann and Carlos were discussing the two S.U.V.'s that had parked behind us, leaving little room for our cars to exit. Exiting was something I desperately wanted to do, but I was merely one little woman. I could tackle but one mountain at a time. Yes, I had backed up vehicles before, but doing it with a trailer hooked on was something I knew wasn't my forte'. Like Scarlett O'Hara, I would worry about that tomorrow.

The girls and I faced off with the kayak first. Charlotte and Emily took one end of it and we rolled it into the trailer behind the Bronco. Not too shabby. When I told them to get Joseph's attention so we could put the canoe in, the girls looked at me as though I had suggested we amputate each other's arms and legs together out here in the woods. I gave them an intense look and they slunk off to get Joseph who was sitting on the muddy ground packing clay into the hole of a Coke can with his little red-stained fingers.

The four of us hefted the canoe as high as our puny arms allowed, but it wasn't enough to lift it into the trailer. Paul limped toward us. Sweaty and still wearing his hat, Paul excused us from the job at hand. With single-handed Herculean strength, he hoisted the canoe into the trailer. I glanced at Ann and Carlos who were holding their breath.

Having spent himself hefting the canoe and fastening it down, Paul stumbled to the back of the Bronco and folded his arms against the back window. Leaning his head against his forearms, Paul rested, heaving heavy breaths. I'd never seen him this way and it scared me more than the ride we just took on the Congaree.

Minutes later, he marched to the driver's seat, climbed in and turned the vehicle and trailer around in hardly a wink. Ann and Carlos, suddenly aware that their mouths hung open, closed them deliberately. Objecting to my offer to drive, he navigated us back home on automatic pilot.

Joy would have filled me at the sight of our house if I hadn't been so wiped out. Our simple desire was to lie down and sleep, but there was the matter of clay sticking all over us. I remember standing in the shower waiting for the silt and clay to rinse off my legs and down the drain, but it was not to be. This was industrial strength clay that didn't move without a brisk measure of elbow grease. I wanted to cry when realized removing it would cost me some energy.

Out of the shower now, my hair was wet, but I was clean and dry. Maybe we'd never have to do this again. The children were sprawled out on the couch in the living room when Paul and I slipped blissfully under our sheets. The hum of our ceiling fan lulled us to slumber.

The next thing I knew, Joseph was knocking at the door.

"No." I remember thinking as my sleep came to an end, "I'm not ready to stop being asleep."

Joseph's little voice sounded alarmed.

"Mommy, Daddy? Somebody's coming. They came in a boat and tied it to the dock. They're walking up our steps, now."

I willed my body to get up and throw clothes on. Sure enough, the doorbell rang and I followed Paul to the door. Our friends, Tim and Gale Bostick had boated over from our old neighborhood. After Paul and I had married, we never missed a Fourth of July with Tim and Gale and their daughter, Morgan. Looking back, they had been a part of so much of our family history: when the twins and Joseph were born, when Betty died, when our teens were in Youth Group. We hadn't seen them since moving to Winnsboro.

We sat at the dining room table catching up on current events and wondering how so much time had passed since we visited. Tim and Gale had been my friends first, all three of us had gone to Spring Valley High School together, but Paul had claimed them in earnest. Dusk began to draw nigh and too soon our dear friends had to float back home.

It was an honor and practically a miracle that they had found our lake house. In a few weeks I would learn they had also come by God's design.

The Lord is near to the broken-hearted and saves those who are crushed in spirit.
Psalm 34:18

Chapter Sixty-One

The first time I saw Psalm 34:18, I was writing at the computer in the office/schoolroom and using my Bible for reference. It just struck a chord so I wrote it down on a scrap of paper and stuck it between some pages. It seemed wise to hide it in my heart, so to speak. I needed to know God was close when my heart broke. The image this verse painted was a lovely illumination of His love.

I was in the office on the computer with my Bible, having just rediscovered the words *The Lord is near to the brokenhearted.* I lost myself for a moment meditating on this. The solitude was broken when Paul shuffled in with his guitar. He was still on medical leave and today he was meandering around in his bathrobe. He loved music. He had found this guitar in a pawn shop for a decent price a few years ago and tried to teach himself to play. So far it hadn't worked. Paul's gifts were so many, so extravagant, yet playing an instrument was not one of them, hard as he tried.

I went back to my writing as Paul sat down across the room and plucked a string.

He did love music. He loved hearing me sing. I could envision him standing at the back of the church with a couple of other ushers, smiling as I sang a solo. I had discovered too late one Sunday morning that I couldn't look at him and sing without getting emotional so I learned to find a focal point just above everyone's heads on the back wall. This eliminated the danger of catching a glimpse of him and losing my composure.

Paul looked at his music book and plucked the string again. I stopped writing and smiled at him across the room. He smiled back and plucked the same string.

Elisabeth played the violin so well. We were both so proud of her. She had started out in her middle school orchestra, continuing in the orchestra at Ridgeview High.

When we moved, she took private lessons. Elisabeth grew out of the loaner violin furnished by the school. We were so broke, but Paul didn't bat an eyelash when she told us her teacher advised we buy her a bigger one. He just located a new violin and wrote the check.

"I'll just work a few extra hours." I recall him saying.

He plucked the string three times in a row and I gave up on writing, certain my brain would explode if I heard the note one more time. I tilted my head and gave him another intolerant smile,

"Hey Counselor."

"Hey."

"I ... wonder if you might play a different note. Heh, heh."

"Am I bothering you?"

"Well, I'm just not good at concentrating when you are ... playing. I mean, I'll be done in just a few minutes."

"No, I'll find something else to do."

Oh, man, I really hadn't wanted to make him mad or hurt his feelings. He picked up his guitar book and dragged his house-slippered feet across the floor and out of the room.

"I'm sorry." I called after him, but he didn't answer.

I finished my writing and checked on my home school-ers. They didn't need a lot of my interaction during their videotaped lessons, but I still had to check their work, grade tests, encourage them and make sure they were really watching the lesson.

I went to the kitchen to make tuna salad sandwiches and tomato soup then called everyone to the table.

"Paul?"

He was lying on his back on the bed staring at the ceiling.

"Hmm?"

"I made you some lunch."

He rose silently and found his place at the table.

We bowed our heads and Paul asked the blessing in his usual way,

"Lord, make us truly thankful for these and all Your other blessings. In Jesus' Name, Amen"

Paul and I dialogued with the children without

acknowledging each other. It was a cooperative avoidance tool we employed. Its effect was meant to postpone a confrontation and hopefully keep the children from witnessing our disagreements. I knew Paul wasn't going to be pleasant and I wasn't going to do anything to provoke him, so for the rest of the day, we passed each other like strangers.

By the end of the day, I was exhausted. I was tired of the entire pretense it took to get along and take care of my duties, too. After supper, Paul went to the computer to do whatever he did on it for hours these days. I knew he was playing Solitaire a lot. I had to get out of here even if it was only for a few minutes

I went to the phone and dialed Barbara's number.
"…Hello?"
"Meet me in the road halfway. I'm bringing the wine."

A startled giggle trickled through the phone before she said,
"Okay. Now?"
"Right now."
"Well, let me get my shoes on."
"Okay, but hurry. The mosquitoes are hungry."

I left all the supper dishes in the sink and asked Elisabeth to keep an eye on things.

The long wooden steps creaked gently against my sandals as I descended into the starry night. I cared little about the threat of bugs flying around out there. The things that threatened my life were much bigger than insects. I felt like I was escaping, and liked the noise of Chardonnay sloshing around in the bottle as I walked. My eyes adjusted to the dark and I thought I could see Barbara's little head bouncing along toward me.

"Are you friend or foe?" I called into the blackness."
"I am your friend." Came her beautiful answer. How true.

We assumed cross-legged seats in the middle of the road and I handed her a red Solo cup. Barbara was giggling. I giggled with her and pulled the cork out of the wine bottle.
"I'm so glad you called." Barbara offered gaily.

"So happy you were free, do forgive the short notice."

"I sensed it was urgent." She replied graciously, playing along. Still, she knew her answer rang true.

I raised my cup, "A toast."

"To what?" She asked.

"To all the things in life that keep us on the map when nothing makes a lick of sense." I said soberly.

We clicked plastic cups. Barbara tucked away the giggles she had brought along, but knowing my need to laugh at trouble, she kept them handy, just in case.

"What happened?"

"…Nothing new." I answered, suddenly aware of pain from a sharp stone boring into my thigh. I picked it out of the dent it had made and felt instantly relieved.

"Paul felt abandoned when he was really little; he was too little to articulate his feelings in words. It's like he's feeling that abandonment now but subconsciously blaming me for it."

"That's deep."

"Yeah, but it's what I've figured out. When his mom died, he grieved for a couple of weeks then transferred all that loss onto me, *even though I was still right by his side.* Not that he would ever admit that, but I believe it. It makes such sense to me and I *need* to understand him."

"Have you talked to him about it?"

"Oh, yes, Barbara. Way back when it first appeared. We finally agreed to disagree on this subject. I don't bring it up anymore. He didn't like the idea that he might have any issues, abandonment or otherwise. He seems to think I am withholding something from him and that's why he can't be happy."

Barbara sighed. "Men sure think differently than we do."

"I know, but is this really a man issue, or something else? It does serve a purpose. As long as he's fixated on me as the source of his discontent, he doesn't have to confront his cancer. I don't know how to reach him. He's miserable. He's depressed. The steroids he has to take make him hungry and mad at every little thing. They keep him from sleeping. He wakes up, sees me sleeping and I guess it makes him mad that I don't sense his agony and wake up. He goes into the computer room and stays up all night. In the morning he won't talk to me. If I try to draw him out, it doesn't help. He thinks I *can* make him happy, but *choose* not to. It's not reasonable. I know he is dying, Barbara. God has given me an understanding that he's really dying this time. I'm not sure what I'm supposed to do but sometimes it's just too big for me. I get so frustrated. The truth is I get really mad at him, but I'm afraid if I say so, I'll bear the guilt forever when he's gone. We were trying to have a conversation earlier today and he said, "You act like this is all about *you*." I said, "I *know* it's not all about me, but *dammit, some of it is.*""

We were so alone in the road that dark evening even the mosquitoes kept their distance. I cried and laughed, vomiting up the words that told my bitter tales of weariness, frustration, loss, hurt, anger, loneliness and fear. The mean things I couldn't say to Paul, the ugly yet truthful things my children wouldn't have understood, the acid rage I felt, at everything, all poured out onto Barbara's dear, open lap.

I sincerely believe she felt the pain in my soul. How compassionately she listened. How non-judgmental were her ears that received every word until there was nothing left to say. Then armed with the sieve of friendship and love, Barbara sifted through my agony to uncover the jewels of truth in the story. Like a gold miner, she shook out all the things I shouldn't have said and all the things I was wrong about. My words, like dust, were caught up by the night wind and flung away to the depths of the sea. We sat together on the asphalt and cried. How unfortunate for Job that his friends didn't have hearts like Barbara's. She reached for my hand and began to pray.

"Lord, I prayed for a friend when we moved here and I was lonely. Thank you for the blessing of my sister in Christ. Look down on her tonight, Lord and supply her with all the grace she needs. Give her a measure of Your patience, Your love and Your wisdom as she cares for Paul and her children. I ask these things of You in the Name of Jesus."

Barbara started to pull her hand away but I held it fast.

"Father God" I invoked, "When Barbara prayed for a

friend You blessed us both. Thank You. I love You, Lord."

Visiting time was almost up. Our respective home duties were pulling at us. Exhausted yet relieved, I headed back to the house, my heart and the wine bottle both just a little lighter. A few steps along I remembered something,

"Hey, Barbara, are you going to your church tomorrow night?"

"Yes, as far as I know. Do you want to come with us?"

"More than anything, but you know my time doesn't belong to me right now."

"I know. Call me if it looks like you can break free."

I don't remember praying about going to Barbara's prayer meeting, yet I must have. There was a mostly constant prayer going on in my head. I noticed at some point the following day, a convenient space had been carved out for me to go. It all happened without any effort on my part which is how I recognized this was something God had worked out.

As I bade farewell to my family and rode with Mike and Barbara to El Bethel church, a sense of expectancy energized me. I had no doubt that God had something in the service for me to hear. We listened to a couple of gospel solos before the preacher stepped out with his message.

"The joy of the Lord is your strength." He announced, his own joy spilling over. "Nehemiah 8:9 tells us that we *should not grieve* because the *joy of the Lord* is our strength."

I thought, "Is this it, Lord? Is this what You want me to know? I don't understand that Scripture. Never have. What does it mean, and what does it mean for me now?"

The pastor continued, calling on the verse in Nehemiah again and again. I left feeling disappointment and confusion, sadness and weakness, not joy, not guidance, not strength. Yet I was sure God had sent me there on purpose. Nehemiah 8:9 really was God's love and guidance and I would recognize soon enough that it *was* meant for me.

Like an open book, you watched me grow from conception to birth; all the stages of my life were spread out before you, the days of my life all prepared before I'd even lived one day. Your thoughts – how rare, how beautiful! God, I'll never comprehend them! I couldn't even begin to count them – any more than I could count the sand of the sea. Oh, let me rise in the morning and live always with you!
Psalm 139:16-18

Chapter Sixty-Two

August first was going pretty well. Having caught him on one of his good days, Paul had agreed to have company tonight. We expected Dave and Nita for supper in a couple of hours, so I was making one of Paul's favorites, country fried steak with rice and field peas. I swept a raw cubed steak through a bowl of egg and milk mixture then dredged it with seasoned flour in another bowl.

Paul walked in holding the Corona I had opened for him earlier.

"Do you need any help?"

"I could use some advice."

I dredged another cube steak which added more flour to my black polo shirt. I always seemed to have on black when I was using flour.

"Advice?"

"This meal is varying colors of brown. Do you have any colorful suggestions besides the tomato I'm going to slice?"

"There might still be some squash out in the garden."

Paul had done battle with his garden this summer. He had bought a used tiller to turn the soil up but the tiller fought back. Unwilling to be bested by a tiller, I had seen him pulling at the crank for thirty minutes at a time until he was exhausted. Sometimes Mr. Jerry would walk over and talk to him, give the crank a pull.

"I already looked."

Our conversation was interrupted by the ringing

phone.

"Just a minute," Paul said, "she's right here."

I washed the flour off my hands and picked up the phone with a kitchen towel.

"It's Jon." Paul whispered.

"Hey, Jonboy."

Jon's voice was excited.

"Mom? He's coming."

"You're sure?"

"We're on the way to the hospital now. Darcie's been having contractions for a few hours and her doctor told her to come on in. I wish you could be here."

Paul's condition being as it was, attending our grandson's birth hadn't seemed to be an option, but as soon as he said the words, I realized we could.

"We're coming."

"What? You are?"

"I think we can. Tell me the name of the hospital and I'll call you if we can make this happen."

"Great. Jon was laughing.

I hung up the phone. Paul was giving me an expectant look.

"Why not?" I giggled. You're on leave, school's still out."

Paul looked at me like I was crazy. "What about dinner?"

"It'll freeze. I'll call Nita. They'll be glad to reschedule. We've got a baby coming, for Heaven's sake."

I dialed Nita's number and held the phone to my ear with my shoulder while stuffing the fried cube steaks into freezer bags.

We were on the road within an hour. Paul wasn't real happy about me driving but Dr. Trip had told him not to drive at his last visit. There had been concern after Paul's fall that he could have seizures.

My mind was racing. "Isn't Sarah staying at her mom's right now?"

"Yes."

"Let's call her. We go right through Atlanta to get to Pensacola. Maybe we can pick her up."

Paul took the cell phone out of his pocket and punched a few numbers. Before he and Sarah hung up, we had a plan. Her mom would drive Sarah to the exit nearest their house when we were getting close.

Jon called us for a travel update from time to time as he waited on his new son. There was a big celebration on the beach this weekend called the "Bushwhacker Festival."

"What's a bushwhacker?" I asked him on the phone.

"Some drink that originated on the beach here." Jon explained. "Every year there's a big to-do and people come from all over.

"Wow. Floridians don't need much of an excuse to celebrate, do they?"

Jon laughed, "Not really. I'm just concerned that you might not be able to find a motel room."

It was late when we got to Pensacola, but Darcie hadn't delivered yet. We stopped at a What-A-Burger drive through before landing at Baptist Hospital. We were the only ones occupying the waiting room, so Sarah climbed into her sleeping bag and went right to sleep. Paul stretched out on the floor, too. I'd brought sleeping bags for Charlotte, Emily and Joseph, but sleep didn't appear to be on their agendas.

In her birthing room, Darcie managed to look beautiful and tiny, despite her full-term pregnancy. Women should all be so lucky. Her mother, Patrice fluttered around Darcie, attending to her needs along with Darcie's sister, Megan. As contractions began to come faster, I joined my family in the waiting room, breathing prayers of safety for Darcie and the little boy we would get to meet soon.

The other side of a wall of windows in the waiting area revealed Jon hurrying down the hall toward us only a few minutes later. I jumped up to meet my smiling son with big tears streaming down his cheeks.

"He's here." Jon told us, his bottom lip quivering. "And he's beautiful."

Beautiful, he truly was. We took turns holding Ian, wrapped like a burrito in his receiving blanket.

By morning Darcie's dad Tiger, her grandparents, Jon's father (also Jon) and Jon's brother, Mark were at the hospital. I wasn't uncomfortable around my ex-husband but

Paul was. I had anticipated events like this that would connect our families but so far there had been only a few. Jon senior was gracious, even offering to let us stay at his house, but we declined.

Without the benefit of marriage, the duplex Jon and Darcie shared seemed a most unlikely place for us, but it was the most practical accommodation. We spent the next couple of days there so I could make some meals to stock their freezer. I made lasagnas, Greek chickens, chili and more, remembering as I cooked the kind people from Christus Victor and Saint Timothy's churches who had performed these same acts of kindness for us.

Paul wasn't sick, but he seemed wooden, rarely showing any emotion. I supposed there was something going on again in the communications area of his brain. Brain bleed, tumor growth, whatever this evil was, it was stealing my husband away from me.

When Ian and his parents arrived from the hospital, we headed back to Winnsboro. I was so thankful it had worked out for us to attend Ian's birth, but I felt an urgency to get my husband home.

"…Mommy?" Charlotte asked as we passed a green exit sign. "What is that word?"

I answered, "It says, "Pintlala.""

"No," argued Paul, "it's PINTALA."

"There's another sign coming up. It's a strange word, but it has two "L's" in it. Pintlala."

"No, it doesn't. Paul continued to argue. "It only has one "L." It's Pintala."

We approached the sign I knew was going to have two "L's" in it. Paul's reading skills were unfailing and I had to know if that was still true.

"What do you see, Paul?" I asked him.

"I see one "L." He said. "It's Pintala."

I drove past the sign and said nothing.

And He said to me, "My grace is sufficient for you, for My strength is made perfect in weakness." Therefore most gladly I will rather boast in my infirmities, that the power of Christ may rest upon me.
2 Corinthians 12:9

Chapter Sixty-Three

August turned into September and Paul was still on leave. School had begun. Paul slept a lot but I wasn't sleeping well at all, which made me tired and unmotivated during the day. I'm sure we were both dealing with depression. Whenever sleep would come, I embraced it, knowing I might be called to do extraordinary things any minute.

Supper was over and I yawned through our ritual bedtime devotion that would lead to individual prayers, ending with The Lord's Prayer in unison: . . . *Thine be the Kingdom, the Power and the Glory forever. Amen.*

I excused myself from the couch to load the dishwasher while Paul read a chapter of Harry Potter to the children. The open style in our house's main area gave me a fly-on-the-wall perspective. Paul's reading style had taken on a sing-song quality over the past few months and I hated myself for letting it grate on my nerves. The Harry Potter chapters are long and Joseph had already fallen asleep on Paul's leg by the time I poured dishwasher detergent in and pressed the *start* button. After brushing my teeth and changing into a nightgown, Paul and I ended up in bed at about the same time. It wasn't long before the hum of our ceiling fan lulled us to sleep.

I woke when I heard Paul stir. In our dark room, I could see the outline of his shadowy frame on the edge of his side of the bed.

"You okay?"

"I'll be all right." He lied.

I fell back to sleep loving the image of his beautiful, broad shoulders. Sometime later, I awoke to the sound of him throwing up in the toilet. I wanted to cry for him, for our children, for me. I emptied some discarded paper out of a plastic trash can and set it on the floor by Paul's side of the bed. In a few minutes he returned and sat down on the bed.

"I'm so sorry, Darlin'" I soothed him.

He was too sick to answer.

"There's a plastic waste basket in case you need it."

As Paul's nausea continued throughout the night, he refused my requests to take him to the hospital. I reached out and laid my hand on him, feeling guilty every time I drifted off to sleep, yet not being able to help myself. I felt sure I would need rest to fight whatever demons awaited us in the daylight. Even still, I imagined Jesus chiding me as He chided His disciples at Gethsemane, *And he cometh, and findeth them sleeping, and saith unto Peter, "Simon, sleepest thou? Couldest not thou watch one hour? Watch ye and pray, lest ye enter enter into temptation. The Spirit truly is ready, but the flesh is weak. Mark 14:37-38*

At the first glimmer of morning, I called Barbara. As soon as she arrived to stay with our sleeping children, Paul and I set off for Dr. Trip's office. I was sure Paul was dehydrated and figured he'd have to get intravenous fluids in the office like he had done after other nights of nausea. I told the receptionist as much upon our arrival but instead of hooking Paul up to an I.V. station, we were told to check into Lexington Hospital. This would be Paul's last trip to the hospital.

The first two days after Paul's admission were pretty routine. With the information I had garnered over these past two years, I imagined another brain bleed was the culprit of his odd conversation. For example, he had referred to the nurse on call as the *administrator*. As a fan of word games, I was getting used to deducing his new, uncommon vocabulary.

I had to call friends and family from the patient waiting area, which is what I was doing when Imogene, Dr. Trip's nurse practitioner found me. I ended my call and gave her my attention. She took my hands in hers.

"Shirley, do you know what's happening to Paul?"

"Is he having a brain bleed?"

"No. Well, yes, probably, but that's only part of it. I need to make sure you understand that he's not coming back this time. I need to prepare you for what's ahead so you can prepare him."

"Okay." I answered as my insides froze.

"There are more tumors in his brain."

"But they respond to the radiation..."

Imogene shook her head slowly.

"Not this time, Shirley. Has Paul been able to talk about dying?"

"Only in a general way." I told her, "We expected him to die at first, but the Lord kept healing him over and over. We really weren't sure what God was doing."

"Do you think Paul knows he is dying?"

"No. I don't think so."

"Then, you have to tell him." She said in earnest. "He's going to lose his ability to talk within the next hours. His organs will to shut down. He will go blind. He deserves to know what's going on."

"I nodded"

Imogene said, "Sweetie, here is what is happening to Paul medically."

She explained how Paul's brain was swelling and this time the process couldn't be reversed. She told me things that would transpire in a certain order because of what the cancer was doing in his brain right then.

"He may not know you at some point. If you can tell him this is the end of his life you'll both have a chance to say goodbye. Help him say goodbye to his children...while he still can."

In her eyes I saw nothing but compassion.

"Then pray for me," I said, standing, "I have to do it now."

She nodded and hugged me. It was the last time I would ever see her.

I first called Barbara and told her to bring the children to the hospital. I then called Sarah, then Fort Jackson as Elisabeth had joined the Army and I had to find out how to get the Red Cross to fly her in from her duty station in Korea.

After that I called Jon in Pensacola, Paul's father in Washington and Danny in North Carolina. Finally I called on God to stay by my side so I could do this hard thing.

Paul was awake when I walked into the room. He smiled, when I sat on the bed facing him. Seeing a tear run down my cheek, Paul reached out and wiped it off, then moved a strand of hair out of my eyes. A beautiful serenity radiated from his eyes and he tilted his head to show me he was sorry I was crying.

"Baby," I began, "Imogene just told me you are going to die this time."

I leaned into his chest and he held me.

I'm going to miss you so much."

My tears bathed his chest and I cried openly. Pulling away, I looked into his face, determined to do this hard thing.

"I know Jesus will do a better job of caring for you, but I'm selfish. I don't want to stop taking care of you. I love you so much."

"I love you, too, Darlin'. You will be fine."

Did he understand me? I couldn't really tell. He wiped another tear off my face and shook his head as though he didn't want me to be sad. I lay my head back on his chest as he stroked my hair. I deeply cherish this memory of his last loving gesture, our final, sweet, interaction of love. I'll always owe Imogene a debt of gratitude for her bold insistence that day.

A soft knock at the door preceded the tentative queue of our tow-headed children. Barbara and Mike ushered Charlotte, Emily and Joseph into Paul's room. Some of the ice cream they had eaten before arriving left little Rorschach images on their shirts. I led them to the right side of their Dad's bed, not really knowing how to do this terrible job. Our time was limited and Paul had already lost a lot of his verbal communication skills, so I began.

"Your daddy, they have told me he will be leaving us. His life is... he is... dying."

Oh, this was hard. They were so little, their hair so silky, their skin so pure and soft. Why was God demanding so much from their beautiful young hearts? So many bad daddies were allowed to live and yet, this loving daddy was not allowed to help his babies grow up.

I remembered the times, watching these little people play, Paul had said, "If I died right now, they wouldn't remember me."

They were old enough to remember some now. As little as he was, even Joseph was old enough to retain a few memories of the past two or three years. I admitted God had been gracious and He promises that His grace is sufficient. I knew it was true. God is sovereign.

Paul reached out to them, they lay their heads on him.

One by one they took turns hugging him.

"I love you, Daddy." Charlotte told him, choking through her tears.

"I love you, Charlotte."

She let go and stepped back, reluctant to leave him, but feeling the same awkwardness as I, not knowing what to do.

"I love you." Joseph's muffled voice said into the crook of his arm. "I love you, Daddy."

"I love you, Joseph."

Emily's tears ran freely. "I love you, Daddy."

"Emily, I love you, too."

The agony we felt was strangely balanced only by the sweetness of love. I'd never felt so much pain and so much love at once. I picture this moment resting securely in the hollow of God's hand.

May nations serve you and peoples bow down to you. Be lord over your brothers, and may the sons of your mother bow down to you. May those who curse you be cursed and those who bless you be blessed.
Genesis 27:29

Chapter Sixty-Four

The Red Cross is efficient. Elisabeth was home from Korea within twenty-four hours. She came directly to the hospital and rested a little after visiting with her daddy and me. Coming sleeplessly into this grave situation from a World away, she struggled to find a place for herself amid the weirdness. Her heart was a paradox; rewound suddenly to a place she knew well, to people she loved, yet unable to respond to the joy of reunion because of fatigue and impending loss. After she slept a little on my cot, I found someone to take her home to her own bed.

Jon, arriving with Ian's mom, Darcie brought baby Ian to Paul's bed. Paul put aside dying for an instant and instinctively reached for our grandson.

"No, Dad," Jon chuckled, "I'll hold him."

Jon related to his step-dad's natural inclination to stop and care for the babies. He had learned so much about being a man and being a father from Paul. Comfortable, knowing Jon could manage on his own, Paul settled back in the bed to die. It was as though Paul was passing Jon a torch with a fatherly message: "I'm leaving you, son, but I go peacefully, knowing a father's heart beats soundly in your chest. Take from your memories the lessons I tried to teach and know that I am so very proud of you."

Jon and his new little family said goodbye and set out for the lake house. I stopped him before he left. He knew what I was thinking without having to speak the words. "Mom, I'm sorry. Austin didn't come. Even Dad encouraged him to come with me, but he just said he couldn't."

I tried not to show the disappointment I felt.

"Take your family to the lake and try to check on the others, especially the little ones. Ian will be a ray of sunshine for them. I love you, sweetie. Please drive carefully."

Jon kissed me on the head.

"I'll watch for deer, Mom. I love you, too."

Jon gently approached his step-daddy and hugged him one last time. "I love you, Dad."

"I love you, too," Paul answered as Jon retreated, tears moistening his cheeks.

Jon shepherded his little family down the hall, clothed in his dad's implied blessing.

Friends and family continued to drop by Paul's room to say goodbye to him. "Look who's here, Paul," I would say as another loved one entered; then I would greet the person by name just in case Paul didn't know or couldn't see. After all, Imogene had warned me that he would probably be going blind.

Paul rarely said much to his visitors, which was probably a blessing. His comments were often inappropriate or not responsive, such as when Sarah's uncle Shawn stopped in. Paul had watched Shawn grow up and was very fond of him. They shared some similarities as adults, too, including being fathers of twin girls.

"Hi, buddy," Shawn said to his old friend.

"Hey," Paul answered; then, "I'm going to kick your butt."

Shawn gave a nervous laugh before answering. "I don't doubt you can, Paul, but let's wait until after you've recovered a little."

Again, Paul repeated his plan. "I'm going to kick your butt."

Shawn approached Paul and took his hand. "I love you, Buddy. I wanted to come by and tell you I love you."

Paul nodded then they embraced. Shawn exited, wiping his eye against his shoulder. Paul closed his eyes and slipped off to sleep or to some foreign place.

I was relieved when Sarah softly pushed the door open a little later. One of my fears this week was that the ones Paul loved best might miss this last chance to see him before he died, but I could see that God was working out these last such gifts for Paul. Danny had made it in from North Carolina earlier and even though it was heartbreaking to watch Paul's baby brother realize Paul was truly going to leave us, I was thankful he got a chance to say, "Goodbye."

"Hey, Daddy," Sarah whispered shakily as she put her slender fingers on his hand. Paul's eyes remained closed. I wondered if they would open again.

I leaned into Sarah, and she hugged me.

"I'm so glad you're here, sweetie."

"I came straight here. I'm prepared to stay, too."

"Good. Thank you. Would you like some time by yourself with your daddy? There's a lady I need to talk to here, a patient advocate, I think. I'm told she can help me get your daddy moved home."

"Go," Sarah insisted. "Do what you have to do, I'll be fine here."

"I know, honey. I'll only be down the hall in the waiting room if you need anything. My cell phone gets pretty good reception in that room, so call me for anything, okay?"

I kissed Paul's forehead. Sarah took his hand and smiled sweetly at her sleeping daddy. "I will, Shirl."

The waiting room was empty. My initial call was transferred to several different people, but my phone calls soon proved productive. A patient advocate was assigned to us and would visit us sometime that afternoon. It appeared that Paul was going home. I let out a sigh that I didn't realize would be so loud.

Remembering my friend, Jane (our movie producer from Charlotte and Emily's birth) I punched her phone number into my phone. The last time I'd seen her, Paul had just had his last surgery. I recalled that she had shown up to hug him on her lunch hour. Paul and I had been pleasantly surprised when she walked in and hugged him soundly.

"Jane," Paul had said, "You're ever faithful."

She had cried when he said that. Dear little Jane. She leaked so easily.

My cell phone clicked, and I heard Jane say, "Hello?"

"Jane? We're at the hospital again. I don't know how long we will be here, but it looks like Paul might get to go home. . . No, that's not good news . . . he's going home to die. They tell me he won't be pulling through this time."

About that time, Sarah burst frantically into the

waiting room. Her voice, pitched high, was accentuated with splayed fingers that stabbed at air.

"Shirley. You have to come quick."

I sucked my breath in: "I have to go, Jane, I'll call you later."

I jumped from my seat and threw the phone in my purse in one motion.

"What?" I asked Sarah, already beginning to hyperventilate.

"It's Dad. He wants you."

"He said that?" I asked, incredulous.

He hadn't really talked, coherently or otherwise, for several hours. I thought he had passed the stage of communication now. He had seized three times already, once during Danny's visit, but Sarah said he was talking, which definitely ruled out a seizure. She tried to explain through her tears. "He woke up. He just woke up and he wants YOU."

"He said that?"

"Yes," Sarah and I were practically running down the corridor. "He told me to go get you."

We reached Paul's door, and I pushed it open. Sarah stayed out in the hall. To my unbelieving eyes, Paul was sitting up in his bed, smiling. His eyes were bright, and he absolutely sparkled at me. I smiled back with genuine joy.

"Hey, there." He greeted me with complete lucidity.

"Hey," I replied, not sure what to say next. I stood there for a couple of seconds trying to acclimate to this newest Paul before me.

"What are you thinking about?" I ventured.

"Thinking about you," Paul continued to smile effervescently.

I giggled, sat beside him and kissed him lightly. He kissed me back.

"What were you thinking?" I asked him, truly wishing to know.

"Thinking about YOU." He repeated.

"Yeah? I'm so happy. What was the thought you had about me?" I asked, starving for a sweet taste of his mind's image.

Paul looked confused and bothered that I didn't

understand: that I wanted more. I realized his coherence was only temporary, and thanks to my wonderful stepdaughter, I had been witness to a rare and beautiful meteor.

I scooted up beside him and lay my head on his shoulder. We rested in each other. This was enough. This was extravagant. This was God's sufficient grace.

Even in laughter the heart may ache and the end of joy may be grief.
Proverbs 14:13

Chapter Sixty-Five

Quoting a little dialogue from movies had become something of an impromptu ritual between Paul and me over the years. This exchange between characters, in *"Airplane."* is a good example of how one of us might respond after hearing the other say the word, "Surely."

Ted Striker: Surely you can't be serious.

Rumack: I am serious... and don't call me Shirley

Raising Arizona had also become one of our favorite movies to quote, but the most recent movie quotes we had added came from *Slingblade*. It wasn't a comedy; however, it was filled with colloquialisms and accents that we quickly added to our repertoire.

Every now and then, as Paul and I waited in his hospital room, he would make a funny movie quote and then smile at me for either approval or the reply of an appropriate movie line. It may sound crazy to think that Paul and I were waiting for the Angel of Death and he was deliberately cracking me up as though this was the most normal thing in the world, but that, he was. Maybe we were both suffering from delirium, but he had been doing this for a while and I had acclimated easily. This kind of silly banter was built in the DNA of our relationship; laughter, a gift from God even now.

Having resigned myself to sharing Paul's hospital bed, it was no sacrifice to give Ruthie my cot in the corner of the room when she arrived that evening. My perch in Paul's bed provided a comfortable enough angle to see and talk to her. She stashed her purse under the cot and sighed,

"I must really love you two."

She looked away and took a breath.

"I haven't been back here since Mama died. I wasn't sure I could ever walk through the doors of this hospital again. It was right down that hall. Did you remember?"

Tears dammed up on my lower lids as the weight of her sacrifice registered. My memory pulled me back to the night Ruthie and I spent here while lung cancer vacuumed the life from sweet Mrs. Louise.

The dam broke and a tear spilled down my right cheek.

"God knew way back in 1969 that we were going to need each other, didn't He, Ruthie?"

"I reckon He did."

As we talked through the night, Ruthie kept biting her bottom lip. I watched her eyes dart around the room as though she felt the need to constantly assess the situation. This behavior seemed out of her character, even under the circumstances.

Finally, I asked her, "Are you okay?"

"Shirley, I'm going to ask you something, and I don't want you to be upset "

"Okay."

"Do you hear Paul?"

"Yeah, Ruthie, I know he can still talk, and all, but that doesn't mean he's improving."

"No, no, I'm not thinking he is… it's just that, do you feel safe in here with him?"

I was totally confused. Ruthie continued,

"Who's Karl? Who's Doyle? Aren't you listening to what he's saying?"

I must have stopped listening to him. I must have become desensitized by all the movie quotes he'd repeated today.

"Shirley. Don't you hear him saying he's going to kill somebody?"

Ruthie's question cued Paul who, using an Arkansas accent, was apparently stuck on *Slingblade* quotes,

"I was fixin' to kill you with this here lawn mower blade. Mmm-hmm. Some call it a Kaiser blade. I call it a sling blade." Paul looked at me, scrunching up his shoulders to emphasize his smile.

I almost choked laughing. It took me fifteen minutes to explain while snorting through my laughter what Paul was doing. Ruthie never shared in our amusement, choosing instead to smile politely and say, "Y'all are crazy."

Eventually, we slept, albeit intermittently. All too soon the light of morning beckoned her to leave us, but I knew she would be back before too long.

As for me, I am already being poured out as a libation, and the time of my departure has come.
2 Timothy 4:6

Chapter Sixty-Six

The first answer to prayer of the day arrived with a knock on our door before noon. The person who entered was the patient advocate. She walked me compassionately through the sheaves of papers necessary for discharging Paul and getting him home via ambulance. It appeared that he would be going home the next day. This thrilled me. There was so very little I could give to him at this point, so I guess this little victory of sending him off to Heaven from his own home, amid his people, would be one of my last gifts to him.

Paul was awake, although he didn't talk so much anymore. I hadn't succeeded in persuading him to eat the last few times the meal cart came around, either. This last afternoon in the hospital found Paul refusing my half-hearted presentations of food from his plate. "This is pudding, Paul." I said, in case the blindness Imogene mentioned had already stolen his eyes. "Looks like vanilla. Do you want to try it?"

Paul's head tilted and he surprised me by looking slightly interested. I put a spoonful to his lips, and his mouth opened to receive the pudding. I laughed with delight.

"You like it. Wonderful!" I gushed, wishing someone else could see this little victory.

Paul opened his mouth again, and again, until I had scraped all the pudding off his plate. The phone rang as I was bestowing the last spoonful. Oh, good, someone to share this new accomplishment with.

"Hi, Shirley?" Joe's Rhode Island brogue greeted me. "The girls and I are headed that way and wondered if we could bring anything."

"Yes. Do you think you could find some pudding? I have just now discovered that Paul will eat pudding."

"Pudding? Sure. Where do you think I could find it?"

"A grocery store, I guess. I think there's a Jell-o brand in little plastic containers."

"We'll look."

God had certainly drawn close. With each tick of the clock, His timing was illuminated in all the details. Even in the detail of pudding. Paul's father Joe and sisters Monica and Michele had flown in from Washington and California, respectively.

Paul's sisters had made themselves busy at our house doing the jobs of servants: scrubbing down our shower, preparing meals for the children, and doing laundry. Their plane would leave tomorrow to return them to their families, but Joe would remain with us indefinitely. The three of them made a welcome sight stepping inside Paul's room. The girls fluttered around Paul, doing their best to bring cheer. Joe reached into a grocery bag and unloaded his treasure trove of pudding.

"You didn't say what kind, so I got what they had. Here's a chocolate, some vanilla, and what's this? Banana."

"Perfect, Granddaddy. Paul's favorite has always been banana. I'll give that a try."

The peel-off lid revealed a banana concoction that only slightly resembled the toasted meringue topped dessert I had seen Paul make himself. No generous chunks of bananas or vanilla wafers lay hidden under this silky parfait, yet this offering proved to be enough for what would be Paul's very last meal.

Not finding Paul responsive to their efforts to engage him, Monica and Michele spoke together loudly enough so that *if* Paul could have joined in, he would have felt included. I could feel their hearts breaking. Tired from their day of cleaning our house, caring for our children, and some residual jet-lag, Joe took Michele and Monica to their motel for a good night's sleep. On the way out, Monica handed me a small bag containing a cassette tape.

"Here's a little gift for you, Shirley. There's music here that I think you'll like."

"Monica. Thank you, sweet girl."

"It's by The Second Chapter of Acts. You probably know them."

I turned the tape over and read a couple of song titles: "No, I've heard of them, but I don't know their music."

Monica hugged me hard. "I wish we didn't have to

leave now."

Michele and Leo's two girls and Monica and David's four children were young, and I was sure this trip had been a loving sacrifice for all.

"Thank you for being here through this time," I said as Michele's arms encircled us both. "You can't possibly know the debt of my gratitude."

Visitors continued to come throughout the day. Another friend named Paul stopped in with a few folks from St. Timothy's and some beautiful music from his mandolin. It was a perfect end to a day that ended with a promise to go home in the morning.

Morning came, bringing Ruthie. She quietly appeared with her usual reason and candor. Before long, we had all my nesting supplies and Paul's flowers ready to put on a wheeled hospital cart. I stood at the foot of Paul's bed, his shaving kit open, trying to figure out what I should put inside it. I'm not sure how many times Ruthie called my name before I finally turned and looked at her.

"Shirley, I know what you're thinking, and it's going to be okay."

I was confused. I already knew she could read my mind – she had been doing it for over thirty years – but right now, even I didn't even know what I was thinking yet. What did she mean?

She read my expression and explained, "Paul's shaving kit. These are his very personal belongings, but he won't need them anymore."

I nodded, trying to focus. I hadn't thought it through, but she was right. Paul wouldn't use the razor in this bag to shave whiskers off his face for work in the mornings ever again. He wouldn't brush his teeth anymore. He wouldn't need anything here.

"It's going to be okay," Ruthie repeated, and I understood why I hadn't been able to do anything more than stare into the open shaving kit.

I accepted that God had already called me to think for Paul, a man who was far more capable in more areas than I. Furthermore, I would soon be responsible, not only for the duties I knew, but also all the duties for which Paul was responsible. I claimed and was aware of this fact, yet didn't know what it would entail any more than I knew how to manage the details of a man's toiletries bag. Whatever duties lay ahead for me, I wouldn't be able to do them like Paul had.

"It's going to be okay." I parroted Ruthie. She put her arms around me and let me cry with a heart that was thankful God had sent her to me all those many years ago. She had to leave before Paul and I were escorted to the ambulance, but left me one last gift, "Shirley?" she whispered. "Do you know what the death rattle is?"

I shook my head, having only heard tales.

"Well, nobody told me about it when mama died, and I wish I had known. I want to make sure you know what to listen for."

Ruthie explained how it begins quietly, sounding kind of like congestion, but different. Over time it becomes louder, louder, then, the breathing stops.

My beautiful friend hugged me once more, and soon I was in the ambulance with Paul, riding home, thanks to intervention by Hospice. I held his hand and balanced myself as the emergency vehicle took the curves that led us home.

"You're going home," I exclaimed, but Paul's eyes remained closed. He wasn't gone, but his eyes wouldn't open ever again. Did Paul hear *Home* instead? Did he slip into the twilight because he was crossing that threshold between Earth and Jesus? Could he really hear me, or was he too far into the chasm that separates the living from Heaven's inhabitants?

The ambulance wheels rolled over our gravel driveway as the beauty of this day exploded around us. The sun shimmered across the bright green of trees as boat and Jet Ski noises buzzed on the river, making a powerful contrast to the stale hospital quiet we had left behind. God had sent a glorious summer day right in the middle of September. Jon and Joseph ran toward us, throwing sparkling drops of lake diamonds behind them.

"Awright. The driver announced. Let's get this big guy home."

He opened his door, jumped out then stood stock still,

assessing the two long flights of steps that he would have to climb in order to get Paul inside. His partner appeared beside him with a long, low whistle. The back door of the ambulance opened, and the driver reached for my hand to help me out. He scratched his head, "Is there another way into your house?"

"I'm afraid that's it," I apologized. "Are you going to be able to navigate it?"

"Oh, yeah." His answer, just a little bit more enthusiastic than necessary, led me to doubt him.

I ran upstairs to make sure the way was clear to get Paul inside and moved a few things around. Opening both French doors wide, I stepped out on the deck just in time to see Paul's ascent almost end in a horrifying crash. Now on the second flight, the two ambulance attendants strained from carrying my Paul this far at such an angle. The Gurney that held him aloft began to teeter, and both men fought hard to hold on to him. The seconds stretched long as they somehow managed to right themselves without falling and get Paul indoors.

Paul was taken to our bedroom where a hospital bed had been situated beside the bed. All our children were there with the exception of Austin. Sarah's boyfriend Matt had accompanied her from Vanderbilt. He would prove to be a wonderful blessing to all of us. Paul's father Joe was there with us, being a fine grandfather to all the kids, young and old. I made a tight nest beside Paul in his hospital bed.

"You made it, Sweetie," I whispered in his ear, but nothing in him responded.

Something more than his eyes had closed. Somewhere between his hospital room and home, another big piece of my darling man had entered the chasm.

A soft knock on the door frame took my attention to Pastor Garry, tiptoeing in. He stood beside us and put his hand on Paul's arm. Frankie lay curled up at Paul's feet, and Kit had mashed herself against his side. They were doing a holy service.

"He's halfway Home." Pastor Garry's words came just barely above a whisper, confirming my lonesome observation.

Hospice had sent a nurse to attend to us. There were reams of papers that required my signature, so she brought a couple of kitchen chairs into our bedroom and offered one to me. I signed each document as fast as I could, not wanting to waste any more time on this that I had to. Finally, she pulled out a page-size poster with, "Do Not Resuscitate" emblazoned across it. "Mrs. Graham, I need for you to sign something now so that this can go over your husband's bed."

"What is it? This isn't right. I don't have to make any decisions about resuscitation. Paul had a Living Will. I can't do this." I sat in the hard chair as this dear little nurse tried vainly to explain this responsibility. I don't know what she said. Something about hospital premises having different requirements from non-hospital premises in initiating CPR and ACLS. Something about, permission of next-of-kin having to make medical decisions of incapacitated relatives. I couldn't process her words. After so many stressful hours, this sign I held in my lap broke loose the dam holding my tears at bay.

"I can't," I cried, "I can't do this."

Nita had arrived just in time for this. She knelt beside me and held my hand.

"Call Pastor Garry, Nita. Ask him to please come back. I can't do this."

In a few minutes, Pastor Garry occupied the kitchen chair to my right. After talking to me about what it meant, I was finally able to provide a shaky signature above the dotted line. When Pastor Garry left our house the second time, I nestled between Paul and the metal rail of his bed. Kit and Frankie hadn't budged from their posts.

The phone rang every few minutes, so when Nita arrived, I asked her to field the calls. I wanted all my attention on my dear husband for whatever minutes were left. Nita walked in holding the phone against her shoulder.

"Shirley, honey? It's Jennifer from church. She just wants to know if you'd like the choir to come over and sing to Paul. What do you want me to say?"

"Tell her yes. Tell her, thank-you. That would be so wonderful. Ask her to call Paul Hayes and Todd. Maybe they would bring their instruments."

In a matter of mere hours, my Saint Tim's choir friends crowded into our bedroom. Paul's mandolin and Todd's guitar made soft background accompaniment to the voices in the room that fell naturally into Heavenly harmonies. I can't describe how utterly beautiful it was. The blended voices were exquisite, yet each voice was a separate masterpiece standing out. Granddaddy Joe's deep musical voice arose from the doorway. Young Matt stood before the wardrobe, his warm tenor notes surprising me with harmonious accuracy. Sarah stood beside him singing softly, soaking in the ethereal majesty of *The Doxology*. My precious choir friends then bade us a good night and disappeared, leaving an aura of God's glory behind.

Throughout the night, Sarah and Matt lay crosswise on the king-size bed in our room, our heads encircling Paul, talking quietly, encouragingly to him and keeping me company. Charlotte, Emily, and Joseph came and went, resting on the bed, just being with us.

When Sarah left the room with Matt, she returned with a glass of water in her hand and a request for my advice.

"Shirl, do you think it would be okay if Matt helped me do a little studying? We could go right there in the living room, and I think I could hear if you called me, if you needed me."

"That's fine, sweetie," I kissed her cheek.

"Thanks, Shirl. Let me know if you need anything."

She'd left Vanderbilt right smack dab in the middle of pre-exam study. Not knowing what to expect, she had brought books and book bags full of notes which called to her unremorsefully. Between jags of tears and time spent with her daddy, she would pull out her books and try beyond comprehension to concentrate.

Something had happened to Sarah and me in the past few hours. The naturally defensive nature of a step-relationship had given way to a sudden, lovely friendship. We'd become sisters, baptized in our shared love for Paul, leaning on and lifting each other through this unknown place. Even as the gates of Heaven opened to receive her daddy, our hearts were opening to one another in a brand new way. Though God allowed the door of Paul's life to close, He opened a large window that loss and mistrust had tried vainly to paint shut.

I left Paul's side to check on the little ones. Before reaching Elisabeth's room, I could hear an animated Elisabeth talking to Charlotte and Emily. I left without intruding and went looking for Joseph, who was easy enough to find in the school room playing games at the computer. No telling how long he had been here, bless his heart. Neither I nor other adults coming and going had the heart to limit this seven-year-old boy whose daddy wouldn't be here to teach him how to be a man. I knelt on the floor beside him.

"Hey, Bubby."

"Hey, Mom." Joseph answered without taking his eyes off the Tetris game. "Do I have to stop playing video games?"

"No, honey. You can play. When you get tired, come in my room. I'll be in there with Daddy."

"Okay."

"Joseph, I have to ask you something. Do you understand that your daddy is dying?"

"Yes, ma'am."

"I'm so sorry."

"Me, too." Joseph's expression remained sober as silence hovered between us.

"Mom?"

"What, darlin'?"

"Will we have to move?"

"No. No, we won't have to move," I said, sure that Paul must have purchased enough life insurance for me to pay off the house.

"What about his clothes?"

"Your daddy's clothes?"

"What will we do with them?"

"Well, nothing at first. Maybe Jonboy would like to have some things. Maybe Uncle Dale. He's about the right size. Maybe I would save some for you. Does that sound like the right thing?"

Joseph nodded, still staring at the computer screen.

It wasn't a shock to hear him ask these questions. I imagined he had plenty of questions and needed honest, candid answers in order to sort them out in his young mind.

"I love you, sweet boy." I kissed him on the head and stood to leave.

"Mom?"

"What, sweetie?"

Will you get married again?"

"Right now, I can't even imagine being married to anyone but your daddy, Joseph; but I don't know what God has in store for us. We're just going to have to trust Him to guide us."

He finally looked at me, and I hugged him hard.

"Come climb in Mom and Dad's bed when you get tired. Okay?"

"Okay."

He did join us later, but only briefly. Charlotte and Emily had wandered into see Paul and ended up lying crosswise on the bed, which had become everyone's style. Sibling rivalry being what it is, refusing to take a vacation even from death, Joseph ended up sleeping with Elisabeth in her room.

I remembered the Second Chapter of Acts cassette Monica had given to me, fished it out of my pocketbook, and slid it into the tape deck in our bedroom. In a heartbeat, the musical strains of beautiful old praise hymns cast life into every corner of the bedroom. I found my small place beside Paul and the cats while *All Creatures of Our God and King, My Jesus I Love Thee, Great Is Thy Faithfulness,* and *Joyful, Joyful, We Adore Thee* summoned the Sandman. Charlotte and Emily drifted off to sleep easily at the foot of Paul's and my big bed.

The room was quiet and I felt alone with Paul now that everyone asleep except for Sarah and Matt studying quietly in the next room. I sang to Paul along with the tape. Every now and again, Sarah cried and I could hear Matt comforting her. They were both quiet now, and I figured one or both of them had fallen asleep.

Adrenaline kept everything so vivid, so sharp. I wasn't tired, wasn't hungry. I couldn't remember the last time I ate, but I couldn't eat. My fight or flight reflex was alive and well. What would tomorrow bring? People would be coming early. What would they need? I got out of the bed again and went to the kitchen. I ran water into the coffeepot and poured it into the coffeemaker. I was on auto-pilot, rinsing out the filter cup, putting a new filter paper in, adding three scoops of coffee, closing the compartment. All of a sudden, an inner voice of reason asked me what I was doing wasting time with this procedure. *Anyone* could do this task. It wasn't urgent. I needed to be with Paul.

    Feeling foolish, I hurried back to the bedroom and turned the cassette over. The words of "Holy, Holy, Holy" followed me gently as I found my niche beside Paul, who remained in the same position he had been in since he had been home: on his back with an oxygen tube gently blowing air into his nostrils. He hadn't liked wearing this thing in the hospital and kept pulling it out. He had no care of it now. I traced his profile with my left index finger. How I loved his profile – the symmetry of his eyebrows; the neat, straight lines of his nose; his high cheekbones; the beautiful deep cleft in his chin. I let my fingertip travel along his eyebrow hair, so smooth. I didn't want to forget. His hands were crossed over his lower rib cage and my right arm rested under his left, our fingers threaded and intertwined. The way our hands clasped caused Paul's fingers to stick out straight. Frankie finally moved from his spot and walked onto the big bed where the children lay. I expected him to find another warm body to snuggle up to, but he didn't. Instead, he made graceful steps to Paul's torso where his arms rested, his fingers pointed straight. Frankie rubbed his face against Paul's fingertips, first to the left, then to the right as though to say, *"Goodbye, my friend."*

    I watched in amazement as this lovely grey and white cat re-traced his steps and returned to his post at Paul's feet. My mind traveled back almost two years to Paul's lung surgery when Frankie was just a tiny puff who slept weightlessly with Paul on top of his healing incision. God had been gracious in letting Paul remain with us. I knew every day he had lived was a miracle after that awful Sunday morning when I thought he was having a stroke. It wasn't logical that he had lived almost two years after melanoma metastases had affected two major organs. Most people in this situation are lucky to last four months. Some would question whether or not God really had healed Paul. Others would argue that Paul wasn't really healed because he died in the end. But, to those I would ask, "Was Lazarus' resurrection any less a miracle because *he* eventually died?"

Still, I wasn't ready to let my husband go. I rested my head on his chest. Alarm shot through me as I heard congestion sounding different from before. I listened to him breathe a minute longer while the panic in my heart increased.

"Matt?" I called quietly.

He was beside me in an instant.

"Do you hear something?" I raised my head, and Matt leaned in.

"It sounds different, doesn't it, Matt?"

"Maybe so. Do you want me to wake Sarah?"

"I hate to wake her. I know she's exhausted."

Paul's breath came evenly. The rattle was almost imperceptible.

"You'll hear me call you, won't you?"

"I'm not going to sleep, Shirley. I'm here to help."

"Thank you so much for being here, Matt."

"Thank you for trusting me here at such a time."

Sarah appeared in the doorway. "Hey."

"Sarah," I said, relieved to see her. "Good, you woke up. Come here, honey."

Sarah came close.

"I hear something in your daddy's breathing. Do you hear it?"

She listened and nodded just a little.

"Sarah, do you remember the Hospice nurse said to call if we had any questions?"

She nodded. "Do you think I ought to call her?"

"Well," I shifted my weight away from the metal bar behind me, "would you ask her if what we hear might be the death rattle?"

"I'm calling right now." Sarah went to the kitchen counter and found the Hospice number. She and Matt returned quickly after making the call.

"The hospice nurse said, "Yes." She told me that is

probably what it is."

I bit my lip. "Ruthie told me about this. She said it means death is imminent, but could still be as far away as twenty-four hours."

I had a flashback of timing labor contractions. Such strange parallels exist between new life and death. Kit rose up as Frankie had done before. She made a soft path to Paul's outstretched fingertips, just like Frankie. Leaning into his fingers, Kit rubbed her face against them; a loving swipe to the left, then to the right to bid her master "Adieu." She followed the path she'd made back to her original spot beside Paul.

"I think it's time for us to gather here, wait and watch." I told them.

Blinking back tears, Sarah climbed up on the bed and scooted as close as possible to her daddy. Matt sat beside her.

"Hey, Daddy," she took hold of her daddy's other hand, "I love you. I love you so much."

We continued talking to Paul and didn't notice when the cassette tape ended. That must have been when we began singing to him, though. We sang *Away in a Manger*; we pieced together the *Twenty-Third Psalm*. Sarah and I shared our memories to him, thanked him for making such a difference in our lives. We told him we loved him over and over.

The death rattle grew in volume over the course of the night, but we journeyed beside him to Heaven's gate, praying the Lord's Prayer aloud. Now and again, our brains would tire and there would be silence. That's how it was when his last loud breath came, then, there was nothing in the room but an enormous pause. I looked at Matt and knew he knew, too. We locked in a gaze, waiting to see if another breath would come.

Sarah seemed deliberately not aware at first that her daddy stopped breathing then panic cast itself across her countenance as the truth of Paul's silence registered. Her eyes, like saucers, darted about, lighting briefly on me, then Matt. Matt held her firmly in his gaze, slowly, gently nodding his head, "Yes" to answer the query in her eyes that knew the truth but begged him for one thread of hope.

Matt had the presence of mind to look at his watch. I didn't understand at first why as he'd said, "Its four-o'clock," but the practical part of him remembered that a time of death would need to be recorded.

Feelings of loss and grieving had been stalking me for months, but what I didn't expect now was a sudden, vibrant sensation of utter pride for my husband. I felt like a spectator, his biggest fan at the end of a finish line. My precious Paul had finished the race. He had gone the distance. He had been a good and faithful servant. I was taken aback by a strange swell of celebration in my heart for him. He was really Home.

I looked around the room, squinting in the dark in the hope of seeing an angel or the rising puff of his soul. What would they look like? I studied the dark corners of our bedroom. God didn't allow me such a visual image but He gave me something else: the vivid knowledge that my Paul is with my Jesus for all of eternity. His life's journey finally over, his suffering finished and inhibitions gone, Paul and Jesus embraced, filled with the joy of Paul's completed task. As my cousin, Beverly, wrote in an email a few days later,

"I know you miss him, Shirley, but just think about this: Paul has actually *seen* the face of Jesus."

The next unexpected feeling was one of thankfulness over being allowed to fulfill my marriage vows. I, an utter failure at two marriages, had finally fulfilled a promise to stand beside my husband in *richer or poorer, better or worse, sickness and health, till death parted us.* Not because I deserved it but because of His love, the Lord had allowed me another chance. Paul and I had needed each other, and in God's mercy, he let us journey together until Paul was standing right before the Pearly Gates of Heaven.

Deja vu. I felt like I had been in this place before; like I had had this sensation, these thoughts before, but that was impossible, wasn't it? I had never witnessed death, but what felt so familiar? Then I remembered the vision I had been given after Paul's mother died. Was it Paul's death God had been foreshadowing? In the vision, I rode ... no, I *flew* with Betty to the closing doors of Heaven where she slipped in and I stayed behind. I believe God allowed me that vision as a gift, something to let me know He's always with me, always in control, guarding me, measuring my steps, holding me in His heart. He knew I would need a personal miracle, something to show me His power on Paul's last day, and that a vision from February, 1995, would send me that message.

Sarah began to cry and left the room with Matt. Charlotte and Emily lay quietly at the foot of the big bed watching me.

"Do you know your daddy is gone?"

They nodded.

"We were awake," Emily revealed, and I wondered if the noise of Paul's dying had woken them. Our pretty little girls had remained still and humble, too little to be losing their big, strong daddy but wise enough to know no one could stop him from dying.

"I'm so sorry," I offered feebly.

Charlotte and Emily slid off the bed together. Our – now *my* – bedroom had become strange and new to them and lacked half the safety it used to provide them. They stole away to find a place that seemed familiar.

Alone again for a few minutes, I looked at Paul's beautiful face. Death had removed all the lines, and he looked young. I traced his profile again: that beautiful straight nose; the forehead that had conveyed such serenity, kindness, and intelligence. I feared time might take away my memory of his face. I would stay there beside him, looking at him as long as I wanted, and I wanted to stay until all his warmth was gone.

> *I have fought the good fight, I have finished the race, I have kept the faith. From now on there is reserved for me the crown of righteousness, which the Lord, the righteous judge, will give to me on that day, and not only to me but also to all who have longed for his appearing. At my first defense no one came to my support, but all deserted me.*
> 2 Timothy 4:7-8

Chapter Sixty-Seven

    Paul's body was carried away to the University of South Carolina Medical School to be studied by medical students. His Earthly body would be making a contribution to medical science even though his Earthly life hadn't allowed it. He was posthumously fulfilling his dream to go to the medical school after all. In two to three years, The Gift of Life Program that enabled Paul to donate his body would send us: his family, his cremains.

    Peace that passed understanding and God's grace, as it worked through our friends and family, brought us through the next days. I planned the music for Paul's memorial service. *Just a Closer Walk with Thee*, Paul's favorite hymn would have to be part of it. He had loved the guitar version sung in the old movie, "Cool Hand Luke." I picked *Holy, Holy, Holy* because that's what Revelations says the saints and angels in Heaven sing. It always makes me feel like some of the veil that shields the Heavenly realm disappears when I sing it, and the presence of the Lord is more vivid. *I Was There To Hear Your Borning Cry*, though impossible to sing without tears, was included because of its absolute truth regarding God's constancy in our lives from birth through death. The choir requested to sing *Go Now in Peace* as their personal tribute to Paul.

    Nita had asked me what I would be wearing to Paul's memoriam.

    "Whatever I wear, I won't ever wear again," I remember telling her.

    "I kind of thought so," Nita had said. "I'll find you something in my closet."

    And so it was that I wore something borrowed to Paul's service.

I enlisted Granddaddy Joe to take my heart-scarred daughters shopping for black dress clothes. A ten-year-old shouldn't ever have to wear black, yet here we were, needing black dresses to fit my littlest girls. Joe couldn't have done this task any more sweetly, encouraging them with grandfatherly words and reminding them they were lovely.

As I planned Paul's last celebration, I had no idea how I would cover the expenses, much less manage our household later. I needn't have worried. The Lord was whispering our burdens into the ears of His people, and all needs were being met. For example, what seemed a chance visit from Tim and Gale just a couple of weeks back now looked a lot more like God's intervention. Besides being our friend, Tim was also an employee of our local newspaper. He called me the day after Paul died. With the memory of our family fresh on his mind, news of Paul's death caught his immediate attention. When we talked on the phone, Tim collected all the information I wanted for Paul's obituary, including a photograph, and posted it in the newspaper the following day. Unbeknownst to me at the time, Tim paid for it himself and refused reimbursement.

It would be a while before we knew how much money could be collected from Paul's life insurance and even longer to know when it was available. We knew there would be some Social Security to collect, but that required some time and documentation. Paul's ability to handle the bills had been impaired in the past few months, and some of the creditors who called me had little patience for the fact that Paul had died. I made a mental note of their insensitivity and vowed to never do business with them again.

Almost immediately I began receiving sympathy cards in the mail with hundred dollar checks in many of them, which was how I was able to pay our bills in the following weeks.

Of the friends who stopped in with gifts of food and sympathy, a visit from the Woolington's stands out in a special way. John and Katie, home-school friends, have their quiver full, a heritage from the Lord. Somber in their entry was this descending queue of precious children: John David, Laura Kaye, Chapman Harry, Hannah Elizabeth, and Sarah Jane with Abigail Louise perched on Katy's hip. Dressed in their Sunday best, they seemed to be acting on loving instructions of how to behave in this strange situation. The sight of them opened my heart to gaping, and I longed to close my arms around their sympathetic purity. I knelt, embracing them one by one. Sarah Jane was last, blonde angel curls making a halo around her pretty face. She lingered, clearly wanting to say something of comfort and value. Even as she spoke, I understood what she *meant* to tell me. Had she been able to draw her words from a larger pool of verbiage, it would have sounded something like this, *I didn't have the pleasure of really knowing Mr. Paul, but I do know and love Charlotte and Emily who are little girls like me. I love my own daddy so my heart grieves for their loss.* But, alas, though her heart was that of a sage, Sarah Jane's vocabulary was only four years old. The sweet consolation she offered was this: "I was sad that Charlotte and Emily's daddy . . . that he was died . . . but I really don't care . . . but I was sad for Charlotte and Emily that he was died." Having articulated a perfect condolence, Sarah Jane joined her family for a collective goodbye.

  Paul's service would be the following day. My sister, Jeanne and her husband were en route. Jeanne would later tell me that Father Ted (the Marianist priest who was most adamantly against closed Communion) had had a complete change of perspective regarding sharing the Host after meeting Paul. Paul hadn't realized what an impact his questions had made.

  Tim and Dale were already in town. Dale had driven to Hartwell to bring Daddy (who was almost entirely bedridden) and Mother (who had been willing to stay or go, depending on Daddy's wishes). So feeble was he that in a mere six months, Daddy would also claim his Home in Heaven, yet he insisted on coming to honor the son-in-law he had come to love and respect.

  The details of the next day were all put together now. I looked forward to its culmination, but just as much, I looked forward to being finished with it. I dressed for bed and hoped I'd be able to sleep some. Paul's hospital bed had been removed from our house now. I lay on my side of the bed very close to the edge. Maybe this would be my new normal now that Paul wasn't on the other side to wrap my arms around. I fell asleep thinking about tomorrow.

  When I awoke, it was still dark. I looked at the alarm clock, still on Paul's side of the bed. Four o'clock in the morning. I didn't know it yet, but dreaming about Paul nightly and waking up on his death hour would become routine for me. I looked around the dusky room. Realizing I wasn't going back to sleep, I sat up, noticed the light coming from the tape player, turned on my bedside light, and went to check it out. I remembered turning it over to the other side as

Paul was dying and suddenly wondered about the last song he must have heard. I read, the last song on side two, rewound it and listened:

> *"He has formed me from the dust and to dust I shall return.*
> *He has made me in His light and to light I shall return.*
> *And I'll be free at last to lay it all down..."*

Where, O death, is your sting? The sting of death is sin, and the power of sin is the law. But thanks be to God, He gives us the victory through our Lord Jesus Christ.
1 Corinthians 15:42-57

Chapter Sixty-Eight

September 20, 2003.

God sent sunshine on the day of Paul's memorial service. I don't remember much about getting ready or arriving at St. Timothy's. I do remember the hole of Paul's absence that physically burned inside my heart and the strangeness of sitting in the pew beside his daddy, Joe. I remember the tragic image of my little daddy-less Joseph seated quietly, silently in the pew wearing his small black dress suit.

As our friends Paul and Todd played a lovely, tinny, meandering mandolin and guitar harmony that complimented how lost we all felt, the church filled up with people who had been touched by Paul. The string duet ended and the string musicians walked away with reddened eyes as Jennifer's piano notes rang a firm, clear directive, *Seek Ye First the Kingdom of God*.

Pastor Garry appeared behind the pulpit: "We are gathered this morning to celebrate the life of Paul Graham." He continued with a Call to Worship from Psalm 101:7. My tired eyes, tight and sore, wandered over to Joseph who was doing a study of his Sunday shoes. He didn't look away from his shoes when I rubbed his back and whispered, "I love you, little man."

Later there would be well-meaning people who would tell him, "You're the man of the house now." But I would always whisper to him aside, "You are the seven-year-old boy of the house, buddy, and that's what we need."

The Doxology came next, sounding more like a funeral dirge than praise, but it was a dirge we needed. Now the lyrics of *Holy, Holy, Holy* came to life, and I had a fine image of Paul casting down his golden crown around the glassy sea. The veil between Heaven and Earth lifted and I could feel Paul near me in that moment.

Joe didn't need the hymnal even when he sang the *...Who, wert and art and evermore shall be* part. I felt so sorry for this man who seemed so strong. He had lost his little boy for so many years, and I knew it hurt him. It seemed so cruel that he now had to give him up again. Joe had poured himself into attending to our needs in these awful days, and that's where he found his comfort.

"*Death is the gate to Eternal Life . . .*" I heard Pastor Garry saying. I tried so hard to follow, but grief is a terrible distraction to one's concentration. He closed with this invitation: "Several family members and friends of Paul's have asked to share their memories of him with us."

My brother, Dale stepped up to the pulpit.

"*I am Shirley's brother, and I'll be sharing the words of Colonel Phil Williams with you.*"

Typically, Phil loved to talk and share his thoughts. He loved telling about the history he and Paul had together, and this was the first time I had ever known him to be unable to speak. As Phil and his Barbara sat stoically beside one another in honor of Paul, Dale read from the script Phil had written that began with a litany of Paul's football nicknames: *"Well, Paul, or J.P. Wangdene, or Garnto, it's tough to say goodbye. It hurts so much to let you go. Those of us who had the privilege to grow up with you, play football with you, and share our lives with each other know that your kind will never pass our way ever again. No man ever loved his family more, had better character or integrity, or loved the Lord more than you did. A popular slogan for today's times is, "What would Jesus do?" Many times in the past, before this phrase became popular and I had a difficult time or decision, I would just ask, "What would Paul do?" because I knew how pure your heart was and I knew how you lived your life and your Christian ideals. What more can you say about a man than this?*

The only thing a man gets to keep when he dies is what he gave away. Your gifts to all of us that shared our lives together are incalculable and will live on with us even though you have gone to be with the Father. To know that you are in Heaven helps me dry my tears and ease the awful pain and sense of loss we all feel. I thank God for the privilege of knowing you, I will cherish all of the things we did together, and I hope that me and Gary and Frankie and Mark and Coach Richardson and everybody else can be on your team in Heaven one day, too.

I love you #31,
Phil"

Dale followed with his own eulogy:

"My sister married Paul. I'm Shirley's brother, and Paul is my brother-in-law, but it wasn't long before Paul turned into my brother. We shared a lot of Christian things, a lot of faith together.

There was a time when I didn't like Paul. I'll tell you a little story about a day when I had been restoring an old Volkswagen and had it towed from Hartwell to Atlanta. That was about a three hour trip. It just had a new paint job, the interior done and I was kind of showing it off. It wasn't all put together, but everybody was looking all around it and saying the car was, "really neat."

Paul kind of pulled me aside and said, "Ah, they kind of short-changed you on the paint job, didn't they?"

I said to myself, "How rude." Here I had just brought this car, and to me it was beautiful. The truth of the matter is, I looked over some of the light spots of the paint and Paul was right-on. But for a while, I just didn't like that. It kind of bothered me.

That kind of grew with my relationship with Paul because if you asked Paul something his answer was always straight up, he really didn't hide anything. By his telling the truth, it was a lot better than . . . what's the saying? "Do you want me to tell you what you want to hear or what it is?" Paul would tell you the way it was and I loved him for that. The last several years we got real close.

And it's nice to know that the breath after the last breath Paul breathed on Earth was the first breath he breathed in Heaven. I know he's waiting just inside the Eastern Gate for me when I get there and that's just a pleasure and an honor. I could talk on and on about Paul. I love him as a brother, and I look forward to seeing him one day."

My brother, Tim approached the pulpit as Dale stepped down.

"A lot of you have never seen me before, but you prayed for me last year when I had cancer."

A collective gasp arose among the prayer warriors of St Timothy's congregation as the meaning of Tim's statement settled in. God's glory was present as we beheld this miracle He had wrought wearing the flesh of my brother.

His voice breaking, Tim continued,

"I have felt the power of your prayers, and I know that Paul, Shirley, and their family feel your prayers. It is through this power manifested in God's miracles that allowed Paul to stay with us as long as he did.

Paul was a unique and special man. Most people would have buckled under the constant treatments and specter of the disease. But he kept fighting, and he was a role model for me while I was going through my treatments. I remember a conversation we had last year right after I had been diagnosed. He said, "God is in the miracle business. I am a walking miracle, and I'm here through the grace of God."

I come here today to celebrate his life. He is a hero to me exemplified by his unwavering determination, his frankness, and his sense of humor. His relationship with God was very deep and strong, and he was proud of it. He also has lots of friends who admire and respect him. That was no accident. As we go through these tough times ahead with the void he has left behind in our lives, it is imperative that we dust off those great memories we have of him. It is also important that we lay the burden of our grief at God's feet and let Him soothe our pain.

Rev. Paul Moore in his book, *A BISHOP'S LIFE IN THE CITY* wrote,

"Many live happily with an undemanding 'Now I lay me down to sleep' God. Then something happens in your life – death, pain, divorce, addiction, mental breakdown – reality comes crashing down and you reach out to a god not large enough or deep enough to respond to the horror and terror of your life. You pray to a Sunday school god and nothing happens. This cozy god should make things better right away

but often does not. However, if you are deeply acquainted with God, you are not frustrated. You open your agony to the agony of Christ hanging on the Cross, you know that God cannot always relieve pain, but you know too that God is there with you in the midst of your pain and that on the other side of this death of pain will be a new life and resurrection."

Paul had broken through the physical bonds of pain here on Earth and has opened the door to his new life in Heaven . . . probably figuring it all out for the next person to come along. He was surrounded by love here on this Earth. He was surrounded by the prayers of those who love and respect him. He is finding the same thing in Heaven now. I will miss him, but will have a lifetime of his memories to sustain me until I get there and he takes me aside and explains how it all works."

Tim descended as Gary Smallen took his place behind the podium. Gary's pregnant pause before speaking called me to pray for his composure as he spoke. This was going to be a hard talk for him to do.

"Bear him up, Lord," I prayed and Gary began: *"Goodbye, my friend. It always seemed that the years and miles kept us from spending enough time together, but the friendship we shared growing up was one of the greatest blessings in my life. I am going to miss the laughs we had reminiscing about those years we were high school best friends. I never got tired of reliving those days. I can hear Coach Richardson crawling all over you right now. I can see Mr. Amaker running us out of the swimming pool. I can hear Colonel Gibbs telling us what time to have the twins home after the prom. I can taste the Krispy-Kremes we scored at Taylor Street Pharmacy. I can still feel you and Phil in 'Bull-In-The-Ring.'*

Of course, as friendships go, I was the lucky one in the deal. You gave me a second family. For the Friday afternoons we spent washing and waxing the ole blue Mustang for the weekend, for the days we slipped down to Mama Graham's cafeteria and ate and ate and ate, for the pool lessons that Daddy Rod gave us, for the road trips to Myrtle Beach, for the door that was always open on Lake Marion Circle. . . I will always miss you, Paul, the best friend a guy could ever have. I am going to miss your competitive spirit. The golf outings these past several years are memories I will always cherish . . . particularly when you split out Frankie's pants. But those matches only hinted at the will to win that was always such a big part of your nature. The years we spent as Dentsville Cougar athletes were a testament to your drive and determination. Now all these years later, to watch you stare death in the eye and beat him back for all that time . . . I am going to miss your fierce sense of pride, Garnto.

And while this will probably surprise everyone who knows us, I am going to miss your love for music. What great times we had listening to the ole guy spin Motown records for us in that little music shop. How "er great" it was to have The Eagles Greatest Hits blaring out of your 8-track player as we passed a record thirteen consecutive cars on the way to the beach . . . and just a moment or so ago, to watch you gaze at Shirley during her rendition of (Patsy Cline's) "Sweet Dreams."

I often wonder what happened to the fortune we made working summer jobs together, painting the barracks at Fort Jackson, counseling those snot-nosed kids at Camp Carolina, lifeguarding for Coach Koty at Columbia Country Club. We should have been rich. But really, Paul, after spending some time with Shirley – and your former teammates and Coach – and to see this wonderful family you gave the World, and to have all these great friends gathered together to celebrate your life and what you gave to us all, you were the richest one of all. And I have a wealth of memories to treasure all of my days.

"Goodbye, my friend."

It is possible that there might have been a dry eye in the congregation before Gary began, but there wasn't one now. The pulpit stood empty for only a few seconds before Marilyn found her place there. Her advice when Paul first became ill still rang in my heart, *"Don't ignore all the little miracles while you are waiting for the big one."*

Marilyn Crosby:

"Henri Nouwen writes about friends and their limitations. 'Friends cannot be made. Friends are free gifts

from God. God gives us friends we need when we need them. Friends cannot replace God; their love is never faultless, never complete, but they are signposts.' Paul was a signpost, and Paul's eyes crinkled, and Paul knew how to pick battles.

I met Paul when we, together, were charter members to build a mission church up in Harbison. Paul was our president. He had quiet faith, but he had vocal leadership; he knew how to pick battles, and his eyes crinkled.

Paul knew how to embrace change; my God, in one day, he went from a single man with a precious little girl, just one, to a brood of four that soon became seven, and . . .,"

Marilyn looked over at baby Ian,

". . . they're still growing.

Henri Nouwen writes about love and the pain of leaving: 'Every time we make a decision to love someone, we open ourselves to great suffering, and the greatest pain comes from leaving.' Paul knew loving, and Paul knew leaving. I was with Paul when he mourned his mother, but Paul loved greatly. Paul loved family, Paul loved his friends, and Paul loved his church, and Paul knew that the risk was worth it.

Paul was like Moses: he traveled through life with a tribe. When he picked his battles – and he picked one in his last days – he picked a battle to live because of his tribe. And he battled. We know he battled.

I had the privilege to be with Paul and pray with him before his first surgery when he couldn't speak and then the next day, he could. His eyes were full of fear, but they still crinkled.

And Henri Nouwen writes about the companionship of the dead: 'It's very important to remember that those who have loved us and those we have loved, letting their spirits inspire us in our daily lives, they become part of our spiritual communities and they gently help us. They become true spiritual companions.' It's important to let go of Paul's body, to let go of the physical. I know that in time, for me the crinkled eyes, the memory of that, will probably disappear. And I will miss him, and you will miss him, and there will be big days in your life that you will miss him; there will be graduations, and there will be babies and weddings. You will miss him, but if you can let go, he will be there with you always. And you will gain the spiritual part of Paul. Your daddy will never leave you. I love you Paul."

Marilyn then passed the torch to Coach Richardson.

"I was fortunate enough to have coached Garnto. I told my wife and daughter, 'I am sure, the way he planned ahead, he must have certainly told Shirley, "Whatever you do, don't let Coach Richardson nor Phil Williams get up and speak because the people will have to go home and eat supper."

I picked that up from one of my players named Phil Williams.

I just told the preacher I am a born-again Baptist. I went to Wake Forest; I almost became a minister, so I sometimes stray from my sermon. If I make a terrible mistake, let me know.

When I received a call about Paul, I know all the things, and I believe in my heart that, yes, we do go on to a better Place. I bit my lips when the person called me, and I did not break down. I went in the house to put the phone up and told my wife and daughter then I grieved and cried until I was dry and hyperventilating. I got over that and went back to the thing with God Who has told us that, yes, there is a better Place. I remembered that and started thinking about it.

I was told I could write a few words that someone else would say about him, which I really didn't think was fair, because I know him. But I wrote sixteen pages, and my sweet daughter said, 'Daddy, a short thing – that's a chapter, not a book.' But I did cut it down and I hope you'll bear with me.

A few little bites: I met Paul in another era when little boys had crew cuts and heroes were not thugs and criminals. That crew-cut little boy was my kind of guy. He had a countenance that could change like the seasons from a stoic face, to a wide-face grin, to an open mouth burst of laughter that allowed you to see all the way down into his heart.

In most athletic environments, he would have been known as a too-fer: too short, too light and too slow. Those who misjudged him would find out there was another too: Too bad. Because he would strike you like a hammer. That *little bag of bones would lay in on you.*

He became a member of an unnamed but very special group that lived in a time and a place that exists now only in the minds and the hearts of those special people. That place was Dentsville High School. His brothers from that place and that brotherhood are here now to honor him. They know who they are and they know what makes them special. They were lumps of coal who became diamonds. One of those diamonds is now mounted in a crown.

Paul was not bone of my bone nor flesh of my flesh, but I loved him like my own child. He was a treasure that God allowed me to share for a short while. I will stick to my script and give you a Madison Avenue summary of Paul:

J-Lo's diamond: Four million dollars.

Two ocean front lots for Oprah Winfrey in Maui: Eleven million dollars.

Ron James shoe contract: fifty million dollars.

To have known, loved and been loved by Garnto: Priceless."

There was one more eulogy to be said and Pastor Garry walked to the podium slowly, deliberately.

"This may be the hardest worship service I have ever done. I'm not sure I can get all the way through it without getting choked up. You see, Paul Graham was my friend. It's hard to talk about his death from this pulpit. Next to his friendship, I will miss his sense of humor the most, I think. The way he would laugh at my bad jokes, as much out of sympathy for me as anything else.

But Shirley reminded me on the day Paul died that this is not only a memorial service for Paul, it is also a service of celebration, a service of praise for God even on a day when we may not feel like praising and giving thanks. So instead of talking about Paul, I want to begin by telling you a little about what I have seen in Paul Graham's house.

In the foyer as you come in the front door to Paul's house is a Nativity Scene and a large Living Bible. There are quotations from Joshua 24:15: As for me and my house, we will serve the Lord. There is another Nativity Scene in the bathroom by the kitchen; this one is on top of the toilet tank. In the kitchen itself is a picture of Jesus, smiling, and a little framed print that quotes Lamentations 3:22-23: "The steadfast love of the Lord never ceases, His mercies never come to an end; they are new every morning; great is your faithfulness." There is a Cross over the front door. There is a Cross over the door to bedrooms. There is a Cross by the master bedroom. There is a Cross in the master bedroom. There is a Cross on the piano. There is a large Cross in the study, made up of thumbprints from members of Christus Victor Lutheran Church in Columbia. There is a sort of sculpture of the Ten Commandments. On bookshelves in the study is the New Testament on tape read by Alexander Scourby. There is a book entitled Bible Truths, and there is another Cross over the door. Shirley, forgive me for snooping. I have to confess that I don't honestly know which of those things were hung on the walls, placed on the shelves and piano and toilet tank by Shirley. It doesn't matter, really. The point is that everywhere in Paul's house, there are reminders of Paul's faith, reminders of the importance to Paul of God's presence, of God's grace and love, reminders that guided Paul as a loving husband and father, as a caring friend, as a congregation council member and as a willing worker in God's vineyard.

And there are reminders of God's love expressed in his life in another ways, too – pictures of parents and brothers and sisters, pictures of Paul and Shirley, pictures of Jon and Austin, of Sarah and Elisabeth, pictures of Charlotte, Emily, and Joseph. Paul was surrounded, not just by symbols and quotes from Scripture – he was surrounded by living images of how God made Himself present through a loving family and loving friends. A wife who cared for him in the hospital and at home as well as anyone I have ever known. A family who were there to help care for him with love and devotion, children whose love I saw expressed over and over in touches, and hugs, and kisses. I remember a wonderful painting of Paul and Joseph: "Muscle Men" hung by the door to the porch. I remember the way Paul's eyes glowed with quiet pride at the sight of all the children.

In his life, Paul Graham had more than one vocation: Pharmacist, Attorney-At-Law, but family was a part of Paul's calling, too. 'He was my brother-in-law,' Dale said to me yesterday, 'but he became my brother.'

Paul was greatly blessed by his family, and he was blessed, too, by friends; friends who have shared their memories of him today, friends who visited him in the hospital and at home, friends who brought both food and prayers. I will always remember Tuesday night when friends gathered to be with Paul and Shirley and to fill his room with hymns and songs, too.

Well. All of this speaks more loudly than I possibly could alone about my friend and brother-in-Christ, Paul Graham, about his character and integrity, about his faith, about his love for Shirley and his children and his family, about his deep caring for his friends and for his colleagues.

But there is more, much more to say. Not only was Paul Graham a loving husband and father, a faithful friend and colleague, Paul Graham was a child of God. Look at the Crosses and quotations and pictures. Just listen to his friends, if you want evidence of it, hear them praying and singing God's praises. Look at his family, at Shirley and his children if you want proof. Watch them loving Paul and each other. Paul Graham was not only blessed, you see; God made him a blessing to us; made his life a blessing to us. So abundantly surrounded he was by love. Look how God has even managed to bring a gleam of light from the darkness of his death, gathering us together to not only remember Paul, not only to support each other, either, but also to celebrate what God has done for Paul and for us in Christ Jesus.

Shirley asked me to quote from the hymn, 'O Sacred Head Now Wounded,' to quote the phrase from the hymn that goes, 'Lord, let me never, never outlive my love to Thee.' But there's another phrase from that wonderful, old hymn that I want to quote, too: 'For he who dies believing dies safely in Thy love.' If Paul's life speaks to us of who we are as God's servants, his death can serve to remind us of whose we are as God's children. Because there is another piece of evidence that is important to pay attention to on this day as we grieve for the loss of our friend, Paul. And that is the evidence of the Resurrection, the evidence that says to us that Christ has risen, that death is a beginning, not an end, that death is not a dead end but a gateway. "Nothing can separate us from the love of God in Christ Jesus," St. Paul said. Nothing. Not even death itself. By God's grace and by our own Baptism into Christ, we will see Paul Graham again; Saint Paul, too, for that matter. It is God Himself Who has promised that.

I began this sermon talking about Paul's home, and I want to end it the same way. The one item hanging on the wall of Paul's home I have not yet told you about is a quotation from John Henry Cardinal Newman. It is about meaning in life. It is about meaning in death too. Cardinal Newman writes:

"God has created me to do Him some definite service;

He has committed some work to me which He has not committed to another.

I have my mission... I am a link in a chain,
A bond of connection between persons.
Therefore, I will trust Him, whatever, wherever I am.
I can never be thrown away.
If I am in sickness, my sickness may serve Him.
If I am in sorrow, my sorrow may serve Him.
He does nothing in vain.
He knows what He is about."

Amen, Paul, Amen."

Our worship continued with Paul's favorite hymn, *Just a Closer Walk With Thee*.

We were seated on the right side of the church. I looked over to the left and saw Paul's brothers Steve and Danny in the front pew with their families. I hadn't seen them look so grim since they lost their mother. A few rows behind them were my parents, Daddy in his wheelchair beside Mother in a pew. It seemed we should have been seated all together.

The hymn ended, and Communion was served. I was only mildly aware of those in charge of these events until our friend Mike Van Brundt scurried over to Pastor Garry and whispered something in his ear. Pastor Garry, front and center, addressed the congregation: "If there are those who would like Communion but are unable to come to the table, please let us know by raising your hand, and someone will bring it to you." My daddy's hand lifted in the air, and Mike rushed over so he could receive the Host and the wine. Thanks to Mike, I was enjoying shared Communion with Daddy one last time before Parkinson's would ingest what was left of Daddy's Earthly body, and he would join Paul and Jesus in Heaven.

Leaving the Sanctuary en route to the Fellowship Hall, Sarah and Matt had displayed an amazing presentation of snapshots from Paul's life on large posters. It proved a lovely place to linger – to reminisce. I stood there for a moment, just smiling at the memories and explaining a couple of the pictures to some who had questions. John Woolington approached the table. He smiled, hugged me then reminded me that he and Katie were as close as a phone call. I marveled at the care God was taking of us through His precious servants.

The beautiful women of Saint Timothy's had prepared a feast in the Fellowship Hall bountiful enough to feed family and friends alike. Paul would have appreciated this cornucopia with its centerpiece of good ol' fried chicken, one of his greatest loves. Except for the heaviness in my chest, it seemed almost like a wedding reception. I drank in these moments, feeling safe here, surrounded by this collective love for Paul, rocking in the cradle of adoration, memories, and the powerful presence of Jesus.

I remembered Mike and Barbara's preacher and the verse in Nehemiah that hadn't made sense to me before. All at once God's message from that evening became clear to me: *the joy of the Lord really was where I found my strength.*

*All things work together for good to those who love God,
who are the called according to His purpose.*
Romans 8:28

Chapter Sixty-Nine

Returning home, the sunshine continued to kiss us with warmth and light. Extended family and a few friends joined us at the house. The children changed into their shorts and played in the yard, swinging on the rope swing Paul had hung from a tree and climbing in and out of the tree house Paul had made out of the deck boards from the old trailer. When a fabulous sunset spread itself across the Wateree River, all those who weren't spending the night bid their goodbyes and the sun soon followed, completely burying itself under the river.

Night brought a strange comfort to our overly stimulated hearts and brains and I found a private peace resting with the soft grays and blues in my bedroom. My soul felt soothed as I lay on my side of the bed, feet dangling off the edge.

As it would be my habit for several months afterward, I was wide awake at 4:00 am. I made a pot of coffee and busied myself around the quiet house for a few hours before settling in front of the computer to check the email. There was a note from John Woolington:

"Dear Shirley,
On the way up to your lake house on Thursday afternoon to see you, I was praying for you and your family and thinking about what to say. I felt God telling me to tell you that He loves you and that He is going to take care of you and your children.

Then, at the memorial service for Paul yesterday, I was standing there reminiscing back to when I first had a personal conversation with you one night outside my driveway. I remember thinking about the Lord's redemption as you shared how you came out of a bad marriage and how God blessed your life with Paul (I love how God works to redeem the Earth and bring about restoration to broken lives). So I am asking myself, "What's so redemptive about this situation? It does not seem right to me."

And I felt God admonish me for looking at this backwards. I felt Him say, "Do you think Paul's death came as a surprise to Me? Do you not realize that I knew Paul would have a shortened life and that I chose for him and crowned him with his beautiful wife, Shirley, to be his soul-mate and help-mate?"

And I thought about that for the first time and felt in my heart the Lord's redemption for Paul. God blessed Paul with you and your children and I am so proud of you for taking such good care of him.

I was blessed to hear what friends had to say about Paul and even more blessed by all the photographs set up at the Church. I know that God is going to take care of you, Shirley, and bring about His redemption of this situation for you and for Charlotte, Emily, and Joseph. In His timing, of course, but I have no doubt that Healing will come. God is continually redeeming our lives and He has not forgotten you. He is going to take good care of you.

In Him,
John Woolington"

When I was finished reading, I realized that I was smiling, feeling a burden lift off my heart. I believed what John had written. In fact, I had already felt the sweet knowledge that God was going to take care of us before I read his note. John's words were a verbal clarification and confirmation to me.

John was right, but for more reasons than he realized. I too believed I had been just right for Paul. For one, I don't know how anybody could have loved that man more than I. But having previously experienced motherhood with only minimal presence of a father, I never felt jealous when our children clamored to be near Paul. I loved it. I loved the role model he was to them. I loved to see them interact. I loved having someone right next to me who was as interested as I in their greater good. Did God choose me for Paul because He knew I would be extravagant in my offering of our children to a father whose Earthly presence would be abbreviated?

Then there was something else I had thought about. Before Paul & I married, I was single with three children, the youngest almost eight. Here I was again, alone with three children, the youngest almost eight. I marveled in the thought that despite my brokenness, God had chosen me for Paul. He also knew before our first date that Paul would be going Home to Him at age fifty-three. Had God, in His redemptive way, sought a wife for Paul who already knew raising children alone would require trusting God to carry us when the load became too heavy? If my life been different, I might have been more frightened about being a widow with young children to raise alone into adulthood. How beautifully God can use everything, our joys and sorrows, our successes, and yes, even our mistakes and failures.

The sun poured into the windows and glinted off the walls. I remembered the pear tree just outside with hundreds of little pears already sprouted on the branches. It had grown to be less lop-sided since we'd begun pruning it in earnest, but truly the damage it endured was what set it on its prolific journey. Paul and I had lived our lives just like that tree. We'd carried on year after year, passing through sunshine and storms and bearing a little fruit in season. Then just like the machine that lopped half the pear tree off, cancer rolled through and cut Paul down to the bark, forcing us to do terribly brave things. Not despite it, but *because* cancer had come barreling into our lives Paul and I had really changed. Helpless, without branches to reach out to God, God reached down to us and made fruit of the Spirit grow in our lives.

Galatians 5:22-23 says, *The fruit of the spirit is love, joy peace, patience, kindness, goodness faithfulness, gentleness and self-control.*

Love. On our wedding day the love we promised bore much fruit, but in the end cancer was the fire that both ended and purified our love. Using both our love and pain God gave us a glimpse into what Jesus suffered on the Cross so that even when we die His purest love remains *forever*. I knew that even though Paul's love was gone, God's love would remain in my fruit basket.

Joy. Even as I sat alone, Paul's absence filling up the house, my heart was full with the joy of knowing he was walking with Jesus, his joy complete. Paul's new Heavenly body would never feel pain and his tears had been dried *forever*. Without God working in our lives through the cancer, how would I know this? Joy was the fruit that was wrought by God's hand through unimaginable loss, so I set it in my basket alongside love.

Peace. God is sovereign. Submitting to God's sovereignty Paul had finally been able to face his life's worst pain, the pain of abandonment. Through admitting and submitting his pain to God in prayer Paul's heart was healed and God brought him immediate peace. The fruit we took from this part of Paul's journey came from seeing firsthand how powerfully God blesses the prayers of a husband and wife. Even though Paul was gone, I knew I could still share this fruit, so I picked it.

Forbearance (or Patience). Patience is perseverance in the face of difficult circumstances. In the book of Job, patience was the fruit God manifested in Job through his trials. When Job realized he had nothing left but God, he was able to see that God was enough. I remembered Marilyn's words right after Paul's first brain tumor, "Don't miss all the little miracles while you're waiting for the big one." What good advice that had been. Our family's patience had been tested for almost two years and yet God kept showing up with miraculous encouragement abundant enough to go another minute, another hour, another day, and another year. Knowing His patience was powerful to endure, I knew it belonged in my basket, too.

Kindness. God used our Christian friends to show us His kindness when we needed it most. I remembered the people God had used through Paul's cancer to show us He was near; like the ones who drove out to the hospital just to pray with us, or to the house to clean up or take my little ones to a movie, or to the ICU waiting room to leave a bank envelope stuffed with one-dollar bills for the vending machines. I could imagine myself serving God this way, now that I knew better. Kindness looked delicious and fit so nicely in my basket with the other fruit.

Goodness. My favorite Bible verse is Romans 8:28 - *And we know that in all things God works for the good of those who love Him: who have been called according to His purpose.*

God uses "*All* things…" for the good of us who love Him and are called by Him. *All* would have to include the deadly disease that took Paul's life, but not his soul. *All* would include anything in the future that was a result of Paul's death; like my loneliness, the fatherless condition my children would continue to suffer and anything else Satan might use to try and crush us. God could *and would* use any of this for our good. This understanding made the prospect of facing tomorrow easier. I claimed God's goodness as more fruit, adding it to my basket along with love, joy, peace patience and kindness.

Faithfulness. Paul was the smartest man I'd ever known and his judgments were usually fair. I wondered how I'd ever get used to not having him around to lean on, yet God's words to Joshua kept coming back to me, "… I will never leave you nor forsake you."

Joshua must have been feeling a lot like me. The Bible says

in the first chapter of Joshua that he was alone, too. Like me, the Lord had trusted him with a whole lot of responsibility. Moses had just died and God had put Joshua in charge of the Israelites. In His wisdom, Our Heavenly Father must have known Joshua needed encouragement to know God hadn't left him.

I picked the fruit of God's faithfulness knowing I couldn't do this job without Him. My basket was almost loaded.

Gentleness. So many Bible passages represent the gentleness of Jesus. He was the Son of the Lord God Almighty and yet He stooped to wash the feet of His disciples, He stopped on the street to heal a woman who touched His garment without His consent, He took Zacchaeus aside and made him a friend, and He called children over to come unto Him. All of these everyday people had been changed by His gentle touch.

It was easy to be gentle to my three youngest children right now but would I still be gentle when they were all three teen agers? I hoped so, but I knew it would be hard. I put gentleness in my basket and prayed that God would show me how to keep it fresh as the years passed.

Self-control. In the English Standard Bible, 2 Timothy 1:7 says, *For God gave us a spirit not of fear but of power and love and self-control.*

God laid this scripture on my heart after Paul's lung surgery so I memorized it. I hadn't really thought about power and love falling into the same category with self-control until then, but these attributes all belong to Jesus. Would His power be perfect without His perfect love and super-natural self-control?

Remembering the passages from the book of John, chapters five and six, I wondered how much self-control it had taken for Jesus to preach and feed fishes and loaves to the multitude so soon after the hideous murder of John the Baptist, his beloved cousin and friend. Jesus hadn't had time to process His grief before the crowd bore down on Him, following Him, pleading for healing and wisdom.

I knew I'd be called on to feed and nurture our remaining family, too, probably long before it seemed I was able. Like the multitudes, my kids would need me even as I grieved. It would take a lot of self-control to put my needs aside, but I knew it would be necessary. The fruit of faithfulness reminded me that Jesus would always be there beside me to show me how to do it. I sure was going to need self-control, so I picked it and let it rest in the basket with all the others.

    I rose from the computer and headed for the shower. Today was Sunday, and we were all going to church, which would probably require some patience, faithfulness and self-control. God would surely supply the love, joy and peace. In His goodness and kindness He was softening the blow of Paul's absence this first Sunday by bringing our family into celebration of Baptism. So, surrounded by my parents, my children, my brothers and my sister Pastor Garry would be baptizing a new little baby boy who had made Paul a granddaddy just in time. God's goodness, as usual, was right on time.

    The words from Nehemiah that God had laid on my heart a few weeks ago resonated again. *The joy of the Lord is my strength* addressed this day perfectly and it would soon address the season of Christmas and the season of Easter. Even in sadness, even in loss, the joy of the Lord remains. It remains because Jesus overcame death and sin so that one day we will all meet in Heaven. Thanks be to God, what a day that will be!

Before I formed you in the womb I knew you, before you were born I set you apart; I appointed you as a prophet to the nations.
Jeremiah 1-5

Epilogue

Humor me now as I go off on a completely imaginary tangent. I'm picturing my Paul a lifetime ago, right before he was born...

Our Heavenly Father is bidding Paul farewell as he heads to Earth for the tour of duty called *Life*.

"Paul?" The Lord looks into Paul's crinkly eyes with a Father's love and compassion.

"Yes, Lord?"

"You'll have to return Here long before you think your tour is over...before you're finished with your fatherly duties. I can grant you some favor if you like."

"Favor, Father? What do You mean?"

"Something to leave behind for the ones who will be left without a husband and father."

Paul takes hold of Our Lord's hand and falls to his knees.

"I'll get to be a father, Lord?"

Jehovah Jirah smiles at Paul with a nod. "I love to give good gifts to my children, Paul. I know your heart better than you do."

Paul thinks a minute before answering. "Thank You, Father. I'm altogether happy to be a dad and I'm glad I won't have to be away from You for too long but..."

Paul's eyebrows knit together as he ponders the loss a child would face by being abandoned by a father through death. Then worry falls away from his face as he realizes the favors he wishes from God Almighty.

"Please cover my family with Your care when I leave them. Free my wife of any fear over raising a child alone because You have granted her the knowledge of Your love and provision. Provide them with reminders that because of what my Brother, Jesus did on the Cross, we'll all be together again one day."

"Granted," proclaims God the Father. "Is there anything else?"

"It's selfish, I know, but... The memories of children, Lord, I know they're short. Will You let me stay at least long enough that my memory remains at least a little?"

"The memories will remain long after you're gone, son, and so will the power of your love and Mine."

Paul grins. "Then I'm ready, Abba! I'm going to do my best to keep it between the ditches for You!"

"You're sure, son?"

"Father, if You're waiting on me, You're backing up! Give me a mama who will born me ready!"

The Lord laughs out loud and gently pushes Paul out the Golden Gate to be born on August 8, 1950.

God Almighty makes the "I love you" sign to Paul who's flying like a hawk toward Earth and He chuckles to Himself.

"I can hardly wait for that boy to find out I put enough love in his heart for seven children!"

Special thanks to all those who have encouraged me as I wrote this book and helped me with the physical job of publishing it.

Some of these dear ones include my children, cousins, aunts and uncles, brothers, sister, nieces, nephews, church family, writer friends, clients and more loyal friends, old and new than I deserve to claim.

I believe the Lord sent you to me and I thank Him for each one of you.